Mustafa Akan and Arman Teksin Tevfik
Fundamentals of Finance

Mustafa Akan and Arman Teksin Tevfik

Fundamentals of Finance

Investments, Corporate Finance,
and Financial Institutions

DE GRUYTER

ISBN 978-3-11-070534-8
e-ISBN (PDF) 978-3-11-070535-5
e-ISBN (EPUB) 978-3-11-070540-9

Library of Congress Control Number: 2020946336

Bibliographic information published by the Deutsche Nationalbibliothek
The Deutsche Nationalbibliothek lists this publication in the Deutsche Nationalbibliografie;
detailed bibliographic data are available on the Internet at http://dnb.dnb.de.

© 2021 Walter de Gruyter GmbH, Berlin/Boston
Cover image: Anton_Petrus/iStock/Getty Images Plus
Typesetting: Integra Software Services Pvt. Ltd.
Printing and binding: CPI books GmbH, Leck

www.degruyter.com

To Perran Akan, always at my side

Mustafa Akan

To Yasemin Tevfik, a supportive wife

Arman Teksin Tevfik

About the Authors

Prof. Dr. Mustafa Akan worked for Booz, Allen and Hamilton in the USA as a consultant and at Interbank and İktisat Banks as manager of the treasury, planning, and economic research departments for five years after his education in electrical engineering, and his MBA, and Ph.D. degrees at Robert College and Northwestern and Bosphorus universities.

He was the Executive Vice President of Garanti Bank in charge of the treasury and investment banking divisions for six years. He established Garanti Securities and served as its first General Manager.

He was appointed as the CEO of Imtas (subsidiary of Union Assurance de Paris, the largest insurance group in Europe at the time) in 1992 and continued serving as the CEO of Generali, Ege, and Liberty Insurance companies for the next 17 years.

Dr. Akan was appointed as Assistant Professor at Haliç University in the Department of Management in 2010. He earned the Associate Professor title in 2015 and the full Professor title in 2019. He teaches finance and quantitative methods courses at Haliç University. His principal research interest is the application of Optimal Control Theory to management, finance, and economics.

He teaches Optimal Control Theory at graduate level in the Industrial Engineering Department of Bosphorus University. He is also a guest lecturer at Technische Hochschule Ingolstadt (THI). He has been a participant and invited speaker in many international conferences and has published numerous articles in international and domestic journals.

Prof. Dr. Arman T. Tevfik is Professor of Finance at Haliç University, Istanbul, Turkey, a position he has held since 2013. He has been the Dean of the Faculty of Business since 2017 at this university. He previously held teaching appointments at Manas University, Bishkek, Kyrgyzstan (2001–2005 and 2008–2011), Beykent University (2005–2008), and Haliç University (2011–).

He received his BA in Business Administration from Anadolu University in 1977, MBA (finance-accounting) from Boğaziçi University in 1983, and Ph.D. in Business from Anadolu University in 1989.

Before entering academia, Arman T. Tevfik worked in the finance industry for almost 20 years. He worked as a controller and head of the corporate finance department for an investment bank. He was awarded the first prize for a research study in a banking competition in 1995.

He is the author or coauthor of 13 books on corporate finance, investments, valuation, and banking.

https://doi.org/10.1515/9783110705355-202

Contents

Part I: Introduction to Finance, Money and Interest Rates, and Time Value of Money

Part II: **Investments and Portfolio Management**

Part III: Financial Management/Corporate Finance

Part IV: Management of Financial Institutions

List of Figures

https://doi.org/10.1515/9783110705355-204

List of Tables

https://doi.org/10.1515/9783110705355-205

Preface

Finance is the study of the acquisition and investment of cash and other financial assets to maximize the value or wealth of the individual or firm. Finance is about monetary choices: how individuals, institutions, governments, and businesses acquire, spend, and manage funds (money and other financial assets). Everyone makes personal financial decisions on a daily basis, from what to purchase for breakfast to investing for retirement. Finance also interacts with various business disciplines. Any marketing or production decision will have financial implications. Finance consists of three overlapping functional areas called the *pillars of finance*: *Institutions and Markets*, *Investments*, and *Financial Management*.

- *Financial institutions and markets* deal with the management of and role played by various financial institutions and markets. We discuss this functional area in the first and the last part of the book.
- *Investments* deal with the analysis of individual financial assets and the construction of well-diversified portfolios.
- *Financial management* (also called *business finance* or *corporate finance*) includes financial planning, asset management, and fund-raising with the goal of increasing an enterprise's value.

Many students in business programs take just a single course in finance with different names such as financial management, business finance, or corporate finance. A course like this, although essential, cannot cover all aspects of finance.

The aim of this book is to provide an introduction to the key topics in finance with a friendly style without burdening the reader with unnecessary detail and complex mathematics.

This book can be delivered in two semesters in Introduction to Corporate Finance and Introduction to Investments classes by choosing appropriate chapters. It can also be used in one semester covering three pillars of finance (corporate finance, investments, and financial markets and financial institutions) by omitting certain sections. The book can also be used in Management of Financial Institutions classes by choosing Chapters 1, 2, 3, 6, 7, 15, and 16. Please contact the publishers at Stefan. Giesen@degruyter.com to request additional instructional material.

This book has been written primarily for students taking a course in finance for the first time either in undergraduate or graduate business programs.

The book consists of four parts:

- Part I: "Introduction to Finance, Money and Interest Rates, and Time Value of Money" focuses on the role financial markets play in the financial system and financial basics that underlie how markets operate.
- Part II: "Investments and Portfolio Management" focuses on the characteristics of stocks and bonds, how securities are valued, the operations of securities markets, formation of optimal portfolios, and derivatives.

https://doi.org/10.1515/9783110705355-206

- Part III: "Financial Management/Corporate Finance" focuses on financial planning, asset management, and fund-raising activities that will enhance a firm's value.
- Part IV: "Management of Financial Institutions" focuses on management of financial institutions in general, and risk management in financial institutions in particular.

No book is the result of individual effort. We benefited from writings of many academics. We did the best we can to provide references for the work of others.

We have enjoyed excellent support from our editors Prof. Dr. Guenter Hofbauer of Technische Hochschule Ingolstadt and Prof. Dr. Leszek Dziawgo of Nicolaus Copernicus University. We received considerable assistance from our colleagues at Haliç University, especially Dr. Melih Atalay, Dr. Şahver Ömeraki Çekirdekçi, and Nurhan Doğan Hüner. We would like to thank them for their suggestions and corrections, and absolve them from any responsibility for remaining errors. We thank our student Arda Dikbiyik for preparing the PowerPoint presentations for the book. We would also like to thank Jaya Dalal, Natalie Jones and André Horn at De Gruyter for their excellent work.

A guide to accompany this book entitled "Excel Models in Fundamentals of Finance" is being prepared to solve all the problems in this book. The models developed in this book can also be used in courses on corporate finance, investments, and financial institutions. This book can also be used alone in a course such as Financial Modeling in Excel, provided that the instructor provides sufficient Excel background in the class.

There are, despite our best efforts, likely to be errors and omissions in the book. For these we take full responsibility. We would be most grateful to have these mistakes pointed out, as well as any suggestions on how to improve the book in the future.

Part I: Introduction to Finance, Money and Interest Rates, and Time Value of Money

1 Introduction to Finance

1.1 Introduction

In this chapter we show that studying finance is a must for business students, and non-business students as well. We define finance and explain pillars of finance – namely, investments, corporate finance, and markets and institutions. In order to understand conceptual foundations of finance, we first present principles of finance. We explain what an effective financial system is and how it functions. Major types of securities traded in markets are also discussed.

1.2 What is Finance?

Finance is the study of the acquisition and investment of cash and other financial assets to maximize the value or wealth of the individual or firm. Finance consists of three overlapping functional areas, called the pillars of finance: *institutions and markets*, *investments*, and *financial management*.

- *Financial institutions and markets* deal with the management of and role played by various financial institutions and markets. We discuss this functional area in the first and the last part of the book.
- *Investments* deal with the analysis of individual financial assets and the construction of well diversified portfolios. We discuss investments in the second part of the book.
- *Financial management* (also called *business finance* or *corporate finance*) includes financial planning, asset management, and fund-raising with the goal of increasing the value of an enterprise for stakeholders. We study corporate finance in the third part of the book.

As shown in Figure 1.1, these areas do not operate in isolation but rather interact with each other.

In addition to this classification, two new finance areas have emerged recently:
- *Entrepreneurial finance*. This is the study of how growth-driven, performance-focused, early-stage firms raise funds and manage operations and assets.
- *Personal finance*. This is the study of how individuals prepare for financial emergencies, protect against premature death and the loss of property, and accumulate wealth.

https://doi.org/10.1515/9783110705355-001

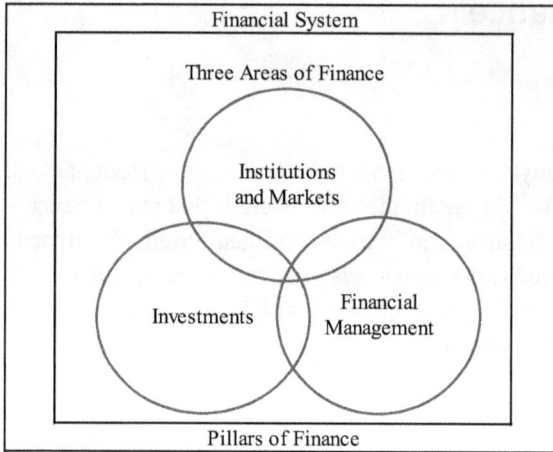

Figure 1.1: Pillars of Finance.
Source: Ronald W. Malicher and Edgar A. Norton, *Finance: Foundations of Financial Institutions and Management*, Wiley, 2007, p. 4.

1.3 Why Study Finance?

Several reasons are suggested as to why students, individuals, and professionals in the area of business should study finance, including the following:[1]

- As an individual, one makes financial decisions every day. Thus, a basic understanding of finance is necessary to make sound financial decisions. The operation of the financial system and the performance of the economy are influenced by policy makers. The voters elect important policy-making bodies such as a Parliament who can pass or change laws, that affects the level of economic activity. Thus, it is important that individuals should be informed when making political and economic choices.
- As a voter, we make decisions regarding the choice of persons to represent us in local and national governmental bodies. Thus, a basic understanding of finance is necessary to understand the ideas presented by the candidates running for such bodies and to question them regarding the feasibility of their ideas and the financial results of their decisions while they are in office.
- As a professional in the business world, a basic knowledge of finance, in addition to other fields, is required to make sound business decisions by keeping in mind that almost every business decision has a financial implication.

---

1 Ronald W. Malicher and Edgar A. Norton, *Finance: Foundations of Financial Institutions and Management*, Wiley, 2007, pp. 2–3. See also Zvi Bodie and Robert C. Merton, *Finance (Preliminary Edition)*, Prentice-Hall, 1998, pp. 3–4.

1.4 Eleven Principles of Finance

Almost all disciplines have principles. Finance is not an exception. There are eleven principles that serve as the foundation of finance:[2]

- *The risk-return trade-off.* As per this principle of finance, every businessperson should be aware of the principle that the return will only increase by taking more risk. If you are not capable of taking risk, you will never get a higher profit or return – that is, *no pain, no gain.*
- *Money has time value.* Money has a time value because the alternative to spending it now is to save it (lend it to someone), postponing consumption to a later date only to be able to consume more later, which can only happen if the lender pays back more money than he borrowed. The difference is the time value of money.
- *Cash is king.* A king is someone who can do what he wants when he wants. In the business world where there are lots of uncertainties, a businessperson can do what the businessperson wants when he wants it only with cash. Thus, cash is king. Or cash makes the businessman king. All other assets are not as liquid as the cash. A large company with very high fixed assets or with high receivables may be helpless in the face of a very profitable project if it does not have enough cash.
- *Incremental cash flows.* As per this principle of finance, a finance manager will always be interested to know incremental cash flows of a project or any other decision. A project should be undertaken only if the net present value of cash flows associated only due to it is positive. Other cash flows unrelated to the project should not be considered.
- *Financial markets are efficient in pricing securities.* Financial markets must be efficient in evaluating and pricing securities and investment opportunities. Markets are said to be information efficient if, at any point in time, the prices of securities reflect all information available to the public. Efficient secondary markets are an essential component of a modern financial system because without them, investors would not be able to transfer ownership easily, firms would not be able to raise capital to grow as easily or as inexpensively, and firm value would be difficult to monitor and evaluate. In sum, efficient markets help an economy to grow and prosper to a far greater extent than would be otherwise possible.
- *The agency problem.* This problem occurs due to divergence of the objectives of the shareholders and the general manager, who is supposed to make decisions to manage the company on behalf of the shareholders. Generally speaking, the

---

2 See Garry Gray, Patrick J. Cusatis, and J. Randall Woolridge, *Valuing A Stock*, Second Edition, McGraw-Hill, 2004, pp. 5–7; Arthur J. Keown, John D. Martin, J. William Petty, and David F. Scott, Jr., *Financial Management: Principles and Applications*, Tenth Edition, Pearson, 2011, pp. 12–22.

objective of the shareholders is to maximize the value of the company in the long run. The general manager makes decisions knowing that they will be in the company for a shorter time than the long run. Thus, the problem for shareholders is to devise plans and develop incentive schemes for the general manager so as to converge the objectives of both parties.

- *Taxes bias business decisions.* Managers, by mistake, may make decisions without considering the effect of tax. Taxes are surely different in different countries and the decisions should be made taking taxes into consideration. A project should be rejected if it yields unfavorable results even without taking taxes into consideration. Every decision relating to investment should be made after taking into effect its tax implications.
- *Diversification.* Every finance manager or investor should understand that different projects and investments have different risks and returns. We have to diversify investments. With this, we can minimize our loss due to the occurrence of risk or maximize our return.
- *Ethics.* An ethical individual or organization treats others fairly, legally, and honestly. A financial manager has to be an ethical person to maintain the trust of all stakeholders.
- *Options are valuable.* Options are valuable principally because they give a choice to the decision maker. Thus, an option holder may reduce risks, costs, and allow the decision maker to take part in high-return projects.
- *There are no arbitrage opportunities in efficient markets.* Financial arbitrage is buying and selling a financial instrument simultaneously when selling price in one market is lower than the buying price in another allowing the trader to make a profit. There would be no arbitrage opportunity if markets were perfectly efficient. Traders would take advantage of a price discrepancy almost immediately.

1.5 The Financial System and its Functions

An effective financial system consists of the following components:[3]
- *Government and policy makers.* There are several sets of policy makers (parliaments, central banks, regulatory bodies) who pass laws and issue regulations and make decisions relating to fiscal and monetary policies.
- *A monetary system.* Basic players are central banks and commercial banks. These institutions help form an efficient monetary system for creating and transferring money from savers to investors.

---

3 Malicher and Norton, *Finance*, op. cit., p. 12.

- *Financial institutions.* Banks, insurance, leasing, factoring, and securities companies are major financial institutions or financial intermediaries. The main role of these companies is to transfer the savings to investors.
- *Financial markets.* Financial markets are arenas that facilitate the transfer of financial assets amongst individuals, institutions, and businesses.
- *Instruments.* Currency, shares, bonds, T-bills, commercial papers are the most common instruments. Instruments such as futures, options, forwards, warrants, and so on are employed mostly in commercial environment.

The financial system is represented in Figure 1.2 as a system that creates money, circulates various financial instruments in the economy, and regulates the system to assure the efficient functioning of the system with a view of meeting the stated objectives of the governments.

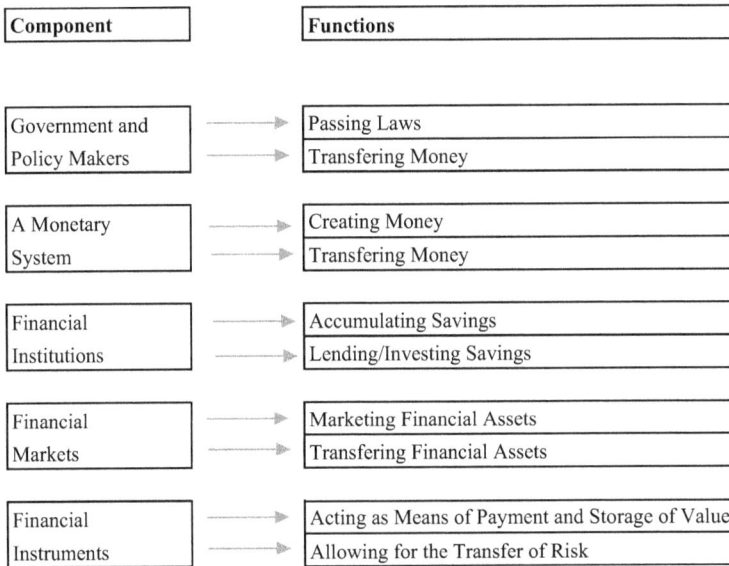

Component	Functions
Government and Policy Makers	Passing Laws / Transfering Money
A Monetary System	Creating Money / Transfering Money
Financial Institutions	Accumulating Savings / Lending/Investing Savings
Financial Markets	Marketing Financial Assets / Transfering Financial Assets
Financial Instruments	Acting as Means of Payment and Storage of Value / Allowing for the Transfer of Risk

Figure 1.2: Components and Functions of the Financial System.
Source: Malicher and Norton, op. cit., p. 12.

The *financial system* is a mix of all components indicated in Figure 1.2 interacting with each other for effectively creating money, transferring savings to investors, and allowing the existence of markets to exchange financial instruments.

The basic financial functions in an effective financial system include creating and transferring money, accumulating savings in financial institutions, lending and investing savings, and marketing and transferring financial assets.

1.6 Types of Financial Institutions

Some of the financial institutions are discussed as follows:

Depository Institutions

There are many types of depository institutions. The most common is commercial banks.

Depository institutions are where the savings of individuals, firms, and governments are deposited to provide basic funding for such institutions. These institutions pay a certain amount of interest to the depositors.

Contractual Savings Organizations

Insurance companies and pension funds are two important contractual saving organizations.

- *Insurance companies.* Insurance companies accept the risks of others (individuals and firms) in exchange for a certain payment (premium). They determine the premiums depending on the nature of risks they accept. They then decide how much of the risks they accept are to be transferred to other insurance companies (reinsurance companies). Out of the premiums and other funds they have (equity, reserves, collected premiums), they pay claims, general expenses, and commissions to sellers of insurance (agents and brokers), and they manage the portfolio of their assets with a view of providing the shareholders a fair return on their investments.
- *Pension funds.* Pension funds provide retirement benefits to the savers. They are subject to certain regulations in terms of length of premium payments, taxation, and age. Savers who fulfilled the requirements can withdraw their accumulated savings without any constraint.

Securities Firms

There are many types of securities firms, such as:
- *Investment trusts.* They sell share to investors and buy securities with the funds collected from shareholders. The value of the investment trusts increases as the value of financial securities in the funds increases. They are established as joint stock companies and they have legal personality.
- *Mutual funds.* They are also called open-end funds. Established and run by financial institutions such as banks. They do not have any legal entity. Mutual

fund advantages are especially important to small investors: professional management, diversification, and low transaction fees.

– *Real estate investment trusts.* They are like investment trusts except they can invest only in real estate and governments securities. They have to distribute certain amounts of their profits.

– *Venture capital trusts.* A venture capital trust (VCT) is a type of publicly listed closed-end fund. They are established in the form of joint stock corporations and they are legal entities. A venture capital trust is designed as a way for individual investors to gain access to venture capital investments via the capital markets. Its objective is to seek out potential venture capital investments in small unlisted firms to generate higher than average, risk-adjusted returns for its investors.

– *Investment bank (IB).* They are like banks except they cannot accept deposits. They can underwrite and distribute new shares and other securities. They are established as joint stock corporations.

– *Brokerage firms.* Firms that assist individuals and institutions who want to purchase new stock issues or who want to sell previously purchased securities on a commission basis. They are established in the form of joint stock corporations.

Finance Companies

Finance companies do not accept deposits. They obtain funds by issuing commercial paper (short-term, unsecured debt) and by borrowing from other financial institutions. They usually generate revenues by making loans.

Factoring Companies

Many companies sell their products on term basis and thus they have significant number of receivables. At times, for various reasons, such as liquidity management, these companies sell their receivables to other companies. The companies that buy these receivables are called *factoring companies*. Factoring allows companies to improve cash flow.

Leasing Companies

Leasing companies enable businesses and individuals to use assets without buying them outright. Leasing companies lend their equipment to other companies that may prefer to lease such equipment for many reasons, including taxation, cash management, and expense management.

Asset Management Companies (AMCs)

An asset management company invests its clients' funds according to the objectives of the clients. AMCs manage mutual funds, hedge funds,[4] and pension plans. They earn income by charging service fees or commissions to their clients. They are also called *portfolio management companies*.

1.7 Types of Financial Markets

A market is a forum for exchange. There are three types of financial markets:
- Securities markets
- Derivative markets
- Foreign exchange markets

On the basis of the maturity of securities traded, they are classified as *money markets*, where securities with maturities of less than one year are traded, and *capital markets*, where longer maturity securities are traded.

Financial markets can also be divided into two categories in terms of *primary* and *secondary* markets, as well:
- *Primary markets* are markets where the initial offering or origination of debt and equity securities takes place.
- *Secondary markets* are markets where the transfer of previously issued bonds, mortgages, and equity securities between investors occurs.

Securities Markets

A security is a tradable financial asset – for example, stocks and bonds. Securities markets can be defined as physical locations or forums of trade of securities. These markets can be divided into two sub-markets:
- *Debt securities markets*. Where money market securities, bonds, and mortgages are sold and traded.
- *Equity securities markets*. Where ownership rights in the form of stocks are initially sold and traded. Important international markets (exchanges) are FTSE (London), DAX (Germany), CAC (France), Nikkei (Japan), Hang Seng (China), SP (USA), Dow (USA), and Nasdaq.

---

4 A hedge fund is an investment fund, structured as a limited partnership or limited liability company, that pools capital from investors or institutional investors and invests in a variety of assets, usually with complicated portfolio-construction and risk management methods.

Derivatives Markets

The derivatives market is where the exchange of derivatives takes place. Derivative is one type of security whose price is derived from the underlying assets. The value of these derivatives is determined by the fluctuations in the value of underlying assets. These underlying assets are most commonly stocks, bonds, currencies, interest rates, commodities, and market indices. As derivatives are merely contracts between two or more parties, anything can be used as underlying assets. The derivatives can be classified as future contracts, forward contracts, options, swaps, and credit derivatives. The derivative market can be classified as *exchange traded derivatives market* and *over the counter derivatives market*. Exchange traded derivatives are those derivatives which are traded through specialized derivative exchanges whereas over the counter derivatives are those which are privately traded between two parties and involves no exchange or intermediary. Swaps and forward contracts are traded in over the counter derivatives market, or *OTC* market.

Foreign Exchange Markets

Currency exchange markets are electronic markets in which banks and institutional traders buy and sell various currencies on behalf of businesses and other clients. They are also referred to as foreign exchange or *FOREX* markets. Foreign exchange markets are truly global as they trade in relative values of many different currencies.

1.8 Types of Securities

Assets are either real (fixed) or financial. Real assets are those that are physically owned, such as land, vehicles, or jewelry. Financial assets are claims that are backed by real assets and include debt and equity, such as mortgages, stocks, and auto loans.

There are many types of securities such as:

- *Money market securities*. Money market securities are the financial instruments with a less than one-year maturity, such as T-bills, commercial papers, and negotiable certificate of deposits.
- *Capital market securities*. Capital market instruments are the financial securities with a maturity of more than one year, such as government bonds, private sector bonds, and shares.
- *Derivatives*. These are instruments whose values depend on the value of other assets, thus they are called derivatives. They derive their value from the values of assets they are based on. Forwards are contracts where the buyer agrees to buy or sell an asset at an agreed upon price at a future date. Futures are forwards

but they are traded on the markets. Options are contracts where the buyer (seller) pays a premium to buy (sell) the right to buy (sell) the asset in the future at an agreed upon price. The seller has to sell the asset at that price if the owner of the option decides to buy the asset. There are various kinds of derivatives which will be discussed in more detail in Chapter 7.

– *International securities*. These are securities (usually bonds) issued by governments or companies denominated in foreign currency. There are basically two types of bonds: *foreign bonds* and *Eurobonds*. For example, if I am a Danish investor and I buy bonds denominated in EUR, JPY, AUD, GBP, etc., I am investing in foreign bonds. They may be Eurobonds or not. Eurobond is one denominated in a particular currency but sold to investors in national capital markets other than the country that issued the denominating currency. An example is an Italian borrower issuing dollar-denominated bonds to investors in the U.S.

1.9 Summary

The study of finance is a requirement for both business students and non-business students. Finance is the study of the acquisition and investment of cash and other financial assets to maximize the value or wealth of the individual or firm.

Finance consists of three overlapping, functional areas, called the pillars of finance: *institutions and markets*, *investments*, and *financial management*.

Almost all disciplines have principles. Finance is not an exception. There are eleven principles that serve as the foundation of finance.

An effective financial system consists of the following components: government and policy makers, a monetary system, financial institutions, financial markets, and instruments.

There are many financial institutions such as depository institutions, contractual savings organizations, securities firms, finance companies, factoring companies, leasing companies, and asset management companies.

A market is a forum for exchange. There are basically three types of financial markets: securities markets, derivative markets, and foreign exchange markets.

Securities are broadly classified as money market securities, capital market securities, derivatives, and international securities.

2 Money and Interest Rates

2.1 Introduction

In this chapter we define money, functions of money, and how to transfer money from savers to business firms. Definition of money supply and control of money supply are also discussed briefly. We explain the relationship between money supply and economic activity. Cost of money (interest rates) and theories regarding interest rates are discussed. The structure of interest rates, as well as nominal and real interest rates are explained. Yield curves and theories regarding yield curves are also discussed. We explain central bank, its goals, actions, tools, and responsibilities. We also show central bank's balance sheet and explain major accounts appearing in the balance sheet.

2.2 Overview of Monetary System

Money is the common denominator used to transact business. It is the accepted means of paying for goods and services and for paying off debts. Money should therefore have the following characteristics:
- Be divisible
- Be relatively inexpensive to store and transfer
- Be reasonably stable in value over time

Money is required to conduct day-to-day activities, facilitate capital investment, and support economic growth.

The three basic functions of money are as a:
- Medium of exchange
- Store of value
- Standard of value (monetary unit)

The four ways money is transferred from savers to business firms are:
- Direct or indirect transfer of individual savings to business firms in exchange for a firm's securities
- Purchase of a firm's securities through investment banking intermediaries
- Purchase of a firm's securities through mutual funds, or other financial institutions
- Depositing with a commercial bank and extending loans to individuals and companies with the deposited funds

https://doi.org/10.1515/9783110705355-002

2.3 The Definitions of Money Supply and Control of Money Supply

Money supply has various definitions as M1, M2, and M3. Their components are presented in Table 2.1.

Table 2.1: Money Supply.

M1	Currency in circulation Traveler's checks Demand deposits at banks Other checkable deposits	
M2	M1	Plus: Savings accounts Small-denomination time deposits Retail money market mutual funds
M3	M1+M2	Plus: Large-denomination time deposits Institutional money market mutual funds Repurchase agreements Eurodollars held by local residents

Demand deposit is a type of deposit which derives its name from the fact that the owner of a deposit account may withdraw all or a portion of the amount in his or her account any time.

Checks are documents used to withdraw, deposit, or transfer money from a bank account.

Traveler's checks are offered by banks and other institutions. They are promises to pay on demand the face amounts of the checks. They are no longer used extensively.

Other checkable deposits include automatic transfer service (ATS) accounts and negotiable order of withdrawal (NOW) accounts at depository institutions.

Money market mutual funds certificates represent the shares of their owner in the mutual funds. The value of the certificate's changes according to the change in the value of the financial instruments in the funds mostly composed of money market instruments.

Repurchase agreement is a way of making a loan. The lender buys an asset, usually securities, from the borrower, thus providing funds to the borrower. The borrower repays by buying back the asset at a prearranged time and price.

Money Creation Mechanism

More money in an economy stimulates consumption and thus stimulate production and investment (higher growth). This in turn lowers unemployment. However, this may result in higher inflation also. Less money in an economy lowers consumption and production resulting in lower inflation rate and lower growth. Thus, the money supply plays a crucial role in an economy.

Central banks control the money supply by using some tools. Some central banks are free to use to choose the tools they have (they are independent of governments) while some are not. Central banks control the money supply by using the following tools:

- Reserve requirements
- Discount rate
- Open market operations

Reserve Requirements. Reserves are required by the central banks in order to be able to control money supply (money generation). It represents the amount of deposits that should be kept at the central bank. The ratio of these reserves to the deposits is called the *reserve ratio*.

An example of how reserve ratio helps create money with €1,000[1] new deposits and 10% reserve ratio:

- Suppose a person deposits €1,000 in bank A. He has €1,000.
- His bank keeps €100 at the central bank and lends €900 as credit to person Y. The person Y who has the credit deposits that money in bank B. He has €900 which is (1,000−100) % of €1,000 or 1,000 × 0.9.
- Bank B increases its reserves at the central bank by 900 × 0.1 = €90 and lends as a credit (900−90) = €810 to person Z which is equal to (900−90)% of €1,000. The person, Z has €810 or 1,000 × 0.81.

This process, theoretically, continues indefinitely.

Thus, the total money (money belonging to all the persons) generated by the initial €1,000 deposit is:

$$M = 1,000 \text{ (original deposit)} + 1,000 \times 0.9 \text{ (money of person Y)} + 1,000 \times 0.81$$
(money of person Z) + ...

$$= 1,000 \times (1 + 0.9 + 0.81 + \ ......)$$

The sum of numbers in the parenthesis can be shown to be equal to 10.

$$= 1,000 \times 10 = 10,000$$

---

1 € is a symbol of euro, the monetary unit of the European Union.

If the reserve ratio was reduced to 5%, the resulting increase in the money supply would be €20,000. If on the other hand, the reserve ratio was 20%, the money supply would be €5,000.

This is the money generation power of central banks through the banking system, which is an important tool to control the money supply in an economy.

Discount Rates. Banks can borrow from central banks. The interest rate that central banks charge to the banks is called the *discount rate*. Reducing this increases reserves and thus increases the money supply. *Interbank funds rate* is related interest rate. The interest that banks charge each other (bank to bank) is called *interbank fund rate*.

Open Market Operations. Central banks buy and sell government securities. Purchasing government bonds increases money supply (persons or corporations selling their bonds have more money) and reduces interest rates. Selling government bonds decreases money supply and increases interest rates.

2.4 Money Supply and Economic Activity

Economists believe that the money supply is important in managing economic activity. Gross domestic product (GDP) is the measure of the output of goods and services in the economy and is sometimes used as an indicator of a country's standard of living. The velocity of money measures the rate of circulation of the money supply and is found by dividing GDP by the money supply (M).

Money supply will be examined from two angles: Monetarist and Keynesian.

Monetarist Economists

Monetarist economists believe that when the money supply increases, the public will spend more, causing an increase in real economic activity and causing the prices to rise (inflation).

In its simplest form, *Quantitative Theory of Money (QTM)*, or *Fisher Equation*, is expressed as:

$$GDP = MV = PT (\text{the Fisher Equation})$$

Each variable denotes the following:

GDP: Gross domestic product, which measures the output of goods and services in an economy.

M = Money supply

V = Velocity of circulation (the number of times money changes hands)

P = Average general price level

T = Volume of transactions of goods and services.

For example,[2] a country's gross domestic product (GDP) is €200 billion and its money supply (M) is €50 billion.
- What is the country's velocity of money (V)?
- If the money supply (M) stays at the same level as last year while the velocity of money "turns over" 4.5 times (V), what would be the level of GDP?
- Assume that the money will turn over 4 times next year. If the country wants a GDP of €220 billion at the end of next year, what will have to be the size of the money supply? What percentage increase in the M will be necessary to achieve the target GDP?

Answer:
- V = PT/M = 200 billion/€50 billion = 4.0 times
- GDP = MV = €50 billion × 4.5 = €225 billion
- M = PT/V = €220 billion/4 = €55 billion which requires an increase of 5 billion in the money supply.
- The percentage increase in the M to achieve target GDP is (55–50)/50=10%.

Nominal GDP increases with:
- An increase in money supply and/or velocity of money
- An increase in real output and/or price level

QTM was a theory advanced by Milton Friedman in the early 1980s and was applied as an economic policy in the U.S. and Great Britain in subsequent years. In later years, it proved to be less successful than was predicted. A huge increase in the money supply was not able to spur growth in almost all European countries and Japan.

Keynesian Economists

Keynesian economic theory states that decisions taken by the private sector may not give rise to efficient macroeconomic results. Governments should interfere in the economic decision-making by proper fiscal policies in addition to monetary policies of the central banks.

Keynesian economists generally claim a managed market economy, predominantly private sector, but with an active role for government intervention during recessions and depressions.

---

2 For another simple example, see John E. Marthinsen, *International Macroeconomics for Business and Political Leaders*, Routledge, 2017, p. 3.

According to Keynesian economists, monetary policy actions by the central bank and fiscal policy actions by the government can help stabilize output over the business cycle.

2.5 Interest: Cost of Money

Interest rate is the cost of *postponing consumption*. It can also be defined as the rent the borrower pays to the lender for the use of their money. The interest rate on deposits is the rent that the banks pay to the depositors for using their money. Interest the borrower pays to a bank is also the rent the borrower pays to the bank.

Benchmark interest rates include the *London Interbank Offered Rate* (or LIBOR), which is a daily reference rate based on the interest rates at which banks offer to lend unsecured funds to other banks in the London wholesale money market (or interbank market). LIBOR will be slightly higher than the *London Interbank Bid Rate* (LIBID), the rate at which banks are prepared to accept deposits.

Interest rates often represent a benchmark rate for comparison with investment opportunities. *Prime rate* was a term applied in many countries to a reference interest rate used by banks. Some variable interest rates may be expressed as a percentage above or below the prime rate. As such, interest rates affect depository institutions (savings and loans), financial institutions (insurance companies and pension funds), financial markets (home mortgages), and securities markets (stocks and bonds).

There are two major theories regarding interest rates:
- *The Loanable Funds Theory*: *Classical or Real Theory*, which explains interest as determined by the demand for and supply of capital.[3]
- *Keynes's Liquidity Preference Theory*, which explains that the rate of interest is higher on securities with long-term maturities.

Loanable Funds Theory

Interest rates are affected by supply and demand of funds, as shown in Figure 2.1. The loanable funds theory suggests that interest rates are a function of the supply and demand for funds earmarked for loans. Savings may also have an effect on interest rates; the volume of saving depends on factors such as income, tax rates, and the demography of the population. Generally, interest rates rise during periods of prosperity, since people increase their level of consumption due to their increased

---

3 For more detailed information, see Peter Howells and Keith Bain, *Financial Markets and Institutions*, Fifth Edition, Pearson Education, 2007, pp. 201–212.

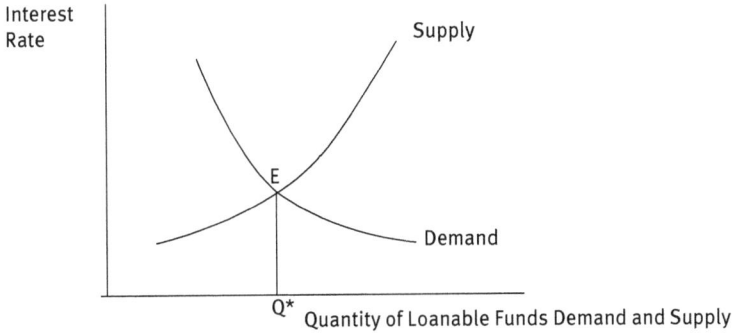

Figure 2.1: Supply and Demand for Funds.

income, and the positive expectations of the future also increase the demand for money, thus increasing the interest rates.

In an economy, interest rate will be determined by the supply of funds (loanable funds) and the demand for loanable funds:

- The supply of funds is a function of savings in the economy.
- When people deposit money in banks, these funds can be lent out to firms for investment in physical capital, or to individuals for consumption.
- Higher interest rates will encourage people to save more.
- Saving will also be dependent upon income and confidence in the future of the economy. A change in these could shift the supply curve.
- A shift in the supply or demand curve will cause a change in the level of interest rate.
- An increase in demand for the loanable fund will cause a shortage of funds causing interest rates to rise. This will encourage an increase in savings.

Liquidity Preference Theory

The liquidity preference theory suggests that an investor demands a higher interest rate, or premium, on securities with long-term maturities, which carry higher risk, because all other factors being equal, investors prefer cash or other highly liquid holdings. According to the liquidity preference theory, interest rates on short-term securities are lower because investors are sacrificing less liquidity than they are by investing in medium-term or long-term securities.

Investors demand progressively higher premiums on medium-term and long-term securities as opposed to short-term securities. In order for the investor to be willing to sacrifice more liquidity, they must be offered a higher rate of return in exchange for agreeing to have their cash tied up for a longer period of time.

According to Keynes, individuals value money for the transaction of current business and for its use as a store of wealth. For this reason, Keynes purports that they tend to relinquish interest earnings on their money in order to spend their money at present. He also suggests that these individuals prefer to keep their money on hand as a precautionary measure. Keynes also theorizes that when higher interest rates are offered, individuals are more willing to hold on to less money in order to obtain an income.

As Keynes describes the liquidity preference theory, he explains three motives that determine the demand for liquidity:

–   The *transactions* motive refers to the fact that individuals have a preference for liquidity in order to guarantee having sufficient cash on hand for basic transactions because income is not always readily available. With this motive, the level of an individual's income determines the amount of liquidity demanded; higher income levels equal a demand for more money to accommodate increased spending.

–   The *precautionary* motive is related to individuals' preference for liquidity as additional security in the event that an unexpected occasion or problem arises that requires a substantial outlay of cash.

–   Individuals may also have a *speculative* motive, based on the belief that bond prices may begin to decrease significantly, thus offering the investor the opportunity to use liquid funds to make an investment offering a more attractive rate of return. Basically, the speculative motive refers to investors' general reluctance to commit to tying up investment capital in the present for fear of missing out on a better opportunity in the future.

2.6 Structure of Interest Rates

The nominal interest rate (NIR) is subject to risks of inflation, maturity, default, and liquidity. As a result, the equation for NIR is as follows:

$$NIR = RRI + IP + DRP + MRP + LP$$

NIR:	Nominal interest rate	RRI:	Real rate of interest
IP:	Inflation premium	MRP:	Maturity risk premium
DRP:	Default risk premium	LP:	Liquidity premium

As a corollary, the risk-free rate of interest (RFRI) is as follows:

$$RFRI(r_f) = RRI + IP$$

The relationship between the real interest rate and the nominal interest rate can be shown as:

$$RRI = (NIR - Inflation)/(1 + Inflation)$$

Let us first define NIR as

$$NIR = (1 + RRI)(1 + IP) - 1$$

Assume that real rate of interest is 2% and inflation rate is 5%, what is the nominal interest rate?

$$NIR = (1.02) \times (1.05) - 1 = 7.1\%$$

$$RRI = (0.071 - 0.05) / (1 + 0.05) = 0.021 / 1.05 = 2\%.$$

Although RRI is often equated to the difference between the nominal rate and the inflation rate. This will be harmless in low-interest rate economies. However, it may lead to serious errors in high-interest rate economies.

The *Treasury bond yields* are often used as a proxy for a risk-free rate because it is extremely unlikely that the government will default on its obligations. However, this was possible in Greece in recent years during the European financial crisis.

Default risk premium (DRP) is the difference between the interest rate on a Treasury bond and a corporate bond of equal maturity and marketability. Default risk premium indicates compensation for the possibility that the borrower will not pay interest and/or repay principal according to the loan agreement. An example is provided as follows: You are considering an investment in a one-year government debt security with a yield of 5% or a highly liquid corporate debt security with a yield of 6.5%. The expected inflation rate for the next year is expected to be 2.5%.

The questions are:
- What would be your real rate earned on either of the two investments?
- What would be the default risk premium on the corporate debt security?

The answers are:
- Government debt rate = real rate + inflation premium
- Real rate = 5% − 2.5% = 2.5% approximately. The exact result is real rate = (1+0, 05) / (1+0.025) − 1 = 2.43%. The error is 0.07%.
- Risky debt rate = government debt rate + default risk premium
- Default risk premium = 6.5% − 5% = 1.5%.

2.7 The Yield Curve

Yield is the profit realized on investments kept to maturity. The yield curve plots yield against time to maturity for default-free securities.

The yield curves:
- Reflect securities of similar default risk
- Represent a particular point in time
- Show yield on a number of securities with differing lengths of time to maturity time

Figure 2.2 shows the hypothetical yield curve for a zero-coupon bond.

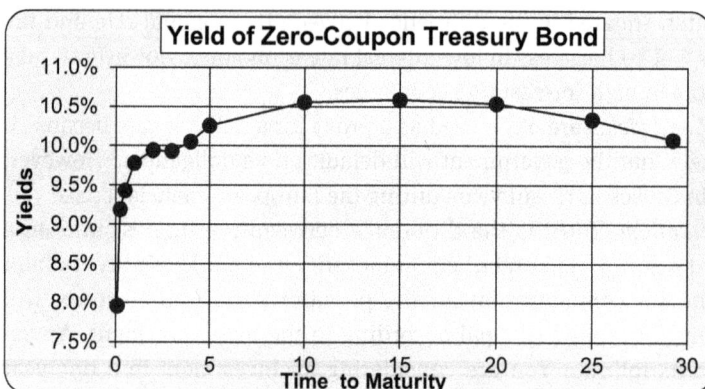

Figure 2.2: Hypothetical Yield Curve.

Yield curves shift upward or downward with changes in economic activity. It typically slopes upward as the economy moves out of a recession, flattens out during expansion, and slopes downward at the peak of economic activity.

Theories of the term structure are discussed as follows.[4]

Expectation Theory

The *expectation theory* suggests that the yield curve shape reflects investor expectations about future inflation rates, allowing interest rate yield curves to be used as a predictive tool.

---

[4] For more explanation see David W. Blackwell, Mark D. Griffiths, and Drew B. Winters, *Modern Financial Markets: Prices, Yields, and Risk Analysis*, Wiley, 2007, pp. 40–45.

Under expectations theory, a long-term rate is the geometric average of current and expected future short-term rates.

Formula for the long-term rate:

$$(1+{}_0r_t)^t = (1+{}_0r_1)(1+{}_1f_2)(1+{}_2f_3)\cdots(1+{}_{t-1}f_t)$$

Where:

r = spot rate,

f = one-period expected future short-term rate,

t = number of time periods in the long-term rate,

prescript is beginning of time period covered by the rate, and postscript is ending of the time period.

An example for a three-year rate is:

$$(1+{}_0r_3)^3 = (1+{}_0r_1)(1+{}_1f_2)(1+{}_2f_3)$$

Timeline of a three-year rate:

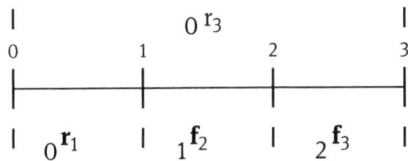

Solving for an expected future short-term rate:

$$(1+{}_0r_t)^t = (1+{}_0r_1)(1+{}_1f_2)(1+{}_2f_3)\cdots(1+{}_{t-1}f_t)$$

Then, solving for ${}_{t-1}f_t$ is

$$(1+{}_{t-1}f_t) = \frac{(1+{}_0r_t)^t}{(1+{}_0r_1)(1+{}_1f_2)\cdots(1+{}_{t-2}f_{t-1})} = \frac{(1+{}_0r_t)^t}{(1+{}_0r_{t-1})^{t-1}}$$

As an example, let us find an expected future rate. The yield for a two-year bond of ABC is 7%. The yield for a one-year zero-coupon bond of a similar zero-coupon bond of the same company yields 9%. What is the yield expectation of a one-year bond next year?

$$(1 + 0.07)^2 = [(1 + 0.09)(1 + {}_1r_2)] - 1$$

$${}_1r_2 = (1.1449/1.09) - 1 = 5.037\%$$

The example shows us that interest rates are going to decline next year. Therefore, the yield is said to be downward sloping. The rate, 5.037%, is also referred to as *forward rate*.

Liquidity Preference Theory

The *liquidity preference theory* suggests that the savers prefer to invest in short-term instruments because they are risk-averse and prefer more liquid assets. This, in turn, increases the demand for short-term investments.

Simply put, investors prefer liquidity. This theory extends expectations theory by assuming that investors are risk-averse and prefer short-term investments.

If investors are asked to extend beyond their preferred short-term time to maturity, they demand a premium for the price risk created by going beyond their preferred time horizon.

Formula for the long-term rate under liquidity preference theory:

$$(1+{}_0r_t)^t = (1+{}_0r_1)(1+{}_1f_2 +{}_1l_2)(1+{}_2f_3 +{}_2l_3)\cdots(1+{}_{t-1}f_t +{}_{t-1}l_t)$$

Where
l = risk premium for increasing time to maturity
and

$$0 \le {}_1l_2 \le {}_2l_3 \le {}_3l_4 \le \cdots$$

As shown in Figure 2.3, liquidity preference theory explains why the yield curve slopes upward most of the time.

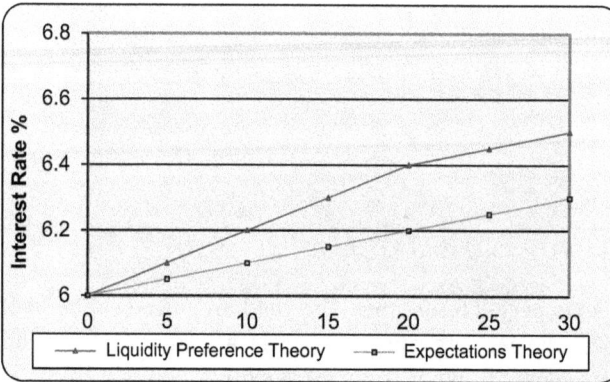

Figure 2.3: Liquidity Preference Theory and Expectation Theory.

Preferred Habitat (Market Segmentation) Theory

The *preferred habitat theory* is a corollary of the market segmentation theory. The *market segmentation theory* says securities of different maturities are not perfect substitutes for each other.

Market segmentation theory assumes that investors have specific maturity preferences that they will not leave regardless of the additional compensation. This assumption is too restrictive.

The *preferred habitat theory* assumes that investors have a desired time to maturity for investment (a preferred habitat), but if adequately compensated for the additional risk of moving from their desired maturity, they will move to other maturities.

The *preferred habitat theory* is the only theory that allows for humps or twists in the yield curve. In other words, it allows for a change in the direction of the slope of the yield curve. This is important because this frequency occurs in plots of market yields.

Other Factors

Other factors that influence interest rate levels or yield curves:

- *The Central Bank policy*. Change in the policy interest rate by the Central Bank directly influences the interest rates. Change in other policy instruments such as the reserve ratio influences the money supply in the economy, thus causing a change in the rates.
- *Budget deficits*. Budget deficits have to be financed by printing money, increasing inflation expectations, thus pushing the rates upward. Governments can also finance the deficit by borrowing from the public. This will also increase interest rates.
- *International factors*. A persistent balance of payments deficit cannot be financed by reserves indefinitely. Thus, it has to be financed by short- or long-term foreign investment (direct investment) in the country. Short-term interest rates have to be kept high to attract short-term capital to finance the deficit.
- *Business activity*. Business conditions influence interest rates. When the economy is strong, the demand for money is higher, since greater spending activity means that there is more need for cash to finance projects. Higher demand, in turn, drives up costs and, in this case, interest rates.

2.8 Central Banks

The *Central Bank* in general, is a government-established organization[5] responsible for supervising and regulating the banking system and for creating and regulating the money supply. The Central Banks are primarily responsible for steering the monetary and exchange rate policies.

The Central Banks, or Federal Reserve System (FED) in the U.S., set monetary policy and to some extent regulate the banking system. Central Bank actions heavily influence interest rates and economic performance. Goals of Central Banks include:
- Stable prices
- Full employment
- Economic growth

In order to achieve these goals, central banks use the following tools:
- Monetary policy
- Bank regulation

Monetary policy refers to the actions of the Central Bank that influence the:
- Money supply
- Credit in the economy

The Central Bank has the following weapons at its disposal for achieving its goals:
- Open market operations (buying and selling of government securities)
- Changing reserve requirements that banks must maintain in their own vaults or on deposit at the Central Bank
- Changing the discount rate (the rate charged by the Central Bank to depository institutions)
- Oral guidance (issuance of public statements)

The Central Banks (CBs) also handle the Treasury's payments, sell government securities, and assist with cash management and investment activities of the governments. In addition, Central Banks supervise commercial banks and process checks and electronic payments. All banks, regardless of size, are subject to the Central Bank's reserve regulations. Internationally, Central Bank actions are designed to facilitate trade and investments overseas as well as allow banks to be competitive worldwide.

---

5 It does not mean that central banks are state/government owned establishments.

The primary objective of the Central Banks is to achieve and maintain price stability. The Bank shall determine, on its own discretion, the monetary policy that will be implemented and the monetary policy instruments that it is going to use in order to achieve and maintain price stability.

Responsibilities of the CBs include:

- Overseeing monetary policy action
- Analyzing domestic and international economic and financial conditions
- Serving on committees that study current issues, such as consumer banking laws and e-commerce
- Exercising control over the financial services industry
- Administering consumer protection regulations
- Monitoring the nation's payment system
- Setting the reserve requirements for depository institutions
- Supervision of the activities of the banks and approving appointments of banks directors

2.9 Central Bank Balance Sheet

A very simplified balance sheet for a Central Bank is shown in Table 2.2. Some of the monetary assets of a Central Bank include:

- *Gold.* Gold purchased from abroad or from domestic sources.
- *Foreign currency Reserves.* Foreign currencies purchased.
- *Government securities.* These are the local Treasury bills and bonds that the Central Bank has purchased in the open market. Purchasing Treasury securities increases the money supply.
- *Government loans.* These are loans made to Treasury. An increase in such loans will also increase the money supply.

Table 2.2: The Central Bank's Balance Sheet.

ASSETS	LIABILITIES & STOCKHOLDERS' EQUITY
Foreign assets	**Currency in circulation**
Gold	**Deposits by banks**
Foreign currencies (Reserves)	**Deposits by government**
Domestic assets	**Stockholders' equity**
Loans to government	Paid-in capital
Loans to banks	Retained earnings

- *Discount loans.* These are loans made to member banks at the current discount rate. Again, an increase in discount loans will also increase the money supply.

Some of the monetary liabilities of the Central Bank include:
- *Currency in circulation (Notes).* The physical currency in the hands of the public, which is accepted as a medium of exchange.
- *Reserves (deposits by banks).* All banks maintain deposits with the Central Bank, known as reserves. The required reserve ratio, set by the Central Bank, determines the reserves that a bank must maintain with the Central Bank. Any reserves deposited with the Central Bank beyond this amount are called *excess reserves.* Since the Central Bank does not pay usually interest on reserves, excess reserves are usually kept to a minimum.
- *Deposits by government.* The Treasury deposits with the Central Bank.

Any action taken by the Central Bank affects its balance-sheet. Table 2.3 shows an example of the impact of open market operation (purchase of bonds) on the Central Bank's balance sheet and on the money supply. *Monetary Base (MB)* is comprised of non-borrowed reserves and currency holdings of the commercial banking system plus public currency holdings.

Table 2.3: Effect of Open Market Operation.

Public		Central Bank	
Assets	Liabilities	Assets	Liabilities
Securities		Securities	Reserves
- €200		+€200	+€200
Deposits			
+€200			

Banking System	
Assets	Liabilities
Reserves	Deposits
+€200	+€200

Should CB purchase securities from the public, reserves and monetary base will increase €200.

Thus, by purchasing bonds held by the public, the Central Bank increased the deposits and therefore the money supply in the economy by allowing the banks to increase their credits, which stimulates growth.

2.10 Banking Regulation and Supervision

The banking industry is a heavily regulated industry. There are three main reasons for regulation:[6]
- *Increasing information to investors.* This is a central reason for regulations of the banking industry since the confidence of the public in the sector is an essential item for the sound functioning of the industry. The public in general does not have sufficient knowledge on the health of individual banks, financial instruments, and the relevant regulations. Thus, providing information to all relevant parties is a very important reason for regulation.
- *Ensuring the soundness of financial intermediaries.* Regulation is also important to ensuring the soundness of financial intermediaries. This is done by issuing strict reporting requirements, restrictions on assets and activities of intermediaries, running the deposit insurance fund, and taking measures to keep the industry competitive.
- *Improving monetary control.* Regulations are necessary to improve monetary control, mostly through reserve policy and capital requirements associated with *Basel Regulations*.

2.11 Summary

Money is the common denominator used to transact business. Money is the accepted means of paying for goods and services and for paying off debts. Money should therefore have certain characteristics.

Money supply has various definitions as M1, M2, and M3. Economists believe that the money supply is important in managing economic activity.

The interest rate is the cost of money. For banks, interest is paid on savings deposits; to consumers, interest is paid on loans and credit card balances. Interest can also be defined as the cost of postponing consumption. The nominal interest rate (NIR) is subject to risks of inflation, maturity, default, and liquidity.

The yield curve plots yield against time to maturity for default-free securities.

---

6 For a complete discussion of bank regulation, see S. Dow, "Why the banking system should be Regulated," *Economic Journal*, 106(436), 1996, pp. 698–707.

The Central Bank in general is a government-established organization responsible for supervising and regulating the banking system and for creating and regulating the money supply. The balance sheet of a Central Bank is an important economic indicator followed by markets.

The banking industry is heavily regulated to inform investors properly, insure soundness of financial intermediaries, and improve monetary control.

3 Time Value of Money

3.1 Introduction

In this chapter we first discuss the reasons of time value of money and its uses in finance. Simple interest concept is introduced. The compound interest (future value) concept is explained. How to calculate present value of a single payment is described. Present and future values of annuities (equal payments) are discussed together with perpetuities. More frequent compound and continuous compounding is studied. Finally, loan amortization and sinking fund schedules are presented.

3.2 Conceptual Background

Financial decisions, individual or commercial, often involve future cash flows. Therefore, future cash flows have to be considered on a common basis: the present value of cash flows. There are various financial issues where future cash flows are involved:
- Valuation of securities and other assets
- Valuation of firms
- Capital budgeting
- Cost of capital
- Working capital
- Buy-lease analysis

The reasons why time value of money exists:
- *Consumption.* Individuals prefer present consumption to future consumption. So they should be offered more in the future.
- *Risk.* As risk of cash flows in the future increases, this risk will lower the value of the cash flows in the future.
- *Expected inflation.* Inflation lowers the purchasing power of money. It is natural that investors demand a high return in inflationary periods to compensate if they lose in terms of purchasing power.

The underlying principle is that the value of one euro that you have in your hand today is greater than one euro you will receive in the future. Conversely, the time value of money (TVM) also includes the concepts of *future value (compounding)* and *present value (discounting).*

Compounding is the technique whereby interest earned each period on the principal amount is added to the principle before reinvesting. Discounting is an arithmetic technique whereby a future value decreases at a compound interest rate

https://doi.org/10.1515/9783110705355-003

over time to reach a present value. Simple interest is interest earned only on the principal amount of the investment.

3.3 Simple Interest

Present value or the future value of a cash flow can be calculated either using simple interest rate or compound interest rate. Interest rate is all the time expressed in yearly terms.

The principal is the amount of money borrowed, lended or invested, the term of a loan is the length of time or number of periods the loan is outstanding, and the rate of interest is the percentage of the principal the borrower pays the lender per time period in the future.

In the simple interest rate case, the interest amount is calculated as the principal times the interest rate without reinvestment of interest earned. In this case, the total interest paid on a principal (PV_0) for years at an interest rate of i is calculated as:

$$I(\text{Interest}) = PV_0 \times i \times n.$$

The future value will be principal plus the total interest amount calculated as in the previous example:

$$FV_n = PV_0 + I$$

$$FV_n = PV_0 + (PV_0 \times i \times n) = PV_0[1 + (i \times n)]$$

For simple interest, the present value of the loan is:

$$PV_0 = \frac{FVn}{[1 + (i \times n)]}$$

Suppose an individual deposits €40,000 in a savings account paying 6% annual interest. What is the amount of interest, and what is the future value of this transaction?

$$I = 40,000 \times 0.06 \times 1 = €2,400$$

$$FV_n = 40,000 \times [1 + (0.06 \times 1)] = €42,400$$

What is the present value of €42,400 if the annual interest rate is 6%?

$$PV_0 = \frac{42,000}{[1 + (0.06 \times 1)]} = €40,000$$

3.4 Compound Interest: Future Value Calculations

Compound interest refers to the process where interest earned on principal is added to principal. In other words, the interest that was earned in previous compounding periods is added to the principal. The amount of interest to be paid in each period is the interest rate times the principal amount at the beginning of the period. In the following formulas, the interest rate is assumed to remain constant throughout the term of the agreement.

For one period, the future value is:

$$FV_1 = PV_0(1+i)$$

And for two periods, the future (compound) value is:

$$FV_2 = FV_1(1+i)$$

$$FV_2 = PV_0(1+i)\,(1+i) = PV_0(1+i)^2$$

In general, the future value at the end of year n for a sum compounded at interest rate i is calculated as:

$$FV_n = PV_0(I+i)^n$$

The term $(1+i)^n$ is referred to as the *future value interest factor* ($FVIF_{i,\,n}$). Appendix D, Table D.3: Future Value Table shows the future value of €1 invested for n years at interest rate i:

$FVIF_{i,n} = (1+i)^n$
The future value of a lump sum can also be written as

$$FV_n = PV_0(FVIF_{i,n})$$

Suppose an individual deposits €40,000 in a savings account paying 6% annual interest. At the end of one year, the account balance will be €42,400 = [€40,000 the original amount + the interest earned (€40,000 × .06)]. If the new amount is left on deposit during year two, interest will be paid on €42,400. The amount at the end of each of the following two years will be as follows.

Applying the formula to the example in Table 3.1:

Table 3.1: Future Value of a Single Sum.

Year	Beginning Amount		Interest	Future Value
2nd year	€42,400.00	+	[(€42,400.00) (.06) = €2,544.00]	= €44,994,00
3rd year	€44,994.00	+	[(€44,994.00) (.06) = €2,696.64]	= €47,640.64

$$FV_2 = 40,000\,(1 + 0.06)^3$$

$$FV_3 = 40,000\,(1.191016) = €47,640.64$$

The *Rule of 72* is a shortcut method used to approximate the time required for an investment to double in value. In order to find time, the interest rate is divided into the number 72. For example, at 10%, the time it would take for an investment to double would be 72/10, or 7.2 years.

The *Rule of 69* is also a shortcut method used to approximate the time required for an investment to double in value. The formula is as follows: 0.35 + 69/i. For example, at 10%, the time it would take for an investment to double would be 0.35 + 69/10, or 7.25 years. The correct answer is 7.273 years.

3.5 Compound Interest: Present Value Calculations

Present value calculations compute present value PV_o, or the amount at time zero of future amount FV_n.

The present value of future amount received in n years discounted at interest rate i is found as:

$$PV_0 = FV_n \frac{I}{(1+i)^n} = FV_n(PVIF_{i,n})$$

Appendix D, Table D.1: Present Value Table includes *present value interest factors* ($PVIF_{i,n}$) that show the present value of €1 discounted at interest rate i for n periods:

$$PVIF_{i,n} \frac{1}{(1+i)^n} \text{ or } 1/FVIF_{i,n}.$$

The present value interest factor is the reciprocal of the future value interest factor shown as $1/FVIF_{i,n}$

If i is in the numerator, the interest rate is referred to as the *compound interest rate* or the *growth rate*. On the other hand, if i is in the denominator, the interest rate is called the *discount rate*.

The present value of €47,640.64 to be received three years hence is €40,000 if the amount could be employed to earn a 6% return annually.

$$PV = FV \times PVIF$$

$$PV = (€47,640.64)(.8396)$$

PV = €39,999.08 (note that differences between two values are due to rounding).

An alternative approach to solving for present value is available by simply expressing the equation as:

$$PV = \frac{FV}{(1+I)^n}$$

$$PV = \frac{47,640.64}{1.191} = 40,000$$

The present value formula can also be used to calculate the interest rate (i) when the present value (PV_0), the future value (FV_n), and the number of periods (n) are given.

If a lender agreed to lend €1,000 now with a lump-sum payment of principal and interest of €1,404.49 at the end of three years, what rate of interest is being charged?

$$i = (FV/PV_0)^{1/n} - 1$$
$$= (1,404.49/1,000)^{1/3} - 1$$
$$= 0.1199 = 11.99\%$$

If a lender agreed to lend €1,000 now at 11.99%, what is the time period (in years) required to reach a lump-sum payment of principal and interest of €1,404.49?

$$n = \frac{ln(FV/V_0)}{ln(1+i)}$$
$$n = \frac{ln(1,404.49/1,000)}{ln(1.1199)} = 3 \text{ years}$$

3.6 Annuities

An *annuity* is a series of periodic equal payments. There are basically two types of annuities. An *ordinary annuity* is one where the payments or receipts result at the end of each period. An *annuity due* is one where payments or receipts result at the beginning of each period.

For an ordinary annuity, the future value at the end of year n ($FVAN_n$) can be found by multiplying the annuity payment (PMT) times the compound value of an annuity interest factor ($FVIFA_{i,n}$):

$$FVAN_n = PMT\ (FVIFA_{i,n})$$
$$\textit{Where } FVIFA_{i,n} = \frac{(1+i)^n - 1}{i}$$

A number of values for FVIFA are shown in Appendix D, Table D.4: Future Value of Annuity Table. This table shows FVIFA of €1 for i percent and n periods. Other values for the interest factor can also be found with a financial calculator, by a spreadsheet program, or by using the formula.

$FVIFA_{i,\,n}$ is the value at time n of €1 invested at the end of each of the next n periods earning interest rate i. For positive interest rates, the value of $FVIFA_{i,n}$ will exceed the value of n (i.e., $FVIFA_{i,n} > n$).

The future value of a 10-year annuity (FV_A) of €4,000 (PMT) per year with each payment invested at 8% would be:

$$FV_A = PMT(FVIFA_{i,n})$$

$$FV_A = €4,000\ (14,487) = €57,948$$

One common use of the FVIFA is to find the annuity amount (PMT) that must be invested each year to produce a future value:

$$PMT = FVAN_n/(FVIFA_{i,\,n}).$$

This is called the *sinking fund* problem.

The *future value of an annuity due* is simply equal to the future value of an ordinary annuity times one plus the interest rate:

$$FVAND_n = PMT(FVIFA_{i,\,n})(1+i)$$

$$= FVAND_n/(FVIFA_{i,\,n})(1+i)$$

For an ordinary annuity, the present value of the annuity (PVAN₀) can be found by multiplying the annuity payment (PMT times the present value of an annuity interest factor (PVIFA$_i$) from Appendix D, Table D.2: Present Value of Annuity Table.

$$PVAN_o = PMT\ (FVIFA_{i,\,n})$$

Where $PVIFA_{i,\,n} = \dfrac{1 - \frac{I}{(1+i)^n}}{i}$

$PVIFA_{i,\,n}$ is the value at time 0 of €1 received or paid at the end of each of the next n periods discounted at interest rate i. The value of $PVIFA_{i,n}$ will be lower than the value of n (i.e., $PVIFA_{i,n} < n$).

PVIFAs can be found in interest factor tables, computed from the formula, or computed on a financial calculator.

The present value of an annuity of €7,000 for four years assuming an interest rate of 6% is:

$$PV_A = €7,000\ (3,465) = €24,255$$

Frequently, the PVFA is used to find the annuity amount that is necessary to recover a capital investment:

$$PMT = PVAN_o/(PVIFA_{i,\,n})$$

This is called the *capital recovery* problem. An example of this problem would be to find the payments necessary to pay off a loan.

The *present value of an annuity due* is equal to the present value of an ordinary annuity times one plus the interest rate:

$$PVAND_0 = PMT(PVFA_{i,n})(1+i)$$

3.7 Perpetuities and Uneven Payment Streams

Some additional cash flow patterns encountered in finance are perpetuities, uneven cash flows, and deferred annuities.

The present value of a perpetuity (which is an annuity with an infinite life) is:

$$PVPER_0 = \frac{PMT}{(1+i)^1} + \frac{PMT}{(1+i)^2} + \frac{PMT}{(1+i)^3} + \dots$$

$$PVPER_0 = \sum_{t=1}^{\infty} \frac{PMT}{(1+i)^t} = \frac{PMT}{i}$$

Where *PMT* is the equal periodic payment and *PVPER_0* is the sum of the present values of these payments from time 1 to infinity.

Find the present value of a perpetuity that pays €100 per year if the current interest rate is 10%.

$$PVPER_o = \frac{100}{0.10} = €1,000$$

An uneven payment stream is a cash flow where the payments in each period are unequal. The present value of an uneven payment stream over *n* periods is given by:

$$PV_0 = \frac{PMT_1}{(1+i)^1} + \frac{PMT_2}{(1+i)^2} + \dots + \frac{PMT_n}{(1+i)^n}$$

Find the present value of an investment that pays €100, €150, and €200 at the end of each year. if current interest rate is 10%.

$$PV_0 = \frac{100}{(1+0.10)^1} + \frac{150}{(1+0.10)^2} + \frac{200}{(1+i0.10)^3} = 365.14$$

A deferred annuity is an annuity that begins in a later period in the future. To find annuities, one should find the future value of the loan. This is considered the new present value of all annuities.

A firm borrows €100,000 from a bank. Payment will start 3 years later. If the annual interest rate is 10%, what are the annual payments (annuities) if the loan is paid off in four years' time? Note that all payments occur at the end of relevant periods.

$$FV_3 = PV_O\,(I+i)^3$$

$$= 100,000\,(1.10)^3 = 100,000 \times 1.331 = €133,100$$

This is the new amount of the loan. What are the annuities?

$$A = PVAN_o/(PVIFA_{0.10,\,4})$$

$$= 133,100/3.1699 = €41,989$$

3.8 More Frequent Compounding

Interest may be subject to compounding more frequently than once per year. When interest compounds frequently, the basic compound interest formula must be corrected. In this case, the periodic interest rate is calculated by dividing the nominal interest rate by the number of compounding periods per year.

The corrected compound value formula is shown as:

$$FVn = PV_0(1+\frac{i_{nom}}{m})^{mn}$$

Where m is the number of compounding periods per year and n is the number of years. Note that periodic interest rate, i_{nom}/m, is compounded m times a year for n years.

For example, the future value of €10,000 after three years at 8% annual interest compounded quarterly would be:

$$FV = 10,000\left(1+\frac{0.08}{4}\right)^{3*4}$$

$$FV = 10,000(1+02)^{12}$$

$$FV = 10,000(1.268) = 12,680$$

The relationship between present and future values in this case will be:

$$PV_0 = FV_n\,\frac{1}{(1+\frac{i_{nom}}{m})^{mn}}$$

The *effective annual interest rate* is also known as the *effective interest rate, effective rate,* or the *annual equivalent rate.* The effective annual rate of interest (i_{eff}) is found by dividing a rate of interest per period, i_m, by m and compounding m times per year:

$$i_{eff} = (1+\frac{i_{nom}}{m})^m - 1$$

For instance, a bank pays 10% yearly interest for a three-month time deposit account. What is the yearly effective rate of interest?

$$i_{eff} = (1 + (0.10/4))^4 - 1$$

$$= 1.1038 - 1 = 0.1038 = 10.38\%$$

The rate of interest per period (where there is more than one compounding period per year), i_{nom}, which results from an effective annual rate of interest, i_{eff}, is found as:

$$i_{nom} = \left((1 + i_{eff})^{1/m} - 1\right) \times m$$

What is nominal rate of interest for this three-month deposit?

$$i_{nom} = ((1 + 0.1038)^{1/4} - 1) \times 4 = 10\%$$

Where i_{nom} is the yearly interest rate (denoted as i), and n number of periods in years.

3.9 Continuous Compounding

Continuous compounding is the case if interest is compounded for a large number of times per year (that is, if m approaches infinity).

The future value (FV_n) of some initial amount (PV_0) compounded continuously is:

$$FV_n = PV_0 e^{in}$$

Find the future value of a €1,000 deposit made today for 5 years if the interest rate is 10%.

$$FV_n = €1,000 \times e^{0.1 \times 5}$$

$$= €1,648.72$$

The present value of a future lump sum discounted at continuous rate i is

$$PV_0 = FV_n/e^{in} = FV_n e^{-in}$$

Find the present value of a €1,648.72 deposit to be collected at the end years if the interest rate is 10%.

$$PV_0 = €1,648.72/e^{0.1 \times 5}$$

$$= €1,000$$

If the nominal interest (or growth) rate is i compounded continuously, the effective annual rate equivalent to this is

$$\text{Effective (annual) rate} = i_{eff} = e^i - 1$$

A bank pays 10% yearly interest. What is the yearly continuous effective rate of interest?

$$i_{eff} = e^{0.10} - 1 = 10.52\%$$

If i_{eff} is a continuous effective rate of interest, the simple rate equivalent to this is:
Simple Rate $(i) = ln(1+i_{eff})$, where ln is the natural logarithm operator.

$$i = ln(1.1052) = 10\%$$

3.10 Amortized Loans

Amortized loans are the loans where the borrower pays an equal amount every period for a fixed number of periods at a given nominal interest rate. Mortgage credits, car loans, consumer credits are such loans. Then the relevant relationship between regular equal payments (*PMT*), number of periods (*n*), original loan amount (*PVA*), and the interest rate (*i*) is:

$$PVA = PMT \left[\frac{1 - \frac{I}{(1+i)^n}}{i} \right]$$

The periodic payment is fixed. However, different amounts of each payment are applied toward the principal and interest. With each payment, you owe less toward principal. As a result, the amount that goes toward interest declines with every payment.

If you want to finance a new machinery with a purchase price of €6,000 at an interest rate of 15% over 4 years, what will your annual payments be at the end of each year?

Payment amount (annuity) can be found by solving for *PMT* using *PV* of the annuity formula:

$$6,000 = PMT\ (2,855)$$

$$PMT = 6,000/2,855$$

$$= €2,101.58$$

The interest for the period 1 is calculated as follows: $6,000 \times 0.15 = €900$. We deduct this amount from the annuity to find out the principal to be paid: $2,101.58-900 = €1,202$. In second period interest is calculated on the balance (€4.798). (See Table 3.2.)

Table 3.2: Amortization Schedule, End of Period (€).

End of period	Interest to be paid	Principal to be paid	Balance
0			6,000
1	900	1,202	4,798
2	720	1,382	3,417
3	512	1,589	1,827
4	274	1,827	0

If payments were made at the beginning of each year, what would be payment amount in each year? (See Table 3.3.)

$$PVAND_0 = PMT(PVFA_{i,n})(1+i)$$

$$6,000 = PMT\ (2,855)\ (1{,}15)$$

$$PMT = 6,000/3.28325$$

$$= 1,827.46$$

Table 3.3: Amortization Schedule, Beginning of Period (€).

Beginning of the period	Interest to be paid	Principal to be paid	Balance
0			
1		1,827	4,173
2	626	1,202	2,971
3	446	1,382	1,589
4	238	1,589	0

3.11 Sinking Fund

A *sinking fund* is created to repay debts easily. The owner of the account sets aside a certain amount of money regularly and uses it only for a specific purpose. Often, it is used by corporations to buy back issued bonds or parts of bonds before the maturity date.

The ABC company will pay of €100M at the end of 3 years. How much money should the company invest in a fund yielding 10% per year at the end of each year?

$$PMT = FVAN_n/(FVIFA_{i,n})$$

$$PMT = €100,000,000/3.31$$

$$= €30,211,480$$

Where,

PMT = Payment

$FVAN_n$ = Future value

$FVIFA_{i,n}$ = Future value interest factor

Transactions in the sinking fund are presented in Table 3.4.

Table 3.4: Schedule of Sinking Fund.

End of Period	Interest Added	Periodic Money Deposited	Increase in Fund	Amount of Fund Accumulated
1	0	30,211,480	30,211,480	30,211,480
2	3,021,148	30,211,480	33,232,628	63,444,109
3	6,344,411	30,211,480	36,555,891	100,000,000

The XYZ company will pay of €100M at the end of 3 years. How much money should the company invest in a fund yielding 6% per year at the beginning of each year?

$$PMT = FVAND_n/(FVIFA_{i,n})(1+i)$$

$$PMT = €100,000,000/(3.18360 \times 1.06)$$

$$= €100.000.000/3.374616 = €29,633,001$$

Transactions in the sinking fund is presented in Table 3.5.

Table 3.5: Schedule of the Sinking Fund.

End of Period	Interest Added	Periodic Money Deposited	Increase in Fund	Amount of Fund Accumulated
1	0	29,633,001	29,633,001	29,633,001
2	1,777,980	29,633,001	31,410,981	61,043,982
3	3,662,639	29,633,001	33,295,640	94,339,623
4	5,660,377	0	5,660,377	100,000,000

3.12 Summary

Business and personal financial decisions that involve cash flows occur at different points in time and require an understanding of the time value of money.

In borrowing or lending money, the amount due in the future can be calculated using simple interest or compound interest. Simple interest is the interest paid on the principal sum only.

Compound interest refers to the process where interest earned on principal is converted into interest-earning principal.

Present value calculations compute present value (PV_o), or the amount at time zero, that is equivalent to some future amount FV_n.

An annuity is a series of periodic payments of equal size. An ordinary annuity is one where the payments or receipts occur at the end of each period. An annuity due is one where payments or receipts occur at the beginning of each period. Perpetuity is an annuity with an infinite life. A deferred annuity is an annuity that begins more than one period in the future.

Interest may be compounded more frequently than once per year. When interest compounded frequency is more than once (annual compounding), the basic compound interest formula must be modified.

Continuous compounding is the case if interest is compounded a large number of times per year.

Loans paid off in equal installments over time, such as home mortgages and auto loans, are called amortized loans. Reducing the balance of a loan via annuity payments is called amortizing.

A sinking fund is a type of fund that is created for repaying debt easily. The owner of the account sets aside a certain amount of money regularly and uses it only for a specific purpose.

Part II: **Investments and Portfolio Management**

4 Bonds and the Markets

4.1 Introduction

Bonds dominate debt securities markets. Thus, we will dwell on bonds rather than other debt securities. Time value of money principle is used extensively in bond valuation. Generally, bonds have contractually-based fixed cash flows, a known time to maturity, and a known principal value at maturity. We first review bond characteristics and the global nature of the bond market. The second part of the chapter discusses valuation principles for bonds and the risks faced by bond investors. Duration and convexity are the major tools used to measure bond risks. Bond portfolio performance is also discussed.

4.2 Bond Terminology and Features of Bond Markets

This section discusses various terms associated with bonds and institutional features of bond markets. Other topics examined include bond income and strategies, global bond markets, and bond ratings.

Bond Terminology

A *bond* is a debt agreement that a corporation or government agency (i.e., municipality) enters into when it wants to borrow money for more than five years.

In the following section, we present important terms for bonds:

- *Par value* is the face value of a bond, the principal to be paid at maturity.
- *Coupon rate* is annual interest divided by face value. Coupon rate times face value equals the coupon interest payment.
- *Maturity date* is the final date on which repayment of the debt principal is due.
- *Indenture* is a legal agreement detailing the issuer's obligations pertaining to a bond issue.
- *Debenture* is an unsecured, long-term corporate bond.
- *Subordinated debenture* is an unsecured bond in which payment will be made to the bondholder only after the holders of senior debt issues have been met.
- *Call feature* is an option that allows the firm to pay off or call a debt issue prior to maturity.
- A *sinking fund* provision requires the issuer to retire specified portions of the bond issued over time by using the fund.
- *Asset securitization* refers to bonds that have coupon and principal payments that are paid from another existing cash flow source.

https://doi.org/10.1515/9783110705355-004

- A *perpetuity* is a bond without a maturity date, in which holders receive interest payments forever.
- *Registered bonds* include bondholders' names and interest payments sent directly to bondholders.
- *Bearer bonds* are bonds of which coupons are clipped from bond certificates and presented to bank or company for payment.
- *Bond covenants* are rules and regulations that impose restrictions on the issuer in order to protect the bondholders' interests.

Bond Quotations

Understanding bond quotations is an important element of how they are valued. A typical quotation as it might appear in a stock exchange is shown as follows.

Frankfurt Stock Exchange provides information with historical prices and volumes of European Investment Bank' bonds (EIB) 7.25% (coupon rate) 17/21 (maturity):

Date	Open	Close	High	Low	Volume €	Volume nominal
08/05/20	104.71%	104.71%	104.71%	104.71%	52,355	50,000

Bond Income and Strategies

The *seesaw effect* is a risk associated with bonds. It means that lower interest rates cause bond prices to rise; higher interest rates mean lower bond prices. A ladder strategy involves investing an equal amount of money in bonds with a wide range of long and short-term maturities so that interest rate cycles will average out. In times of declining interest rates, discount bonds, or bonds sold at a discount, are issued; when interest rates rise, then premium bonds, or bonds sold at a premium, are sold. This strategy is shown figuratively in Figure 4.1. Inflation poses a great risk to bond investors, as an unexpected increase in inflation can lower returns.

Figure 4.1: Relationship between Current Interest Rates and Bond Prices: The Seesaw Effect.
Source: Malicher and Norton, op. cit., p. 470.

Global Bond Markets

The global bond market includes global bonds, Eurodollar bonds, and Yankee bonds.

Global bonds are those that are usually denominated in U.S. dollars and marketed globally, offering sizes typically exceeding $1 billion.

Eurodollar bonds are dollar-denominated bonds sold outside the U.S. These bonds escape from SEC review, somewhat reducing the expense of issuance. Typically, Eurodollar bonds have fixed coupons, annual coupon payments, and most mature in five to ten years (relatively short-term). Additionally, most Eurodollar bonds are debentures.

Yankee bonds are U.S. dollar-denominated bonds that are issued in the U.S. by a foreign issuer. These bonds can have maturities up to 30 years.

Bond Ratings

Bond ratings are credit risk assessments by independent bond rating agencies, such as Moody's and Standard & Poor's. Basic features of ratings are as follows:
- Ten different ratings plus modifiers
- Moody's uses capital and lowercase letters with numerical modifiers
- S&P uses capital letters only with +/- modifiers

There two types of bonds in terms of default:
- *Investment grade bonds*. Rated Baa or above (Moody's), BBB or above (S&P).
- *High-yield (junk) bonds*. Rated below investment grade. If downgraded to "junk," bonds are called "fallen angels."

There is an inverse relationship between bond ratings and bond promised rates of return: If ratings go down, yields go up. The following are the factors that affect default risk and bond ratings:
- *Financial performance*. Measured by the following ratios: debt ratio, coverage ratios, such as interest coverage ratio or EBITDA coverage ratio, and current ratios.
- *Features of the bond*. Secured versus unsecured debt, senior versus subordinated debt, guarantee provisions, sinking fund provisions, and debt maturity.
- *Other factors*. Measured by the following factors: earnings stability, regulatory environment, potential product liability, and accounting policies.

The rating systems of three major rating companies are summarized in Table 4.1.

Table 4.1: Comparative Ratings of the Three Major Credit Rating Companies.

Explanation	S&P	Fitch	Moody's	Quality	Grade
Prime – highest safety	AAA	AAA	Aaa	High	Investment
High Quality	AA+	AA+	Aa1		
	AA	AA	Aa2		
	AA-	AA-	Aa3		
Upper medium credit	A+	A+	A1		
	A	A	A2		
	A-	A-	A3		
Lower medium credit	BBB+	BBB+	Baa1		
	BBB	BBB	Baa2		
	BBB-	BBB-	Baa3		
Speculative – low quality	BB+	BB+	Ba1	Lower	Speculative
	BB	BB	Ba2		
	BB-	BB-	Ba3		
Highly speculative		B+	B1		
	B	B	B2		
		B-	B3		
Very high risk – poor quality	CCC+	CCC+	Caa	Low	Highly Speculative
	CCC	CCC			or Default
May be in default soon	CC	CC	Ca		
	C	C	C		
No interest being paid	CI				
Default	D	DDD			
		DD			
		D			

Source: PinoyMoneyTalk, *Credit Ratings by S&P, Moody's, and Fitch Ratings,* https://www.pinoymoneytalk.com/meaning-of-credit-ratings/

Above all, credit ratings affect the cost of borrowing,[1] that is, the interest rate that will have to be paid by the issuer to attract buyers. The interest cost to the issuer is the coupon the investor will earn.

The most creditworthy issuers – say, large states with diverse economies, blue-chip corporations with very little debt, or governments – borrow at a lower cost. Less creditworthy clients have to pay higher interest. Consequently, bonds with the highest quality credit ratings always carry the lowest yields, and bonds with lower credit ratings yield more. Note that the yield, in a sense, provides a scale of credit-worthiness. Higher yields generally indicate higher risk – the higher the yield, the higher the risk.

4.3 Bond Valuation

The value of an asset is based on the expected future cash inflows its owner will receive over the life of an asset. The value of any financial asset is based on the ex-pected cash flows it will generate over the holding period. The capitalization-of-cash flow method of valuation determines the value of an asset as the present value of the stream of future cash flows discounted at an appropriate required rate of return.

Algebraically;

$$P_0 = \sum_{t=1}^{n} \frac{CF_t}{(1+k)^t}$$

where CF_t is the expected cash flow at time t, k is the required rate of return or dis-count rate, n is the number of the holding period, and P_0 is the value (price) of the asset.

The required rate of return (k) on an asset is a function of the asset's risk as well as the risk-free interest rate. If the asset's returns are known with certainty (there is no risk), the investor's required rate of return is the risk-free rate. Otherwise, it will include default risk premium (spread).

The market value of an asset is determined by the demand for and the supply of that asset. The transaction price at which an asset is sold is the market price. As investors' required rates of return or expected returns from an asset change, the price will also change.

---

1 For real functions of bond rating agencies, see MacDonald Wakeman, "The Real Function of Bond Rating Agencies," in *The Revolution in Corporate Finance*, Editor: Joel M. Stern and Donald H. Chew, Jr, Blackwell, 1998, pp. 25–28. The author, while stressing the importance of rating, states that grading does not matter because the market, having made evaluations on the firm, determines interest cost before rating is released.

Bonds may be valued using the capitalization of cash flows method. The future cash flows consist of the interest payments and the principal value repaid at the end of maturity. The discount rate (required rate of return) depends upon the risk-free rate and the default risk premium of the particular bond.

Using the capitalization-of-cash flow method, the value of a bond (if the interest payments are different at every period) is:

$$P_0 = \frac{I_1}{(1+k_d)^1} + \frac{I_2}{(1+k_d)^2} + \ldots + \frac{I_{n-1}}{(1+k_d)^{n-1}} + \frac{I_n + F}{(I+k_d)^n}$$

where P_0 is the present value of the bond, I is the interest payment at time t, n the time to maturity, F the principal payment (face value) at maturity, and k_d the investor's required rate of return for the bond.

The value of the bond can be expressed using the summation notation as:

$$P_0 = \sum_{t=1}^{n} \frac{I_1}{(1+k_d)^t} + \frac{F}{(I+k_d)^n}$$

Using present value factors, the value of the bond is

$$P_0 = I\left(PVIFA_{k_d, n}\right) + F\left(PVIF_{k_d, n}\right)$$

It is clear that there is an inverse relationship between the price of the bond and the required rate of return. An equal change in the required rate of return changes the value of a long-term bond more than that of the value of a short-term bond.

Bonds are subject to interest rate risk and reinvestment rate risk, which refers to the potential loss that an investor could experience from a reduction in a bond's market price due to a change in market interest rates. Reinvestment rate risk occurs when a bond issue matures (or is called) and because of a decline in interest rates, the investor has to reinvest the principal at a lower coupon rate.

Most bonds pay interest semi-annually. Bonds which pay interest semi-annually have a value of:

$$P_0 = \sum_{t=1}^{2n} \frac{I/2}{(1+k_d/2)^t} + \frac{F}{(1+k_d/2)^{2n}}$$

A perpetual bond, or perpetuity, promises to pay interest indefinitely and has no maturity date. The general valuation formula for a perpetual bond that pays interest (I) per period forever and has a required rate of return k_d is:

$$P_0 = \sum_{t=1}^{\infty} \frac{I}{(1+k_d)^t} = \frac{I}{k_d}$$

The yield to maturity of a bond is the expected rate of return earned on a bond purchased at a given price and held to maturity.

The yield to maturity is found by solving the following formula for k_d, given values for Po, I, F, and n.

$$P_0 = \sum_{t=1}^{n} \frac{I}{(1+k_d)^t} + \frac{F}{(I+k_d)^n}$$

If sold prior to maturity, the *realized rate of return* for a bond will generally differ from its *yield to maturity*. Variation in the market value of a fixed-income security (and in realized rates of return) due to fluctuations in interest rate levels is called *interest rate risk*.

Suppose we have a ten-year, €1000 par value bond with €80 coupon payments per year. Suppose interest rate (k_d) = coupon rate = 8% = (€80/€1000). Then the value of the bond (V_b) = €80 $(1–1/(1.08)^{10})/(0.08)$ + €1000/(1.08)^{10}$ = €536.8065 + €463.1935 = €1000.

Suppose interest rate drops to 5% – that is, (k_d) = 5%. Then V_b = €80$(1–1/ (1.05)^{10})/$ (0.05) + €1000/(1,05)^{10}$ = €617.7388 + €613.9133 – €1231.65. The previous bond is more attractive than the new one, with coupon payments of €50 per year. So, the demand for the old bond goes up, all other things being constant, so the price of the old bond goes up; the bond sells at a premium, and the bond is called a *premium bond*.

Suppose the interest rate goes up to 10% – that is, (k_d) = 10%. Then V_b = €80 $(1–1/(1.10)^{10}/(0.10)$ + €1000/(1.10)^{10}$ = €491.5654 + €385.5433 = €877.1087. This bond sells at a discount and it is called a *discount bond*.

Valuation of bonds on non-interest dates is a little bit complicated. The process can be summarized as follows:
- Calculate the value the bond at the next coupon date.
- Add the coupon payment to be received at the next interest data to the value of the bond calculated in the previous stage.
- To calculate the present value of the bond, discount this sum by using the market interest rate.
- Adjust this computed value for the accrued interest amount.

A bond with a face (maturity) value of €1,000 pays 9% interest. There are 13 (semi-annual) interest payments in the future, and 120 days since the last interest payment. What is this price of the bond if yield to maturity is 11%?

Let us define the variables:

Discount rate = 0.11/2 = 0.055 = 5.5%

Face value (F) = €1,000

Coupon payment per period = 90/2 = €45

Now let us do the necessary calculations:

- Price (value) of the bond at the end of next coupon payment data will be calculated as follows:

$$P = C_t/2\left(PVIFA_{kd/2, 2n}\right) + M\left(PVIF_{kd/2, 2n}\right)$$

$$= 45 \times \left(PVIFA_{0.055, 12}\right) + 1,000 \times \left(PVIF_{0,055,12}\right)$$

$$= 45 \times 8.6185 + 1,000 \times 0.526$$

$$= 387.83 + 526.00$$

$$= €913.83$$

- At the second stage, we add the next coupon payment to the value:

$$P + C_t = 913.83 + 45$$

$$= €958.83$$

- At the third stage, the present value/dirty price of the bond at the date of valuation is calculated as follows:

$$D = 958.83 \times PVIF_{0,055,40/180}$$

$$= €947.47$$

This is the price on which the bond trades. This is called the *dirty price* of the bond. *Day count* conventions vary. Since the number of days in a year is assumed 360 days in this case, the number of days in a semi-annual period will be 180 days.

- At the fourth stage, let us calculate accrued interest and deduct it from the dirty price to reach the clean price:

Accrued interest = ((180−40)/180) × 45 = €35

$$\text{Clean price} = \text{Dirty price} - \text{Accrued interest}$$

$$\text{Clean price} = 947.47 - 35 = €912.47$$

4.4 Pure Discount Bonds

A *pure discount bond* is a security that promises to pay a specified single cash payment (*face value* or *par value*) at its maturity date and there is no cash flow associated with interest. Pure discount bonds are purchased at a discount from their face or par value.

The pure discount bond is an example of the present value of a lump sum equation that we analyzed in Chapter 3. Solving this, the yield-to-maturity (YTM) on a pure discount bond is given by the following relationship:

$$F_n = P_0(1+k_d)^n \quad \Rightarrow \quad i = \left(\frac{F_n}{P_0}\right)^{\frac{1}{n}} - 1$$

$$P_0 = F_n / (1+k_d)^n$$

$$P_0 = F_n\left(PVIF_{k_d, n}\right)$$

In this equation, P_0 is the present value or price of the bond, F_n is the face or future value, n is the investment period, and k_d is the yield-to-maturity.

For example, if you purchase a pure discount bond for €4,500, and it matures in two years with a face value of €5,000, its VTM (i) will be:

$$k_d = \left(\frac{5,000}{4,000}\right)^{\frac{1}{2}} - 1 = 11.80\%$$

$$F_n = 4,000 \times /(1+0.1180)^2 = €5,000$$

For zero-coupon bonds that pay no interest over their lives, the only payment to holders is the principal payment at maturity. The yield to maturity on a zero-coupon bond can be found directly from the following relationship:

$$P_0 = \frac{F_n}{(1+k_d)^n} = F_n\left(PVIF_{k_d, n}\right)$$

The yield to maturity for a perpetual bond is $k_d = I/P_0$.

4.5 Bond Price Changes

The bond price changes over time due to interest rate changes. This and the effect of maturity on bond price will be discussed below. These are summarized as the following theorems:[2]

- *Theorem 1.* Bond prices move inversely to bond yields. As the yield increases, the bond price decreases. Or as the yield decreases, the bond price increases.

---

2 These are known as bond price theorems. For more information, see Burton G. Malkiel, "Expectation, Bond Prices, and the Term Structure of Interest Rates," *Quarterly Journal of Economics*, 76, May 1962, pp. 197–218. Arman T. Tevfik and Gürman Tevfik, *Lotus 1-2-3 ile Menkul Değer Yatırımlarına Giriş*, Ekonomik Araştırmalar Merkezi, 1996, pp. 77–90.

- *Theorem 2.* For a given change in market yield, changes in bond prices are greater for longer term maturities – bond price volatility is directly related to term to maturity.
- *Theorem 3.* Price volatility of bonds increases at a diminishing rate as the term to maturity increases.
- *Theorem 4.* The lower the coupon interest rate, the more sensitive the price is to interest rate changes.
- *Theorem 5.* For a given bond, capital gain due to a decrease in yield is greater than the capital loss due to an equal increase in yield.

4.6 Measuring Bond Price Volatility: Duration

In managing a bond portfolio, the most important consideration is the effect of yield changes on the prices and the rates of return for different bonds. The problem is that a given change in interest rates can result in very different percentage price changes for the various bonds that investors hold.

In order to equate bonds with different characteristics, a measure is needed that accounts for the entire pattern (both size and timing) of the cash flows over the life of the bond. This would measure the effective maturity of the bond.

Such a concept was devised over 50 years ago by *Frederick Macaulay*, known as *duration (Macaulay duration)* which measures the weighted average maturity of a bond's cash flows on a present value basis. That is, the present value of the cash flows is used as the weight in calculating the weighted average maturity.

Duration is the number of years needed to fully recover the purchase price of a bond, given the present values of its cash flows.

Calculate Duration

To calculate duration, it is necessary to calculate a weighted time period. The present values of the cash flows serve as the weighting factors to apply to the time periods. The sum of the weighting factors will be one, indicating that all the cash flows have been accounted for. Algebraically:

$$D = \frac{\sum_{t=1}^{n} \frac{C_t(t)}{(1+k_d)^t}}{\sum_{t=1}^{n} \frac{C_t}{(1+k_d)^t}} = \frac{\sum_{t=1}^{n} t \times PV(C_t)}{\text{Market Price}}$$

where D = Macaulay duration, t = the time period at which the cash flow is expected to be received, n = the number of periods to maturity, PV (CF_t) = present value of the cash flow in period t discounted at the YTM (k_d), and market price = the bond's current price or present value of all the cash flows.

This formula is derived by first calculating the derivative of the price with respect to the yield:

$$D = \frac{\frac{dP}{dk_d}}{P}$$

An example of calculating the duration of a bond using a 10% coupon rate, five-year maturity bond priced at €100 and paying an annual interest of €10 is shown in Table 4.2.

Table 4.2: Calculation of Duration.

(1)	(2)	(3)	(4)	(5)	(6)
Years	Cash Flow	PV Factor	(2) × (3)	(4)/Price	(1) × (5)
1	€10	0.909	€9 09	0.0909	0.0909
2	€10	0.826	€8.26	0.0826	0.1652
3	€10	0.751	€7.51	0.0751	0.2253
4	€10	0.683	€6.83	0.0683	0.2732
5	€110	0.621	68.31	0.6831	3.4155
				Duration =	4.1701

Notice that the fifth-year cash flow of €110 (€10 coupon plus €100 return of principal) accounts for 68% of the value of the bond and contributes 3.41 years to the duration of 4.17 years. The duration of 4.17 years is less than the term to maturity of five years. Duration will always be less than the term to maturity for bonds that pay coupons.

Understanding Duration

Checking out the equation for duration will show us that duration depends on three factors:
- final maturity of the bond (1)
- coupon payments (2)
- yield to maturity (3)

Holding 2 and 3 constant, duration expands with time to maturity but at a decreasing rate. For a zero-coupon bond, duration is equal to time to maturity.

Holding 1 and 3 constant, we find that coupon is inversely related to duration, which is logical as higher coupons lead to quicker recovery.

Holding 1 and 2 constant, yield to maturity is inversely related to duration, which is logical as higher coupons lead to quicker recovery.

Holding 1 and 2 constant, yield to maturity is inversely related to duration.

Why Is Duration Important?

The reasons for the importance of duration are:
- It tells us the difference between the effective lives of alternative bonds. Bond A and B, with the same duration but different years to maturity, have more in common, but bonds C and D with the same maturity but different durations have less in common.
- The duration concept is used in certain bond management strategies, particularly *immunization* as we will discuss later.
- Duration is a measure of bond price sensitivity to interest rate movements, which is a very important part of any bond analysis.

Estimating Bond Prices Using Duration

As noted earlier, duration is positively related to maturity and negatively related to coupon rate. However, bond price changes are directly related to duration. The percentage change in a bond's price, given a change in interest rates, is proportional to its duration. Therefore, duration can be used to measure interest rate exposure.

The term *modified duration* refers to the Macaulay duration equation divided by $(1+k_d)$, or

$$\text{Modified duration} = D^* = D/(1+k_d)$$

Where k_d is the bond's yield to maturity.

The modified duration can be used to calculate the percentage price change in a bond for a given change in the k_d. This is shown by the following:

Percentage change in bond price $\approx [-D/ (1+k_d)]$ *times the percentage point change in* k_d

$$\text{or } \Delta P/P \approx -D \times \Delta k_d$$

Where
  ΔP = change in price
  P = the price of the bond
  $-D^*$ = modified duration with a negative sign
  Δk_d = the instantaneous change in yield

Following an instantaneous yield change of 20 basis points (+0.0020) in the YTM from 10% to 10.2%, what is an estimation of the new bond price? The modified duration of the bond is 3.79.

$$\Delta P/P \approx -3.79 \times (+0.0020) \times 100 = -0.758\%$$

Given the original price of the bond of €100, this percentage price change would result in an estimated bond price of 100(1−0.00758) = €99.24. For very small changes in yield, this equation produces a good approximation. This is due to the non-linear relationship between price and yield. An adjustment for this convexity must be included if the instantaneous yield change is large.

Although duration is an important measure of bond risk, it is not necessarily always the most appropriate one. Duration measures volatility, which is important but is only one aspect of the risk in bonds.

4.7 Convexity

We can see from our example using duration to estimate that the percent change in the value of a bond is less than perfect, as shown in Figure 4.2. The straight line denotes the duration based bond value while the nonlinear curve denotes convex and duration based bond price.

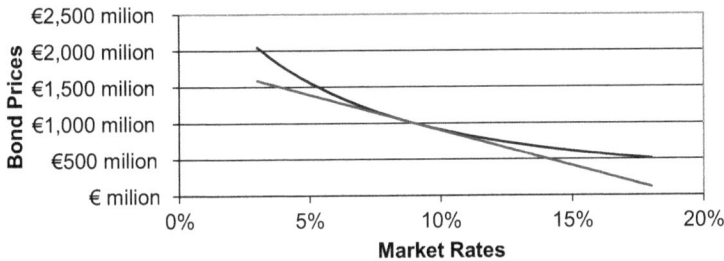

Figure 4.2: Duration-Based and Convexity-Based Bond Prices.

While the linear curve estimates duration-based bond prices, the non-linear curve shows real prices that can be obtained via convexity.

Empirical evidence shows that duration works well in estimating the percent change in value of relatively short-term bonds with relatively small changes in interest rates.

We can improve the process by including convexity as a correction factor in the ΔP/P formula:

$$C = \frac{\frac{1}{(1+k_d)^2}\left[\sum_{t=1}^{N}\frac{C_t}{(1+k_d)^t}(t^2+t)\right]}{P}$$

Note that the convexity formula is the second derivative of the bond's price with respect to interest rate:

$$C = \frac{\frac{d^2P}{dk_d^2}}{P}$$

The convexity correction factor changes the $\Delta P/P$ formula to:

$$\frac{\Delta P}{P} = -D\frac{\Delta k_d}{(1+k_d)} + \frac{1}{2}\ Convexity\ \Delta k_d^2$$

Our estimate improved, but it is not exactly correct, so why go through this trouble to estimate the percent change in the value of a bond?

The answer is that in the financial markets, duration and convexity are tools to manage bond portfolios and the math is the same for one bond or one portfolio, so we showed all our examples with one bond to keep the numbers simpler.

As shown in Table 4.3, our new bond with a 9% coupon rate, €1,000 face value, 25 years to maturity, a discount rate of 9%, and a duration of 10.71 has a convexity of 159.17. If yield increases by 25 basis points, then the estimate of the percent change is:

Table 4.3: Duration and Convexity Numbers.

Dirty price of bond	1,000.00
Duration of bond (year)	10.707
Modified duration of bond (year)	9.823
Convexity	159.173
New price of bond	975.93

$$\frac{\Delta P}{P} \approx -10.707 \times (0.0025/1.09) + 1/2 \times 159.173 \times 0.0025^2 \approx -0.0245 + 0.0005 \approx$$
$$-0.0240 \approx -2.40\%$$

Given the original price or the bond of €1,000, this percentage price change (in this case increase) would result in an estimated bond price of (1,000−0.024 × 1,000≈) 975.93.

4.8 Immunization

Immunization is a strategy that matches durations of assets and liabilities so as to make net worth unaffected by interest rate movements.

In order to achieve immunization, the following equation should be sought:

Duration of assets = Duration of liabilities

Immunization guarantees a specific percent return on investment (and thus total euro return) assuming one yield change. How can this be? The two types of risks, price risk and reinvestment risk, offset each other:

- When rates go up, you lose on bond price but gain on reinvestment.
- When rates fall, you gain on price but lose on reinvestment.

An insurance company issues a guaranteed investment contract (GIC) for 1,000 with 4-year maturity and a guaranteed rate of 12%.

The insurance company has to pay the following amount at the end of four years:

$$1,000 \times (1+.12)^4 = €1,573.52$$

This is similar to a zero-coupon bond. Duration of the liability can be calculated as follows:

(1)	(2)	(3)	(4)	(5)	(6)
Years	Cash Flow	PV Factor	(2) × (3)	(4)/Price	(1) × (5)
4	€1573.52	0.6355	1,000	1	4

$$D = 4 \text{ years}$$

Let us check that the company will immunize its payment if it invests in a bond with five-year maturity, a 12% coupon paid annually and YTM = 12%. You can verify that the duration of the bond is four years, which matches the duration of the liabilities of the company. This is illustrated in Tables 4.4 and 4.5.

Table 4.4: Case 1: The Interest Rate Remains at 12%.

1. Coupon payments	Future value in year 4	
Year 1	$120 \times (1+.12)^3$	= 168.59
Year 2	$120 \times (1+.12)^2$	= 150.53
Year 3	$120 \times (1+.12)^1$	= 134.40
Year 4	120	= 120.00
2. Sale of bond in year 4	$P = (1,000+120)/(1+.12)$	= 1,000.00
Total:		1,573.52

Note: Possible slight differences are due to rounding and convexity.

Table 4.5: Case 2: The Interest Rate Falls to 10%.

1. Coupon payments	Future Value in year 4	
Year 1	$120 \times (1+.10)^3$	159.72
Year 2	$120 \times (1+10)^2$	145.20
Year 3	$120 \times (1+.10)^1$	132.00
Year 4	120	120.00
2. Sale of bond in year 4	P= (1,000+120)/ (1+.10)	1,018.18
Total:		1,575.10

Note: Possible slight differences are due to rounding and convexity.

4.9 Bond Portfolio Management Strategies

There are basically four strategies: passive portfolio strategies, active management strategies, core-plus bond management strategies, and matched-funding techniques. We will discuss each briefly.

Passive Portfolio Strategies

Passive strategies emphasize buy-and-hold, which is a low-energy management. Funds following this strategy try to earn the market return rather than beating the market return. There are two ways to achieve this strategy:
- *Buy-and-hold.* A portfolio of bonds is bought and held to maturity. The portfolio can be modified by trading into more desirable positions.
- *Indexing.* Funds try to match the performance of a selected bond index. Performance analysis involves examining tracking errors for differences between portfolio performance and index performance.

Active Management Strategies

Active management strategies attempt to beat the market. Mostly the success or failure can occur from the ability to accurately forecast future interest rates. The methods are:
- *Interest-rate anticipation.* This is a risky strategy, relying on uncertain forecasts of future interest rates and adjusting portfolio duration.
- *Valuation analysis.* This is a form of fundamental analysis which selects bonds that are thought to be priced below their estimated intrinsic value.

-   *Credit analysis.* Fund managers determine expected changes in default risk. They try to predict rating changes and trade accordingly. Bonds with expected upgrades are bought. Bonds with expected downgrades are sold.
-   *Bond swaps.* This is selling one bond and buying another simultaneously. Pure yield pickup swap is swapping low-coupon bonds into higher coupon bonds. Substitution swap is swapping a seemingly identical bond for one that is currently thought to be undervalued. Tax swap is used to manage tax liability.

Core-Plus Bond Management

This approach combines passive and active bond management styles. A large part of the portfolio is passively managed in one of two sectors. The rest of the portfolio is actively managed. In actively managed portfolio, managers:
-   Often focus on high-yield bonds, foreign bonds, or emerging market debt
-   Diversify the portfolio to manage risks

Matched-Funding Techniques

Classical immunization strategies attempt to earn a specified rate of return regardless of changes in interest rates. The portfolio must balance the components of interest rate risk. There are two types of risks:
-   Price risk: problem with rising interest rates
-   Reinvestment risk: problem with falling interest rates

Immunize a portfolio from interest rate risk by keeping the portfolio duration equal to the investment horizon. A duration strategy is superior to a strategy based only on maturity since duration considers both sources of interest rate risk.

Dedicated portfolios can also be analyzed under this caption. This is designing portfolios that will service liabilities. There are many different types of dedicated portfolios:
-   *Exact cash-match.* This is a conservative strategy, matching portfolio cash flows to needs for cash and is useful for sinking funds and maturing principal payments.
-   *Dedication with reinvestment.* It does not require an exact cash flow match with a liability stream. Flexibility can aid in generating higher returns with lower costs.

– *Horizon-matching.* This is a combination of a cash-matching and immunization strategies. With multiple cash needs over specified time periods, we can duration-match for the time periods while cash-matching within each time period.

4.10 Bond Portfolio Performance Measurement

There are many ways to measure the performance of a bond portfolio. We provide here a simple technique based on duration. The performance of a bond portfolio can be measured by calculating the excess return to relative duration where the measure of risk is the duration, as follows:[3]

$$ER = \frac{r_p - rf}{d_p / d_m}$$

where

r_p = Portfolio return
r_f = Risk-free return over the same period
d_p = Duration of the portfolio
d_m = Duration of market or benchmark portfolio
ER = Excess return to relative duration
An example with data is given below.

Portfolio	Portfolio return (%)	Portfolio duration (years)	Market durations (years)
A	12	14	7
B	10	7	7

Assuming the risk-free rate is 5%:

$$ER_A = \left(\frac{12-5}{14/7}\right) = 1.0$$

$$ER_B = \left(\frac{10-5}{7/7}\right) = 5.0$$

On a duration-adjusted basis, portfolio B outperformed portfolio A.

4.11 Summary

A bond is a debt agreement that a corporation or government agency enters into when it wants to borrow money for more than one year.

---

3 Christine Bretani, *Portfolio Management in Practice*, Elsevier, 2004, p. 79.

Bond ratings assess both the collateral underlying the bonds as well as the ability of the issuers to make timely payments of interest and principal.

The seesaw effect is a risk associated with bonds and means that lower interest rates cause bond prices to rise and higher interest rates mean lower bond prices.

The global bond market includes the following: global bonds, Eurodollar bonds, and Yankee bonds.

The capitalization-of-cash-flow method of valuation determines the value of an asset as the present value of the stream of future cash flows discounted at an appropriate required rate of return.

A pure discount bond is a security that promises to pay a specified single cash payment (face value or par value) at a specified date called its maturity date.

Bond price changes over time. Bond price changes as a result of interest rate changes, and the effect of maturity on bond price is also important. In managing a bond portfolio, the most important consideration is the effect of yield changes on the prices and the rates of return for different bonds.

To measure the effects of yield changes on prices, two tools are used: duration and convexity. A strategy that matches durations of assets and liabilities so as to make net worth unaffected by interest rate movements is called immunization.

There are basically four bond portfolio strategies: passive portfolio strategies, active management strategies, core-plus bond performance strategies, and matched-funding techniques.

The performance of a bond portfolio can be measured by calculating the excess return to relative duration where the measure of risk is the duration.

5 Stocks and the Markets

5.1 Introduction

This chapter presents some of the features of stock and markets. We first review types of common stocks. Next, we review various forms of stock transactions. Then we examine initial public offering. Trading securities in secondary markets is also discussed. To understand the trend in the market, stock market indexes are created and are followed by investors. Finally, we discuss valuation principles for stocks and risks faced by investors.

5.2 Types of Common Stock and Stockholders' Rights

Common stock represents ownership shares in a corporation and can be divided into special groups, generally class A and class B:
- *Class A* shares its class of common stock, usually retained by a company's founders at the time a company goes public, carrying certain rights not granted to stock available to the public. These are super voting shares to retain control.
- *Class B* shares its class of common stock, usually issued at initial public offering (IPO) or if a company issues new stock at a later date.

Foreign companies' shares trade in many countries such as the U.S., Poland, and England as a means of securing new funding and a way to finance assets overseas. Some securities are listed on several markets globally. *American Depository Receipts* (ADR) represent shares of common stock that trade on a foreign stock exchange. *Global Depository Receipts* (GDR) represent shares of common stock that are listed on the *London Stock Exchange.*

Ownership gives common stockholders certain rights that bondholders do not have. These rights are as follows:
- Shareholders (stockholders) vote to select the corporation's board of directors, who exercise general control over the company's business operations.
- Shareholders vote on major issues concerning the firm, such as mergers and acquisitions.
- Shareholders have a claim on business profits, but only those that remain after holders of all other classes of debt and equity are satisfied.

There basically two voting systems for electing the board of directors:
- *Majority voting system.* The holders of the majority of stock can elect all directors.
- *Cumulative voting system.* Minority stockholders (own less than 50% of stock) can elect some of the directors. The stockholders can cast one vote for each share of

https://doi.org/10.1515/9783110705355-005

stock owned times the number of directors to be elected. The following formula may be employed to determine the number of shares needed to elect a given number of directors under cumulative voting.

$$No.\,of\,shares = \frac{No.\,of\,directors\,desired \times No.\,of\,shares\,outstanding}{No.\,of\,directors\,being\,elected + 1} + 1$$

If number of stock is 1,000M, and five board members are to be elected, the stockholder group who owns 51% of votes will elect all board members in a majority voting system. In this case, each candidate will have received 501M votes.

Let us determine the number of stocks needed to elect one board member in a cumulative voting system:

$$No.\,of\,shares = \frac{1 \times 1,000}{5 + 1} + 1$$

$$No.\,of\,shares = 168$$

Now let us determine the number of board members in a cumulative voting system, assuming that the minority stockholders own 499M shares:

$$No.\,of\,board\,members = \frac{(No.\,of\,shares\,owned - 1) \times (Total\,number\,of\,board\,members + 1)}{No.\,of\,stocks}$$

$$No.\,of\,board\,members = \frac{(499 - 1) \times (5 + 1)}{1,000}$$

$$No.\,of\,board\,members = 2.98$$

Since the number is less than three, the minority group will be able to elect just two board members.

A dividend is a payment to the owner of a share of a corporation's stock, which represents the owner's portion of the profits.

Dividend decisions are voted at the general meeting of the company. Dividends are declared by a corporation's board of directors and may not be declared at all. Dividends are subject to double taxation.

Upon liquidation of the business, common stockholders have the lowest standing. Creditors, bondholders, and preferred stockholders must be paid in full before common stockholders are paid.

Common stock is assigned a par or stated value, but this value has little bearing on the price or book value of the stock.

Preferred stock is an equity security that has a preference, or senior claim, to the firm's earnings and assets and usually carries a stated fixed dividend. Preferred stockholders cannot force payment of dividends.

5.3 Inside Information and Stock Transactions

Capital markets are successful in allocating capital because of their confidence in such markets. Should investors lose confidence in the markets, everyone loses. Two breaches of investor confidence are as follows:

–   *Insider trading.* This is the illegal practice of buying and selling stocks based on information that is known only by corporate officers and is not available to the public. Insider trading is prohibited under the *Securities Exchange Legislations* all over the world.

–   *Churning.* This is when a broker constantly buys and sells securities from a client's portfolio in an effort to generate commissions.

The *bid price* is the price the buyer is willing to pay for the securities; the *ask price* is the price at which the owner is willing to sell the securities.

An investor can purchase securities in the following ways:

–   By placing a *market order,* which is an order for immediate purchase or sale at the best possible price,

–   By placing a *limit order,* an order in which the maximum buying price (*limit buy*) or the minimum selling price (*limit sell*) is specified by the investor:

    –   Limit orders may be placed to expire at the end of 1 day, 1 week, 1 month, or on a good-until-canceled basis.

    –   Limit orders may not be completed, depending on what the limit is and how the security trades.

–   By placing a *stop-loss order,* which is an order to sell stock at the market price when the price of the stock falls to a specified level. It is used to protect gains or limit losses.

Under the system of *T+2* settlement, accounts must be settled within 2 days of the transaction, meaning that funds must be available within 2 days. In the U.S., accounts are settled within 3 days of transaction.

When a trade takes place, the information is sent to a central computer system that sends the information to display screens across the country.

Stock Quotations

Understanding stock quotations is an important element of how stocks are valued. A typical quotation as it might appear in *Frankfurt Stock Exchange* is shown in Table 5.1.

Table 5.1: Historical Prices and Volumes Wirecard AG.

Date	Open	Close	High	Low	Volume €	Volume units
08/05/20	86.84	91.84	93.45	83.20	6,616,541	75,079

Margin Trading

Buying stocks on margin means that the investor borrows a portion of the purchase price of the stock from a broker. *Margin* is the portion of the purchase price contributed by the investor. The remaining part is borrowed.

Let us define important terms:

$$\text{Percentage margin} = \text{Equity in account}/\text{Value of stock}$$

$$\text{Market value of the stock} = \text{Price}/\text{share} \times \text{Number of shares.}$$

Equity in account (the equity value of the account or net worth) = Market value of stock – Amount borrowed

Assume that the initial margin is 50%. The investor pays €3,500 to purchase 1,000 shares of corporation × worth €7 each. *Initial position*:

$$\text{Value of stock} = €7 \times 1,000 = €7,000 (\text{Asset})$$

$$\text{Loan from broker} = €3,500 (\text{Liability})$$

$$\text{Equity} = €3,500 (\text{Owners' equity})$$

$$\text{Initial margin\%} = \text{Equity}/\text{Value of stock}$$

$$= 3,500/7,000 = 0.5 \text{ or } 50\%$$

Let's say the stock price falls to €6 per share. *New position*:

$$\text{Value of stock} = €6 \times 1,000 = €6,000 (\text{Asset})$$

$$\text{Loan from broker} = €3,500 (\text{Liability})$$

$$\text{Equity} = €2,500 (\text{Owners' equity})$$

$$\text{Margin\%} = €2,500/€6,000 = 0.4167 \text{ or } 41.67\%$$

Maintenance margin is defined as the minimum level of the equity margin that must be retained. *Margin call* means a call for more equity funds when the maintenance margin is not met.

If the maintenance margin were 40%, how far could the stock price (P) fall before a margin call?

$$(1000 \times P - €3,500)/1000P = 40\%$$

$$P = €5.83$$

Let us explain why people buy on the margin. In the previous example, assume that you pay an annual interest rate of 10% on the loan from the broker and the stock price rises by 20% to €8.40/share at the end of the year.

$$\text{Value of stock (at the end of the year)} = €8.4 \times 1,000 = €8,400$$

$$\text{Pay interest on the broker's loan} = 10\% \times 3,500 = €350$$

$$\text{Principal payment} = €3,500$$

Net income = Value of stock − Interest − Principal = (8,400 − 350 − 3,500) = 4,550
Rate of return = ((4,550 − 3,500)/3,500) × 100 = 30%

Short Sales

The purpose of short sales is to make a profit from a decline in the price of a stock or a security.

Let's say you are pessimistic (bearish) on Z Corp. You sell short 500 shares at P = €4.00

$$\%\text{margin} = \text{Equity/Value of stock owed} = 75\%$$

$$\text{Sale proceeds (value of stock owed)} = €4.00 \times 500 = €2,000$$

If the broker has a 75% initial margin on short sales:

$$\text{Equity} = \%\text{margin} \times \text{value of stock owed} = 75\% \times 2,000 = €1,500$$

Assume that stock price falls to €3.60. You buy 500 shares to cover your position:

$$\text{Purchase cost} = €3.60 \times 500 = €1,800$$

$$\text{Profit} = \text{Sale proceeds} - \text{Purchase cost} = 2,000 - 1,800 = €200$$

5.4 Initial Public Offering (IPO) and Costs of IPOs

An *initial public offering* (IPO) is a sale of securities to the investing public or a sale of securities to a small group of private investors. *Capital Market Boards* (similar to the SEC in the U.S.) regulates the public offering process. Investment banking firms identify candidates for an IPO. The investment bank conducts a detailed study, called *due diligence*, of the issuing firm to determine the best way of raising funds for the issuer. The investment bank typically recommends types, terms, and the offering price of securities to be sold. The banker also aids the company in preparing registration and informational materials such as the *prospectus*, which outlines the issuer's business and finances, and must be provided to each buyer. Companies go public to raise money for long-term growth and for the prestige of being publicly traded.

An investment banker enters into an underwriting agreement with the issuer. The investment banker can commit to buy the shares (*commitment agreement*) or can agree to do its best to sell the shares to others (*best-effort selling*). In a firm commitment underwriting, the investment bankers purchase shares at a pre-determined price and then sell the securities to the investors at the offer price. The difference between an offer price and a price paid by the investment bank (spread) is the revenue to the bank. In a best-effort agreement, the investment bankers try to sell the securities of the issuing corporation but assume no risk for the possible failure of the sale or the flotation. The bankers take a commission on the securities they sell. The IPO process is described in Figure 5.1.

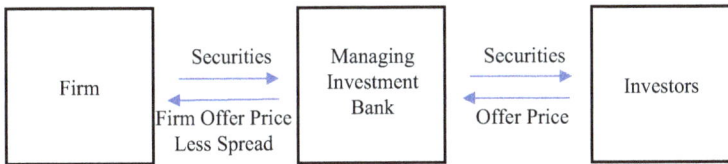

Figure 5.1: Diagram of a Firm Commitment Underwriting.

In addition to selling stock through public offerings, firms may also do so by *private placements*. Firms may do a private placement to:

- Prevent a hostile takeover by selling a large block of voting stock to friendly hands
- Fulfill a need for an emergency infusion of equity

Sometimes, under the charters of some corporations, existing stockholders have the first right to buy shares if additional shares are to be issued. This is done so that existing stockholders can maintain a proportional share of ownership. This is called a *right offering*.

In general, securities issues require *competitive bidding* by investment bankers before underwriting agreements are awarded. A variation of competitive bidding called the *Dutch auction bidding process* enables smaller firms and individual investors to purchase securities.

Retail selling is selling to individual investors. Institutional investors are large investors such as insurance companies, pension funds, investment companies, and other large financial institutions.

Tombstones are announcements of securities offerings placed in newspapers or other publications. These announcements are not offering to sell or buy the securities. The underwriters of the offering, called the syndicate, are listed in order of importance at the bottom of the tombstone with the lead underwriters occupying positions of prominence.

After the new issue is initially sold to the public, the *secondary market* commences. During this time, the syndicate, in a process called *market stabilization*, is allowed to step into the aftermarket to purchase securities if the market price falls below the offer price. During this time, *syndicate members* may not sell securities for less than the offering price. The lead underwriter decides when the syndicate is allowed to break up, freeing members to sell at the prevailing market price.

IPOs are costly due to the following items:
- Accountants' fees
- Lawyers' fees
- Printing expenses
- Filing fees (fees paid to stock exchange)
- Road show expenses

Additionally, the firm faces two additional costs, which represent the difference between the market value of a firm's shares in the aftermarket and the actual proceeds received from underwriters. The costs are:
- Underpricing
- Flotation costs

Underpricing represents money left on the table, or money the firm could have received had the initial offer price been set higher and more accurately estimated the aftermarket value of the stock. In general, IPOs are underpriced if:
- It is a small stock issue
- The firm has venture capital investment
- The firm is a technology firm
- The underwriters are prestigious

The flotation costs of an IPO:
- Consist of direct costs, the spread, and underpricing
- Depend on the size of the offering, the issuing firm's earnings, the industry, and the condition of the stock market
- Are usually lower, on a relative basis, for a firm commitment offering rather than a best-effort offering

5.5 Trading Securities and Trading Commissions

The secondary markets provide liquidity to investors who wish to sell securities. There are two types of secondary markets:
- Organized security exchanges which have physical trading floors, such as the *NYSE trading floor* on *Wall Street*; and
- *Over-the-counter* (OTC) markets, such as *National Association of Securities Dealers Automated Quotation System* (NASDAQ), which are networks of independent dealers and agents who communicate and trade electronically rather than on a trading floor.

To qualify for listing its security, a corporation must meet certain requirements regarding profitability, the total value of outstanding stock, or the stockholder's equity. Traditionally, the NYSE and other exchanges attract *blue-chip* companies that are large and more established. NASDAQ has a reputation for attracting high-technology companies.

The OTC market is also regulated in the U.S. by the *Maloney Act of 1938*. Under this legislation, the *National Association of Securities Dealers* (NASD) was created as a national self-regulating trade association reporting to the SEC. The NASD has established rules and regulations intended to ensure fair practices and responsibility from its members.

A comparison between organized exchanges and the OTC market appears in Table 5.2.

Table 5.2: A Comparison between Organized Exchanges and the OTC Markets.

Organized Exchange	OTC Market
has a central location floor	has telecommunications network linking brokers and dealers that trade OTC stocks
has specialists that make markets and control trading m listed stocks	does not have any specialists: OTC dealers buy and sell from their own account to the public and to the dealer
has stocks from primarily larger firms	has stocks from primarily smaller firms

The third kind of market is for large blocks of listed shares and it operates outside the confines of the organized exchanges. This market exists for institutions to trade blocks of shares. The fourth market is comprised of electronic communications networks, which are computerized trading systems that automatically match, buy, and sell orders at specific prices.

Stock commissions vary from brokerage firm to brokerage firm, depending on what services are also being offered.

- Full-service brokerages assist with trades and have research staffs that analyze firms and make *sell-side* recommendations on what stocks to buy or sell.
- Discount brokerages (deep-discount brokerages) just execute stock transactions without offering recommendations or doing research.

Online trading has increased the access to exchanges and caused commissions to fall. Commissions are generally lower on more liquid securities, those that are more actively traded or those securities with a popular secondary market. Commissions are higher for smaller trades that involve fewer shares or lower-priced shares. Some firms charge minimum commissions and transaction fees.

Investors may also buy directly from the issuer in a process called *direct investing*. Some companies have *dividend reinvestment* plans that allow for reinvestment of dividends and purchasing shares.

5.6 Stock Market Indices

A market index consists of a list of companies that are believed to represent the stock market; as such an index is a proxy for the profile of the economy. Common indices include the *Standard & Poor's 500 Stock Index* (S&P500), the *NYSE index, FTSE 100, Euronext 100*, CAC 40, and DAX. Indexes have also been constructed by industry or by geography. Stocks included in can change.

In addition to indices, averages are also computed to reflect general price behavior in the market using the arithmetic average.

Indices are believed to reflect the general price behavior of the market relative to a base value. Such indices are market-value weighted.

S&P 500 index is a market value-weighted index made up of 500 large company stocks, and is believed to reflect the overall market profile:

$$\text{S\&P indexes} = \frac{\sum \text{Current closing market value of stocks}}{\sum \text{Based period closing market value of stocks}} \times 100$$

Market value (Market capitalization) = market price × number of shares outstanding

Averages are believed to reflect general price behavior in the market using the arithmetic average, and such indices are price weighted.

Dow Jones Industrial Average (DJIA) is a stock market average made up of 30 high-quality industrial stocks and believed to reflect the overall stock market.

$$\text{DJIA} = \frac{\text{Closing } P_1 + \text{Closing } P_2 + - - - - - - + \text{Closing } P_{30}}{\text{DJIA divisor}}$$

Using the following information, let us calculate the S&P-type index and Dow Jones Industrial Average (DJIA) with data presented in Table 5.3.

Table 5.3: Information about Stocks.

Date	Stock price			# of shares outstanding		
	X*	Y	Z	X*	Y	Z
0	$5.00	$5.00	$5.00	100	100	100
1	$2.60	$5.10	$5.10	200	100	100
2	$2.70	$5.20	$5.20	200	100	100

*Stock X has a 2-for-1 stock split before trading on day 1. Date 0 is the base date. The current divisor is 3.0 and the base value for an S&P type of index is supposed to be 10.

The following is an S&P-type index example: What would be the value of an S&P-type index at the end of date 1?

$$S\&P\ index_1 = \frac{2.60 \times 200\ +\ 5.10 \times 100\ +\ 5.10 \times 100}{5.00 \times 100\ +\ 5.00 \times 100\ +\ 5.0 \times 100} \times 100 = 10.27$$

$$\text{Rate of return on date1} = (10.27/10) - 1 = 2.7\%$$

What would be the value of an S&P-type index at the end of date 2?

$$S\&P\ index_2 = \frac{2.70 \times 200 + 5.20 \times 100 + 5.20 \times 100}{5.00 \times 100 + 5.00 \times 100 + 5.00 \times 100} \times 100 = 10.53$$

$$\text{Rate of return on date two}: 10.53/10.27 - 1 = 2.53\%$$

$$\text{Rate of return on two days} = (10.53/10) - 1 = 5.3\%$$

The following is an example of a DJIA-type average: What would be the value of a DJIA-type average at the end of date 2?
At the end of date 0: DJIA-type average = (5.00 + 5.00 + 5.00) / 3 = 5.00
Before date 1: DJIA type average = (2.50 + 5.00 + 5.00) / d = 5.00, solve for d = 2.5
(Note: A 2-for-1 stock split for stock X will split the price in half, but it should not affect the average itself. Therefore, the divisor should be adjusted.)
At the end of date 2: DJIA type average = (2.70 + 5.20 + 5.20) / 2.5 = 5.24
Rate of return on two days = ((5.24 / 5.00) − 1) × 100 = 4.8%

5.7 Evaluating the Corporation

A company's profits are determined by the following items:
- Sales revenues
- Expenses
- Taxes

In evaluating a company's profit-making ability, the following factors are important:

- *Competition.* In a competitive market, it will be difficult for a firm to increase its revenues. This decreases a firm's ability to pay its bond interest and stock dividends and/or reinvest for growth.
- *Overseas influences.* Two main overseas influences also have an effect on local firms. The growth in foreign economies increases the demand for exports of local firms. Exchange rates affect profitability by influencing sales, price competition, expenses, and domestic interest rates.
- *Disposable income.* The consumer makes a choice as to how money is spent. Consumption spending for items such as food, cars, clothes, or computers form much of the *gross domestic product* (GDP) of the country. Higher disposable incomes (after taxes) lead to higher levels of spending. Economic growth, among other factors, results from increased spending.
- *Government spending.* Governments shape the domestic economy by spending, taxation decisions, and monetary policy. For example, a change in interest rate may affect consumers' ability to take on more debt. Interest rates typically affect industries such as banks and housing more profoundly.
- *Changes in supply.* Changes in the cost and availability of raw materials, labor, and energy can affect a firm's competitive place in the market and, ultimately, its profitability.

These five factors will determine the profitability, investment spending, and financing pattern of the company. All these factors at the same time will also determine the inputs of the valuation models, which we discuss in the following section.

5.8 Stock Valuation: Dividend Discount Model (DDM)

Valuation of common stock is based on the same concept underlying the valuation of bonds. The value of common stock is the discounted value of the stock's expected stream of returns.

The valuation of common stock is more difficult than other securities. The returns from owning common stock are a sum of future dividends and capital gains (losses). Dividends are not constant and expected to grow over time. The future returns from common stock are much more unknown than the returns from bonds.

The present value of a share of common stock is based on the expected dividends to be received during the investor's holding period and the expected selling price at the end of the holding period.

The one-period dividend valuation model is as follows:

$$P_0 = \frac{D_1}{1 + k_e} + \frac{P_1}{1 + k_e}$$

Where k_e is the required rate of return, D_1 is the expected dividend at time 1, and P_1 is the expected selling price at time 1. Expressing P_1 exactly as we did P_0 and rearranging, we get the two-period dividend valuation model as:

$$P_0 = \frac{D_1}{(1+k_e)^1} + \frac{D_2}{(1+k_e)^2} + \frac{P_2}{(1+k_e)^2}$$

where the investor receives dividends for two periods and the stock is sold at the end of the second period. The multiple-period dividend valuation model can be similarly written as:

$$P_0 = \frac{D_1}{(1+k_e)^1} + \frac{D_2}{(1+k_e)^2} + \dots + \frac{D_n}{(1+k_e)^n} + \frac{P_n}{(1+k_e)^n}$$

or

$$P_0 = \sum_{t=1}^{n} \frac{D_t}{(1+k_e)^t} + \frac{P_n}{(1+k_e)^n}$$

where the investor receives dividends for n periods and P_n is the selling price after n periods.

The value of the stock at the end of the holding period (P_n) depends on the value of future dividends after time n. The value of common stock at time zero (P_0) depends directly on dividends received during the holding period and indirectly on dividends after the holding period (through their effect on P_n). The general dividend model simply establishes the value of a firm's common stock to the investor to be equal to the present value of the expected future dividend stream:

$$P_0 = \sum_{t=1}^{\infty} \frac{D_t}{(1+k_e)^t}$$

What happens to P_n? Since the present value of P_n at the constant growth period is so small, it is ignored in the calculations.

The general dividend valuation model can be simplified if the dividends follow a regular pattern. Three patterns considered are *zero growth*, *constant growth*, and *nonconstant growth*.

Zero-Growth Stock

The *zero growth* dividend models are the simplest dividend valuation model. If the dividends are expected to be constant forever, the general valuation model is:

$$P_0 = \sum_{t=1}^{\infty} \frac{D}{(1+k_e)^t} = \frac{D}{k_e}$$

This is perpetuity formula and can also be visualized as a special case of the constant growth model (presented in the following section) where g = 0.

What is the value of a stock that is expected to pay dividends of €0.75 per share forever and has a required rate of return of 15%?

$$P_0 = \frac{0.75}{0.15} = €5.00$$

Constant Growth

The *constant growth* dividend valuation model assumes that dividends grow at a constant rate g per year forever.

The future dividend at time t is $D_t = D_0 (1 + g)^t$.

The general dividend model becomes the following:

$$P_0 = \sum_{t=1}^{\infty} \frac{D_0(1+g)^t}{(1+k_e)^t}$$

Assuming $k_e > g$, this model reduces to:

$$P_0 = \frac{D_1}{k_e - g}$$

where D_1 is the next period's dividend, $D_1 = D_0 (1 + g)$.

What is the value of a stock that is expected to pay dividends of €0.75 per share with an expected constant growth rate of 6% and has a required rate of return of 15%?

$$\hat{P}_0 = \frac{D_0(1+g)}{k_e - g}$$

$$= \frac{0.75(1.06)}{.15 - .06} = 8.83 \approx €8.83$$

This constant growth dividend model is usually referred to as the *Gordon model*. If P_0, g, and D_1 are given, the Gordon model can be used to find the investor's required rate of return on equity:

$$k_e = \frac{D_1}{P_0} + g$$

implying that the return of the investor is equal to the rate he will earn if the dividends remained constant plus the growth rate.

Value of growth is defined as follows:

Value of growth = Value of constant growth stock – Value of zero-growth stock

$$= 8.83 - 5 = €3.83$$

The take home message of this result is that growth in cash flows (here dividends) has an important effect on the value of an asset!

Nonconstant Growth Stock

The *nonconstant growth* model allows for varying dividend patterns over various future time periods.

One example of this model is where the firm's dividends fluctuate over the next few years and then grow at a constant rate after that. The value of this stock is:

$P_0 =$	*Present value of expected dividends during nonconstant growth period*	+	*Present value of the expected dividends after the nonconstant period discounted back at cost of equity back to present*

If the dividends fluctuate until time m and then grow at a constant rate during period $m + 1$ and after, the value of the stock at time m is P_m, which is:

$$P_m = \frac{D_{m+1}}{k_e - g_2}$$

If P_m is discounted back for m periods, this is the second half of the equation for P_0.

A special case of the nonconstant growth model occurs if there is rapid above-normal growth of dividends for a period of time after which the growth rate of dividends is lower. Assume that dividends grow at a rate g_1 over the first m years and that dividends grow at a rate g_2 after that. The value of the stock can be expressed as:

$$P_0 = \sum_{t=1}^{m} \frac{D_0(1+g_1)^t}{(1+k_e)^t} + \frac{P_m}{(1+k_e)^m}$$

This gives the present value of the first m dividends plus the present value of the value of the stock at end of year m (P_m).

Because dividends will grow at a constant rate g_2 beginning in year $m + 1$, the Gordon model may be used to find the stock value in year m: $P_m = D_{m+1}/(k_e - g_2)$. By substituting this into the equation for P_m, the above-normal growth, dividend valuation model becomes:

$$P_0 = \sum_{t=1}^{m} \frac{D_0(1+g_1)^t}{(1+k_e)^t} + \frac{1}{(1+k_e)^m}\left(\frac{D_{m+1}}{k_e - g_2}\right)$$

What is the value of a stock that is expected to pay dividends of €0.50 per share with an expected growth rate of 20% for the next 3 years and then a constant growth rate of 6% and has a required rate or return of 15% (see Table 5.4)?

Table 5.4: Inputs for Dividend Discount Valuation Method.

k	15%
m_s	3
g_s	20%
g_u	6%
D_0	€0.50

Step 1: Calculate the PV of the dividends during nonconstant growth period (see Table 5.5).

Table 5.5: Calculation for Non-Constant Growth Period.

Year	Dividend	PV
1	€0.600	€0.52
2	€0.720	€0.54
3	€0.864	€0.57
4	€0.916	

P_0=0.52 + 0.54 + 0.57= €1.63

Step 2: Calculate the price of the stock at the beginning of the constant growth period.

$$\hat{P}_3 = \frac{0.916}{15\% - 6\%}$$

$$\hat{P}_3 = €10.18$$

$$\hat{P}_0 = €10.18/1.15^3$$

$$\hat{P}_0 = €6.69$$

Step 3: Combine PV from Step 1 and Step 2.

$$P_0 = €1.63$$

$$P_0 = €6.69$$

$$P_0 = €8.82$$

5.9 Stock Valuation: Relative Valuation Model

Instead of pricing stocks in isolation by the DDM, investors can also price stocks by comparing them to similar stocks in the market. With everything else being equal, two identical stocks should have identical prices. Therefore, investors can price stocks by observing the prices of similar stocks in the market today, or the prices of similar stocks in the past.

There are many methods used.[1] One of the widely used methods is *price-earnings ratio* (PER). The formula for PER is as follows:

$$\text{Price per share} = \text{Forecasted EPS} \times P/E$$

where:

EPS = Earnings per share
P/E = Price/earning ratio
Key estimates are as follows:
- *P/E ratio.* How many euros you are willing to pay today for one euro of expected future earnings of your company.
- *Expected future earnings.* Expected future earnings are usually calculated over the following 12-month period.

To estimate the P/E ratio, you should analyze the implicit ratios for the company, its industry, and for the market in general. If your firm is similar to the other firms in the industry, or similar to the market, it should have a similar P/E ratio.

Implicit P/E = Current Market Price/Consensus 12-month ahead earnings

The implicit P/E measures the prevailing attitude of investors towards a stock's value.

Using the DDM, you can see that a security's P/E ratio is a function of three factors:

$$P_0 = D_1/(k_e - g)$$
$$P_0/E_1 = (D_1/E_1)/(k_e - g)$$

Everything else equal,
- The higher the dividends payout ratio, the higher the P/E ratio.
- The higher the discount rate k_e, the lower the P/E ratio.
- The higher the growth rate g, the higher the P/E ratio.

In order to estimate EPS, estimate company sales by using pro-forma financial statements or/and industry forecasts. Once you have estimated next year's sales,

---

1 For a detailed treatment of relative valuation, see Aswath Damodaran, *Dark Side of Valuation*, Financial Times Prentice Hall, 2002, and Aswath Damodaran, *Investment Valuation*, Wiley, 1996.

you can use the estimated future profit margin to calculate expected earnings for next year: E(EPS) = E(PM) × Estimated sales per share.

Earnings per share of ABC Inc. is €0.40 and it is expected to grow 10% per year. It is also determined that the normal P/E ratio is 7. What is the value of one share of ABC?

$$\text{Projected EPS} = 0.40(1+0.10) = €0.44$$

Expected value of one share therefore will be:

$$0.44 \times 7 = €3.08$$

The multiples approach is a comparable analysis technique that seeks to value similar companies using the same financial metrics. Firm value multiples and equity multiples are the two categories of valuation multiples. We examined P/E ratio, one of the most commonly used equity approaches.

5.10 Stock Valuation: Free Cash Flow to Firm Method

Instead of trying to forecast dividends or earnings, one can estimate the future operating free cash flows. Forecasting operating free cash flow is generally easier than estimating dividends or earnings per share.

Total firm value (V)

= Long-term debt (D) + Shareholder value (E).

= PV of net cash flows from operations in the *forecast period*.

+ PV of terminal value from operations.

+ PV of excess assets (from non-operations, e.g., marketable securities, excess cash). Algebraically:

$$V = \sum_{t=1}^{T} \frac{NCF_t}{(1+r)^t} + \frac{TV_T}{(1+r)^T}$$

Three big important issues are:

- Net cash flows (NCF). Therefore the first term on the righthand side of this formula indicates the present value of all cash flows in the future. The second term is the present value of the terminal value from operations.
- (Opportunity) cost of capital (r)
- Estimation period (T).

Both NCF and k must be estimated out for five, seven, or ten years in most practical applications.[2]

---

2 For estimation of forecast period, see G. Gray, P. J. Cusatis, and J. R. Wollridge, *Valuing a Stock*, McGraw Hill, 1999, pp. 47–49.

Modern methodology is to use the discounted cash flow (DCF) method to estimate total firm value (V) and then deduct the long-term financial debt (D) to derive the shareholder value (E):[3]

- *Step 1:* Estimate the after-tax CFs of the firm.
- *Step 2:* Discount the CFs from Step 1 at the *weighted average cost of capital* (WACC).[4] This gives the value of the firm.
- *Step 3:* Subtract the value of the debt to get the value of the equity: E = V – D. The value of the equity is then divided by the total shares outstanding to net the stock price per share.

Estimate Net Cash Flows (NCFs) in the Forecast Periods

Cash flow estimates should be unbiased. Cash flows are usually forecasted for a period of five to ten years, or until the firm is expected to reach its long-run competitive equilibrium. Thus, it usually requires an analysis of the firm, its industry, and the overall macro-economic environment. Net cash flow (NCF) is defined as follows:

$$NCF = EBIT \; (1-t) + Depreciation - Investment$$

$$= NOPAT + Depreciation - Investment$$

The calculation process is as follows:
- Estimate net revenue (sales).
- Estimate operating margin (OM): OM = EBIT/Net revenue

  EBIT = Earnings before interest and taxes, also called *operating profit* or *operating income.*
  EBIT = Net Revenue × Operating margin
- Estimate Net Operating Profit after Tax (NOPAT) as NOPAT = EBIT(1–t)

  t = Corporate marginal tax rate.
- Estimate depreciation expense.

---

3 For a detailed treatment of free cash flow stock valuation model, see Arman T. Tevfik, *Hisse Senedi Değerlemesi*, Literatür, 2005; Arman T. Tevfik, *Excel ile Hisse Senedi Değerlemesi*, Literatür, 2012; Phillip R. Davies, Michael C. Ehrhardt, and Ronald E. Shieves, *Corporate Valuation: A Guide for Managers and Investors*, Cengage Learning, 2004; G. Gray, P. J. Cusatis, and J. R. Wollridge, *Valuing a Stock*, McGraw Hill, 1999; Aswath Damodaran, *Investment Valuation: Tools and Techniques for Determining the Value of Any Asset*, 3rd Edition; Wiley, 2012.
4 WACC is discussed later in this chapter and in Chapter 11.

– Estimate investments to be made in the future. Investments include capital expenditures and incremental working capital (WC). Both are considered as cash outflows. Investment in incremental *WC = Changes in Accounts Receivable + Changes in Inventory – Changes in Accounts Payable*. A common method to estimate *investment in incremental WC* is to estimate the average ratio *R* which is equal to *R = (current assets – current liabilities)/net sales*. Then the estimated investment in *incremental working capital = R × Forecasted change in net revenue*. It can be also estimated as *incremental working capital = R × Net working capital*.

Estimate Terminal Value (TV or Residual Value)

The TV captures the present value of all cash flows beyond the forecast period. During this period, the firm is assumed to reach its long-run competitive equilibrium and is expected to grow at a constant (steady) rate. Usually it is assumed that depreciating will be equal to investments.

$$TV_T = \frac{NCF_{T+1}}{k-g}$$

where

k = WACC (Weighted average cost of capital)

g = Estimated long-term nominal growth rate (the inflation rate plus the real growth rate)

For example, consider the constant-growth model. Assume a 6-year forecast period:

$$TV_{T=6} \frac{NOPAT_{T=6} \times (1+g)}{k-g}$$

Estimate Excess Assets

Firm value includes excess cash, marketable securities, the market value of real estate which is not used in operations, and the value of unconsolidated subsidiaries or other assets not required in the firm's daily business operations.[5] You should take tax effects into consideration. Some authors claim that initial net working capital should be included to firm value.[6]

---

5 For more information see Nuno Fernandes, *Finance for Executives: A Practical Guide for Managers*, Nuno Fernandes, 2014, pp. 215–216.
6 For more information see G. Gray, P. J. Cusatis, and J. R. Wollridge, *Valuing a Stock*, Second Edition, McGraw Hill, 2004, pp. 116–122.

Estimate Cost of Capital – WACC

Use the following formula to estimate weighted average cost of capital:

$$k = WACC = \frac{D}{V} \times k_D \times (1 - t) + \frac{E}{V} \times k_e$$

where:

(D/V) = Long-run target leverage ratio in terms of market values.

k_e is estimated by CAPM: $k_e = r_f + \beta_E \times (r_m - r_f)$

All returns all nominal. The risk-free rate (r_f) is Treasury bond of long duration. β_E (beta)[7] can be obtained from a regression study.

An over-simplified example will clarify the discussion made in Tables 5.6–5.8.

Table 5.6: Data for FCFF Valuation Model (€ in millions).

Company name	ABC
Last year	20X8
Net sales	€3,448.3
EBIT (1-t)	124.1
Depreciation	258.6
Cash flow from operations	**382.7**
Net working capital investment	(34.5)
Net capital expenditures	(86.2)
Free cash flow to firm (ECFF)	262.0
Growth rate after planning horizon	5.0%
Planning horizon (years)	5
Weighted cost of capital (discount rate)	15.00%
Present value of financial debt	2,093.0
Number stock (million)	200.0

---

7 Beta measures the sensitivity of change in a security's return to the return of the market portfolio. In statistical sense, it's the regression coefficient when we regress the (excess) return of a security on the (excess) return of the market. Beta is discussed more fully in Chapter 6 and Appendix C.

Table 5.7: Output Obtained from Actual Data.

Output: Calculated values	
EBIT(1-t)/Net sales	3.6
Depreciation/Net sales	7.5%
Net working capital/Net sales	1.0%
Net capital expenditures/Net sales	2.5%
Inputs: To be used in forecasts	
EBIT (1-t)/Net sales	3.6%
Depreciation/Net sales	7.5%
Net working capital/Net sales	1.0%
Net capital expenditures/Net sales	2.5%

Table 5.8: Input Output and Valuation.

Periods	0	1	2	3	4	5
Years	20X8	20X9	20X0	20X1	20X2	20X3
Growth rate in net sales (input)	–	15%	15%	15%	15%	15%
Net Sales	€3,448.3	€3,965.5	€4,560.4	€5,244.4	€6,031.1	€6,935.8
EBIT (1–t)	124.1	142.8	164.2	188.8	217.1	249.7
Depreciation	258.6	297.4	342.0	393.3	452.3	520.2
Cash flow from operations	382.7	440.2	506.2	582.1	669.5	769.9
Net working capital investment	(34.5)	(39.7)	(45.6)	(52.4)	(60.3)	(69.4)
Net capital expenditures	(86.2)	(99.1)	(114.0)	(131.1)	(150.8)	(173.4)
Free cash flow to firm (ECFF)	262.0	301.4	346.6	398.6	458.4	527.1
Terminal (residual) value)	–	–	–	–	–	5,534.7
Expected FCFF	–	301.4	346.6	398.6	458.4	6,061.9
Present value interest factors	–	0.8696	0.7561	0.6575	0.5718	0.4972
Discount FCFF	–	262.1	262.1	262.1	62.1	3,013.8
Corporate (firm) value	4,062.1	–	–	–	–	–
Present value of financial debts	(2,093.0)	–	–	–	–	–

Table 5.8 (continued)

Periods	0	1	2	3	4	5
Present value of equity	€1,969.1	–	–	–	–	–
Number of stocks (million)	200.0	–	–	–	–	–
Stock value per share	€9.85	–	–	–	–	–

Value Enhancement

Using the DCF framework, there are four basic ways in which the value of a firm can be enhanced:[8]

- The cash flows from existing assets to the firm can be increased by either increasing after-tax earnings from assets in place or reducing reinvestment needs (net capital expenditures or working capital).
- The expected growth rate in these cash flows can be increased by either increasing the rate of reinvestment in the firm or improving the return on capital on those reinvestments.
- The length of the high-growth period can be extended to allow for more years of high growth.
- The cost of capital can be reduced by reducing the operating risk in investments/assets, by changing the financial mix, or by changing the financing composition.

5.11 Summary

Common stock represents ownership shares in a corporation and can be divided into special groups, generally Class A and Class B.

Capital markets are successful in allocating capital because of their integrity. Should investors lose confidence in the markets, everyone loses. Two breaches of investor confidence are: insider trading and churning.

An investor can purchase securities by placing a market order, a limit order, or a stop-loss order. Buying stocks on margin means that the investor borrows part of

---

8 See Bill Neale and Trofer McElroy, *Business Finance: A Value Based Approach*, Prentice-Hall, 2004, pp. 397–448; Aswath Damodaran, *The Dark Side of Valuation: Valuing Old Tech, New Tech and New Economy*, Financial Times/Prentice-Hall, 2001, pp. 403–452.

the purchase price of the stock from a broker. The purpose of short sales is to profit from a decline in the price of a stock or a security.

An *initial public offering* (IPO) is a sale of securities to the investing public or a sale of securities to a small group of private investors.

The secondary markets provide liquidity to investors who wish to sell securities. The secondary market has two components: organized security exchanges and over-the-counter (OTC) markets.

A *market index* is a list of companies that are believed to represent the stock market; as such, an index is a proxy for the health of the economy. Averages reflect the general price behavior in the market by using the arithmetic average, price weighted.

A company's profits are determined by the following items: sales revenues, expenses, and taxes. In evaluating a company's profit-making ability, many factors – such as competition, overseas influences, disposable income, government spending, and changes in supply – are considered.

The present value of a share of common stock is based on the expected dividends to be received during the investor's holding period and the expected selling price at the end of the holding period.

Investors can also price stocks by comparing them to similar stocks in the market.

Instead of trying to forecast dividends or earnings, it is easy and better to estimate the future operating free cash flows. The present value of a share of common stock is based on the expected free cash flows minus financial obligations.

6 Risk, Rate of Return, and Portfolio Theory

6.1 Introduction

Return and risk are two key dimensions for investment decisions. To maximize investment returns for a given level of risk, or equivalently, to minimize investment risk for a given level of return, is the ultimate goal of investors. A way to achieve this goal is to construct a portfolio. It is also under the framework of portfolio theory that the relationship between return and risk can be quantified in equilibrium. This is the famous *Capital Asset Pricing Model* (CAPM), which is also known as the *Sharpe-Lintner-Mossin* form of Capital Asset Pricing Model.[1]

6.2 Efficient Markets

This section explains why market efficiency is the key element to the economic well-being of societies and discusses three aspects of market efficiency.[2]

- *Allocational efficiency.* Allocational efficiency exists when funds flow to their highest valued use. Directing funds to highest NPV (profitable) projects benefits not only corporations and their employees, but also consumers who benefit from lower prices and governments that collect more taxes on higher profits. Societies with high levels of corruption tend to have low allocational efficiency and, as a result, tend to be poorer societies.
- *Operational efficiency.* An operationally efficient market has the lowest possible transaction cost. In addition to the cost of trade (such as commissions), transaction costs also include search costs, information costs, and opportunity costs. The lower the transaction cost, the more freely investable funds will flow to their most productive use.

---

1 For more information, see: John Lintner, "The Aggregation of Investor's Diverse Judgements and Preferences in Purely Competitive Security Markets," *Journal of Financial and Quantitative Analysis*, IV, no. 4, Dec. 1969, pp. 347–400; Jan Mossin, "Equilibrium in Capital Asset Market," *Econometrica*, 34, Oct. 1996, pp. 768–783; and W.F. Sharpe, "Capital Asset Prices: A Theory of Market Equilibrium Under Conditions of Risk," *Journal of Finance*, Sept. 1964, pp. 425–442.
2 Efficient market was first introduced by Eugene Fama. See Eugene Fama, "Random Walks in Stock Market Prices," *Financial Analysts Journal*, Sep.–Oct. 1965, p. 4; Eugene Fama, "The Behavior of Stock Market Prices," *Journal of Finance*, Vol. 38, No. 1, Jan. 1965, pp. 34–105. There are also some authors that claim markets are not efficient. See Robert A. Haugen, *The New Finance: The Case against Efficient Markets*, Second Edition, Prentice-Hall, 1999; Robert A. Haugen, *The Inefficient Stock Market: What Pays Off and Why*, Prentice-Hall, 1999.

https://doi.org/10.1515/9783110705355-006

- *Informational efficiency.* Informational efficiency exists when the investors have sufficient, timely, and accurate information about assets being considered. This allows to value assets correctly.

The most important of these market efficiency types is the informational efficiency, which is explained in the following section.

Informational Efficiency

Prices on securities change over time because prices are determined by the pattern of expected cash flows and discount rates. An efficient market is a market in which prices adjust quickly after the arrival of new information and the price change reflects the economic value of the information, on average. In an efficient market, only unexpected news or surprises should cause prices to fluctuate wildly. Expected events should have already been incorporated into the price.

A random walk means that prices appear to fluctuate randomly over time, driven by the random arrival of new information. Informational efficiency exists when the investors have sufficient, timely, and accurate information about assets being considered. This allows assets to be valued correctly.

The reasons why markets are efficient can be explained as follows:
- The existence of large number of rational, profit-maximizing investors. They actively participate in the market.
- Individuals cannot affect market prices.
- Information is costless, widely available, generated in a random or independent fashion.
- Investors react quickly and fully to new information.

The levels of informational efficiency are:
- *Weak-form efficiency.* This hypothesis implies that all information about past prices is reflected in the security price. Investors cannot consistently beat the market using historical information. Prices reflect all past price and volume data. History of price information is of no value in predicting price changes. Technical analysis, which relies on past price history, is of no value in assessing future changes in price. The market adjusts or incorporates this information quickly and fully.
- *Semi-strong-form efficiency.* This hypothesis implies that all publicly available information is reflected in the security price. Investors cannot consistency beat the market using current publicly available information. Investors cannot benefit from new public information after its announcement.
- *Strong-form efficiency.* This hypothesis implies that all information (public and private) of every kind is reflected in the security price. Even insiders cannot

consistently outperform (beat) the market by exploiting their private information. It encompasses weak and semi-strong forms as subsets. Investors who believe in strong-form efficiency should be passive investors.

Research shows that developed markets (such as U.S. markets) tend to be semi-
strong-form efficient. It is important to stress here that the different levels of informational efficiency are not separate from each other. The market cannot be strong-form
efficient but at the same time not semi-strong-form efficient.

These three forms of efficiency and their relationship are indicated in Figure 6.1.

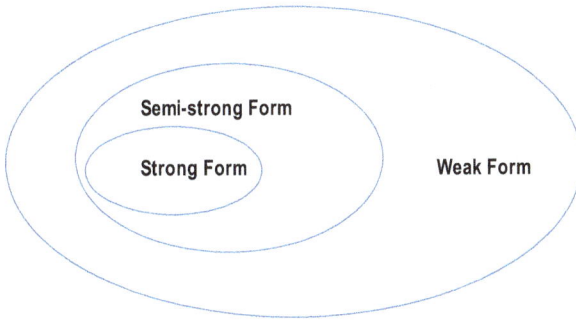

Figure 6.1: Three Forms of Market Efficiency.

In contrary to the belief in market efficiency, the following facts are some of the
market anomalies:[3]

- *Calendar effects.* Stocks returns may be closely tied to the time of year or time
  of week. Some examples are: the January effect and the weekend effect.
- *Small-firm effect.* The size of a firm impacts stock returns. Small firms may offer
  higher returns than larger firms, even after adjusting for risk. (This is the market impact of trading.)
- *Post-earnings announcement drift (momentum).* Stock price adjustments may
  continue after earnings adjustments have been announced. Unusually good
  quarterly earnings reports may signal buying opportunity.
- *Value effect.* Uses P/E ratio to value stocks. Low P/E stocks may outperform
  high P/E stocks, even after adjusting for risk.

---

3 See Tahsin Özmen, *Dünya Borsalarında Gözlemlenen Anomoliler ve İstanbul Menkul Kıymetler
Borsası Üzerine Bir Deneme*, Sermaye Piyasası Kurulu, no. 61, 1997.

6.3 Behavioral Finance

Behavioral finance suggests that various *psychological traits* influence investor pricing of securities.[4] *Modern portfolio theory* (MPT) assumes investors are rational, risk averse, and considers investment decisions in a portfolio context. *Behavioral finance* assumes investors are irrational, loss averse, and make separate investment decisions.

Behavioral finance makes the following assumptions:
- Emotions and biases affect markets
- Investors make errors, markets overreact or underreact
- Investors could profit from others' errors

There are many biases on the part of investor. Some of the biases include:[5]
- *Overconfidence.* Investors tend to be overconfident in their judgment, leading them to underestimate risks.
- *Self-attribution bias.* Investors tend to take credit for successes and blame others for failures. Investors will follow information that supports their beliefs and will disregard conflicting information. These two biases may cause investors to trade too often.
- *Loss aversion.* Investors dislike losses much more than they like gains. Investors will hang on to losing stocks hoping they will bounce back.
- *Representativeness.* Investors tend to draw strong conclusions from small samples. Investors tend to underestimate the effects of random chance.
- *Narrow framing.* Investors tend to analyze a situation in isolation, while ignoring the larger context.
- *Belief perseverance.* Investors tend to ignore information that conflicts with their existing beliefs.
- *Familiarity bias.* Investors buy stocks that are familiar to them without regard to whether the stocks are good buys or not.

6.4 Measures of Return and Risk (The Case of a Single Security)

Investments almost always involve an expectation of return in the future. However, the future is always risky. Investors therefore use historical data to predict the future to estimate the return on their investment. We will begin this section by evaluating the return and risk characteristics of individual assets.

---

4 For an introductory treatment of behavioral finance, see Keith Readhead, *Introducing Investments: A Personal Finance Approach*, Prentice Hall Financial Times, 2003, p. 30, and Lukasz Snopek, *The Complete Guide to Portfolio Management*, Wiley, 2012, pp. 151–165.
5 See D. Kahneman, A. Tvorski, "Prospect Theory: An Analysis of Decisions under Risk," *Econometrica*, XLVII, pp. 263–291.

Measures of Return

To facilitate the comparison of desirability of different securities, we usually use the rate of return, instead of the amount return. Rate of return is equal to € return divided by the € value of initial investment.

Holding-period return (HPR) or *r* is the rate of return over a given investment horizon:

$$HPR = \frac{V_1 - V_0 + C}{V_0}$$

Where

V_1 is the value of your investment at the end of the horizon,

V_0 is the value of your investment at the beginning of the horizon,

C is the intermediary cash payment from the security during the horizon (for example, cash dividend for a stock or coupon payment for a bond).

For example, compute the holding period return if you purchased a stock for €50, received a €5 dividend, and sold the stock for €55.

$$HPR = (55 - 50 + 5)/50 = 20\%$$

Measures of Average Return over Multiple Periods

There are many measures such as arithmetic average return, geometric average return, time-weighted return, money-weighted return, and log return.

Arithmetic Average Return and Geometric Average Return. *Arithmetic average return* is the return on investment calculated by simply adding the returns for all sub-periods and then dividing it by the total number of periods. It overstates the true return and is only appropriate for shorter time periods.

$$Arithmetic\ Average\ Return = \frac{r_1 + r_2 + \ldots + r_n}{n}$$

Where $r_1, r_2 \ldots r_n$ denote returns of period 1, 2, . . ., n, and n is the number of holding periods.

The stock's HPR's for the last 4 years are as follows: 10%, 25%, -20%, and 25%. What is the arithmetic average return?

$$Arithmetic\ Average\ Return\ (AAR) = \frac{10\% + 25\% - 20\% + 25\%}{4} = 10\%$$

Geometric average return is the average rate of return on an investment which is held for multiple periods such that any income is compounded. In other words, the geometric average return incorporates the compounding nature of an investment.

Geometric Average Return $(GAR) = \sqrt[n]{(1+r_1)(1+r_2)\ldots(1+r_n)} - 1$

Using these numbers, let us calculate geometric average return:

$$GAR = \sqrt[4]{(1+0.10)(1+0.25)(1-0.20)(1+0.25)} - 1 = 8.29\%$$

We can also calculate geometric return using price or wealth data as follows:

$$GAR = (W_n/W_0)^{1/n-1}$$

Where W_n, W_0, represent terminal and initial wealth (prices), respectively.

Assume that the stock prices for the last 4 years were as follows: 100, 110, 121, and 133.1. Using the second formula, calculate the geometric average return. Note that there are 3 periods in the formula.

$$GAR = (133.1/100)^{1/3} - 1 = 10\%$$

Arithmetic mean captures typical return in a single period. Geometric mean reflects compound, cumulative returns over more than one period.

Difference between geometric mean and arithmetic mean depends on the standard deviation of returns, s:[6]

$$(1+GAR)^2 \approx (1+AAR)^2 - s^2$$

One more new concept is *nominal return vs. real return*. Real return takes into account the effect of inflation. Approximately, real return (r) is equal to the difference between nominal return (R) and inflation rate (i):

r ≈ R−i or the correct form is:

$$r = (1+R)/(1+i) - 1$$

Last year, while inflation rate was 5%, nominal return was 15%, what was the real return of this investment?

$$r = (1+0.15)/(1+0.5) - 1 = 9.52\%$$

These two average return measures both assume there is no change of the amount of your investment during the n-periods. If there are period-to-period variations of your investment funds, the more proper measures of average return are *time-weighted returns* and *money weighted average returns*.

Time-weighted Return (TWR). First, separate the timeline into sub-periods where cash flows occurred. Let's say there are T such periods. Second, compute the return per sub-period. This return is the *holding period return* with end cash flow.

---

6 s denotes the standard deviation of returns, which is more fully explained in Appendix C.

$$r_{t,i} = \frac{\left(MV_{i,END} - CF_{i,END}\right) - MV_{i,BEG}}{MV_{i,BEG}}$$

Where

$MV_{i,END}$ = Month-end value

$MV_{i,BEG}$ = Month-beginning value

$CF_{i,END}$ = Month-end cash flow

Then the time-weighted return is defined as:

$$r_{twr} = (1 + r_{t,1})\,(1 + r_{t,2}) \quad \cdots \quad (1 + r_{t,T}) - 1$$

A €1,000,000 account recorded a month-end value of €1,080,000. The account has received two cash flows during a month: a €30,000 contribution on day 5 and a €20,000 contribution on day 16. Using a daily pricing system, we know that the account value was €1,045,000 and €1,060,000 on days 5 and 16, respectively. What is the TWR?

Three sub-periods: days 1–5, days 6–16, days 17–30

For each sub-period, the holding period return is:

- Days 1–5: r_1 = [(1,045,000–30,000) – 1,000,000]/1,000,000
- Days 6–16: r_2 = [(1,060,000–20,000) – 1,045,000]/1,045,000
- Days 17–30: r_3 = [(1,080,000–1,060,000]/1,060,000

Then, the TWR for the month is:

$$r_{twr} = (1 + r_{t,1})\,(1 + r_{t,2})\,(1 + r_{t,3}) - 1 =$$

$$= (1 + 0.0150)\,(1 + -0.0048)\,(1 + 0.0189) - 1 = 0.0292 = 2.92\%$$

Money-weighted Return (MWR). The *money-weighted return* is defined as the rate that solves the following equation:

$$MVR(r) = MV_0(1+r)^m + CF_1(1+r)^{m-L(1)} + \cdots + CF_n(1+r)^{m-L(n)}$$

Where

m = number of time units in the evaluation period

CF_i = the ith cash flow

L(i) = number of time units by which the ith cash flow is separated from the beginning of the evaluation period

A €1,000,000 account recorded a month-end value of €1,080,000. The account has received two cash flows during a month: a €30,000 contribution on day 5 and a €20,000 contribution on day 16. Using a daily pricing system, we know that the account value was €1,045,000 and €1,060,000 on days 5 and 16, respectively. What is the MWR?

The MWR would solve:

By trial-and-error we have: r = 2.90%

We can set this up in Excel:
- First, create three columns: one for dollar values, one for time passed, and one for present value, which incorporates dollar values and time.
- Then the sum of all present values should be zero.

Log Returns in Finance. If €100 grows to €120, what is the single-period return? Discretely, we say +20% because 120/100−1 = 20%. But in quantitative finance, we more typically use log returns expressed as $\ln(P_1/P_0)$. In this case, ln (120/100) equals about 18.2%. (If the asset paid dividends, we would include them in the numerator.)

The benefits of log return can be summarized as follows:
- *Time additive.* Note that the two-period log return is identical to the sum of each period's log return. This would be *really* convenient since, to get the n-period log return, we can simply add the consecutive single period log returns. Conversely, notice the simple return is not time additive.
- *Mathematically convenient.* Logs and exponents are easier to manipulate with calculus. Financial models tend to assume, unrealistically but conveniently, continuously compounded rates of return.
- *Approximately good.* For short periods (e.g., daily), the log return approximates the discrete return anyway

Some drawbacks of log return are:
- *Not linear in portfolio return.* We would like to be able to say that portfolio return is a weighted sum of returns of the assets in the portfolio. However, we cannot say this under log returns. The log return is not linearly additive across portfolio components. But the discrete return is linearly additive.
- *Unrealistic.* Markets tend to quote discrete returns.

Measure of Risk

We use standard deviation to measure the level of risk for a security, because as we know in basic statistics, variance or standard deviation measures the degree of variation of an uncertain value. The greater the standard deviation, the more volatile of the return, and thus the riskier the stock is.

Consider the following example in Table 6.1. You are considering buying a stock. Although you don't know exactly the rate of return for the stock during the following year, you can estimate the stock's returns under three different economic scenarios with their relevant probabilities.

Table 6.1: Three Scenarios.

	Scenario (s)	Probability p(s)	Rate of Return(s)
Boom	1	0.25	44%
Normal growth	2	0.50	16%
Recession	3	0.25	−20%

The average return you expect (expected return) to obtain is:

$$E(r) = \sum_{s=1}^{3} p(s).r(s) = 0.25 \times 44\% + 0.5 \times 16\% + 0.25 \times (-20\%) = 14\%$$

Variance (var) is defined as follows:

$$var(r) \equiv \sigma^2 = \sum_{s=1}^{3} p(s).[r(s) - E(r)]^2$$

$$= 0.25 \times (44\% - 14\%)^2 + 0.5 \times (16\% - 14\%)^2 + 0.25 \times (-20\% - 14\%)^2 = 0.0516$$

$Standard\ deviation \equiv \sigma = \sqrt{var(r)} = \sqrt{0.0526} = 0.2272 = 22.72\%$

6.5 Historical Risk and Return for Asset Classes

Historical returns and standard deviations of returns from different assets during the period of 1926 to 2017 for USA are shown in Table 6.2.

Table 6.2: Historical Returns and Standard Deviations of Returns: USA.

Arithmetic Average	S&P 500 (includes dividends)	3-month T-bill	Return on 10-year T. Bond	Geometric Average Inflation Rate
1928 –017	11.53%	3.44%	5.15%	3.03%
1968–2017	11.41%	4.82%	7.17%	4.06%
2008–2017	10.27%	0.42%	4.29%	1.47%
Geometric Average				
1928–2017	9.65%	3.39%	4.88%	
1968–2017	10.05%	4.77%	6.76%	
2008–2017	8.42%	0.41%	3.86%	

Table 6.2 (continued)

Arithmetic Average	S&P 500 (includes dividends)	3-month T-bill	Return on 10-year T. Bond	Geometric Average Inflation Rate
Standard Deviation				
1928–2017	19.51%	3.04%	7.68%	
1968–2017	16.52%	3.27%	9.44%	
2008–2017	18.05%	0.55%	9.43%	

Source: Adapted from Aswath Damadoran, http://pages.stern.nyu.edu/~adamodar/New_Home_Page/datacurrent.html, April 2018 and *U.S. Inflation Rate, $1 in 2008 to 2017*, http://www.in2013dollars.com/2008-dollars-in-2017?amount=1

Table 6.3 is a sample of historical, inflation-adjusted, risk and return numbers.

Table 6.3: Annualized Inflation Adjusted Risk Return Estimates: 1973–2013.

Asset Classes	Return (%)	Standard Deviation (%)
Fixed income	0.9	1.2
Intermediate term bond	3.1	4.6
Long-term bond	4.6	10.1
High-yield bonds	6.3	8.4
International government bonds	4.8	10.5
Commodities	4.8	19.9
Large capitalization equity	6.9	15.7
Middle capitalization equity	9.3	17.7
Small capitalization equity	11.3	21.6
International equity	5.9	17.6
Emerging market equity	12.0	24.1
REITs	9	19.1

Source: http://ralphwakerly.com/investing/the-risk-return-tradeoff/ fi360 Asset Allocation Optimizer: Risk-Return Estimates.

Each instrument class has a different average annual return and standard deviation. It must be remembered that market returns are not always positive. Investing in one class would be the equivalent of putting all of one's eggs in one basket. *Diversification* in asset classes mitigates risk.

6.6 Measures of Return and Risk (The Case of a Portfolio)

The case of two-risky-asset portfolio and the case of many-risky-asset portfolio will be discussed respectively in the following sections.

The Case of Two-Risky-Asset Portfolio

We begin with the simplest case. There are only two assets in the economy: stock i and stock j, and you decide to invest 40% of your fund in the first asset and 60% in the second asset, respectively. Thus the weight of stock i, $W_i = 40\%$, and the weight of stock j, $w_j = 60\%$. Also assume there are three scenarios for the economy in the following year, and the rates of return for the stock i and stock j under the three scenarios are as follows:

First, we compute the expected return, variance, and standard deviation for the stock i and stock j respectively, as we did in the single security case. The results are shown in Table 6.4. Then we compute the expected rate of return for your portfolio as follows:

Table 6.4: Three Scenarios for Two-Risky-Asset Portfolio.

Scenario (s)	P	Return for stock r_i	Return for stock r_j
Recession	0.25	10%	6%
Normal	0.50	11%	13%
Boom	0.25	12%	14%
E(R)		11%	11.5%
S		0.707%	3.202%
s^2		0.0000499849	0.0010252804

$$E\left(r_p\right) = w_i \cdot E(r_i) + w_j \cdot E\left(r_j\right) = 0.4 \times 11\% + 0.6 \times 11.5\% = 11.30\%$$

The variance of the return of the portfolio is:

$$s_p^2 = w_i^2\, s_i^2 + w_j^2\, s_j^2 + 2\, w_i\, w_j\, cov\left(r_i, r_j\right)$$

$$\text{or } s_p^2 = w_i^2\, s_i^2 + w_j^2\, s_j^2 + 2\, w_i\, w_j\, p.s_{i.}s_j$$

and the covariance of the return of the stock and the bond is calculated as:

$$cov\left(r_i, r_j\right) = s_{ij} = \sum_{s=1}^{3} p(s)\, [r_i(s) - E(r_i)]\, [r_j(s) - E\left(r_j\right)]$$

$$cov(r_i, r_j) = (0.10 - 0.11)(0.06 - 0.115)(0.25) + (0.11 - 0.11)(0.13 - 0.115)(0.5)$$
$$+ (0.12 - 0.11)(0.14 - 0.115)(0.25) = 0.0002$$

Substitute the covariance into the expression for variance of the portfolio, we have;

$$s_p^2 = 0.4^2 \times 0.0000499849 + 0.6^2 \times 0.0010252804 + 2 \times 0.4 \times 0.6 \times (0.0002)$$

$$= 0.000473099$$

$$s_P = \sqrt{0.000473099} = 2.175\%$$

From this example, we see the desirable *diversification effect* of a portfolio. The risk of the portfolio (standard deviation) is less than both that of the stock i and the stock j, and the expected return of the portfolio, although less than that of the stock j, is larger than that of the stock i.

Correlation coefficient is defined as:

$$p = \frac{cov(r_i, r_j)}{s_i.s_j} = \frac{0.0002}{0.00707 \times 0.03202} = 0.8835$$

No matter which scenario the economy is in, the return of the portfolio will be relatively stable.

The extreme case occurs when the coefficient of correlation between the two assets achieve its minimal value -1. In this case, the portfolio will become risk-free and will get the risk-free rate of return.

More specifically, we can break down the risk of a portfolio, or the standard deviation of the portfolio, into two parts:

- *Systematic risk (non-diversifiable risk).* The part of risk that is common to all the securities in the market, and that cannot be diversified away by constructing a portfolio. *Purchasing power risk, interest rate risk,* and *market risk* are the sources of systematic risk.
- *Unique risk (firm-specific risk, nonsystematic risk, or diversifiable risk).* The part of risk that is specific to an individual security and that can be diversified away by including more securities into the portfolio. *Operating, liquidity,* and *default* risks are the sources of unsystematic risk.

Generally speaking, when the number of securities included in a portfolio increases, the unique risk of the component securities will be reduced gradually, and in the limit, there is only market risk remaining in the portfolio. This is indicated graphically in Figure 6.2.

What is the question to be asked at this point? What is the combination of portfolio having the lowest variance (risk)? Or what combination maximizes portfolio return? Using the following data in Table 6.5, we can determine the least risky portfolio combination.

portfolio variance

asset
variance
terms

diversifiable risk

covariance
terms

systematic risk

No. of assets
in portfolio

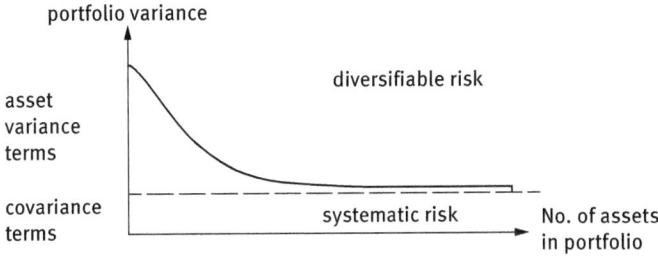

Figure 6.2: Diversification Effects.

Table 6.5: Data for Two Assets.

	Stock A	Stock B
Expected return	10%	15%
Standard deviation	15%	25%
Correlation coefficient	−1	

We will use the following formula to find the optimal risk portfolio:

$$S^2{}_p = W_i{}^2 s_i{}^2 + W_j{}^2 s_j{}^2 + 2W_i W_j\, s_{ij} \times s_i \times s_j$$

After taking the differential of this function with respect to W_i, and if we let the new equation equal to 0, risk minimizing weights can be found:

$$W_i = \frac{2 s_j{}^2 - 2r_{ij} \times s_i \times s_j}{2 s_i{}^2 - 4 r_{ij} \times s_i \times s_j + 2 s_j{}^2}$$

$$W_j = 1 - W_i$$

$$W_i = \frac{2 \times 0.25^2 - (2 \times (-1) \times (0.5 \times 0.25))}{2 \times 0.15^2 - (4 \times (-1) \times (0.15 \times 0.25) + 2 \times 0.25^2)}$$

$$W_i = \frac{0.125 + 0.075}{0.045 + 0.15 + 0.125}$$

$$W_i = \frac{0.20}{0.045 + 0.15 + 0.125}$$

$$W_i = 0.625 = 62.5\%$$

$$W_y = 1 - W_I = 1 - 0.625 = 0.375 = 37.5\%$$

By investing 67.5% in stock A, 37.5% in stock, the investor will minimize her risk. We can show how the businessperson can minimize her risk.

$$s^2_p = W_i^2 s_i^2 + W_j^2 s_j^2 + 2W_i W_j r_{ij} \times s_i \times s_j$$

$$s^2_p = (0.625^2 0.15^2) + (0.75^2 \times 0.25^2) + (2 \times 625 \times 0.375)(-1) \times (0.15 \times 0.25)$$

$$s^2_p = (0.0088 + 0.0088 - 0.0176) = 0$$

$$s_p = 0^{0.5} = 0$$

Now let us calculate the return of the portfolio:

$$E(R_p) = W_i R_i + W_j R_j$$

$$E(R_p) = 0.625 \times 0.10 + 0.375 \times 0.15 = 0.1188 = 11.88\%$$

This solution method is applicable if there are only two financial assets.

The Case of Many-Risky-Asset Portfolio

As number of assets increase, matrix algebra is a must.[7] Now let us give the general formula for a portfolio variance having n number of assets:

$$s^2_P = \left[\sum_{i=1}^{N} \sum_{j=1}^{N} w_i \, w_j \, s_{ij} \right] \text{ or, } s^2_P = \sum_{j=1}^{N} w_i^2 s_i^2 + \left[\sum_{i=1}^{N} \sum_{j=1, j \neq i}^{N} w_i \, w_j \, s_{ij} \right]$$

Matrix algebra can be a useful tool in this case. First it simplifies the calculation, then it can be used in an Excel environment.

A matrix is a rectangular array of numbers such as the following:

$$A = \begin{bmatrix} 5 & 3 & 0 \\ 2 & 4 & -5 \\ -9 & 8 & 10 \end{bmatrix}$$

A is a 3×3 matrix with 3 rows, 3 columns.

Vectors are matrices consisting of one row or one column: $a = [2 \quad 3 \quad 6]$ $b = \begin{bmatrix} 4 \\ -3 \end{bmatrix}$, a is a 1×3 row vector, b is a 2×1 column vector.

Matrices can be added, deducted, and multiplied. We are here interested only in the multiplication of two matrices.

If the number of columns in the first matrix is equal to the number of rows in the second matrix, these two matrices can be multiplied. For instance, if $a(1 \times 3)$

---

7 For more information about matrix algebra, see Appendix B.

and b (3×3), these two matrices can be multiplied, the resulting c matrix will be a 1×3 matrices. In this case, c will be calculated as follows:

$$ab = \begin{bmatrix} 2 & 3 & 6 \end{bmatrix} \begin{bmatrix} 5 & 3 & 0 \\ 2 & 4 & -5 \\ -9 & 8 & 10 \end{bmatrix} =$$

$$[(2 \times 5) + (3 \times 2) + (6 \times -9) \quad (2 \times 3) + (3 \times 4) + (6 \times 8) \quad (2 \times 0) + (3 \times -5) + (6 \times 10)]$$

$$= \begin{bmatrix} -38 & 66 & 45 \end{bmatrix}$$

Now let us show how variance can be calculated for a portfolio consisting of financial assets. In $s^2 = W'\Omega W$, here W denotes portfolio weight vector, Ω variance-covariance matrix. Using the previous inputs, one can calculate two-asset portfolio variance, as shown in Table 6.6.

Table 6.6: Data for Portfolio.

State	P	Return Stock A	Return Stock B
1	0.25	10%	% 6
2	0.50	11%	%13
3	0.25	12%	%14
E(R)		11%	%11,5
S		0,707%	%3,202

$$\text{Cov}(A, B) = (0.10 - 0.11)\,(0.06 - 0.115)\,(0.25) + (0.11 - 0.11)\,(0.13 - 0.115)\,(0.5)$$
$$+ (0.12 - 0.11)\,(0.14 - 0.115)\,(0.25) = 0.0002$$

$$\text{Variance-covariance matrix: } \Omega = \begin{bmatrix} VarA & Cov(A, B) \\ Cov(A, B) & VarB \end{bmatrix}$$

$$\text{Variance-covariance matrix: } \Omega = \begin{bmatrix} 0.0000499849 & 0.0002 \\ 0.0002 & 0.0010252804 \end{bmatrix}$$

$$\text{Weight vector: } W = \begin{bmatrix} 0.40 \\ 0.60 \end{bmatrix}$$

The matrices will be set up as follows:

$$W'\Omega W = \begin{bmatrix} 0.40 & 0.60 \end{bmatrix} \begin{bmatrix} 0.0000499849 & 0.0002 \\ 0.0002 & 0.0010252804 \end{bmatrix} \begin{bmatrix} 0.40 \\ 0.60 \end{bmatrix}$$

$$W'X\Omega W = 0.000473098525s = \sqrt{0.000473098525} = 0.17508 \text{ or } \%2.175$$

Now let us show how the variance-covariance matrix is made with a figure, as shown in Figure 6.3.

Bold cells show variance terms, other cells covariance terms.

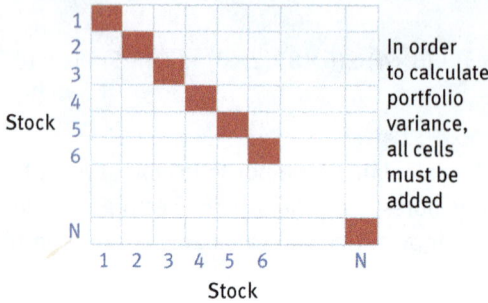

Figure 6.3: Variance-Covariance Matrix.

In our example, we can change the weights of the stock and the bond continuously and calculate the corresponding expected rate of return and standard deviation of the portfolio. We graph all the combinations in an $E(r_p)$-σ_p space. The resulting graph is a parabola, called the *feasible frontier*. The upper portion is called the *efficient frontier*, and the lower portion is called the *inefficient frontier*. This is what Harry M. Markowitz, who won the Nobel Prize in Economics in 1990 (with William Sharpe), has shown us.[8]

The feasible frontier is also a parabola, although in many-asset cases, not all the portfolios of the existing securities lie on the frontier, and some of the portfolio lie within the frontier. But the portfolios lying within are dominated by at least one portfolio on the frontier (see Figure 6.4).

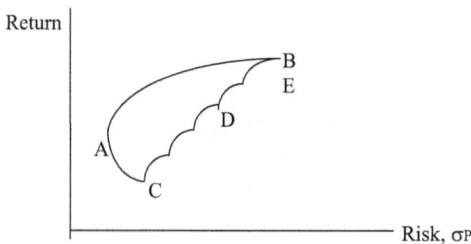

Figure 6.4: Efficient Portfolio: A.

---

8 See Harry M. Markowitz, "Portfolio Selection," *Journal of Finance*, March 1952, pp. 77–91; Harry Markowitz, *Portfolio Selection: Efficient Diversification of Investments*, Wiley, 1959.

The mathematical model used to find optimal portfolios (points) can be stated as follows:

Maximization of return:

$$Maximize\ E(R_p) = \sum_{i=1}^{n} W_i R_i$$

$$Subject\ to:\ s^2{}_p = \sum_{i=1}^{i=n} \sum_{j=1}^{i=n} W_i W_j Cov(R_i, R_j) \le s^2$$
$$i \ne j$$

Minimization of risk:

$$Minimize\ s^2{}_p = \sum_{i=1}^{i=n} \sum_{j=1}^{i=n} W_i W_j Cov(R_i, R_j)$$
$$i \ne j$$

$$Subject\ to\ E(R_p) = \sum_{i=1}^{i=n} W_i R_i > = E(R)$$

where
  s^2 = Required variance level by the investor
  $E(R)$ = required rate of return by the investor
  In the maximization and minimization problem, a short sale is possible. If short sale is not adopted, the following constraint should be added to the model:

$$Subject\ to\ W_i = \sum_{i=1}^{n} W_i = 1$$

In case of *short sales*, the model can be solved via *matrix algebra*. Otherwise, the solution method is *quadratic programming*.[9] These two topics will not be discussed in this book. But we can explain quadratic programming intuitively: the program seeks to find the minimum risky portfolio (having lowest variance) or the maximum return portfolio by varying the weights of individual securities, taking the con-straints into consideration.

Diversification is key to risk management. Asset allocation is the most impor-tant single decision in portfolio theory, and this is done by using Markowitz princi-ples through the following steps:

- Step 1: Identify optimal risk-return combinations using the Markowitz analysis: Inputs: Expected returns, variances, covariances.
- Step 2: Choose the final portfolio based on your preferences for return relative to risk.

---

9 The quadratic programming technique is discussed in management science (operations manage-ment) texts. For Excel-based sources, see the following books: Cliff T. Ragsdale, *Spreadsheet Modelling and Decision Analysis: A Practical Introduction to Management Science*, Course Technology, 1995, pp. 285–328; Simon Benninga, *Financial Modelling*, Fourth Edition, The MIT Press, 2014, pp. 291–303.

Assumptions on portfolio theory are:
- A single investment period (one year)
- Liquid position (no transaction costs)
- No taxes
- Preferences based only on a portfolio's expected return and risk

The efficient frontier is the set of all mean/variance efficient (optimal) portfolios such that their returns dominate the return of all other portfolios. An optimal portfolio on the efficient frontier has a maximum return for a given level of risk or a minimum risk for a given level of return.

In Figure 6.4, efficient frontier or efficient set is shown by the curved line from A to B. The global minimum variance portfolio is represented by point A. Portfolios on AB dominate those on AC.

Another way to use the Markowitz Model is with asset classes – that is, allocation of portfolio to asset types. Because:
- Asset class, not individual security, is most important for investors.
- Different asset classes offer various returns and levels of risk.
- Correlation coefficients may be quite low.

The Single-Index Model

Developed by William Sharpe[10] to reduce the number of inputs required by the Markowitz Model, the model relates returns on each security to the returns on a common index, such as the *S&P 500 Stock Index*. The model is expressed by the following equation:

$$R_i = \alpha_i + \beta_i R_M + e_i$$

Divides return into two components
- A unique part, α_i
- A market-related part, $\beta_i.R_M$

β measures the sensitivity of a stock to stock market movements:

$$\beta = \frac{Cov(R_i, R_M)}{s_M^2}$$

10 See William Sharpe, "A Simplified Model for Portfolio Analysis," *Management Science*, Vol. 9, Jan. 1963, pp. 277–293.

If securities are only related in their common response to the market. Securities co-vary together only because of their common relationship to the market index. Security covariances depend only on market risk and can be written as:

$$s_{ij} = \beta_i \beta_j \sigma^2_M$$

A single-index model helps split a security's total risk into:

$$\text{Total risk} = \text{market risk} + \text{unique risk}$$

$$\sigma^2_i = \beta^2_i [\sigma_M] + s^2_{ei}$$

According to the Market Index Model, the expected return and risk of a portfolio can be estimated as:

$$E(R_p) = W_i E(R_i) = W_i E[a_i + \beta_i E(R_M)]$$

$$Var(R_p) = \beta_p^2 Var(R_M)$$

Expected return and risk of a portfolio can be estimated as:

$$E(R_p) = W_i E(R_i) = W_i E[a_i + \beta_i E(R_M)]$$

$$VAR(R_p) = \sum_{i=1}^{n} W_i^2 Var(e_i) + [\sum_{i=1}^{n} W_i^2 b_i] \ VAR(R_M)$$

The first term is called nonsystematic risk, the second term is the systematic risk portion of the portolio variance.

In order to find optimal weight in a portfolio, as in the Markowitz Model, either R_i's should be maximized or, σ^2's should be minimized.

Capital Asset Pricing Model (CAPM)

From now on, we introduce a risk-free asset, such as the *treasury bill*, into the model, in addition to many risky assets such as stocks and corporate bonds. The risk (standard deviation) for the risk-free asset is, of course, zero. It can be shown that any portfolio that combines the risk-free asset and a risky portfolio on the feasible frontier must satisfy the following[11]:

$$E(r_p) = r_f + \frac{E(r_D) - r_f}{\sigma_D} . \sigma_P$$

---

11 William Sharpe, "Capital Asset Prices: A Theory of Market Equilibrium under Conditions of Risk," *Journal of Finance*, Vol. 19, Sep. 1964, pp. 425–442.

This is simply the straight line that connects the risk-free asset and the portfolio D. This means that the investor will choose to hold a portfolio of risky and risk-free assets that lie on this line. But the investor will not be satisfied with such a portfolio. When we raise the line with r_f fixed, until it is *tangent* to the efficient frontier at point M. We note that for any point on the line r_fD, there is always at least one point on the line r_fM that dominates it. r_fM becomes the efficient frontier when the risk-free asset is added (see Figure 6.5).

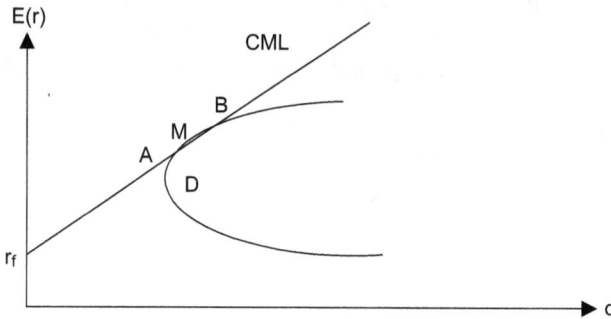

Figure 6.5: Feasible Frontier and Capital Market Line.

The tangent portfolio M is held by all the investors in equilibrium. It is therefore an index portfolio that replicates the composition of all the risky securities in the market. We call portfolio M as *market portfolio*, and the line r_fM as *capital market line (CML)*. The equation for CML is, as before:

$$E(r_p) = r_f + \frac{E(r_M) - r_f}{\sigma_M} \cdot \sigma_P$$

where $E(r_M)$ and σ_M denote the expected rate of return and the standard deviation of the market portfolio, respectively.

In equilibrium, an investor will hold a portfolio that lies on the CML, depending on her risk attitude. All investors hold a combination of two funds: risk-free asset and market portfolio. We call this *two-fund separation*.

Let us make the following assumptions:

Expected return of market portfolio = 0.15

Standard deviation of market portfolio = 0.20

Risk free rate of return = 0.05

Money to be invested: €100

Assume further that the investor invests 50% of his/her money in a risk-free asset and 50% in market portfolio. What is the expected return and standard deviation of this portfolio?

$$E(R_p) = W_1 rf + W_2 P_m$$

$$= 0.5 \times 0.05 + 0.5 \times 0.15$$

$$= 0.025 + 0.75 = 0.10 = 10\%$$

$$s^2{}_p = W_{RF}{}^2 \, s \, rf^2 + W_{Pm}{}^2 s_M{}^2 + 2W \, rf \, W_{Pm} \, Cov \, (rf, \ P_m)$$

Since $Cov \, (rf, \ P_m) = 0$,

$$s^2{}_p = W_{PM}{}^2 s_m{}^2$$
$$s_p = W_{Pm} s_m$$
$$= 0.50 \times 0.20$$
$$= 0.10$$

This portfolio is a *lending portfolio*. Now let us calculate the expected value and standard deviation of a *borrowing portfolio*. Let us assume that the investor borrows €50 and invests €150 in market portfolio. What is the expected return and standard deviation of this portfolio?

$$E(R_p) = - (0.5 \times 0.05) + (1.5 \times 0.15)$$

$$= - 0.025 + 0.225$$

$$= 0.20 = 20\%$$

$$s_p = W_{Pm} s_m$$

$$= 1.5 \times 0.20$$

$$= 0.30$$

One can reach the same conclusions using the capital market line formula. This line now is called the *capital allocation line*. The investment decision about which risky portfolio to hold is separate from the financing decision. The financing decision depends on the investor's preferences.

Market Line

The CML equation gives the equilibrium condition for a well-diversified portfolio held by an investor. The next question is: What's the equilibrium risk-return trade-off for an individual security?

Using the CML formula, but writing it in a different way, we can write the equilibrium risk-return tradeoff for an individual security. We know the following equation:

$$(r_p) = r_f + \frac{E(r_M) - r_f}{s_M} \times s_P$$

We can write the equation as follows:

$$E(r_i) = r_f + \frac{E(r_M) - r_f}{Cov_{M,M}} \times COV_{i,M}$$

Since $Cov_{M;M}$, represents variance of market portfolio (or σ_M^2) and beta is defined as $\beta = Cov_{i,M}/ s_M^2$, *security market line* or *capital asset pricing* formula can be derived easily:

$$E(r_i) = r_f + \beta_i \cdot [E(r_M) - r_f]$$

In the case of individual stocks or less diversified portfolios, we will no longer use standard deviation (the total risk) in the formula. We know the total risk consists of two parts: systematic/market risk and idiosyncratic/unique risk. When the security is included in a well-diversified portfolio, its unique risk will be diversified away, and only the market risk will remain. In other words, in equilibrium, only market risk will be rewarded, and unique risk will not be rewarded. Thus, we should replace standard deviation σ_i by a measure of market risk. We call the measure of market risk as *Beta* of the security β_i.

Beta measures the sensitivity of change in a security's return to the return of the market portfolio. In a statistical sense, it's the regression coefficient when we regress the excess return of a security on the excess return of the market:

$$r_i - r_f = a_i + \beta_i (r_M - r_f) + e_i$$

here $\beta_i = \frac{cov(r_f, r_M)}{s_M^2}$ is the regression coefficient.

Since $\beta_M = 1$, we have the following relationship between the expected return and the systematic risk for any individual securities or portfolios:

$$E(r_i) = r_f + \beta_i \cdot [E(r_M) - r_f]$$

This equation is known as the capital asset pricing model (CAPM), first derived by William Sharpe, who won the Nobel Prize in Economics in 1990 for this contribution.

The CAPM simply says that the risk premium of a security is proportional to its market risk β_i. The greater its market risk, the greater its expected return will be. Unique risk is irrelevant for security pricing. We can graph the relationship in E(r)-β space. The resulting straight line is called the *security market line* (SML), as shown in Figure 6.6.

The CAPM specifies the relationship between risk and the required rate of return on assets when they are held in well-diversified portfolios. Some of assumptions of this model are:

- All investors focus on a single holding period and seek to maximize the expected utility of their terminal wealth by choosing a portfolio among many on the basis of each portfolio's expected return and standard deviation.

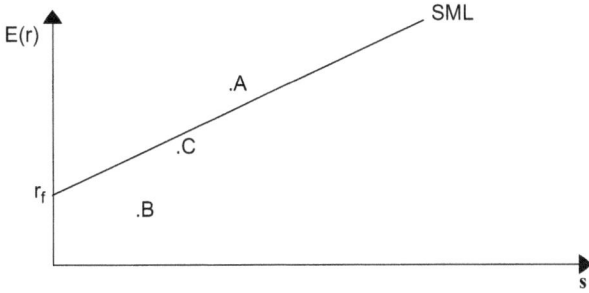

Figure 6.6: Security Market Line.

- All investors can borrow or lend an unlimited amount at a given risk-free rate. There are no restrictions on short sales.
- All investors have identical estimates of the expected returns, variances, and covariances among all assets.
- All assets are perfectly divisible and perfectly liquid.
- There are no transaction costs and no taxes.
- All investors are price-takers.

CAPM plays an important role in financial decisions. It is often used to calculate the cost of capital, which in turn is used as the discount rate for capital budgeting and firm valuation. CAPM is one of the most important discoveries in the field of finance even though most of these assumptions are not true.

6.7 Investment Analysis and Portfolio Management

This section is, in a way, a conceptual summary of what we have covered in Chapters 4, 6, and 7. In addition to these chapters, Chapter 9 is also related with investment analysis and portfolio management.

We can do two things with money: spend it or save it. Investment can be defined as setting aside funds with the expectation of receiving more funds in the future. When we invest, we expect to earn returns that will compensate us for:
- Time the money is invested (real risk-free rate of interest)
- Expected inflation over the investment time horizon
- Risk of the investment

Reasons why people invest can be explained as follows:
- *Income.* Investors want to receive dividends or interest. Some investors purchase annuities, which promise regular payments over a period of time.

- *Capital preservation.* Investors want to maintain purchasing power and want a return that matches inflation.
- *Capital appreciation.* Investors want growth, primarily through capital gains.
- *Total return.* Investors want growth, via capital gains and reinvesting income.
- *Minimize taxes.* Investors want to protect the return from taxes to increase future spending.

Traditional investments cover:
- *Security analysis.* Involves estimating the merits of individual investments.
- *Portfolio management.* Deals with the construction and maintenance of a collection of investments.

Security analysis is a three-step process:
- The analyst considers the prospects for the economy, given the state of the business cycle.
- The analyst determines which industries are likely to fare well in the forecasted economic conditions.
- The analyst chooses particular companies within the favored industries.

Literature supports the *efficient markets paradigm* in portfolio management. On a well-developed securities exchange, asset prices accurately reflect the tradeoff between relative risk and potential returns or a security:
- Efforts to identify undervalued securities are fruitless
- Free lunches are difficult to find

A properly constructed portfolio achieves a given level of expected return with the least possible risk. Portfolio managers have a duty to create the best possible collection of investments for each customer's unique needs and circumstances.

Portfolio management primarily involves *reducing risk* rather than increasing return. Consider two €10,000 investments:
- Earns 10% per year for each of ten years (low risk). Terminal value is €25,937. Standard deviation of returns is 0%.
- Earns 9%, -11%, 10%, 8%, 12%, 46%, 8%, 20%, -12%, and 10% in the ten years, respectively (high risk). Terminal value is €23,642. Standard deviation of returns is 16.10%.

The secret to successful investing: buy low, sell high. But how easy is this? It is quite difficult to do so consistently in markets where information is quickly disseminated and incorporated into asset prices.

In applying investments knowledge, the following should be considered:[12]
- Investor life cycle
- Creating an investment policy statement
- An investment policy statement
- Portfolio management process
- Constraints that affect the investment policy
- Investment strategies

Investor Life Cycle

Net worth typically transitions from negative to positive and then declines after retirement:
- *Accumulation phase.* This is the period when the individuals save money in appropriate funds.
- *Consolidation phase.* The years in the middle of working life.
- *Spending phase.* Starts when one retires.

Creating an Investment Policy Statement

Investment objectives depend on risk and return. These go together, since risk determines expected returns. What is the investor's risk tolerance, and how will that affect his/her investment strategy? Consider the following:
- Ability to handle risk
- Willingness to take risk
- Risk tolerance or appetite

Portfolio Management Process

The five steps of portfolio management are as follows:[13]
- *Set portfolio objectives.* It is difficult to accomplish your objectives until you know what they are. The separation of investment policy from investment management is a fundamental tenet of institutional money management. The board of directors or investment policy committee establishes policy. Policy outlines

---

12 Ali Ceylan and Turhan Korkmaz, *Uygulamalı Portföy Yönetimi*, Ekin, 1993, p. 13.; William F. Sharpe and Gordon J. Alexander, *Investments*, Fourth Edition, Prentice Hall, 1990, pp. 9–12.
13 Ali Ceylan and Turhan Korkmaz, *Uygulamalı Portföy Yönetimi*, op. cit., p. 13.; William F. Sharpe and Gordon J. Alexander, *Investments*, Fourth Edition, Prentice Hall, 1990, pp. 9–12.

the return requirements, investor's risk tolerance, and constraints under which the portfolio must operate. The investment manager implements policy.

- *Formulate an investment strategy.* Formulate an investment strategy based on the investment policy statement. Portfolio managers must understand the basic elements of capital market theory such as informed *diversification, naive diversification,* and *beta.* Valuation for individual securities must be made at this stage, then securities must be screened. A *screen* is a logical protocol to reduce the total number of securities to a workable number for closer investigation.
- *Have a game plan for portfolio revision.* Conditions change, and portfolios need maintenance. At this stage, there are two portfolio approaches: passive and active. Passive management has the following characteristics: follow a predetermined investment strategy that is invariant to market conditions or do nothing. Active management requires the periodic changing of the portfolio components as the manager's outlook for the market changes.
- *Evaluate performance.* The performance of the manager has to be evaluated at a pre-determined period using the appropriate tools which will be discussed in the following sections.
- *Protect the portfolio when appropriate.* Portfolio protection was called portfolio insurance prior to 1987. It is a managerial tool to reduce the likelihood that a portfolio will fall in value below a predetermined level. Among other tools, derivatives are usually used for protection.

Constraints That Affect the Investment Policy

Five constraints affect the investment policy:[14]
- *Liquidity needs.* Is there any need for quick access to funds?
- *Time horizon.* Generally, investors who can invest for longer time frames can invest in riskier assets (for example, stocks).
- *Taxes.* Marginal tax rate, average tax rate, tax deductions, and tax deferral issues should be taken up.
- *Legal/regulatory factors.* Many rules govern the process of investing and retirement planning.
- *Unique needs and preferences.* Social/moral preferences of investors, investors' time, and expertise to manage investments affect the process.

---

14 Zvi Bodie, Alex Kane, and Alan J. Marcus, *Investments*, Third Edition, Irwin, 1996, pp. 864–866. Donald E. Fischer and Ronald J. Jordan, *Security Analysis and Portfolio Management*, Sixth Edition, Prentice-Hall, 1995, pp. 616–617.

Asset Allocation Decisions

There are two sets of decisions in creating a portfolio investment strategy:
- What asset allocation to use and what securities to purchase.
- Whether to use active investing or passive investing.

Asset allocation process is as follows:
- Determining what asset classes to use (stocks, bonds, international securities, real estate).
- What percentage of the portfolio should be invested in each asset?
- What specific securities to purchase in each allowable asset class?

Active and passive investment can be defined as follows:
- *Active investing.* Investor can select securities that will earn higher returns and/ or have lower risk than a corresponding index – trade securities in an attempt to buy low, sell high.
- *Passive investing.* Invest in an index representing each allowing asset class. Allocation changes only if the financial market outlook changes or rebalancing is needed.

Finally, there are four truths of investing:
- Risk determines expected returns: the risk-return tradeoff.
- Most financial markets are fairly efficient.
- Try to minimize investment expenses and tax consequences of investments.
- Diversify your portfolio.

Risk and Performance Measurement

Risk differences cause portfolios to respond differently to market changes. The total risk is measured by the standard deviation of portfolio returns. Non-diversifiable risk is measured by a security's beta. The *coefficient of determination* (R^2) denotes the degree of diversification.

Performance measurement tools (benchmarks) should be:
- Unambiguous
- Specified in advance
- Appropriate
- Investable
- Measurable

There are many performance measures, some of which are discussed as follows.

Sharpe (reward-to-variability) ratio. It measures the excess return per unit of risk (σ_p). The higher the ratio, the better the performance. This provides a ranking measure for portfolios.

$$Sharpe\ ratio = \frac{[\overline{r_p} - \overline{rf}]}{\sigma_p} = excessreturn/risk$$

Where:

$\overline{r_p}$ = Average return of portfolio

$\overline{r_f}$ = Average return of risk – free asset

The Treynor ratio. Replaces standard deviation with beta

$$Treynor\ measure = \frac{[\overline{r_p} - \overline{rf}]}{\beta_p}$$

Jensen's Alpha. The estimated a coefficient in $R_{pt} - RF_t = a_p + b_p [R_{Mt} - r_{ft}] + e_{pt}$ is a means to identify superior or inferior portfolio performance. CAPM implies a is zero. The estimated a measures the contribution of the portfolio manager. If $a > 0$, $a < 0$, a=0), this implies that the manager has superior, inferior, and neutral performance, respectively. But statistical significance is rarely achieved.

If the portfolio is completely diversified, Sharpe, Treynor, and Jensen agree on ranking. The Sharpe ratio evaluates performance on the basis of both return and diversification. Jensen's measure must be adjusted to rank portfolios.

Using the numbers in Table 6.7, we can calculate Jensen Alpha for both A and B, respectively:

Table 6.7: Comparison of Sharpe and Treynor Methods.

Fund	Return r_p, %	Excess Return r_p-r_f, %	Standard Deviation SD_p, %	Sharpe Ratio $(\overline{r_p} - \overline{r_f})/ SD_p$	Beta b_p	Treynor Ratio $(\overline{r_p} - \overline{r_f})/ b_p$
A	8	6	19	0.347	067	9
Market, M	9	7	21	0.333	100	7
B	10	8	32	0.250	133	6
		R_F= %2				

$$E(r_p) = r_f + b_p[E(r_M) - rf]$$

$$= 0.02 + 0.67\ (0.09 - 0.02) = 6.7\%$$

$$a_p = 0.08 - 0.067 = 1.3\%$$

While Fund A has earned 1.3% alpha return, Fund B has earned -2.64%. M's alpha return is zero (0).

In order to be statistically significant, the alpha return should be tested. Because the variable in equation comes from the following regression:

$$E(r_p) - r_{ft} = a_p + b_p\,[R_{Mt} - r_{ft}] + E_{pt}$$

Naturally, the values for a_p, b and E are obtained from regression analysis. An alpha value with a t value of 2 or above shows that the alpha value is statistically significant.

To use Jensen measure for ranking purposes, another measure, called the *modified Jensen* (J_m), is used:

$$J_m = a_p/b$$

Which Measure Is Appropriate? It depends on investment assumptions:
- If the portfolio is well-diversified, the Treyner Index is better.
- If no, then the Sharpe Index should be used.

If many alternatives are possible, use the Jensen or the Treynor measure.

Market Timing. Market timing involves shifting funds between a market index and a safe asset. When the market is up, the portfolio beta will be higher, because more funds are invested in the risky assets. When the market is down, the portfolio beta will be lower, because more funds are invested in the safe asset.

This can be tested by adding a quadratic term in the *security market line* regression. If the coefficient on squared market excess returns is significant, then timing ability exists:

$$r_P - r_f = a + b(r_M - r_f) + c(r_M - r_f)^2 + e_P$$

If c is statistically greater than 0, then we conclude that the portfolio manager has market timing ability.[15]

6.8 Summary

Efficiency is the key element to the economic well-being of societies. The three aspects of market efficiency are allocational efficiency, operational efficiency, and informational efficiency. An informational efficient market is a market in which prices adjust quickly after the arrival of new information and the price change reflects the economic value of the information, on average. The levels of informational efficiency are weak-form efficiency, semi-strong-form efficiency, and strong-form efficiency.

---

15 See Appendix C for testing regression coefficients.

Behavioral finance suggests that various psychological traits influence the investor pricing of securities.

The *holding-period return* (HPR) is the rate of return over one given investment horizon. There are many measures such as arithmetic average return, geometric average return, time-weighted return, money-weighted return, and log return over multiple periods.

Each instrument class has a different average annual return and standard deviation in various countries in the world.

If we form a portfolio, the risk of the portfolio (standard deviation) might be less than the individual assets. The source of the diversification effect is the negative correlation between assets.

We can explain *quadratic programming* intuitively: The Markowitz model seeks to find the minimum risky portfolio (having the lowest variance) or the maximum return portfolio by varying the weights of individual securities, taking the constraints into consideration.

The single-index model was developed by Sharpe to reduce the number of inputs required by the Markowitz Model. The model relates returns on each security to the returns on a common index, such as the S&P 500 Stock Index.

The Capital market line equation gives the equilibrium condition for a well-diversified portfolio held by an investor.

The security market line gives equilibrium risk-return tradeoff for an individual security. Investment can be defined as: setting aside funds with the expectation of receiving more funds in the future.

The five steps of portfolio management are setting portfolio objectives, formulating an investment strategy, having a game plan for portfolio revision, evaluating performance, and protecting the portfolio when appropriate.

To measure the performance of a portfolio, some performance measures are used that take risk (standard deviation or beta) into consideration.

7 Basic Derivatives

7.1 Introduction

We have seen several ways in which individuals and institutions can design their investments to take advantage of future market conditions. We have also seen how investors can control the volatility associated with their stock and bond positions by forming well-diversified portfolios of securities to reduce or eliminate a portfolio's systematic risk. A derivative is a security, the value of which depends on the underlying security or asset. There are essentially four types of derivatives, though there are many variants. A forward contract is an agreement to buy or sell an asset at a fixed time in future for a predetermined price. Futures are contracts to be executed at a future date, involving the sale of an asset or security according to the terms of the contract. Options contracts are the rights to buy or sell an asset or security according to the terms of the contract. A call option is a right to buy, while the put option is the right to sell. A swap contract involves the exchange of assets or securities now with the understanding that the transaction will be reversed later. Derivative securities are not used by corporations to raise funds. Rather, they serve as a useful tool for managing certain aspects of firm risk.

7.2 Forward Contracts

A *forward contract* is an agreement to buy or sell an asset at a fixed time in the future for a predetermined price. A futures contract, like a forward contract, is an agreement between two parties to buy or sell an asset at a certain time in the future for a prespecified price. Unlike forward contracts, futures contracts are traded on an exchange and they are standardized.

In this section, we will focus on FX forward contracts and forward rate agreements, instruments of over-the-counter markets.

Currency Forwards

Currency forwards are OTC contracts traded in forex markets that lock in an exchange rate for a currency pair.

They are generally used for hedging and can have customized terms, such as a particular notional amount or delivery period.

Unlike listed currency futures and options contracts, currency forwards don't require up-front payments when used by large corporations and banks.

https://doi.org/10.1515/9783110705355-007

Determining a currency forward rate depends on the interest rate differentials for the currency pair in question.

FX rates applied to future transactions are called *forward exchange rates*. At present, \$1= dk.5.3500.[1] What should the exchange rate be in 90 days' time? Interest rates are 6% and 2% in Denmark and the U.S., respectively. In order to answer this question, let us examine the equation used in calculating forward FX rates:[2]

$$F = S \times (1 + (r_d - r_f) \times (t/T))$$

Where:

S = Spot FX rate (the value of 1 unit of foreign currency in terms of local currency)

R_h = Risk-free interest rate in home country,

R_f = Risk-free interest rate in a foreign country,

t = Maturity of the contract,

T = Number of days in a year (generally 360 days).

F = 5.35000 × (1+(0.06(90/360)))/ (1+(0.02(90/360)))

= 5.3500 × (1.015/1.005) = dk.5.40323

Importers and exporters generally use currency forwards to hedge against fluctuations in exchange rates. A currency forward settlement can either be on a cash or a delivery basis, provided that the option is mutually acceptable and has been specified beforehand in the contract.

In forex trading, a long position is one in which a trader buys a currency at one price and aims to sell it later at a higher price. In this scenario, the trader benefits from a rising market. A short position is one in which the trader sells a currency in anticipation that it will depreciate. Assume that the bank agrees to sell one US dollar for dk.5.40323 after 90 days. In this case, the bank takes a short position in dollars. The importer takes a long position in dollars.

Assume that FX rate stood at dk.5.40. This bank will buy dollars at dk.5.6000 and sell dollars at dk.5.40323. Assume further that the amount of dollars to be delivered to the importer was \$100,000. Instead of paying dk.560,000, the importer will pay dk. 540,032, thus making a profit of dk.19,968.

Forward Rate Agreements (FRAs)

A *forward rate agreement* is an instrument to make a settlement in the future. With this agreement, one agrees to pay or receive at a future date the difference between

---

1 dk. (DKK) is the symbol of Danish krone.

2 This is the *interest rate parity* formula, which is discussed in Chapter 14.

the agreed upon interest rate and the rate prevailing on the settlement date times the notational amount. This not an exchange product, but an over-the-counter product. The parties involved are clients and banks.

The company that needs a loan 90 days later wants to lock in an interest rate of 7% for three months and requests its bank to write an FRA with a notational amount of €100,000. On the settlement, data interest rates have fallen 6.5%. In this case, the client will make up the difference on the agreement. If the market rate were above the contract rate, then the client would receive the difference.

$$\text{Settlement Amount} = PV\,(r_c - r_s) \times P \times t/T$$

$$= (r_{s-} - r_c) \times P \times t/T/(1 + (r_c \times t/T))$$

Where,

$r_c =$ Contract interest rate
$r_s =$ Realized interest rate (generally LIBOR)
P= Notational principal
t = Contract period
T= Number of days in a year (generally 360)
    Settlement Amount = ((0.065−0.07) ×100.000×90/360)/ (1+(0.065×90/360)
        = −125/1.01625 = −€123

If the payment amount is positive, the FRA seller pays this amount to the buyer. Otherwise, the buyer pays the seller. The notional amount of €100,000 is not exchanged. Instead, the two companies involved in this transaction are using that figure to calculate the interest rate differential.

7.3 Futures

A futures contract represents an obligation to carry through a transaction, while the option contract is a choice and does not obligate the owner of the contract to actually conclude the transaction. Both contracts are used to lock in prices and reduce risks.

Futures can be traded. Exchange-traded futures are standardized as to terms and conditions, such as the quality and quantity of the underlying asset and expiration dates. A reversing trade is one that mitigates risk. A buyer of a futures contract can counteract that obligation by selling the identical type of contract. At the close of each trading day, *a settlement price*, or *approximate closing price* of the future, is determined by a *special exchange committee* in a process called *marking to the market*.

Using futures and forwards:

- Investors can hedge the uncertainty faced by producers of certain products.
- Producers and consumers can eliminate their risks by entering a forward or futures contract, which calls for the producers to deliver the product to consumers for a predetermined price at a future date.

Key differences between futures and forwards:
- There is secondary trading – liquidity for future contracts.
- Future contract is valued marking-to-market or *pay-as-you-go*.
- Future contracts are standardized contract units.
- In futures trading, *Clearinghouse* warrants performance.

Types of contracts:
- Agricultural commodities
- Metals and minerals (including energy contracts)
- Foreign currencies
- Financial futures
  - Interest rate futures
  - Stock index futures
  - Individual stock futures

The first commodity futures market was established in Japan in the Tokugawa period (17th century) for rice contracts. Today, the Chicago Board of Trade (CBOT), established in 1848, is the largest in the world.

Trading Mechanics and Margins

Clearinghouse acts as a counterparty to all buyers and sellers. It is obligated to deliver or supply delivery. Clearinghouse requires a margin from traders in futures.
    How to close out positions:
- Reversing the trade
- Take or make delivery

Most trades are reversed and do not involve actual delivery. Margin and trading arrangements are as follows:
- *Initial margin.* Funds deposited to provide capital to absorb losses.
- *Marking-to-market.* Each day, the profits or losses from the new futures price are reflected in the margin account.
- *Maintenance or variance margin.* The value below which the margin is not allowed to fall.

The other important terms regarding a futures contract are:
- *Convergence of price.* When maturity approaches the spot and futures price converge.
- *Delivery.* Some contract is the actual commodity of a certain grade with a delivery location or, for some contracts, cash settled.

- *Basis.* The difference between the futures price and the spot price is called basis. Over time, the basis will likely change and will eventually converge.
- *Basis risk.* The variability in the basis that will affect profits and/or hedging performance.

Marking-to-Market

When a position is established, each party deposits with the clearing house to absorb potential losses. From then on, *marking-to-market* will occur. The profit and losses will be reflected in each investor's account each day. The party that has opened a long position will collect profits whenever the spot price goes up, and incur losses when the spot price decreases. Let us develop a hypothetical example. Let's say you are long in $/dk. worth of $100,000 futures contract, established at an initial settle price of dk.5.45. Your initial margin to establish the position is dk.54,500 and the maintenance margin is dk.40,875 for all 100 contracts. Over the subsequent five trading days, the settlement prices are dk.5.55, dk.5.60, dk.5.40. dk.5.50, and dk.5.20, respectively. Compute the balance in your margin account at the end of each of the five trading days, and compute your total profit or loss at the end of the trading period. See Table 7.1.

Table 7.1: Hypothetical Euro Futures Margin Account.

Date	Rate	Futures Position	Initial Margin	Maintenance Margin	Profit/ Loss Account*	Margin Account	Margin Call
14.07.2018	5.45	545,000	54,500	40,875	–	54,500	–
15.07.2018	5.55	555,000	54,500	40,875	10,000	64,500	–
16.07.2018	5.60	560,000	54,500	40,875	5,000	69,500	–
17.07.2018	5.40	540,000	54,500	40,875	−20,000	49,500	–
18.07.2018	5.50	550,000	54,500	40,875	10,000	59,500	–
19.07.2018	5.20	520,000	54,500	40,875	−30,000	29,500	−25,000

*Futures Position$_t$-Future Position$_{t-1}$.

- Day 1: New position value = $5.45 \times 100,000 =$ dk.545,000. The initial margin to establish the position is dk.54,500 and the maintenance margin is dk.40,875. The balance of the margin account is dk.54,500.

- Day 2: New position value = 5.55 × 100.000 = dk.555,000. Since there is a rate increase, a profit of dk.10,000 goes to the margin account. In this case, the balance of the margin account amounts to dk.54,500.
- Day 3: Since there is a rate increase, a profit of dk.5,000 goes to the margin account.
- Day 4: Since there is a rate decrease, a loss of dk.20,000 goes to the margin account. The balance of margin account is now dk.49,500
- Day 5: Since there is a rate increase, a profit of dk.10,000 goes to the margin account. Now the margin account amounts to dk.59,500.
- Day 6: Since there is a rate decrease, a loss of dk.30,000 goes to margin account. The balance of margin account is now dk.29,500. Since this is less than 75% of initial margin, the investor is required to compensate the rest, which is equal to (€54,500 – dk.29,500=) dk.25,000.

In sum, the investor has incurred a loss of dk.25,000. We will not show the futures margin account of an investor who opened a short position. But it is sufficient to say at the moment the investor will have earned dk.25,000.

Trading Strategies

Trading strategies and payoffs are as follows:
- Speculation:
  - *Short.* You believe the price will fall.
  - *Long.* You believe the price will rise.

- Hedging:
  - *Long hedge.* Protecting against a rise in price.
  - *Short hedge.* Protecting against a fall in price.

Suppose that you have a long position in gold futures with a delivery date in three months. The delivery price is $1,800. What is your payoff if the gold price in three months is $1,500, $1,800, or $2,100?

If the ending gold price is $1,500, you buy an ounce of gold that is worth $1,500 for $1,800. You lose $300. If the ending gold price is $1,800, you buy an ounce of gold that is worth $1,800 for $1,800. You break even.

If the ending gold price is $2,100, you buy an ounce of gold that is worth $2,100 for $1800. You make $300.

So, when you long a futures contract, the higher the future price is, the higher your payoff. See Figures 7.1–7.3.

Suppose that you agree to sell an ounce of gold in three months for $1,800. If the ending gold price is $1,500, you sell an ounce of gold that is worth $1,500 for

Payoff

Payoff $= S_T - F_0$

0

F_0

S_T

Long Position

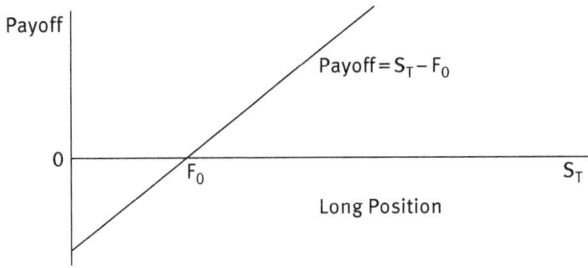

Figure 7.1: Payoffs from Forwards & Futures: Long Position.

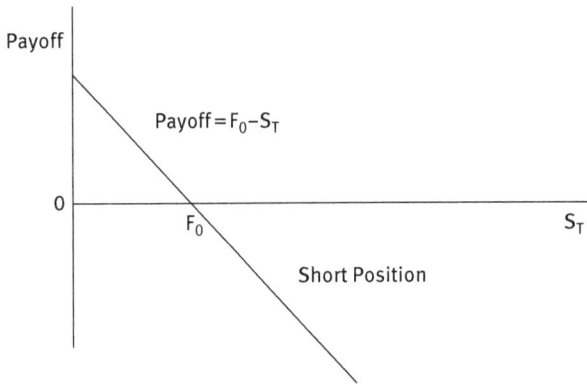

Payoff

Payoff $= F_0 - S_T$

0

F_0

S_T

Short Position

Figure 7.2: Payoffs from Forwards & Futures: Short Position.

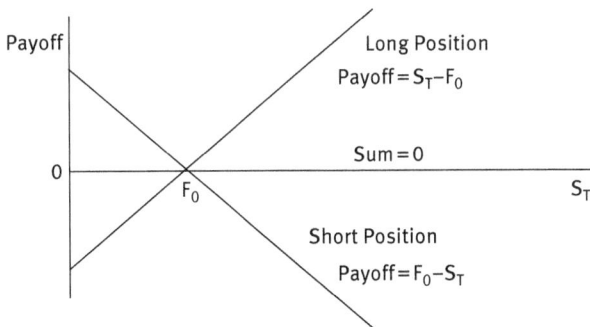

Payoff

Long Position
Payoff $= S_T - F_0$

Sum $= 0$

0

F_0

S_T

Short Position
Payoff $= F_0 - S_T$

Figure 7.3: A Zero-Sum Game.

$1,800. You make a profit of $300. If the ending gold price is $1, 800, you sell an ounce of gold that is worth $1,800 for $1,800. You break even. If the ending gold price is $2,100, you sell an ounce of gold that is worth $2,100 for $1,800, and you lose $300.

You may have noticed that what the long position wins is exactly what the short position loses, and vice versa.

$$(S_T - F_0) + (F_0 - S_T) = 0$$

Where:

S_T represents the spot price at the end of the contract period.

F_0 represents the future price set in the beginning of contract period.

This is a *zero-sum* game.

Futures Pricing

We can determine the futures price of many contracts by imposing the no arbitrage condition. There are two ways to acquire an asset for some date in the future:

- Purchase it now and store it.
- Take a long position in futures.

The *Spot-Futures Parity Theorem* says that these two strategies should have the same market-determined costs.

As an initial example, consider gold. Assume that it has no storage costs. We have the following strategies:

- Strategy A: Buy the gold and hold it for a year.
- Strategy B: Put funds aside today and buy a gold futures contract with one year to maturity.

$1,500 is the current gold price per ounce, and S_T is the gold price at T, which is of course unknown at t. As shown in Table 7.2, $1,650 is the futures price (the risk-free rate is 10%).

Table 7.2: Strategies: Numerical Example.

Strategy A	Action	Cash Flow at t	Cash Flow at T
	Buy gold	($1,500)	S_T
Strategy B	**Action**	**Cash Flow at t**	**Cash Flow at T**
	Long gold futures	0	$S_T - \$1,650$
	Invest $1500 in T-bill	($1,500)	$1,500(1.1) =$1,650
	Total for B	($1,500)	S_T

Strategy A and B have the same cash flow at t and T. The key here is that the futures price $1,650 is exactly $1,500 (1+10%).

This model can be expressed as in Table 7.3.

Table 7.3: Strategies: Formula Example.

Strategy A	Action	Cash Flow at t	Cash Flow at T
	Buy gold	$-S_t$	S_T

Strategy B	Action	Cash Flow at t	Cash Flow at T
	Long gold futures	0	$S_T - F_t$
	Invest $F_t/(1+r_f)$ T^t in T-bills	$-F_t/ (1+r_f)^{T\text{-}t}$	F_t
	Total for B	$-F_t/(1+r_f)^{T\text{-}t}$	S_T

Strategy A and Strategy B give identical payoffs at T, regardless what the future gold price is. Hence, they should cost the same at t.

$$-S_t = \frac{-F_t}{\left(1+r_f\right)^{T-t}}$$

$$\Rightarrow F_t = S_t\left(1+r_f\right)^{T-t}$$

$$\$1,650 = \$1,500(1+10\%)$$

This is the *cost of carry* formula, as the futures price is the spot price plus the cost of carry for the gold.

Note that for gold, the futures price is always higher than the spot price regardless of your expected future gold price.

Stock Futures

Assume a 3-month stock futures contract on ABC exists. Suppose that the annual dividend yield (q) is 3%, and the risk-free interest rate (r) is 8%. If the stock currently stands at €8, then the futures price will be:

$$F_0 = S_0 e^{(r-q)T}$$

$$= 8 \times e^{(0.08 - 0.03)\,(3/12)}$$

$$= €8,101$$

Or the futures price in discrete form will be

$$F_0 = S_0(1+r-d)^T$$

$$= 8(1+0.08-0.03)^{3/12}$$

$$= €8,098$$

Hedging Stock Market Risk (Cross-hedging Using Index Futures)

Assume a 3-month futures contract on an index exists. Suppose that the annual dividend yield (q) is 3%, and the risk-free interest rate (r) is 8%. If the Index currently stands at 8,000, then the futures price will be:

$$F_0 = S_0 e^{(r-q)T} = 8,000 e^{(0.08-0.03) \times \frac{3}{12}} = 8,101$$

Suppose that $F_0 > 8,101$ then you can go long in the index and sell the futures contract and lock in an arbitrage profit. And if $F_0 < 8,101$, you short the index and take a long futures position.

To protect against a decline in level stock prices (systematic risk), we can short the appropriate number of futures index contracts. It is less costly and is quicker to use the index contracts. Use the beta for the portfolio to determine the hedge ratio. Inputs are portfolio value, beta, and index contract value.

The properties of a well-diversified portfolio may be relatively similar to some index portfolios. The CAPM tells us that the return on a portfolio is:

$$r_p = r_f + \beta(r_m - r_f)$$

We can thus alter the risk profile of a portfolio by changing its beta. A simple way of doing this is to take positions in index futures.

Hedging can be interpreted as *setting the beta equal to zero*. Then the question is: What is the expected return of a zero-beta portfolio? As a reasonable approximation, we can assume that the futures contract and the Index (such as the DAX-30) have the same beta. Assume that the DAX-30 is a close proxy for the market portfolio. What is the number of contracts to hedge stock market risk?

$$N = \left(\frac{B_t - B_p}{B_f}\right)\left(\frac{V_p}{P_f^* m}\right)$$

β_t: ? We want to set β_t to 0
β_p: Given as 0.8 (actual beta of our portfolio)
V_p: Current portfolio value
N: Unknown target quantity (number of futures contracts)
P_f: Current futures price (Value of the Index, such as DAX-30)
m: Multiplier (# of times the index is to be multiplied, which is €25 in our case)
β_f: Assumed here to be equal to 1 (beta of futures contracts)

For example, if V_p = €200M, Dax-30 Index is 8,000, and β_p is 0.80, you need:

$$N = \left(\frac{0-0.8}{1}\right)\left(\frac{200{,}000{,}000}{25*8{,}000}\right)$$

$$N = -800\ contracts$$

For this transaction, the investor will deposit the initial margin and take a short position.

Assume that beta of futures contract (β_f) were 1.1. What would be the number of contracts to hedge stock market risk?

$$N = \left(\frac{0-0.8}{1.1}\right)\left(\frac{200{,}000{,}000}{25\times8{,}000}\right)$$

$$N = -727.27\ contracts$$

Suppose instead of *hedging* we would like to increase returns by doubling the risk (beta) of our portfolio to 1.6. How many futures contracts should we buy?

$$1.6\times200{,}000{,}000 = 200{,}000{,}000\times1.6 + N\times8{,}000\times100\times1 = 40{,}000\ \text{contracts.}$$

For this transaction, the investor will deposit the initial margin and take a long position.

Hedging Foreign Exchange Risk

Currency contracts are valued by using the interest rate parity formula:[3]

$$F_0 = S_0\left(\frac{1+r_l}{1+r_f}\right)^T$$

where:
  F_0 is the forward price,
  S_0 is the current exchange rate.

$r_l = 8\%$ $r_f = 3\%$ $S_0 = €5,50$ per dollar $T = 2/12$ yr.

$$F_0 = 5.50\left(\frac{1.08}{1.03}\right)^{2/12} = €5.5436$$

---

3 *Interest rate parity* is discussed in Chapter 14.

A Danish firm expects to receive 2 million dollars in three months. The firm wants to protect against a decline in profit that would result from a decline in the dollar.

To do this, the firm sells dollars for future delivery. That is, the firm enters a futures contract that agrees to sell 2 million dollars (2,000 futures contracts[4]) in three months, at say, dk.6 per dollar. While the spot rate of $/dk. now is dk.5.8, June contracts, as said before, trades at dk.6.

At the end of contract period, the firm will sell dollar futures at €6 per dollar.

If the dollar goes up to dk.6.6/$ in three months, what happens?
- $2 M is worth dk.13.2 M
- You lose $(6.6-6.0) \times 2\,M = dk.1.2\,M$
- Your total payoff is dk.12 M

If the dollar drops to dk.5.4/$ in three months, what happens?
- £2 M is worth dk.10.8 M
- You win in futures $(6-5.4) \times 2\,M = €\,1.2\,M$

Your total payoff is dk.12 mil. This guarantees that that firm will receive dk.12 million in three months regardless of the future exchange rate.

7.4 Options

In the following section, we will examine payoffs, profits from options transactions, trading strategies using options, and, finally, option valuation.[5]

Options can be created and sold in exchange markets. A *call option* is a contract for the purchase of a security at a specified price within a specified time frame. A *put option* is a contract for the sale of a security at a specified price within a specified time frame.

The price of the option is called the *option premium*. The option may be exercised or may expire.

Options contracts are capital market instruments that give the holder the right, but not the obligation, to buy or to sell an underlying asset at a specified price on or before a predetermined date where such right is exercised by registered delivery or cash settlement. The holder of an option has only the right to buy or sell the underlying security itself.

4 Contract size is assumed to be $1,000.
5 Some parts of this section were adapted from André Farber, *Corporate Finance Lecture Notes*, Vietnam, 2004. http://www.ulb.ac.be/cours/solvay/farber/vietnam.htm, 01.05.2005; Aswath Damodaran, *Applied Corporate Finance*, Wiley, 1999, pp. 196–212.

Definition and Classification

An *option* gives its holder the *rights* (but not the obligation) to buy or sell an asset for a pre-specified price (*exercise price* or *strike price*) *on* or *before* a future date (*expiration date* or *maturity date*).

The seller of an option contract is called the *writer* of the option. The writer has the obligation to sell or buy the underlying asset if the holder of the option chooses to exercise the option and buy or sell the asset.

The price the buyer or holder of an option pays to the writer to buy or sell the option is called the *premium* of the option.

According to whether the option gives the rights to buy or to sell an asset (underlying security), options can be classified into:
- *Call options* → rights to buy
- *Put options* → rights to sell

According to when the holder can exercise the options:
- *European options* → only on maturity date
- *American options* → on or before maturity date

According to the relationship between exercise price and the underlying asset's price:
- *In-the-money options*
  For call options: exercise price < current asset price
  For put options: exercise price > current asset price
- *At-the-money options*
  For call and put exercise price = current asset price
- *Out-of-the-money options*
  For call options: exercise price > current asset price
  For put options: exercise price < current asset price

According to the assets, the underlying asset is traded in the option contracts:
- Stock options
- Stock index options
- Futures options
- Foreign currency options

According to whether options are traded in organized exchanges or not:
- Exchange-traded options: standardized options.
- OTC options: traded in the over-the-counter market, tailored to customers' specific needs. For example, interest rate caps and interest rate floors.

Time Value of Option

The price (premium) of an option can be divided into two components: *intrinsic value* and *time value*. *Intrinsic value* is the payoff if the option were to be exercised immediately. Intrinsic value is always greater than or equal to zero. For example, if a stock is trading for €30, the yearly standard deviation of stock is 25%, and the exercise price is €25, what is the call premium for this one-year call option? What is the intrinsic value of this call option? What is the time value of this option?

Using the *Black-Scholes* model, the call premium will be €6,852.[6] The intrinsic value of the call will be (30–25=) €5. The time value of this call will be (6,852–5,000=) €1,852.

Usually the price of an option in the marketplace will be higher than its intrinsic value. The difference between the market value of an option and its intrinsic value is called the *time value* (or extrinsic value) of an option. An option is trading at parity when the price of the option is equal to its intrinsic value, implying that the time value is zero.

An option which has a positive intrinsic value is considered to be *in-the-money* by the amount of the intrinsic value. If a stock is trading at €50, a €40 call is €10 in-the-money. A €50 call on the same stock would be considered to be *at-the-money*, and a €55 call would be considered to be *out-of-the-money*.

Put-Call Parity

Put-call parity specifies the difference in value between a European call option and a European put option. Necessary conditions for this are that the stock does not pay dividends and that the options have the same exercise price and expiration date.

The put-call parity relationship is:

$$C_0 - P_0 = S_0 - Xe^{-rT} = S_0 - PV(X)$$

where r is the continuously compounded interest rate

Strategy 1: Buy a call option and write a put option with the same exercise price.

Payoff at

expiration if	$S_T < X$	$S_T > X$
Call option	0	$S_T - X$
Put option	$-(X - S_T)$	0
Total payoff	$S_T - X$	$S_T - X$

---

6 The Black-Scholes model is discussed later in this chapter.

Strategy 2: Buy stock on margin.
Borrow the present value of the exercise price, Xe^{-rT}.

$$\text{Cost} = S_0 - Xe^{-rT}$$

Payoff at expiration is $S_T - X$.
    Since the payoffs are equal, equilibrium requires that

$$C_0 - P_0 = S_0 - Xe^{-rT}$$

Payoffs and Profits from Options

Payoff means strictly what one gets paid excluding the premium, which was presumably paid up front. but if asked for *profit*, then one should include the premium in the calculation. We consider the payoffs and profits (payoffs net of premium) from a European option for the holder and writer of the option *at the maturity date*. For American options, the payoffs and profits before the maturity date can be derived in a similar way.
    Payoff and profit for a call option:

Payoff to call holder
$$\begin{cases} S_T\text{-}X & \text{if } S_T > X \\ 0 & \text{if } S_T \le X \end{cases}$$

Profit to call holder
$$\begin{cases} S_T\text{-}X\text{-}C & \text{if } S_T > X \\ \text{-}C & \text{if } S_T \le X \end{cases}$$

Payoff to call writer
$$\begin{cases} X\text{-}S_T & \text{if } S_T > X \\ 0 & \text{if } S_T \le X \end{cases}$$

Profit to call writer
$$\begin{cases} X\text{-}S_{T+}C & \text{if } S_T > X \\ C & \text{if } S_T \le X \end{cases}$$

Payoff and profit for a put option:

Payoff to put holder
$$\begin{cases} 0 & \text{if } S_T \geq X \\ X\text{-}S_T & \text{if } S_T < X \end{cases}$$

Profit to put holder
$$\begin{cases} \text{-P} & \text{if } S_T \geq X \\ X\text{-}S_T\text{-}P & \text{if } S_T < X \end{cases}$$

Payoff to put writer
$$\begin{cases} 0 & \text{if } S_T \geq X \\ S_T\text{-}X & \text{if } S_T < X \end{cases}$$

Profit to put writer
$$\begin{cases} P & \text{if } S_T \geq X \\ S_T\text{-}X\text{+}P & \text{if } S_T < X \end{cases}$$

Using the inputs in Table 7.4, one can form a graph of option payoffs and option profits/losses.

Table 7.4: Inputs for Option Payoffs.

Symbol of the underlying stock	ABC
Exercise price	€3.50
Option premium	€0.50
Number of stocks	100
Maturity of the option	21.09.18

Calculation of option payoffs, option profit/loss, and the total profits are shown in Tables 7.4–7.8 and Figures 7.4–7.7.

Trading Strategies Using Options

Options can be used for a speculative purpose and also for the purpose of risk management. Since one only pays the premium (much less than the stock price) for the option, the resulting leverage effect could make the active use of options very risky.

Table 7.5: Calculations of Option Payoff and Option Profit/Loss for Buy Call (€).

Type of option	Buy Call										
Price of ABC at 21.09.18	0.00	0.70	1.40	2.10	2.80	3.50	4.20	4.90	5.60	6.30	7.00
Option payoff	0.00	0.00	0.00	0.00	0.00	0.00	0.70	1.40	2.10	2.80	3.50
Option profit/loss	−0.50	−0.50	−0.50	−0.50	−0.50	−0.50	0.20	0.90	1.60	2.30	3.00
Total profit/loss	−50.00	−50.00	−50.00	−50.00	−50.00	−50.00	20.00	90.00	160.00	230.00	300.00

Table 7.6: Calculations of Option Payoff and Option Profit/Loss for Sell Call (€).

Type of option	Sell Call										
Price of ABC at 21.09.18	0.00	0.70	1.40	2.10	2.80	3.50	4.20	4.90	5.60	6.30	7.00
Option payoff	0.00	0.00	0.00	0.00	0.00	0.00	−0.70	−1.40	−2.10	−2.80	−3.50
Option profit/loss	0.50	0.50	0.50	0.50	0.50	0.50	−0.20	−0.90	−1.60	−2.30	−3.00
Total profit/loss	50.00	50.00	50.00	50.00	50.00	50.00	−20.00	−90.00	−160.00	−230.00	−300.00

Table 7.7: Calculations of Option Payoff and Option Profit/Loss for Buy Put (€).

Type of option	Buy Put										
Price of ABC at 21.09.18	0.00	0.70	1.40	2.10	2.80	3.50	4.20	4.90	5.60	6.30	7.00
Option payoff	3.50	2.80	2.10	1.40	0.70	0.00	0.00	0.00	0.00	0.00	0.00
Option profit/loss	3.00	2.30	1.60	0.90	0.20	−0.50	−0.50	−0.50	−0.50	−0.50	−0.50
Total profit/loss	300.00	230.00	160.00	90.00	20.00	−50.00	−50.00	−50.00	−50.00	−50.00	−50.00

Table 7.8: Calculations of Option Payoff and Option Profit/Loss for Sell Put (€).

Type of option	Sell Put										
Price of ABC at 21.09.18	0.00	0.70	1.40	2.10	2.80	3.50	4.20	4.90	5.60	6.30	7.00
Option payoff	−3.50	−2.80	−2.10	−1.40	−0.70	0.00	0.00	0.00	0.00	0.00	0.00
Option profit/loss	−3.00	−2.30	−1.60	−0.90	−0.20	0.50	0.50	0.50	0.50	0.50	0.50
Total profit/loss	−300.00	−230.00	−160.00	−90.00	−20.00	50.00	50.00	50.00	50.00	50.00	50.00

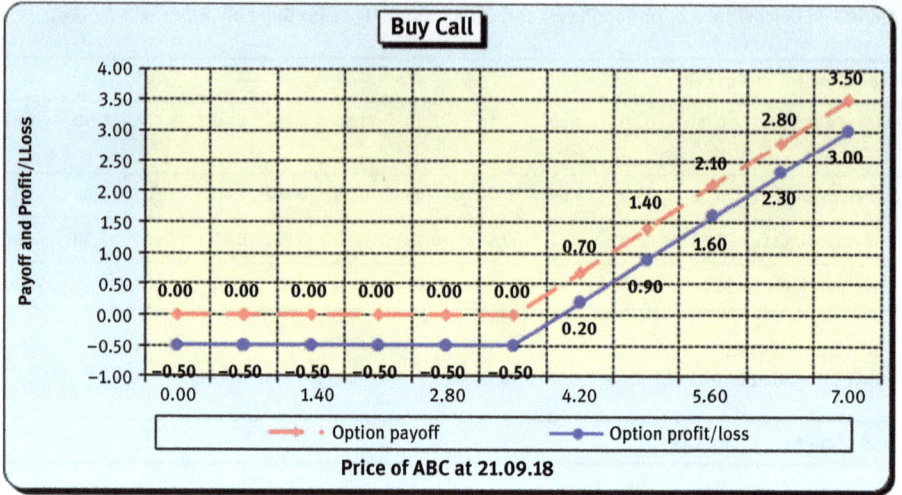

Figure 7.4: Option Payoff and Option Profit/Loss for Buy Call.

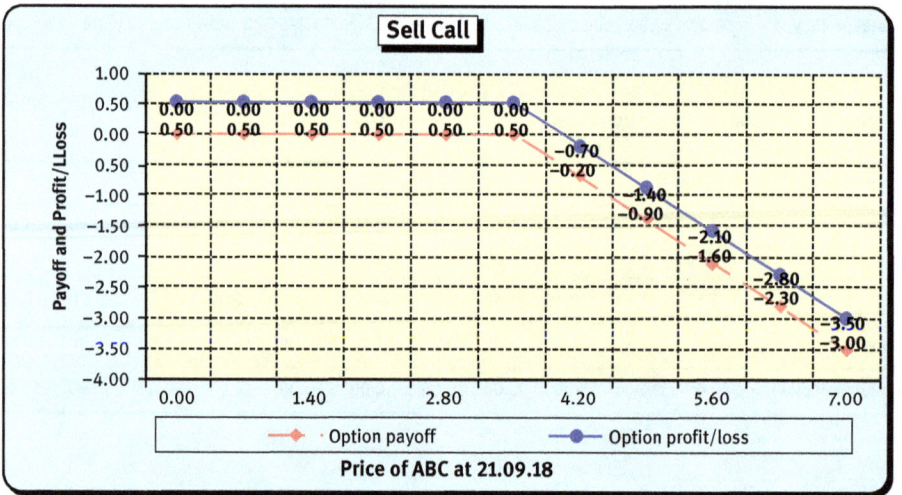

Figure 7.5: Option Payoff and Option Profit/Loss for Sell Call.

Some combinations of options and the underlying stocks or combinations of different options can reduce one's exposure on the options or the underlying stocks and, at the same time, increase profit opportunities. We will review a few of these trading strategies.

Protective Put. The strategy of *protective put* is the combination of a long position on a stock and a long position on the put option on this stock with the maturity

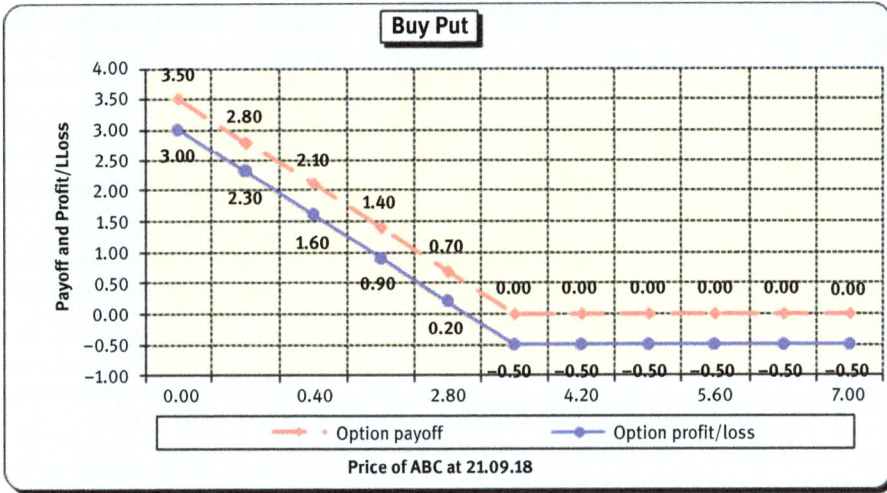

Figure 7.6: Option Payoff and Option Profit/Loss for Buy Put.

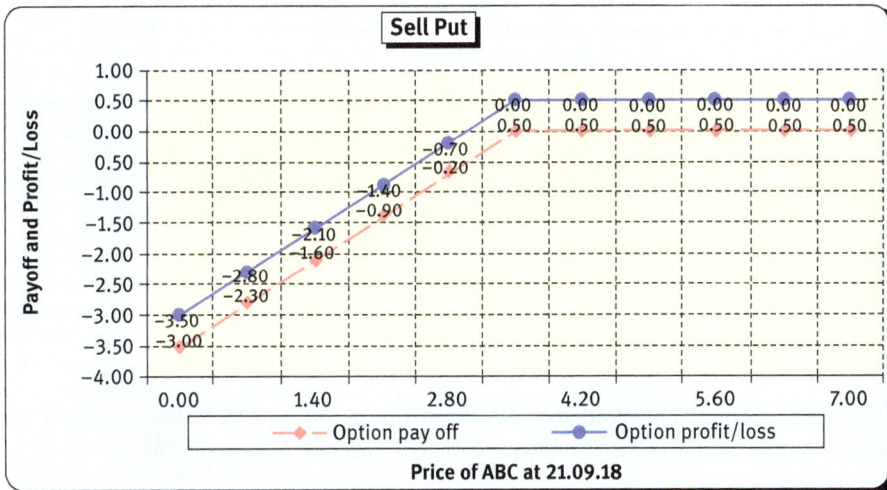

Figure 7.7: Option Payoff and Option Profit/Loss for Sell Put.

date equal to the holding horizon of the stock. Protective put is a part of the so-called *portfolio insurance* programs.

Suppose you expect ABC stock is going to rise, so you buy 100 shares of the stock. But at the same time, you're worried that if your prediction is wrong and the ABC stock price goes down instead, you will incur large losses. In this case, you can buy a put option contract (one contract involves 100 shares of stock) at the same time you buy the stock. Then you can limit your losses when the stock price declines and simultaneously take advantage of the likely upside movement of the stock price.

For example, the current price of ABC stock is €30 per share, and you want to hold it for 3 months. You can then buy a 3-month maturity put option on ABC stock with exercise price X = €30. Suppose the cost (premium) of the put is €1.

When the stock price falls, your maximum loss is only €1; when the stock price rises substantially, you will not miss the profit opportunity.

Synthetic protective puts. When you are holding a stock, you could buy a put on that stock to protect your investment value. But when you're holding a portfolio, you may find the put option on a portfolio is simply not available in the market, and at best you could only find a put option on a market index. Practitioners deal with this issue by creating *synthetic protective puts*: selling a proportion of shares equal to the put option's delta (a concept discussed in the following sections and placing the proceeds in risk-free T-bills. The problem, however, with synthetic portfolio insurance technique is that when the market crashes, stock prices change so fast that you may not be able to compute the delta correctly and sell your shares in a timely manner. The 1987 stock market crash is a good case in point.

Covered Call. The combination of a long position in a stock with a short position in the call option on this stock is called a *covered call*. Suppose you have written (sold) a call option on a stock. If the stock price increases, you may incur large losses. To minimize this risk, you can buy the underlying stock so that when the stock price rises, the profits from your stock position can offset the losses from your call option position. The cost: You may miss the profit opportunity at the time of large upward movement of the stock price. The compensation: the premium you collect from the buyer of the call option.

Risk Sensitivities (Greeks)

Traders will often talk about the *Greeks* in relation to securities with optionality. What do they mean? The Greeks are five letters used to describe an option's behavior:

– *Delta* (also known as the *hedge ratio*) is the sensitivity of an option's theoretical value to a change in the price of the underlying contract.

Delta = Change in the option price/Change in the stock price

Calls have deltas ranging from zero to one hundred. Puts have deltas ranging from Delta to negative one hundred. An underlying contract always has a delta of one hundred.

– The *Gamma* of a portfolio of derivatives on an underlying asset is the rate of change of the portfolio's delta with respect to the price of the underlying asset.

Gamma = Change in the value of the portfolio × Change in time / Change in stock price

If the gamma is large, the delta is highly sensitive to the price of the underlying asset.

- The *Theta* of a portfolio of derivatives is the rate of change of the value of the portfolio with respect to time with all else remaining the same.

Theta = Change in the value of the portfolio / Change in time

It is sometimes referred to as the time decay of the portfolio.

- The *Vega* of a portfolio of derivatives is the rate of change of the value of the portfolio with respect to the volatility of the underlying asset.

Vega = Change in the value of the portfolio / Change in the volatility of the underlying asset

Vega is also known as lambda, kappa, or sigma.

- The *Rho* of a portfolio of derivatives is the rate of change of the value of the portfolio to the interest rate.

Rho = Change in the value of the portfolio / Change in interest rates

- It is a measure of the sensitivity of the portfolio's value to interest rates. See Table 7.9 for reference to the option Greeks.

Table 7.9: Option Greeks.

	Call	Put
Delta	$\frac{dC}{dS} = \Delta_C 0 \leq \Delta_C = N(d_1) \leq 1$	$-\frac{dp}{dS} = \Delta_p$ $-1 \leq \Delta_p = N(d_1)-1 \leq 0$
Gamma	$\frac{d\Delta_C}{dS} = \frac{d^2C}{dS^2} = \Gamma_C > 0$	$\frac{d\Delta_p}{dS} = \frac{d^2p}{dS^2} = \Gamma_p > 0$
Theta	$\frac{dP}{dT} = \Theta_{P,\text{Amerikan}} > 0$	$\frac{dP}{dT} = \Theta_{P,\text{Amerikan}} > 0$
Vega	$\frac{dP}{d\sigma} = V_P > 0$	$\frac{dP}{d\sigma} = V_P > 0$
Rho	$\frac{dP}{dr} = \rho_P < 0$	$\frac{dP}{dr} = \rho_P > 0$

Determinants of Option Values

There are 6 key factors that influence the value (premium) of an option. The relationship between option value and these factors are shown in Table 7.10 (assuming other factors don't change):

Table 7.10: The Relationship between Option Value Factors.

Factors	Value of call option (C)	Value of put option (P)
Stock price S ↑	↑	↓
Exercise price X ↑	↓	↑
Volatility of stock price σ ↑ ↑		↑
Time to maturity T ↑	↑ (American)	↑(American)
Interest rate r ↑	↑	↓
Dividend yield q ↑	↓	↑

Binomial Option Pricing Model

The intuition behind the option pricing formulas can be introduced in a two-state option model known as the *binomial model*,[7] Let S be the current price of a non-dividend paying stock.

Suppose that, over a period of time (say, 6 months), the stock price can either increase (to uS, u>1) or decrease (to dS, d<1).

Consider a X = €100 call with 1-period to maturity.

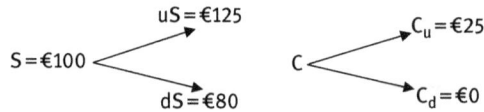

It is possible to create a *synthetic call* that replicates the future value of the call option as follows:
- Buy Delta shares
- Borrow B at the riskless rate r (i.e. 5% per annum)

Choose Delta and B so that the future value of this portfolio is equal to the value of the call option:
- Delta uS – (1+r Δt) B = C_u *Delta 125–1.025 B = 25*
- Delta dS – (1+r Δt) B = C_d *Delta 80–1.025 B = 0*

(Δt is the length of the time period in years, e.g., 6-months means Δt=0.5)

---

7 See John C. Cox, Stephen Ross, and Mark Rubinstein, "Option Pricing: A Simplified Approach," *Journal of Financial Economics*, 7, Sep. 1979, pp. 229–263.

In a perfect capital market, the value of the call should then be equal to the value of its synthetic reproduction, otherwise arbitrage would be possible:

$$C = Delta \times S - B$$

This is the *Black-Scholes model*. We now have 2 equations with 2 unknowns to solve.

$$[Eq1] - [Eq2] \Rightarrow Delta \times (125 - 80) = 25 \Rightarrow Delta = 0.556$$

Delta is the sensitivity of call price to stock price. We call it *hedge ratio*, or simply the call option's delta. Delta gives the number of shares or the underlying stock you need to buy (for a short position in call or long position in put) or sell (for a long position in call or short position in put) in order to make your combined positions in options and the underlying assets risk-free. The delta for the portfolio is therefore made to be zero, or *delta-neutral*. This procedure is called *delta hedging*.

Replace Delta by its value in [Eq2] $B = 43.36$

$C = $ Delta $S - B = 0.556 \times 100 - 43.36$ $C = €12.20$

$C = [p \times C_u + (1-p) \times C_d] / (1+r\Delta t)$ with $p = (1+r\Delta t - d)/ (u-d)$

P is the probability of a stock price increase in a risk-neutral world where the expected return is equal to the risk-free rate.

In a risk-neutral world: $p \times uS + (1-p) \times dS = 1+r\Delta t$

$P \times C_u + (1-p) \times C_d$ is the expected value of the call option one period later, assuming risk neutrality.

The current value is obtained by discounting this expected value (in a risk-neutral world) at the risk-free rate.

In our example, the possible returns are:

+ 25% if stock up

– 20% if stock down

In a risk-neutral world, the expected return for 6-months is 5%× 0.5= 2.5%. The risk-neutral probability should satisfy the equation: $p \times (+0.25\%) + (1-p) \times (-0.20\%) = 2.5\%$ which implies that $p = 0.50$

The call value is then: $C = 0.50 \times 15 / 1.025 = €12.20$

Multi-Period Model: European Option. For a European option, follow the same procedure:

– Calculate at maturity the different possible stock prices, the corresponding values of the call option, and the risk neutral probabilities.

– Calculate the expected call value in a risk-neutral world.

– Discount at the risk-free rate.

For example, valuing a 1-year call option:
  Same data as before: X = €100, r = 5%, u = 1.25, d = 0.80. Call maturity = 1 year (2-period).

Stock price evolution   Risk-neutral probabilities

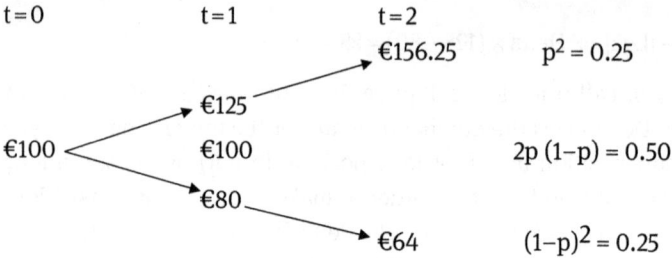

t = 0   t = 1   t = 2

                                           €156.25 $p^2 = 0.25$

                      €125

€100   €100   2p (1–p) = 0.50

                      €80

                                           €64 $(1-p)^2 = 0.25$

Current call value: C = 0.25 × 56.25/ (1.025)² = €13.38

  The value of a call option is a function of the following variables:
  - Current stock price S
  - Exercise price X
  - Time to expiration date t
  - Risk-free interest rates
  - Volatility of the underlying asset

Note: In the binomial model, u and d capture the volatility (the standard deviation of the returns) of the underlying stock.
  Technically, u and d are given by the following formula:

$$u = e^{\sigma\sqrt{\Delta t}}, \; d = 1/u, \; and$$

$$p = \frac{(1+r\times t)^{1/n} - d}{u - d}$$

where,
  u = Upward movement in multiplicative form
  d = Downward movement in multiplicative form
  p = Probability
  σ = Volatility
  t = Time to maturity in terms of years
  n = Number of time periods in binomial tree
  r = Yearly interest rate

After solving these three formulas, a binomial tree is set up. By reading probabilities, the call value is calculated. In addition, in order to calculate the present value of the call value, the call value is discounted with the risk-free rate.

The value of a call or of a put option is an increasing function of volatility (for all other variables unchanged).

Intuition: A larger volatility increases possible gains without affecting loss, since the value of an option is never negative.

Let us value a call option using the following data: X=100, E=100, r=5%, u=1, 25, d=0, 80, s=62.13% and n=8. See Table 7.11.

Table 7.11: Solution of Multi-Period Binomial Model.

Type of point	Call
Discounting	Continuous
Period	0.125
Riskless rate of interest per period	0.63%
Upward movement/period	25.00%
Downward movement/period	−20.00%
Risk neutral probability	45.84%
Number of periods	8
Call Premium	€25,934

In order to solve a multiple-period binomial model, the *backward induction* method is used. First, option values at the last nudge (8th period) are calculated. For instance, the first value is calculated using the formula Max $[S_T - E, 0]$, as Max (596.139 − 100.000 =) €496.139. In the period starting €496,139, 9 option (call) values are calculated. See Table 7.12.

The option will be calculated by using a backward sweep procedure starting with relevant values in the 7th period. The value of the option in the 7th period is calculated as:

$$(P \times Cu + (1-p) \times C_d)/(1 + r_f^{e(t/n)})$$

$$(0.4584 \times 496.139 + 0.5416 \times 281.514)/(EXP(0.05/8) = €377.531.$$

This process will be pursued until period 0. Call value in this case will €25,934.

Black-Scholes Option Pricing Model

Using the same ideas as in the *binomial pricing model* – that is, the no-arbitrage pricing argument – assume the state of the stock price is continuous and follows a

Table 7.12: Solution of Multi-Period Binomial Model.

	Now								Maturity
Period	0	1	2	3	4	5	6	7	8
Time	0.000	0.125	0.250	0.375	0.500	0.625	0.750	0.875	1.000
Stock	100,000	125,002	156,256	195,324	244,160	305,205	381,514	476,902	596,139
		79,998	100,000	125,002	156,256	195,324	244,160	305,205	381,514
			63,998	79,998	100,000	125,002	156,256	195,324	244,160
				51,197	63,998	79,998	100,000	125,002	156,256
					40,957	51,197	63,998	79,998	100,000
						32,765	40,957	51,197	63,998
							26,211	32,765	40,957
								20,969	26,211
									16,775
Call	25,934	41,915	65,818	100,027	146,629	207,063	282,756	377,525	496,139
		12,710	22,171	37,629	61,747	97,181	145,402	205,828	281,514
			4,851	9,346	17,654	32,474	57,498	95,947	144,160
				1,103	2,422	5,317	11,673	25,625	56,256
					0,000	0,000	0,000	0,000	0,000
						0,000	0,000	0,000	0,000
							0,000	0,000	0,000
								0,000	0,000
									0,000

specific, continuous stochastic process. *Black, Scholes, and Merton*[8] derived a closed-form pricing formula for European call options:

$$C = S_0 \cdot e^{qT} \cdot N(d_1) - X \cdot e^{rT} \cdot N(d_2)$$

---

8 See F. Black and M. Scholes, "The Pricing of Options and Corporate Liabilities," *Journal of Political Economy*, May–June 1973, pp. 637–654.

$$d_1 = \frac{\ln\frac{S_0}{K} + \left(r - q + \frac{\sigma^2}{2}\right).T}{\sigma.\sqrt{T}}, d_2 = d_1 - \sigma.\sqrt{T} \tag{1}$$

Where

S_0 = current price of the stock,

X = exercise price,

r = risk-free interest rate,

q = annual dividend yield,

σ = standard deviation of the rate of return of the stock,

T = time to maturity (years) of the option,

N (d) = cumulative probability at value of d under standard normal distribution. (See Appendix E.)

There is a relationship between the price of a European call and a European put on the same stock with the same exercise price X and the same time to maturity T.

$$C - P = S_0 - X \cdot e^{-r \cdot T}$$

This relationship, as said before, is called put-call parity. For a European *put* option, the pricing formula is:

$$P = X.e^{-rT}.[1 - N(d_2)] - S_0.e^{-qT}.[1 - N(d_1)]$$

If we use the Black-Scholes model, the data for a European call option on a non-dividend-paying stock (q = 0) is simply N (d_1), and the delta for a European put option on a non-dividend-paying stock is simply N (d_1) – 1.

Assume the following:

S = €90

X = €95

T = 50 days (50/365 year = 0.137 year)

r = 7% (per annum)

σ = 35% (per annum)

What is the value of the call?

$$Ke^{-rT} = 95e^{(-0.07)\,(50/365)} = (95)\,(0.9905) = \$94.093.$$

$$d_1 = \frac{\ln(S/X) + (r + \sigma^2/2)T}{\sigma\sqrt{T}} = \frac{\ln(90/95) + (0.07 + 0.1225/2)0.137}{0.35\sqrt{0.137}}$$

$$= \frac{\ln(0.947368) + 0.01798}{(0.35)(0.3701)} = \frac{-0.05407 + 0.01798}{0.12955} = -0.2786$$

$$d_2 = d_1 - \sigma T^{.5} = -0.2786 - (0.35)\,(0.137)^{.5} = -0.4082$$

The d values can be read from the Appendix E or obtained from the Excel function =NORMSDIST ().

Using Excel functions:

$$= \text{NORMSDIST} (-0.2786) = 0.3903$$

$$= \text{NORMSDIST} (-0.4082) = 0.3416$$

$$C = S \, N \, (d_1) - X e^{-rT} \, N \, (d_2)$$

$$= (90) \, (0.3903) - (94.0934) \, (0.3416) = 35.127 - 32.142$$

$$= €2.98.$$

Applying put-call parity, the put price is:

$$P = C - S + X e^{-rT} = 2.98 - 90 + 94.0934 = €7.08.$$

Let us value a call and put option using the data in binomial example: S=100, E=100, r=5%, t=1, and s=62.13%. See Table 7.13.

Table 7.13: Results of Calculations for Option Value.

Stock price	100.0000
Exercise price	100.0000
Time to maturity (year)	1.0000
Treasury bond interest rate	0.0500
Variance	0.3860
d1	0.3911
N(d1)	0.6521
d2	−0.2302
N(d2)	0.4090
Call value	26.3116
Put value	21.4345

If the dividend yield (*dividend/current stock value*) is assumed to be constant during the life of the option, the Black-Scholes model can be defined as follows:

$$C = S e^{yt} N(d_1) - X e^{-rt} N(d_2)$$

Where:

$$d_1 = \frac{\ln(S/E) + (r - y + (\sigma^2/2))\,t}{\sigma\sqrt{t}}$$

$$d_2 = d_1 - \sigma\sqrt{t}$$

$$y = \text{dividend yield}$$

According to put-call parity, put value can be expressed as follows:

$$P = K \times e^{-rt} N(-d_2) - S N(-d_1)$$

Implied Volatility

The stock volatility has the highest potential to impact the option's value. Thus, the stock volatility (s) is a variable of considerable interest within the options industry.

Using the Black-Scholes model and an observed market price of an option, we can solve for volatility. This is called an *implied volatility* because it is the value implied by the other five variables in the Black-Scholes formula. Implied volatility can be calculated in Excel with Solver.

Portfolio Insurance Using Put Options

Consider for example a fund manager with €100 million portfolio whose value reflects the value of a *Stock Market Index*. Suppose that the Stock Market Index is at a level of 1000 and the manager wishes to insure against the value of the portfolio dropping below €90 million in the next six months.

One approach is to buy 100,000 six-month option contracts on the Stock Market Index with a strike price of 900 and maturing in six months. If the Index drops below 900, the put options will become in-the-money and will provide the manager with compensation for the decline in the value of the portfolio.

Buy 100,000 put options with strike of 900. If the Stock Market Index goes up to 1,200:
- Your portfolio is worth approximately €1.20 million.
- Your option is out-of-the-money, hence it is worthless.
- Your total value is €120 million.

If the Stock Market Index drops to 800:
- Your portfolio is worth approximately €80 million.
- You option is in-the-money and it is worth (900–800) × 100,000 = €10 million.
- Your total value is €90 million.

Of course, insurance is not free. In this example, the put options could cost the portfolio manager as much as €2 million.

Valuation of FX Options

In valuing FX option, a model similar to the dividend-paying Black-Scholes model is being used.[9]

$$c = Se^{-r_f T} N(d_1) - Xe^{-r_d T} N(d_2)$$

$$p = Xe^{-r_d T} N(-d_2) - Se^{-r_f T} N(-d_1)$$

where:

$$d_1 = \frac{\ln(S/X) + \left(r_d - r_f + \sigma^2/2\right)T}{\sigma\sqrt{T}}$$

$$d_2 = d_1 - \sigma\sqrt{T}$$

Two minor and two major adjustments are necessary for the Black-Scholes model. Minor adjustments are:
-   S = Spot price of domestic currency for a unit price of a foreign currency.
-   X = Exercise price of domestic currency for a unit price of foreign currency.

Major adjustments are:
-   S is adjusted by $e^{r_f T}$ with, where (r_f) denotes riskless rate of return.
-   d_1 is adjusted in order to obtain $(r_f) - (r_d)$.

Foreign currency call options have the following properties:
-   As the value of the foreign currency increases against local currency, the call value increases.
-   As the interest rate of local currency increases, so does the call price.
-   As the interest rate of foreign currency increases, the call price will decrease.
-   As time to maturity increases, so does the call price.
-   As the volatility of foreign currency increases, so does the call price.

The call price calculated for a foreign currency will be equal to the put price of a foreign currency, provided that they have the same exercise price and maturity date.

---

9 M. Garman and S. Kohlhagen, "Foreign Currency Option Values," *Journal of International Money and Finance*, 2, 1983, pp. 231–237.

Let us show how to calculate call and put prices with hypothetical data. What is the call price of USD having an exercise price of 1,500 CAD (Canadian dollars) and a maturity of six months? CAD, in this case, represents domestic (national) currency. Other data are as follows:

Spot rate of = CAD 1.5000.

Riskless rate of return in Canada (r_d or r_{CAD}) = 5%

Riskless rate of return in in USA (r_f or $r_\$$) = 7%

Maturity or the option = 6 months (0.5 year)

CAD/$ volatility = 40% (yearly)

First let us calculate the forward rate:

$$F = S_t e^{(r_{CAD} - r_\$)T} = 1.50 e^{(0,05 - 0,07)0,50} = 1.485075$$

Now let us calculate d_1 and d_2.

$$d_1 = \frac{\ln(F/E) + 0.5\sigma^2 T}{\sigma\sqrt{T}} = \frac{\ln(1.485075/1.50) + 0.5(0.4)^2 0.5}{0.4\sqrt{0.5}} = 0.106066$$

$$d_2 = d_1 - \sigma\sqrt{T} = 0.106066 - 0.4\sqrt{0.5} = -0.176878$$

$$F = 1.485075$$

$$d_1 = 0.106066$$

$$d_2 = -0.176878$$

$$N(d_1) = N(0.106066) = 0.5422$$

$$N(d_2) = N(-0.1768) = 0.4298$$

$$C_0 = [F \times N(d_1) - E \times N(d_2)]e^{-r_{CAD}T}$$

$$C_0 = [1.485075 \times 0.5422 - 1.50 \times 0.4298e^{-0.05 \times 0.5} = 0.157 CAD$$

Using the simple formula, we can easily calculate the put premium:

$$P_0 = [C_0 + (E - F)]e^{-r_{TL}T}$$
$$P_0 = [0.157 + (1.50 - 1.485075] \times e^{-0.05 \times 0.5} = 0.171 CAD$$

If the contract size is USD 1,000, the premium to be paid will be 0.1044 × 1.000 implying a CAD of 104.4. Similar calculations can be made for the put premium.

7.5 Swaps

A *swap* is an agreement to provide a counterparty with something they want in exchange for something that you want with the understanding that the process will be reversed at an agreed upon future date.

In a swap contract, two counterparties exchange one stream of cash flows for another. The cash flow streams are usually liabilities – for example, fixed dollar interest payments swapped with floating yuan interest payments. However, the concept works just as well with financial assets. There are many types of swaps. We will review two of them:

- *Interest rate swap*. An agreement to exchange interest payments for a specific period of time on a principal amount. Most interest rate swaps are fixed-for-floating. Only the interest payments are exchanged, so the principal is merely notional. Only the difference check needs to be exchanged.
- *Currency swap*. An agreement to exchange a principal amount of two currencies and, after a pre-arranged length of time, re-exchange the original principal. Unlike interest rate swaps, the notional principal may or may not be exchanged. Interest payments typically are exchanged, although sometimes the difference in value is settled with a difference check.

Pricing and Valuing Swaps

A swap is equivalent to an asset and a liability. An at-market swap has zero value, ignoring the impact of bid-ask spread, when it is originated. To determine the fixed price for a swap, find the present value of the swap's fixed payments and the swap's floating payments. The price that equates the two present values results in a zero-net value for the two parties.[10] To make a profit in their service as a market maker, the swap dealer can adjust the price to quote a bid-ask spread.

Fixed-Floating Interest Rate Swap. The following equation will be satisfied: Present value of fixed payments = Present value of floating receipts.

Important variables are:

$r\ (0, t)$ = spot interest rate for a zero-coupon bond maturing at time t,

$fr\ (t_1, t_2)$ = forward interest rate from time t_1 to time t_2.

As an example, suppose $r\ (0,1) = 5\%$. $r\ (0,2) = 6\%$. $r\ (0,3) = 7.5\%$. $fr\ (1,2) =?$ Solve the equation $(1.06)^2 = (1.05) \times (1+fr\ (1,2))$, yielding $fr\ (1,2) = 0.0701$. $fr\ (2.3) =?$ Solve the equation $(1.05)^3 = (1.06)^2 \times (1+fr\ (2.3))$, yielding $fr\ (2.3) = 0.1056$. Assume that the *pure expectations hypothesis* is true. So the forward rate = expected future spot rate. Assume a notional value of $100 million. So expected cash flows are as follows: $CF_1 = 0.05 \times \$100 = \$5$. $CF_2 = 0.0701 \times \$100 = \$7.01$. $CF_3 = 0.1056 \times \$100 = \$10.56$. The present value of the floating cash flows is $\$5/ (1.05)^1 + \$7.01/ (1.06)^2 + A/ (1.075)^3 = \$19.5039$.

---

10 All models discussed are adapted from Mark Legge Muzere, *Multinational Financial Management Lecture Notes*, Sawyer School of Management, 2004, http://www.suffolkfin.org/mmu zere, 10.10.2005.

Assuming fixed cash flows A, we solve $19.5039 = A/ (1.05)^1 + A/ (1.06)^2 + A/ (1.075)^3$. We get $A = \$7.3674$. Thus, the fixed interest rate is 7.3674%.

Fixed-Fixed Currency Swap. In a plain currency swap, principal amounts, expressed in two different currencies are exchanged at origination at the prevailing exchange rate. This initial exchange of principal amounts has no pricing consequences. For example, let the spot exchange rate to be \$1.250/€1. Exchanging \$10 million for €8 million is currently a valueless transaction from the point of view of both parties.

So, for example: Maturity = 3 years. Principal = \$10 million. Dollar interest rate = 10%. Annual payments = \$1 million. Current exchange rate = \$1.250/€1. Euro principal = €8 million. What is the fixed euro rate? Suppose dollar spot interest rates on a zero-coupon instrument are $r (0.1) = 4\%$, $r (0.2) = 5\%$, $r (0.3) = 7\%$. Suppose euro spot interest rates on a zero-coupon instrument are $r (0.1) = 5\%$, $r (0.2) = 6\%$, $r (0.3) = 7\%$. The present value of the dollar cash flows is given by \$1 million $/ (1.04)^1 +$ \$1 million $/ (1.05)^2 +$ \$1 million $/ (1.06)^3 +$ \$10 million $/ (1.06)^3 = \$11.10438$ million.

To compute the euro fixed interest rate, we solve r× €8 million $/ (1.05)^1 +$ r×€8 million $/ (1.06)^2 +$ r×€8 million $/ (1.07)^3 +$ €8 million $/ (1.07)^3 = $ €11.10438 million $/$ 1,250. Thus, 21,269,402.15×r + 6,530,383,015 = 8,883,500 which gives r = 2,353,116,985/ 21,269,402.15 = 11.06%.

Fixed-Floating Currency Swap. Find the fixed interest rate that makes the present value of the fixed cash flows equal to the present value of the floating cash flows. Consider two parties, one is U.S.-based and the other is EU-based. Suppose the U.S. counterparty receives fixed cash flows and the European Union counterparty receives floating cash flows.

Suppose the spot rates on zero-coupon debt instruments are given. Since the floating cash flows are unknown, they are typically estimated by forward prices, which are given by the formula $f = e \times (1+r_h)^t / (1+r_f)^t$.

To solve the swap pricing problem, the forward EU interest rates must be computed using the formula $(1+r (0.t))^t = (1+r (0.t\text{-}1))^{t\text{-}1} \times (1+fr(t\text{-}1.t))$.

7.6 Credit Default Swap

A *credit default swap* (CDS) is effectively an insurance product, whereby the consequences of a bankruptcy (default) of a reference party are transferred in return for a periodic payment. Take, for example, a party that wishes to purchase or has already purchased a bond but wants to avoid the (further) risk that the seller will go bankrupt. By concluding a CDS, any loss sustained in the case of default is compensated or paid off in return for a periodic payment, the premium for the CDS.

The CDS is valued in much the same way as its cousin, *the interest rate swap.*[11] In an interest rate swap, the exchange of fixed and variable interest cash flows is valued by estimating the amount of the future cash flows in advance. These cash flows are then discounted at the market interest rate applicable at that time and added up. In the case of a CDS, two types of cash flows are also exchanged. First, a series of cash flows from the risk seller to the risk buyer, including the periodic payment of the premium. Second, these cash flows are then exchanged for a (possible) cash flow from the risk buyer to the risk seller in the event of a default. The periodic payment ceases immediately if that bankruptcy actually takes place.

7.7 Summary

A derivative is a financial contract which derives its value from the performance of another entity called the *underlying*. Nowadays, derivatives which are based on equity, index, foreign exchange, T-bill, bond, commodity, gold, energy, and so on are traded on the exchanges all over the world.

A forward contract is an agreement to buy or sell an asset at a fixed time in the future for a predetermined price.

A futures contract, like a forward contract, is an agreement between two parties to buy or sell an asset at a certain time in the future for a pre-specified price. Unlike forward contracts, futures contracts are traded on an exchange and they are standardized. Clearinghouse acts as a counterparty to all buyers and sellers. When a position is established, each party deposits with the clearinghouse to absorb potential losses. From then on, marking-to-market will occur. The profit and losses will be reflected in each investor's account each day. We can determine the futures price of many contracts by imposing the no-arbitrage condition. There are two ways to acquire an asset for some date in the future: purchase it now and store it or take a long position in futures. The *spot-futures parity theorem* says that these two strategies should have the same market-determined costs.

Options for stock can be created and sold in exchange markets. A call/put option is a contract for the purchase/sale of a security at a specified price within a specified time frame. The price of the option is called the *option premium*. The option may be exercised or may expire. The premium, or price of an option, can be divided into two components: intrinsic value and time value. Intrinsic value is the payoff if the option were to be exercised immediately. Intrinsic value is always greater than or equal to zero. Put-call parity specifies the difference in value

---

11 For information about valuation of CDS, see John C. Hull, *Fundamentals of Futures and Options Market*, Fifth Edition, Pearson Prentice-Hall, 2005, pp. 449–463 and https://zanders.eu/en/latest-insights/how-do-you-value-a-credit-default-swap/, 21.10.2020.

between a European call option and a European put option. Options can be used for speculative purpose and also for the purpose of risk management. Since you only pay the premium (much less than the stock price) for the option, the resultant leverage effect could make the active use of options very risky. Traders will often talk about the Greeks in relation to securities with optionality. The Greeks are five letters used to describe an option's behavior. There are two methods in valuing options: the binomial model and the Black-Scholes model.

A swap is an agreement to provide a counterparty with something they want in exchange for something that you want. In a swap, two counterparties exchange one stream of cash flows for another. The cash flow streams are usually liabilities, such as fixed-dollar interest payments swapped with floating yuan interest payments. However, the concept works just as well with financial assets. There are many types of swaps. An interest rate swap is an agreement to exchange interest payments for a specific period of time on a principal amount. Most interest rate swaps are fixed-for-floating. Only the interest payments are exchanged, so the principal is merely notional. A currency swap is an agreement to exchange a principal amount of two currencies and, after a pre-arranged length of time, re-exchange the original principal.

A credit default swap (CDS) is effectively an insurance product, whereby the consequences of a bankruptcy (default) of a reference party are transferred in return for a periodic payment.

Part III: **Financial Management/Corporate Finance**

8 Basics of Corporate Finance

8.1 Introduction

The goal of any firm is to maximize the wealth of its shareholders. Corporate finance is built on three principles: the investment principle, the financing principle, and the dividend principle. In a functional organization, the key financial positions are vice president for finance, treasurer, and controller. The three principal forms of business organization are the sole proprietorship, partnership, and corporation. Every form has certain advantages and disadvantages. The mission statement declares the organization's purpose and the vision statement indicates what the firm wants to achieve. An agency relationship is created when the owner (a principal) of a business hires an employee (an agent). Better corporate governance reduces agency costs. Ethics are society's standards for judging whether an action is right or wrong.

8.2 Overview of Corporate Finance

We begin with the objectives of a corporation: maximization of the value of the firm. A narrower objective is to maximize stockholder wealth. When the stock is traded and markets are viewed to be efficient, the objective is to maximize the stock price.

Because:[1]
- Employees are also stockholders in many firms.
- Firms that maximize stock price generally are profitable firms that can afford to treat employees well.
- Maximizing stock price does not mean that customers are not critical to success. Making and keeping customers happy is the road to stock price maximization.
- Stock price is easily observable and constantly updated.
- If investors are rational, stock prices reflect the wisdom of decisions, short-term and long-term, instantaneously.

Every discipline has its principles – corporate finance is not an exception. All of corporate finance is built on three principles: the investment principle, the financing principle, and the dividend principle. These principles can be summarized as follows:
- *Investment principle.* Invest in projects that yield a return greater than the minimum acceptable hurdle rate. The hurdle rate should be higher for riskier projects and reflect the financing mix used, owners' funds (equity), or borrowed money

---

1 Aswath Damodaran, *Corporate Finance Lecture Notes Packet 1*, pp. 4–5. People.stern.nyu.edu, 29.22.2019.

https://doi.org/10.1515/9783110705355-008

(debt). Returns on projects should be measured based on cash flows generated and their timing. They should also consider both positive and negative side effects of these projects.

- *Financing principle.* Choose a financing mix that minimizes the hurdle rate and matches the assets being financed.
- *Dividend principle.* In case there are not enough investments that earn the hurdle rate, cash should be returned to stockholders. The form of returns, dividends, and stock buybacks will depend upon the stockholders' characteristics.

Finance managers are assumed to apply these principles. All these principles will be discussed in Chapters 9, 10, 11, 12, 13, and 14. The decisions made by finance managers are investment decisions, financial decisions, and dividend decisions, as shown in Figure 8.1.

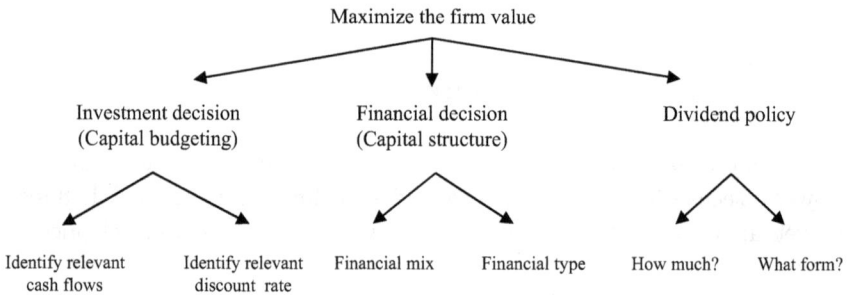

Figure 8.1: Corporate Finance Decisions.

Approaching corporate finance from a *balance-sheet view,* we reach the following: capital budgeting involves the *asset* side, while capital structure and dividend policy involve *liabilities and owners' equity* side.

8.3 Financial Manager

In a functional organization, the key financial positions in a corporation are *vice president for finance, treasurer,* and *controller.*

Vice president for finance is responsible for managing the overall financial affairs of the corporation. To accomplish this responsibility, the vice president for finance must work closely with other managers.

The treasurer is responsible for forecasting, cash and credit management, capital budgeting, acquisition of new financing, and maintaining a good relationship with the investment community. In short, the treasurer is responsible for financial management tasks.

The controller is responsible for measuring costs, inventory control, budgeting, financial accounting, payroll, profit analysis, and internal control. In short, the controller is responsible for accounting tasks.

The functions of the financial manager can be summarized as follows:

– Analysis and planning include understanding the firm's current financial situation and planning for its future under different economic scenarios. This is discussed in Chapter 9.
– Asset management requires decisions on the optimal levels of fixed (non-current) assets, which is discussed in Chapter 10 and current assets such as cash and marketable securities, account receivables (credit), and inventory levels, which is discussed in Chapter 12.
– Financial structure management requires decisions on the amount of short-term debt versus long-term debt and the amount of debt versus equity. This is discussed in Chapters 11, 12, and 13. Chapter 14 examines financing and investment decisions of international financial managers.

8.4 Business Organizations

The three principal forms of business organization are the sole proprietorship, partnership, and corporation.

Sole Proprietorship

A sole proprietorship is simply a business owned by one person. Advantages of the sole proprietorship are as follows:

– Simple to create
– Least costly form to begin
– Profit incentive
– Total decision-making authority
– No special legal restrictions
– Easy to discontinue

Disadvantages of the sole proprietorship are:

– Unlimited personal liability
– Limited skills and capabilities
– Feelings of isolation
– Limited access to capital
– Lack of continuity

Partnership

A partnership is a business organization of two or more persons. Partnership may be classified as either *general* or *limited partnership*. In a general partnership, each partner has *unlimited liability* for all the obligations of the business. In a limited partnership, one or more general partners have *unlimited liability* and one or more limited partners have *limited liability* (the extent to which is spelled out in the partnership agreement). When one partner quits or dies, the partnership is dissolved and another one must be formed.

Advantages of the partnership are:
- Easy to establish
- Complementary skills of partners
- Sharing of profits
- Larger pool of capital
- Ability to attract limited partners
- Little government regulation
- Flexibility
- Taxation

Disadvantages of the partnership are:
- Unlimited liability of at least one partner
- Capital accumulation
- Difficulty in disposing of partnership interest
- Lack of continuity
- Potential for personality and authority conflicts

Corporation

A *corporation* is a legal entity composed of one or more persons and is separate and distinct from these persons. As a legal entity, a corporation can purchase and own assets, borrow money, sue, and be sued. The owners of a corporation are called *shareholders* or *stockholders*. The money shareholders invest in the corporation is called *capital stock*.

Advantages of the corporation are:
- Limited liability of stockholders
- Ability to attract capital
- Ability to continue indefinitely
- Transferable ownership

Disadvantages of the corporation are:
- Cost and time of incorporating
- Double taxation
- Potential for diminished managerial incentives
- Legal requirements and regulatory *red tape*
- Potential loss of control by founder(s)

In theory, the board of directors is responsible for managing the corporation. The board of directors is elected by the shareholders. The board in turn hires officers who do the actual managing of the company on a daily basis. The officers are considered to be agents of the corporation who act on behalf of the owners (shareholders) of the company. The officers might include a president, one or more vice presidents, a treasurer, and a secretary.

Corporations issue debt and equity securities to fund corporate operations. Debt securities promise periodic interest payments as well as the return of the principal amount of the debt. Common stockholders are the true residual owners of the corporation. Their claims on earnings and assets of the firm are considered only after all other claims have been met. Common stockholders possess several specific rights including dividend rights, asset rights, voting rights, and preemptive rights.

8.5 Mission and Vision

Mission states the reason of existence of a company. Therefore, the company's organization, plans, and the way it does business must all be consistent with its mission. A company's mission statement should be compatible with its operating plans and the way that the company does business. Note also that this mission statement incorporates important values such as honesty, fairness, and integrity.

The *vision* statement indicates what the firm wants to achieve, produce, distribute, provide, or sell (in the future). The vision shows what the organization wants to become. Frequently, a vision is incorporated into the mission statement.

A companion statement often created with the vision and mission is a statement of *core values*. Core values show how the company will behave during the strategic management process.

Once the vision is identfied and how it will be achieved, as well as the mission, the next step is develop a series of statements such as:
- *Strategies*. Strategies are one or more ways to use the mission statement in order to achieve the vision statement. Although an organization will have just one vision statement and one mission statement, it may have several strategies.
- *Goals*. These are general statements of what needs to be accomplished to implement a strategy.

- *Objectives*. Objectives provide specific milestones with a specific timeline for achieving a goal.
- *Action plans*. These are specific implementation plans of how to achieve an objective.

Capital budgeting, which will be discussed in the next chapter, follows strategic planning. The investment decision will be influenced by the strategy of the firm. Investment in a project will require financing, a topic covered in Chapter 11, and will affect the capital structure of the firm. Project proposals cannot be generated in isolation with the firm's corporate goals, mission, and vision.

8.6 The Goal of the Firm, Agency Relationship, Corporate Governance, and Ethics

In this section, we will review four related concepts: the goal of the firm, agency relationship, corporate governance, and ethics.

The Goal of the Firm

Maximizing the price of a firm's stock will maximize the value of a firm and the wealth of its shareholders. The source of a firm's value is positive cash flows.

The reasons are:
- Positive residual cash flow may be paid to firm shareholders as dividends or invested in new assets.
- As explained in Chapter 5, the larger the positive residual cash flow, the higher the value of a firm.
- Negative residual cash flow, in the long run, leads to financial failures such as bankruptcy or closing a business.

Agency Relationship

An agency relationship is created when the owner (a principal) of a business hires an employee (an agent). The owner surrenders some control over the enterprise and its resources to the employee. Separating ownership from control creates the potential for agency conflicts. Shareholders own the corporation, but managers control the firm's assets and may use them for their own benefit.

In large corporations, shared ownership amongst many stockholders may result in relatively little control over management.

Agency costs arise from conflicts-of-interest between a firm's stockholders and its managers. This may reduce positive residual cash flow, stock price, and shareholder wealth.

Managers tend to focus on wealth maximization when their compensation depends on stock price. This is one of the incentives. Others might be sharing of profits, giving agents the right incentive.

Corporate Governance

Better corporate governance reduces agency costs by requiring more effective monitoring of managers' activities programs that promote appropriate behavior by managers, penalizing those who do not conduct their fiduciary responsibilities.

The single most important objective of corporate governance is the optimization of the returns to shareholders over time.

In order to achieve this goal, good governance practices should focus the attention of the board of directors on developing and implementing strategies that ensure corporate growth and improvement in the value of the corporation's equity.

The most widely accepted statement of good corporate governance practices has been established by the OECD:

- *Shareholder rights*. Shareholders are the owners of the firm and their interests should take precedence over other stakeholders.
- *Board responsibilities*. The board of the company is recognized as the individual entity with final, full legal responsibility for the firm, including proper oversight of management.
- *Equitable treatment of shareholders*. Equitable treatment is specifically targeted toward domestic versus foreign residents as shareholders, as well as majority and minority interests.
- *Stakeholder rights*. Governance practices should formally acknowledge the interests of other stakeholders such as employees, creditors, communities, and government.
- *Transparency and disclosure*. Public and equitable reporting of operating and the financial results of firms should be done in a timely manner, and should be available to all interested parties.

Ethics

Ethics is a society's standards for judging whether an action is right or wrong. Business ethics are society's standards for acceptable behavior that are applied to business and financial markets. Examples of ethical conflict in business are:

- *Agency cost*. An example might be an employee's unacceptable use of the employer's asset, such as a computer.

- *Conflict of interest.* A purchasing manager of a refrigerator company whose uncle owns a steel company faces a conflict of interest if his uncle participates in bidding for the company's steel purchases.
- *Information asymmetry.* The seller knows about prior damage to the vehicle, but the potential buyer does not.

Regulation and market forces are not enough to maintain integrity in the marketplace. Business norms must be based on ethical beliefs, customs, and practices.

The consequences of unethical behavior are:
- Inefficiency in the economy and costs to society
- High legal and social costs
- Problems such as the recent financial crises in the U.S. and Europe

8.7 Summary

The objective of a corporation is maximization of the value of the firm. A narrower objective is to maximize stockholder wealth. When the stock is traded and markets are viewed to be efficient, the objective is to maximize the stock price.

Every discipline has its own principles. All of corporate finance is built on the investment principle, the financing principle, and the dividend principle.

In a functional organization, the key financial positions in a corporation are vice president for finance, treasurer, and controller. The functions of the financial manager are analysis and planning, asset management, and financial structure management.

The three principal forms of business organization are the sole proprietorship, partnership, and corporation. A sole proprietorship is simply a business owned by one person. A partnership is a business organization of two or more persons. A corporation is a *legal person* composed of one or more natural persons and is separate and distinct from these persons.

The mission statement declares the organization's purpose and reasons for being. The vision statement indicates what the firm wants to achieve, produce, distribute, provide, or sell.

Maximizing the price of a firm's stock will maximize the value of a firm and the wealth of its shareholders (owners).

An agency relationship is created when the owner (a principal) of a business hires an employee (an agent). Agency costs arise from (incurring and preventing) conflicts-of-interest between a firm's owners and its managers. Better corporate governance reduces agency costs. Ethics are society's standards for judging whether an action is right or wrong. Business ethics are society's standards for acceptable behavior that are applied to business and financial markets.

9 Financial Analysis and Financial Planning

9.1 Introduction

Managers within the firm as well as the firm's lenders (e.g., banks, bondholders) and owners keep track of the firm's performance by reviewing its financial statements (income statement, balance sheet, and statement of cash flows). These financial statements show the trends facing the firm; the results of management's decisions; and debt obligations and shareholder needs that can be met. Thus, financial institutions, markets, and investors, as well as the firm's managers, are interested in reviewing and interpreting a firm's financials. We show how to analyze financial statements. The techniques discussed here will be used both by the firm's own analysts (as they study their own firm and its competitors) and by outside evaluators such as stock and bond investors, competitors, bond rating agencies, and lenders such as banks. Financial ratio analysis examines historical data to pinpoint a firm's strengths and weaknesses. Financial planning uses historical and expected financial ratios and financial statement relationships to estimate a firm's future asset and financing needs, as well as future earnings levels.

9.2 Overview of Financial Statements

A firm's basic financial statements include the film's *balance sheet* (statement of financial position), *income statement*, and *statement of cash flows*. Financial statements are usually prepared and issued at the end of each quarter. In analyzing these statements, it is critical to include trend analysis tracking the changes from one period to another across time in order to detect changes in business conditions that are reflected in the financial statements. The comparison of a firm's financial statements with those of competitors provides a vital look into the firm's standing within the industry. Benchmarking the firm's performance (stock) against standard metrics such as indexes or interest rates also provides an indicator of how the financial markets view the firm.

Financial statements are prepared by the firm's management team. Even through the statements generally have to be prepared according to *generally accepted accounting principles* (GAAP) or *international financial reporting standards* (IFRS), management does have a great deal of leeway in preparation of statements. GAAP/IFRS are a set of guidelines as to the form and manner in which accounting information should be presented. Additionally, certain industries may prepare statements in a certain way. Different industries may feature various distinguishing characteristics on the financial statements of companies within those industries. At the end of the day, the accounting represents the language of the financial statements. As long as students understand that language, analysis is possible.

https://doi.org/10.1515/9783110705355-009

9.3 Annual Reports

A corporation's annual report includes detailed information on:
- Operating and financial performance
- Current and future business opportunities
- Financial statements

One of the ways that managers of a business communicate with the owners of a business is through the financial statements. Corporations are required to prepare annual financial statements for the shareholders. Public corporations are required to file annual and quarterly reports required by regulatory bodies. The contents of the annual reports are governed by IFRS/GAAP. Annual reports contain descriptive information about the company, financial statements, management biographies, the company's capital structure, a discussion on past performance, an industry overview, and a preview of future opportunities.

As mentioned before, three important financial statements provided in the annual report are the *balance sheet, income statement,* and *cash flow statement.* There is one more financial statement called *statement of changes in stockholder equity* which is not covered in this book. Notes to the financial statements are considered an integral part of the statements.

Financial statements are prepared according to generally accepted accounting principles (GAAP), which is established by the Financial Accounting Standards Board (FASB) in the U.S. The European Union (EU), among other countries, follows international financial reporting standards (IFRS).

9.4 Balance Sheet (Statement of Financial Position)

The balance sheet is a statement of a company's financial position as of a particular date; it is a snapshot in time. The balance sheet contains:
- Assets
- Liabilities
- Owner's equity

Assets are financial and physical items owned by the company. Liabilities are the creditor's claims on the business. Owner's equity is the net worth of the business.

The basic accounting equation is as follows:

$$Assets = Liabilities + Owners\ Equity$$

Assets are grouped by liquidity, or by the ease at which the particular asset can be converted into cash. Assets are also grouped into current assets and fixed assets. Current assets are expected to be converted into cash within one year or one operating cycle; they are expected to satisfy the normal operations of a business. Typical current assets include cash, accounts receivable, and inventory. Accounts receivable are amounts owed to the company due to purchases on credit. Fixed assets are physical facilities used in production, storage, display, and distribution of the products or services of the firm. Fixed assets are expected to last for a number of years. Typical fixed assets are property, plant, and equipment. Fixed assets are usually depreciated, or lose value, according to the useful life of the asset.

Liabilities are the debts of the business. They are ordered by liquidity and are grouped into short- and long-term liabilities. Current liabilities are obligations that must be paid in one year or one operating cycle, including accounts payable, notes payable, and accrued liabilities. Current assets are expected to satisfy current liabilities. Accounts payable are debts owed by the company for purchases of supplies and inventory made on credit. Long-term debt is an example of long-term liabilities. See Table 9.1.

Table 9.1: Balance Sheet.

DEM Inc. December 31 Balance Sheets (€ in millions)

	20X8	20X7
Assets		
Cash and equivalents	€50	€15
Short-term investments	€0	€65
Accounts receivable	€375	€305
Inventories	€575	€385
Total current assets	€1,000	€770
Net plant and equipment	€1,000	€870
Total assets	€2,000	€1,640
Liabilities and equity		
Accounts payable	€64	€35
Notes payable	€110	€60
Accruals	€140	€130
Total current liabilities	€314	€225
Long-term bonds	€750	€575
Total debt	€1,064	€800
Common stock (130 million shares)	€130	€130

Table 9.1 (continued)

DEM Inc. December 31 Balance Sheets (€ in millions)		
Retained earnings	€806	€710
Total common equity	€936	€840
Total liabilities and equity	€2,000	€1,640

Owner's equity is the investment of the owners or the owner in the business. For a corporation, owner's equity is usually broken out into three accounts: *preferred stock*, which is not common in some countries, *common stock*, and *retained earnings*. The first two reflect how the company has financed itself through stock offerings; the last reflects the accumulated undistributed earnings within the corporation over time. Retained earnings are not cash, as the cash has already been invested in the firm.

The way a balance sheet is formatted is different in some countries. In some countries, accounts are listed in the order of liquidity, or how quickly and easily they can be converted to cash. The items are arranged in descending order (most liquid to least liquid): current assets, non-current assets, current liabilities, non-current liabilities, and owners' equity. Under IFRS, the order is usually reversed (least liquid to most liquid): non-current assets, current assets, owners' equity, non-current liabilities, and current liabilities.

9.5 Income Statement

The *income statement*, or *profit and loss statement*, reports revenues (sales) and expenses of a firm over an accounting period.

Revenues are the euro value of the products sold or services rendered over the given period of time. Expenses are the costs incurred by the firm over the given period of time. Profit is the difference between revenues and expenses over the given period of time.

There are four basic measures of profit:
- *Gross profit* equals sales less cost of goods sold. *Cost of sales* are costs directly related to those sales.
- *Operating profit* is gross profit minus operating expenses.
- *Profit before taxes* is operating profit plus other income minus interest expenses.
- *Net profit* is profit after tax. A net loss is where the total expenses are higher than the total revenue and a net profit is where the total revenue is greater than the total expense.

Examples of an income statement and statement of retained earnings are presented in Tables 9.2 and 9.3.

Table 9.2: Income Statement.

DEM Income Statements for Years Ending December 31 (€ in millions)		
	20X8	20X7
Income Statements		
Net sales	€3,010.0	€2,860.0
Cost of sales	€2,454.6	€2,338.3
Gross profit	€555.4	€521.7
Operating expenses	€271.6	€258.7
Earnings before interest and taxes (EBIT)	€283.8	€263.0
Less interest	€92.0	€64.0
Earnings before taxes (EBT)	€191.8	€199.0
Taxes	€38.3	€39.8
Net income	€153.5	€159.2
Additional Information (€ in millions)	20X8	20X7
Common dividends	57.5	53.0
Addition to retained earnings	95.9	106.2
Depreciation charges	90.0	80.0
Per-share Data	20X8	20X7
Market value per share	€15.00	€14.00
Earnings per share (EPS)	€1.18	€1.22
Dividends per share (DPS)	€0.44	€0.91
Book value per share (BVPS)	€7.20	€6.46

Table 9.3: Retained Earnings.

	20X8
Balance of Retained Earnings, Dec. 31, 20X7	€710.0
Add: Net income, 20X8	€153.5
Less: Dividends to common stockholders	-€57.5
Balance of Retained Earnings, Dec. 31, 20X8	€806.0

9.6 Cash Flow Statement

A statement of cash flows provides a summary of the cash sources that come into the company and the cash that goes out of the company during an accounting period. The cash flow statement consists of three sections: operating activities, investing activities, and financing activities. Cash flows are determined as in Table 9.4.[1]

Table 9.4: Determinants of Cash Flows.

Operating Activities	Investing Activities	Financing Activities
– Net income (loss)	– Purchase of property, plant, equipment	– ssuance of capital stock
– Depreciation		– Repurchase of capital stock
– Increase in accounts receivable	– Sale of property, plant, equipment	– Debt increase (decrease)
– Increase in inventories		– Dividends
– Increase in accounts payable		

Sources (cash inflows):
- Amount of net income plus amount of depreciation
- Decrease in an asset account
- Increase in a liability account
- Increase in an equity account

Uses (cash outflows)
- Increase in an asset account
- Decrease in a liability account
- Decrease in an equity account
- Amount of cash dividends

Cash is not equal to net income. In fact, it is possible for a company to be profitable and cash-starved at the same time. A financial manager is concerned with cash and not necessarily income. An example of statement of cash flow is presented in Table 9.5.

---

1 There are two methods of preparing a statement of cash flows: direct and indirect. Here, we explain the indirect method.

Table 9.5: Statement of Cash Flows (€ in millions).

DEM Statement of Cash Flows for Year Ending Dec. 31, 20X8 (in millions of euros)	
Operating Activities	
Net income	€153.5
Noncash adjustments	
Depreciation and amortization	€90.0
Due to changes in working capital	
Increase in accounts receivable	-€70.0
Increase in inventories	-€190.0
Increase in account payable	€29.0
Increase in accruals	€10.0
Net cash provided by operating activities	€22.5
Long-term investing activities	
Cash used to acquire fixed assets	-€220.0
Financing Activities	
Sale of short-term investments	€65.0
Increase in notes payable	€50.0
Increase in bonds	€175.0
Payment of common dividends	-€57.5
Net cash provided by financing activities	€232.5
Net change in cash and equivalents	€35.0
Cash and securities at beginning of the year	€15.0
Cash and securities at end of the year	€50.0

9.7 Free Cash Flow to Firm

Free cash flow to firm (FCFF) is defined as cash flow that is free and available to distribute to the firm's investors. It is obtained after a firm has paid off all its operating expenses and taxes, and has made all of its investments in operating working capital and assets. See Table 9.6.

FCFF = *Earnings before interest and taxes (1-t) + Depreciation – change in operating working capital – Change in gross fixed assets*

Table 9.6: DEM Statement of Free Cash Flows to Firm for Year Ending Dec. 31, 20X8 (€ in millions) .

Earnings before interest and taxes (1-t)	€ 227.04
Depreciation and Amortization	€ 90.00
Operating Working Capital Investment	-€ 256.00
Cash Used to Acquire Fixed Asset	-€ 220.00
Free Cash Flow to Firm	-€ 158.96

Earnings before interest and taxes (1-t) = €283.8 – (€283.8×0.2) = €227.04
Net operating working capital = *Total current assets – Account payable – Short-term investments – Accruals*

Net operating working capital$_{20X8}$ = 1,000 – 64 – 140 = 796
Net operating working capital$_{20X7}$ = 770 – 35 – 65 – 130 = 540
Change in operating working capital = Net operating working capital _ Net operating working capital $_{t-1}$

Change in operating working capital$_{20X8}$ = – (796–540) = – 256
Change in gross fixed assets = – (Net plant and equipment + Depreciation – Net plant and equipment $_{t-1}$)

Change in gross fixed assets$_{20X8}$ = – (€1,000 +90-870) = –220

FCFF = €227.04 + 90 – €256 – €220 = – €158.96 million

What can a firm do with free cash flow to the firm? The firm can:
- Pay interest to lenders
- Pay dividends to stockholders
- Decrease its interest bearing long-term or short-term debt
- Repurchase stock from current shareholders

Does positive or negative free cash flow maximize shareholder wealth? We need more information to answer this question. We need to consider the trend in cash flows and also analyze the possible causes of positive or negative free cash flows. Specifically, we need to look closely at cash flows relating to operations, working capital, long-term assets, and financing.

9.8 Economic Value Added (EVA) and Market Value Added (MVA)

How is shareholder value created? If the firm earns a return on capital that is higher than the investors' required rate of return.

EVA^2 attempts to measure a firm's economic profit, rather than accounting profit. EVA recognizes a cost of equity in addition to the cost of debt (interest expense).

$$EVA = (r - k) \times A$$

where:

r = Operating return on assets

k = Total cost of capital

A = Amount of capital (or total assets used)

Operating return on assets = Operating profit after tax/ Total asset used $_{t-1}$

Net Operating profit after tax $_{20X8}$ = Operating profit (EBIT) − Taxes

$$= €283.8 - (€283.8 \times 0,20) = €227$$

Net Operating profit after tax $_{20X7}$ = €263.0 − (€263.0 × 0,20) = €210.4

Total asset used $_{20X7}$ = Net operating working capital + Fixed assets

$$= €540 + €870 = €1.410, \text{ or}$$

Total operating capital (Total asset used) $_{20X7}$ = Stockholders' equity + Interest bearing liabilities − Short-term investments

$$= €840 + €60 + €575 - €65 = €1,410$$

Operating return on assets $_{20X8}$ = €227/ €1,410= %16.10

Assume that the cost of debt is 8% and the cost of equity is 20%. Assume also that the financial liabilities' market value is equal to the book value (€60 + €575 = €635). The market value of equity amounts to (14×130=) €1,830 million. Let us calculate the average cost of capital (see Table 9.7).

Table 9.7: Cost of Capital Calculation.

Items (A)	Market values (B)	Weight (C)	After tax cost (D)	Weighted cost (C × D)
Financial liabilities	€635	0.2576	0.08 × (1−0.2) = 0.064	0.01649
Equity	€1,830	0.7424	0.20	0.14818
Total	2,465	1.0000		0.16497

$$EVA = (r - k) \times A$$
$$= (0.1610 - 0.16497) \times €1,410 = -€5.60 \text{ million}$$

---

[2] EVA® is a registered trademark of Stern Stewart Co. For more information, see G. Bennett Stewart III, *The Quest for Value*, HarperCollins, 1991; Pamela P. Peterson and David R. Peterson, *Company Performance and Measures of Value Added*, The Research Foundation of The Institute of Chartered Financial Analysts, 1996; James L. Grant, *Foundations of Economic Value Added*, Frank Fabozzi and Associates, 2002.

Some results of the calculation are presented in Table 9.8.

Table 9.8: Calculated Data: DEM's Operating Performance and Cash Flows (€ in millions).

	20X8	20X7
Net operating working capital (NOWC)	€796.0	€540.0
Total operating capital	€1,796.0	€1,410.0
Net Operating Profit After Taxes (NOPAT)	€227.0	€210.4
Net Cash Flow (Net income + Depreciation)	€243.4	€239.2
Operating Cash Flow (OCF)	€317.0	€290.4
Free Cash Flow (FCF)	(€159.0)	N/A

Market value added represents the wealth generated by a company for its investors since inception. Market value added (MVA) is a calculation that shows the difference between the *market value* of a company and the capital contributed by investors, both bondholders and shareholders. In other words, it is the sum of all capital claims held against the company plus the market value of debt and equity. It is calculated as:

$$MVA = Company's\ Market\ Value - Invested\ Capital$$

$$MVA = (Market\ Value\ of\ Debt + Market\ Value\ of\ Equity) - (Book\ Value\ of\ Debt$$
$$+ Book\ Value\ of\ Equity)$$

Assuming the book values of financial debts are equal to market values, the MVA for 20X7 and 20X8 can be calculated as follows:

$$MVA_{20X8} = (Market\ Value\ of\ Equity_{20X8}) - (Book\ Value\ of\ Equity_{20X8})$$
$$MVA_{20X8} = (15 \times 130) - 806 = €1,144\ million$$
$$MVA_{20X7} = (14 \times 130) - 710 = €1,110\ million$$

9.9 Overview of Financial Statement Analysis

Financial statements are used by financial market participants who analyze statements for different purposes. Financial statements incorporate the external (i.e., inflation, government policy, exchange rates) and internal environments (i.e., management, organization structure, corporate culture, cost control, operations) of a firm. Ratio analysis performed on financial statements can reveal how a company is doing, how it is making profits, and what its standing is among its peers. *Ratio analysis* is a financial technique that involves dividing various financial statements numbers into one another. Financial statements analysis can therefore assess the success or failure of a company's strategies and operations. The way that investors view the results of analysis often depends on the current state of the economy.

Common-size financial statements (Tables 9.9, 9.10) express balance sheet numbers as a percentage of total assets and income statement numbers as a percentage of revenue in order to enable comparisons between firms of different sizes. Common-size statements should reveal how a firm has chosen to run its business in terms of dealing with suppliers to how a firm has historically financed itself in terms of debt, equity, and internally driven growth. Common-size statements also

Table 9.9: Common-Size DEM's Balance Sheets.

Assets	20X8	20X7
Cash and equivalents	0.9%	2.5%
Short-term investments	4.0%	0.0%
Accounts receivable	18.6%	18.8%
Inventories	23.5%	28.8%
Total current assets	47.0%	50.0%
Net plant and equipment	53.0%	50.0%
Total assets	100.0%	100.0%

Liabilities and equity	20X8	20X7
Accounts payable	2.1%	3.2%
Notes payable	3.7%	5.5%
Accruals	7.9%	7.0%
Total current liabilities	13.7%	15.7%
Long-term bonds	35.1%	37.5%
Total debt	48.8%	53.2%
Common stock (130,000,000 shares)	7.9%	6.5%
Retained earnings	43.3%	40.3%
Total common equity	51.2%	46.8%
Total liabilities and equity	100.0%	100.0%

Table 9.10: Common-Size DEM's Income Statements.

	20X8	20X7
Net sales	100.0%	100.0%
Cost of sales	81.8%	81.5%
Gross profit	18.2%	18.5%
Operating expenses	2.8%	3.0%
Earnings before interest and taxes (EBIT)	9.2%	9.4%
Less interest	2,2%	3,1%
Earnings before taxes (EBT)	7.0%	6.4%
Taxes (20%)	1.4%	1.3%
Net Income available to common stockholders	5.6%	5.1%
Common dividends	1.9%	1.9%
Addition to retained earnings	3.7%	3.2%

allow the comparison between firms to see if a particular firm is operating within industry or competitive parameters.

9.10 Ratio Analysis

Ratio analysis is a financial technique that involves dividing various financial statement numbers into another. Three basic categories of ratio analysis are used:
- *Trend or time-series analysis.* This category evaluates performance over time. It is a measure that uses ratios to evaluate a firm's performance. It is also referred to as time series analysis.
- *Cross-section analysis.* Makes comparisons with different companies at the same point in time.
- *Industry-comparative analysis.* Compares a firm's ratios for companies in some industry.

Performing ratio analysis also comes with the following words of caution:
- Understand how industry averages are constructed.
- Large firms may have multiple businesses in different industries.
- Assess industry mix to see if true apples-to-apples comparisons are being made.
- Different people define ratios differently.
- Different people interpret ratios differently, depending on perspective.

Ratios are grouped into five basic categories:
- Liquidity ratios
- Asset management ratios
- Financial-leverage ratios
- Profitability ratios
- Market-value ratios

Data to calculate the ratios are taken from a firm's income statements and balance sheets as well from stock market data.

Liquidity Ratios

Liquidity ratios indicate the ability to meet short-term obligations to creditors as they mature or become due. The net working capital of a firm is its current assets minus current liabilities. Two ratios are commonly used to gauge a firm's liquidity:
- Current ratio
- Quick ratio, or acid-test ratio,

The current ratio is a measure of a company's ability to pay off its short-term debt as it becomes due and is defined as current assets divided by current liabilities. Generally, a high value is desired. However, too high of a value may indicate that funds are not being efficiently deployed within the firm. The quick ratio, or acid-test ratio, is defined as the sum of cash, marketable securities, and accounts receivable divided by current liabilities. The quick ratio eliminates inventory from the calculation because inventories are often the least liquid of the current assets.

$$\text{Current Ratio} = \frac{\text{Current Assets}}{\text{Current Liabilities}}$$

$$\text{Current ratio}_{20X8} = 1000/314 = 3.18$$

$$\text{Current ratio}_{20X7} = 770/225 = 3.42$$

$$\text{Quick ratio}_{20X8} = 425/314 = 1.35$$

$$\text{Quick ratio}_{20X7} = 385/225 = 1.71$$

Asset-Management Ratios

Asset-management ratios, or activity or utilization ratios, indicate the extent to which assets are used to supports sales. Four ratios are commonly used to gauge a firm's activity:

- Total-assets turnover ratio
- Fixed-assets turnover ratio
- Average collection period
- Receivables turnover

Total-assets turnover ratio is found by dividing net sales by total assets and indicates how efficiently a firm is using its assets to produce sales; generally, the more efficient the asset use is, the higher a firm's profits are. For example, a capital-intensive company may have a relatively low asset turnover ratio of 0.33, indicating that it requires €3 of investment to produce €1 in revenue. In general, a higher ratio is more desirable.

$$\text{Total Assets Turnover} = \frac{\text{Sales}}{\text{Total Assets}}$$

$$\text{Total Assets Turnover}_{20X8} = 3{,}010/2000 = 1.51$$

$$\text{Total Assets Turnover}_{20X7} = 2{,}860/1{,}640 = 1.74$$

The *fixed assets turnover* is found by dividing net sales by fixed assets and indicates the extent to which long-term assets are being used to produce sales. Because investment in plant and equipment is usually expensive, unused or idle capacity is often costly and is a major contributor to a firm's poor operating performance. In general, a higher ratio is more desirable. High turnover numbers here are not necessarily a good thing, as a high ratio can be obtained by the use of obsolete equipment with reduced book value due to accumulated depreciation.

$$\text{Fixed Assets Turnover}_{20X8} = 3{,}010/1000 = 3.01$$

$$\text{Fixed Assets Turnover}_{20X7} = 2{,}860/870 = 3.29$$

The *average collection period* (ACP) or days sales outstanding (DSO) is found by taking the year-end accounts receivable divided by the average net sales per day, indicating the average number of days it takes to collect credit sales. A shorter number is preferred to a longer number – the sooner the cash is in hand, the better off the firm is. Receivables turnover is found by dividing annual sales, preferably credit sales, by the year-end accounts receivable. This ratio provides essentially the same information as the average collection period.

$$\text{ACP or DSO} = \frac{\text{Receivables}}{\dfrac{\text{Sales}}{365}} \text{ or ACP or DSO} = \frac{\text{Receivables}}{\dfrac{\text{Cost of Goods Sold}}{365}}$$

$$\text{ACP}_{20X8} = 375/(2{,}454.6/365) = 55.80 \text{ days}$$

$$\text{ACP}_{20X7} = 315/(2{,}338.3/365) = 47.58 \text{ days}$$

The inventory turnover ratio is found by dividing the cost of goods sold by year-end inventory and gives an indication as to how efficient the amount of inventory is being managed. In general, a higher ratio is more desirable. Too low inventory turnover may suggest obsolete inventory. However, too high inventory turnover could lead to stock-outs and lost sales.

$$Inventory\ Period = \frac{365}{Inventory\ Turnover}$$

$$Inventory\ Turnover_{20X8} = 2{,}454.6/575 = 4.28$$

$$Inventory\ Turnover_{20X7} = 2{,}338.3/385 = 6.07$$

$$Inventory\ Period_{20X8} = 365/4.27 = 85.48\ days$$

$$Inventory\ Period_{20X7} = 365/6.07 = 60.13\ days$$

The average payment period is found by dividing year-end accounts payable by the firm's average cost of goods sold per day. This ratio shows the number of days it takes for the firm to pay its suppliers:

Average payment period = Accounts payable / (Cost of goods sold / 365)

The operating cycle is the inventory conversion period plus the average collection period. The cash conversion cycle is the operating cycle minus the average payment period.[3]

Leverage (Debt Management) Ratios

Financial-leverage ratios indicate the extent to which borrowed or debt funds are used to finance assets. Five ratios commonly used to gauge a firm's financial leverage are:
- Total-debt-to-assets ratio
- Total-debt-to-equity ratio
- Equity multiplier ratio
- Interest coverage, or times-interest-earned ratio
- Fixed-charge-coverage ratio

Total-debt-to-assets ratio is found by dividing the total debt or total liabilities of a firm by its total assets. This ratio reflects the portion of the total assets financed by debt and creditors. In general, a low ratio is desired, for too much debt results in higher interest payments and the inability to produce further debt funding on top

---

3 See Chapter 12 for more information.

of the existing capital structure. However, because interest is deductible for tax purposes, having too little debt may not be the answer either.

$$\text{Total Debt Ratio} = \frac{\text{Total Debt}}{\text{Total Assets}} = \frac{\text{Total Assets} - \text{Total Equity}}{\text{Total Assets}}$$

$$\text{Total Debt Ratio}_{20X8} = 1{,}064/2{,}000 = 53.20\%$$

$$\text{Total Debt Ratio}_{20X7} = 800/1{,}640 = 48.78\%$$

Total-debt-to-equity ratio is found by dividing the total debt of a firm by its shareholder's equity. This ratio is a capitalization ratio in that it compares how the firm has been financed – by debt or by equity. A lender would likely look upon a low ratio favorably. As a practical matter, companies that have a low ratio here may do so because debt financing was not available to them.

Debt-to-Equity Ratio $_{20X8}$ = 936/1,064= 87.97%

Debt-to-Equity Ratio $_{20X7}$ = 800/840= 95.24 %

The *equity multiplier* (EM) *ratio* is found by dividing total assets (TA) by equity (E) and gives another way of looking at a firm's debt burden (D). This ratio is equivalent to one plus the debt-to-equity ratio. A large reliance on debt results in a larger equity multiplier ratio.

$$\text{Equity Multiplier} = \frac{\text{Total Assets}}{\text{Equity}} \quad or \quad EM = 1 + \frac{D}{E} = \frac{1}{1 - \frac{D}{TA}}$$

$$\text{Equity Multiplier}_{20X8} = 2{,}000/936 = 2.14$$

$$\text{Equity Multiplier}_{20X7} = 1{,}640/840 = 1.95$$

Interest coverage, or *times-interest-earned* (TIE) *ratio*, is found by dividing the firm's operating income (or EBIT) by the annual interest expense. This ratio is often included in loan covenants. Generally, a higher coverage is more desirable. Analysts may include certain fixed charges, such as lease payments or sinking fund payments, into this calculation as well.

$$\text{Times Interest Earned}_{20X8} = 283.8/92 = 3.08$$

$$\text{Times Interest Earned}_{20X7} = 263/64 = 4.11$$

Earnings before interest, tax, depreciation, and amortization (EBITDA) coverage ratio is calculated as follows:

$$\text{EBITDA Coverage Ratio} = \frac{\text{EBITDA} + \text{Lease Pmt.}}{\text{Interest} + \text{Lease Pmt.} + \text{Principal Repayments}}$$

$$\text{EBITDA Coverage Ratio}_{20X8} = (283.8 + 90 + 28)/(92 + 28 + 20) = 2.72$$

$$\text{EBITDA Coverage Ratio}_{20X7} = (263 + 80 + 20)/(64 + 20 + 15) = 3.76$$

Profitability Ratios

Profitability ratios indicate the firm's ability to generate returns on its sales, assets, and equity. Five ratios commonly used to gauge a firm's profitability are:
- Operating profit margin
- Net profit margin
- Operating return on assets
- Net return on total assets
- Return on equity

Operating profit margin is found by dividing the earnings before interest and taxes (EBIT) by net sales and indicates the firm's ability to control operating expenses relative to sales.

$$\text{Operating Profit margin}_{20X8} = 283.8/3.000 = 9.46\%$$

$$\text{Operating Profit margin}_{20X7} = 263.8/2.850 = 9.26\%$$

Net profit margin is found by dividing net income by net sales and indicates the ability to earn a return after meeting interest and tax obligations.

$$\text{Profit Margin (ROS)} = \frac{\text{Net Income}}{\text{Sales}}$$

$$\text{ProfitMargin (ROS)}_{20X8} = 153.4/3,010 = 5.10\%$$

$$\text{Profit Margin (ROS)}_{20X7} = 159.2/2,860 = 5.57\%$$

Operating return on assets is found by dividing EBIT by total assets and measures how well assets are working to generate an operating return (ignoring taxes and how the firm is financed).

$$\text{Basic Earning Power}_{20X8} = 283.8/2,000 = 14.19\%$$

$$\text{Basic Earning Power}_{20X7} = 263.0/1,640 = 16.04\%$$

Net return on total assets is found by dividing net income by total assets and measures how well assets are working to generate return.

$$\text{Net Return on Total Assets} = \frac{\text{Net Profit}}{\text{Total Assets}}$$

$$\text{Net Return on Total Assets}_{20X8} = 153.5/2,000 = 7.67\%$$

$$\text{Net Return on Total Assets}_{20X7} = 159.2/1,640 = 9.71\%$$

Return on equity (ROE) is found by dividing net income by the shareholder's equity and measuring the return that shareholders earned on equity invested in the firm.

$$ROE_{20X8} = 153.5/936 = 16.39\%$$

$$ROE_{20X7} = 159.2/840 = 18.95\%$$

Market-Value Ratios

Market-value ratios indicate the willingness of investors to value a firm in the marketplace relative to financial statement values. Three ratios commonly used to gauge a firm's market-value are:
- Price/earnings ratio (P/E)
- Price to book value ratio
- Price to cash flow ratio

The *price/earnings ratio* (P/E), or P/E ratio, is the market price of a firm's common stock divided by the firm's annual earnings per share (EPS). A firm's value is linked to factors such as the firm's profitability, risk, competitive position, future prospects, and management. All of these factors are reflected in the financial statements by efficient financial markets.

$$\text{Price} - \text{Earnings Ratio} = \frac{\text{Market Price per Share}}{\text{EPS}}$$

$$\text{Price} - \text{Earnings Ratio}_{20X8} = 15/1.18 = 12.71$$

$$\text{Price} - \text{Earnings Ratio}_{20X7} = 14/1.22 = 11.48$$

Price to book value ratio is the market price of a firm's common stock divided by the firm's book value (assets minus liabilities). In general, higher market-value ratios reflect a firm with higher-quality financial statements.

$$\text{Market Value} - \text{Book Value}_{20X8} = 15/7.2 = 2.08$$

$$\text{Market Value} - \text{Book Value}_{2017} = 14/6.46 = 2.17$$

Stock prices depend on a company's ability to generate cash flows. Consequently, investors often look at the price/cash flow ratio, where cash flow is defined as net income plus depreciation and amortization:

$$\text{Price} - \text{cash flow ratio} = \frac{\text{Price per share}}{\text{Cash flow per share}}$$

$$\text{Price} - \text{Cash Flow Ratio}_{20X8} = 15/((153.5+90)/130) = 8.01$$

$$\text{Price} - \text{Cash Flow Ratio}_{20X7} = 14/((159.2+80)/130) = 7.61$$

DEM's price/cash flow ratio is also above the industry average, once again suggesting that its growth prospects are above average, its risk is below average, or both.

Du Pond Method of Ratio Analysis

The Du Pont system focuses on:
- Expense control (PM)
- Asset utilization (TATO)
- Debt utilization (EM)

It shows how these factors combine to determine the ROE. The Du Pont analysis is the technique of breaking down return on total assets and return on equity into their component parts and is illustrated as follows:

$$\left(\frac{Pr\,ofit}{m\arg in}\right)\left(\frac{TA}{turnover}\right)\left(\frac{Equity}{multiplier}\right) = ROE$$

$$\frac{\text{Net Income}}{\text{Sales}} \times \frac{\text{Sales}}{\text{Total Assets}} \times \frac{\text{Total Assets}}{\text{Common Equity}} = ROE$$

Let's discuss how we obtained this formula:

If we divide nominator and denominator in sales, we obtain the following:

$$\frac{\text{Net Income}}{\text{Sales}} : \frac{\text{Common Equity}}{\text{Sales}} = ROE$$

$$\frac{\text{Net Income}}{\text{Sales}} \times \frac{\text{Sales}}{\text{Common Equity}} = ROE$$

Sales/Common Equity gives us equity turnover. If we divide the nominator and denominator in total assets, we obtain the following:

$$\frac{\text{Sales}}{\text{Common Equity}} = \frac{\text{Sales}}{\text{Total Assets}} : \frac{\text{Common Equity}}{\text{Total Assets}}$$

$$\frac{\text{Sales}}{\text{Common Equity}} = \frac{\text{Sales}}{\text{Total Assets}} \times \frac{\text{Total Assets}}{\text{Common Equity}}$$

As shown before, our final equation will be:

$$\frac{\text{Net Income}}{\text{Sales}} \times \frac{\text{Sales}}{\text{Total Assets}} \times \frac{\text{Total Assets}}{\text{Common Equity}} = ROE$$

$$ROE_{20X8} = 16.39\% = 5.10\% \times 1.51 \times 2.14 = 16.39\%$$

$$ROE_{20X7} = 18.95\% = 5.57\% \times 1.74 \times 1.95 = 18.95\%$$

Return on equity can be increased by increasing net profit margin, by using asset more efficiently, and by using more debt. Note that determining how much debt should be used is a financial decision, which is discussed in Chapter 11.

Tables 9.11 and 9.12 show per share data and calculated ratios.

Table 9.11: DEM's Calculated Data: Per-Share Information.

Calculated Data: Per-Share Information	20X8	20X7
Earnings per share (EPS)	€1.18	€1.22
Dividends per share (DPS)	€0.44	€0.41
Book value per share (BVPS)	€7.20	€6.46
Cash flow per share (CFPS)	€1.87	€1.84
Free cash flow per share (FCFPS)	(€1.22)	N/A

Table 9.12: DEM's Calculated Data: Some Ratios.

	20X8	20X7	Industry Average	Comment
Liquidity ratios				
Current Ratio	3.18	3.42	4.20	Poor
Quick Ratio	1.35	1.71	2.10	Poor
Asset Management ratios				
Inventory Turnover	4.27	6.07	9.00	Poor
Days Sales Outstanding	55.8	47.6	36.00	Poor
Fixed Asset Turnover	3.01	3.29	3.00	Ok
Total Asset Turnover	1.51	1.74	1.80	Low
Debt Management ratios				
Debt Ratio	53.20%	48.78%	40.00%	High
Times Interest Earned	3.08	4.11	6.00	Poor
EBITDA Coverage Ratio	4.17	6.03	8.00	Low
Profitability ratios				
Profit Margin	5.10%	5.57%	5.00%	Acceptable
Basic Earning Power	14.19%	16.04%	17.20%	Acceptable
Return on Assets	7.68%	9.71%	9.00%	Ok
Return on Equity	16.40%	18.95%	15.00%	Ok
Market Value ratios				
Price-to Earnings Ratio	12.70	11.43	12.50	Ok
Price-to-Cash Flow Ratio	8.01	7.61	6.80	Ok

Table 9.12 (continued)

		20X8	20X7	Industry Average	Comment
Market-to-Book Ratio		2.08	2.17	1.70	Ok
		Du Pont Analysis			
	ROE =	P.M. ×	T.A.T.O. ×		Equity Multiplier
DEM Inc.	2020	16.40%	5.10%	1.51	2.14
DEM Inc.	2019	18.95%	5.57%	1.74	1.95
Industry Average		15.00%	5.00%	1.80	1.67

9.11 Long-Term Financial Planning

Financial managers employ financial analysis techniques in the company's financial planning process. Financial planning requires foresight. Long-range plans should project growth in sales, assets, and employees. Such plans should also anticipate developments in the economy and competition from others.

Financial models support the financial planning process by making it easier and cheaper to construct forecast financial statements. Components of financial planning models are as follows:

– *Inputs.* A firm's current financial statements and its forecasts about the future; the principal forecast is growth in sales, how a change in sales affects costs, working capital, and fixed assets.
– *Planning model.* This calculates the implications of the manager's forecasts for profits, new investment, and financing.
– *Outputs.* Financial statements such as income statements, balance sheets, and cash flow statements are called proformas, meaning they are forecasts based on inputs and assumptions.

Percentage of sales model is a special case of a financial planning model. Sales are the driving variable and most other variables are proportional to sales. Steps in this context are as follows:

– Project the company's sales.
– Project operational expenses (e.g., cost of goods sold, SGA) using the common-size income statement, including various margin analysis. Suggestion: Forecast gross profit margin to determine COGS and gross profit.
– Estimate the level of investment in inventory and receivables using the appropriate asset utilization ratios. Project the payables using average payment period (days).
– Project the level of property plant and equipment.

- Forecast interest expense.
- Project short-term and long-term debt exclusive of any new financing.
- Adjust any miscellaneous balance sheet and income statement items.
- Adjust equity (exclusive of buying back shares or issuing additional stock) based on net income and forecasted dividends.
- At this step, it is acceptable to have a negative cash balance. A company should never have a negative cash balance. With pro forma financial statements, a negative cash balance means the company may need additional financing. In reality, a company will borrow to update the negative cash balance to the required level of cash balance.
- Determine financing needs.

Let's take a simple example using the financials of DEM presented in Tables 9.13–9.16. The ratios (Forecast 20X9) will be used in projected financials.

Table 9.13: DEM's Pro Forma Ratios.

	Actual		Historical Average	Industry Composite	Forecast 20X9
	20X7	20X8			
Costs / Sales	81.76%	81.55%	81.65%	81.06%	81.06%
Operating expenses / Sales	9.05%	9.02%	9.03%	9.00%	9.00%
Depreciation / Net plant & equipment	10.34%	100.00%	55.17%	10.20%	10.20%
Cash / Sales	0.52%	1.66%	1.09%	1.00%	1.00%
Accounts Receivable / Sales	10.66%	12.46%	11.56%	10.00%	10.00%
Inventory / Sales	13.46%	19.10%	16.28%	11.11%	11.11%
Net plant & equipment / sales	30.42%	3.32%	16.87%	33.33%	33.33%
Accounts Payable / Sales	1.22%	2.13%	1.68%	1.00%	1.00%
Accruals / Sales	2.10%	3.65%	2.88%	2.00%	2.00%

If required operating assets are less than the sources of financing, the difference is plugged to short-term investments.

If required operating assets are more than sources of financing, the difference is plugged to notes payable.

In order to calculate the balance of either of notes payable or short-term investments, we need to know interest expense and income, thus net income. So, it is like solving simultaneous equations problems. Fortunately, the automatic calculation

Table 9.14: Other Inputs.

Sales growth rate	10%
Tax rate	20%
Dividend growth rate	8%
Interest rate on notes payable and short-term investments	13%
Interest rate on long-term bonds	11%

Table 9.15: DEM, Inc.: Actual and Projected Income Statements (€ in millions).

	Actual	Forecast	Forecast
	20X8	Basis	20X9
	(1)	(2)	(3)
Sales	€3,010	110%	€3,311
Cost of sales	€2,455	81.00%	€2,682
Gross profit	€555		€629
Operating expenses	€272	9.00%	€298
EBIT	€284		€331
Less Interest	€92	0.13–0.11	€109
Earnings before taxes (EBT)	€192		€222
Taxes (20%)	€38	20.00%	€44
NI available to common	€154		€177
Shares of common equity	€130		€130
Dividends per share	€0	108%	€0
Dividends to common	€53	108%	€57
Add. to retained earnings	€101		€120
Depreciation	€100	10%	€116

option in Excel will do it for us. Interest expense and income has been calculated on average of two years' balances of respected balance sheet items.

An advantage of the percentage of sales model is that it is a first approximation for financial planning. A disadvantage of the percentage of sales model is that

Table 9.16: DEM, Inc.: Actual and Projected Balance Sheets (€ in millions).

	Actual	Forecast	Forecast
	20X8	Basis	20X9
	(1)	(2)	(3)
Assets			
Cash	€50	0.50%	€16.6
ST investments	€ 0	"plug" if needed	€0,0
Accounts receivable	€375	13.00%	€430.4
Inventories	€575	20.00%	€662.2
Total current assets	€1.000		€1.109.2
Net plant and equipment	€100	35.00%	€1.158.9
Total assets	€1.100		€2.268.0
Liabilities and equity			
Accounts payable	€64	2,00%	€66.2
Accruals	€110	3,70%	€122.5
Notes payable	€140	"plug" if needed	€273.2
Total current liabilities	€314		€461.9
Long-term bonds	€ 750	Same: no new issue	€750.0
Total liabilities	€1,064		€1,211.9
Common stock	€130	Same: no new issue	€ 130.0
Retained earnings	€806	RE_{t-1} + Additions RE_t	€ 926.1
Total common equity	€936		€1,056.1
Total liabilities and equity	€2,000		€2,268.0
Required assets			€2,268.0
Specified sources of financing			€1,994.8
Additional funds needed (AFN)			€273.2
Additional short-term investments			€0.0

Table 9.16 (continued)

	Actual	Forecast	Forecast
Interest on notes payable			€ 26.9
Interest on long term bonds			€ 82.5
Interest on short term investments			€ 0.0
Total interest expense			€ 109.4

many variables will not be proportional to sales – for example, labor and materials. Plant and equipment can be purchased in lumpy amounts. If costs are projected as *Total cost = Fixed cost + Unit variable cost × Volume*, then the model output will be more meaningful.

Suppose in 20X9 fixed assets had been operated at only 60% of capacity.

$$\text{Capacity sales} = \text{Actual sales}/\% \text{ of sales}$$

$$= 3{,}010/0.60 = €5{,}017$$

With the existing fixed assets, sales could be €5,017. Since sales are forecasted at only €3,311, no new fixed assets are needed. This will lower additional funds needed (AFN). In our case, the company did not need any additional funds.

On the other hand, if there are economies of scale, this will lead to less than proportional asset increases. If the company invests lumpy assets, this will lead to large periodic AFN requirements and recurring excess capacity.

9.12 Cost-Volume-Profit Analysis

Cost-volume-profit analysis is used by managers for financial planning to estimate a firm's operating profits at different levels of unit sales. Break-even analysis (see Figure 9.1) estimates how many units of product must be sold in order for the firm to break even, or generate zero profit. Costs are either variable or fixed. Variable costs vary according to the number of units sold, while fixed costs are the same irrespective of how many units are sold. Earnings before interest and taxes (EBIT) are calculated by the following equation:

$$\text{EBIT} = \text{Sales} - \text{Variable Costs} - \text{Fixed Costs}$$

$$= (P)\,(Q) - (VC)\,Q - FC$$

Where P is the price per item, Q is the quantity sold, VC is the variable cost per unit, and FC is fixed costs.

Figure 9.1: Break-Even Analysis Graph.

Quantity break-even (Q_{BE}) is the number of units that have to be sold to break even and is found by the following equation:

$$(P)(Q) = (VC)\,Q - FC$$

$$(P)(Q) - (VC)\,Q = FC$$

$$Q_{BE} = FC/(P - VC)$$

Find the break-even quantity for a firm whose fixed costs are €200,000, variable cost per unit is €8, and sales price per unit is €20. See Table 9.17.

Table 9.17: Data for Break-Even Analysis.

Sales Quantity	Total Revenue	Variable Costs	Fixed Costs	Total Costs	Operating Profit
0	€0	€0	€200.000	€200.000	−€200.000
5.000	100.000	40.000	200.000	240.000	−140.000
10.000	200.000	80.000	200.000	280.000	−80.000
15.000	300.000	120.000	200.000	320.000	−20.000
20.000	400.000	160.000	200.000	360.000	40.000
25.000	500.000	200.000	200.000	400.000	100.000

$$Q_{BE} = €200,000/(€20 - €8) = 16,667 \text{ units}$$

In order to find the break-even sales revenue (SR), we multiply the break-even quantity by sales price per unit:

$$Q_{SR} = 16,667 \times 20 = €333,340$$

Break-even analysis can also be used to find the operating profit targeted. In this case, the formula used to find desired sales quantity $Q*$ is as follows:

$$Q* = \frac{FC + operating\ profit,\ targeted}{(P - VC)}$$

In order to find *necessary sales revenue* (NSR), we multiply $Q*$ quantity by sales price per unit. Assume that the company wants to achieve €30,000 operating profit. What is the desired sales quantity $Q*$ and sales revenue?

$$Q* = (200,000 + 30,000)/(20 - 8) = 19,167 \text{ units}$$

$$NSR = 19,167 \times 20 = €383,340.$$

A multi-product break-even analysis is more relevant, since most firms produce more than one product. The analysis is same as in one product case. A requirement is that the ratio of the quantity of one product to the total quantity of products has to be given (sales mix). The following example will clarify the methodology with the following data:

   Sales mix: 40% product A; 60% product B.
   P_1=Price of product A=€10; P_2=Price of product 2=€5.
   V_1=Variable cost per unit of product A=1; V_2=Variable cost per unit of product B=2.
   F = Fixed costs = €500
The formula for the breakeven point is;

$$\text{Profit} = P_1 \times Q_1 + P_2 Q_2 - (F + V_1 Q_1 + V_2 Q_2) = 10 \times Q_2 + 5 \times Q_2 - (500 + 1 \times Q_1 + 2 \times Q_2) = 0$$

Dividing both sides of this equation by the total number of products (Q_1+Q_2) and rearranging, we find;

$$10 \times 0.4 + 5 \times 0.6 - (500/(Q_1 + Q_2) + 1 \times 0.4 + 2 \times 0.6), \text{ or;}$$

$Q_1 + Q_2 = 500/8.6 = 58$ units. Therefore $Q_1 = 23$ units (+ 40% of 58) and, $Q_2 = 35$.

9.13 Operating and Financial Leverage

Operating leverage arises when a firm has *fixed operating costs* (e.g., rent, property taxes, salaries). *Degree of operating leverage* (DOL) is a measure of the sensitivity of the firm's EBIT to fluctuations in sales. An example of calculation of DOL is presented in Tables 9.18 and 9.19.

Table 9.18: Inputs and Outputs of Degree of Operating Leverage.

	Decreased sales	Base case	Increased sales
% change from base case	−20%		+20%
Sales	€800,000	€1,000,000	€1,200,000
Variable costs @ 40%	(320,000)	(400,000)	(480,000)
Gross profit	480,000	600,000	720,000
Fixed cost	(120,000)	(120,000)	(120,000)
EBIT	€360,000	€480,000	€600,000
% change from base case	−25%		25%

Table 9.19: Inputs and Outputs of Degree of Financial Leverage: Case 2.

	40% debt case		
	Decreased EBIT	Base case	Increased EBIT
% change from base case	−25%		+25%
EBIT	€360,000	€480,000	€600,000
Interest	(€40,000)	(€40,000)	(€40,000)
EBT	€320,000	€440,000	€560,000
Taxes @ 20%	(€64,000)	(€88,000)	(€112,000)
EAT	€256,000	€352,000	€448,000
Shares outstanding	60,000	60,000	60,000
EPS	€4.27	€5.87	€7.47
% change from base case	−27.27%		27.27%

Calculation of DOL:

$$DOL_{base\ case} = \frac{\Delta\%in\ EBIT}{\Delta\%in\ sales} = \frac{.25}{.20} = 1.25$$

or

$$DOL_{base\ case} = \frac{sales - variable\ cost}{EBIT} = \frac{€1,000,000 - €400,000}{€480,000} = 1.25$$

Financial leverage arises when firms have fixed financial costs (such as interest). *Degree of financial leverage* (DFL) is a measure of the responsiveness of the firms EPS to changes in EBIT.

Calculating DFL base case:

$$DFL_{base\ case} = \frac{\Delta\%EPS}{\Delta\%EBIT} = \frac{.2727}{.25} = 1.091$$

or

$$DFL_{base\ case} = \frac{EBIT}{EBIT - interest} = \frac{€480,000}{€480,000 - €40,000} = 1.091$$

By combining DOL and DFL, we can measure the relationship between changes in sales and changes in EPS. This combination is called the *degree of combined leverage* (DCL).

The degree of combined leverage is calculated as follows:

$$DCL_{base\ case} = DOL \times DFL = 1.25 \times 1.091 = 1.364$$

or

$$DCL_{base\ case} = \frac{\Delta\%\ in\ EPS}{\Delta\%\ in\ sales} = \frac{.2727}{.20} = 1.364$$

or

$$DCL_{base\ case} = \frac{sales - variable\ cost}{EBIT - interest} = \frac{€1,000,000 - €400,000}{€480,000 - €40,000} = 1.364$$

If sales increase by 20%, what happens to the net income? The net income will increase by (1.364×0.20=) 27.27%. You can check this result by comparing EATs:

Percentage change in net income = (*EAT* 20% *increase in sales/EAT base case*) − 1
= (€448,000/€352,000) − 1 = 27.27%.

If sales decrease by 20%, what happens to the net income? The net income will decrease by (1.364 × 0.20=) 27.27%. You can check this result by comparing EATs:

Percentage change in net income = (€256,000/€352,000) − 1 = − 27.27%.

9.14 Summary

A firm's basic financial statements include the balance sheet, income statement, and statement of cash flows.

A corporation's annual reports include detailed information on operating and financial performance, current and future business opportunities, and financial statements.

The balance sheet (statement of financial position) is a statement of a company's financial position as of a particular date; it is a snapshot in time. The balance sheet contains assets, liabilities, and owner's equity.

The income statement, or profit and loss statement, reports revenues (sales) and expenses of a firm over an accounting period.

A statement of cash flows provides a summary of the cash sources that come into the company and the cash that goes out of the company during an accounting period. The cash flow statement consists of three sections: operating activities, investing activities, and financing activities.

EVA attempts to measure a firm's economic profit, rather than accounting profit. If the firm earns a return on capital that is greater than the investors' required rate of return, the company is said to be profitable. EVA recognizes a cost of equity in addition to the cost of debt (interest expense).

Financial statements are used by financial market participants who analyze statements for different purposes.

Common-size financial statements express balance sheet numbers as a percentage of total assets and income statement numbers as a percentage of revenue in order to enable comparisons between firms of different size.

Ratio analysis is a financial technique that involves dividing various financial statement numbers into one another. Three basic categories of ratio analysis are used: trend or time-series analysis, cross-section analysis, and industry-comparative analysis.

Ratios are grouped into five basic categories: liquidity ratios, asset management ratios, financial leverage ratios, profitability ratios, and market-value ratios. Financial managers use financial analysis in the company's financial planning process.

Financial planning requires foresight. The percentage of sales model is a special financial planning model. Sales is the driving variable and most other variables are proportional to sales.

Cost-volume-profit analysis is used by managers for financial planning to estimate a firm's operating profits at different levels of unit sales. Break-even analysis, a variation of cost-volume-profit analysis, estimates how many units of product must be sold in order for the firm to break even, or generate zero profit.

The degree of operating leverage (DOL) is a measure of the sensitivity of the firm's EBIT to fluctuations in sales.

The degree of financial leverage (DFL) is a measure of the responsiveness of the firm's EPS to changes in EBIT.

By combining DOL and DFL, we can measure the relationship between changes in sales and changes in EPS. This combination is called the degree of combined leverage (DCL).

10 The Basics of Capital Budgeting

10.1 Introduction

We now focus on investment principle (capital budgeting). The capital budget must relate to the firm's mission and its abilities to meet competitive challenges. Information from marketing, finance, and production analyses are put together to form cash flow estimates of proposed projects. Project risk considerations enter the capital budget analysis because higher-risk projects should be expected to earn higher returns than lower-risk projects. The capital budget evaluation is done with the goal of identifying projects that will increase shareholder wealth. This chapter examines the process of evaluating projects and determining the inputs that are used to form the cash flow estimates.

10.2 Data and Stages in Capital Budgeting

The capital budget must relate to the firm's mission and its abilities to meet competitive challenges. Information from marketing, finance, and production analyses are put together to form cash flow estimates of proposed projects.

Capital budgeting is the process of identifying, evaluating, and implementing a firm's investment opportunities.[1] Various methods of capital budgeting are available. However, it is the continuous planning and feedback cycles of capital budgeting that allow a company to grow and prosper. Capital budgeting helps companies in the following areas:

- better working capital, the capital used for day-to-day expenses
- profit maximization due to proper budgeting of funds
- an increase in firm value when cash flow benefits exceed capital expenditures
- proper investment in assets that generate earning power and profitability

Capital budgeting decisions can involve mutually exclusive or independent projects. Mutually exclusive projects mean that selecting one project precludes others from being undertaken. Independent projects are not in direct competition with one another.

The *market (intrinsic) value* of an investment is the present value of future cash flows associated with that investment. The net benefit is also called the *net present value* (NPV) which is the present value of a project's cash flows minus its cost. A good situation is where the NPV is greater than the capital outlay.

---

1 Capital budgeting is covered fully in project appraisal texts. See, for example, Arman T. Tevfik, *Yatırım Projeleri*, Literatür, 2012; Prassanna Chandra, *Projects: Planning, Analysis, Financing, Implementation, and Review, Implementation*, Fifth Edition, Tata McGraw-Hill, New Delhi, 2002.

https://doi.org/10.1515/9783110705355-010

The five stages of capital budgeting are:
- *Identification.* Finding potential capital investment opportunities.
- *Development.* Estimating relevant cash inflows and outflows, as well as assessing pros and cons.
- *Selection.* Applying appropriate capital budgeting techniques to determine project feasibility.
- *Implementation.* Executing on plans for accepted projects.
- *Follow-up.* Periodic review of performance to decide whether or not to continue.

Multinational corporations must also assess political and economic risks while evaluating overseas projects.

Capital budget decisions require three types of information to be generated and compiled:
- Internal financial data:
  - Investment costs
  - Market studies and estimates of revenue, costs, and cash flows
  - Financing cost
  - Transportation costs
  - Data on competitors
- External economic and political data:
  - Business cycle stages
  - Inflation trends
  - Interest rate trends
  - Exchange rate trends
  - Freedom of cross-border currency flows
  - Political stability and environment
  - Regulations
  - Taxes
- Nonfinancial data:
  - Distribution channels
  - Quantity and quality of labor force by geography
  - Labor-management relations
  - Technological change
  - Potential reaction from competitors

10.3 Capital Budgeting Techniques

To evaluate projects, six methods of capital budgeting are widely used:
- Net present value (NPV)
- Internal rate of return (IRR)
- Profitability index

- Payback period
- Accounting rate of return
- Modified internal rate of return

Net Present Value

The *net present value* (NPV) of a project is calculated as the present value of all cash flows for the life of the project minus the cost of the initial investment. In order to apply the NPV method, we need to know the amounts and the timing of estimated future cash flows as well as the required rate of return, or cost of capital. A positive NPV means that the project's cash inflows are sufficient to repay the initial investment costs and cover the financing costs.

What does NPV represent?

- NPV represents the euro gain in time zero (0) in shareholder wealth from undertaking the project.
- If NPV > 0, accept the project, as shareholder wealth rises.
- If NPV < 0, reject the project, since it reduces shareholder wealth.

Net present value (NPV) is shown mathematically as:

$$NPV = CF_0 + \frac{CF_1}{(1+k)^1} + \frac{CF_2}{(1+k)^2} + \frac{CF_3}{(1+r)^3} + \ldots + \frac{CF_N}{(1+k)^N}$$

CF_0 denotes the initial investment (negative value), and CF_is denote periodic cash flows, some of which may be negative. A key input in NPV analysis is the discount rate (cost of capital), k, which represents the minimum return that the project must earn to satisfy investors. The discount rate, r, varies with the risk of the firm and/or the risk of the project.

Internal Rate of Return

The *internal rate of return* (IRR) method finds the return that causes the NPV to be zero. This is the point where the present value of future cash flows equals the project's initial investment. In general, a higher cost of capital will lead to a lower NPV. NPV and IRR methods will always agree on whether a project increases or decreases shareholder wealth.

The formula for the internal rate of return (IRR) is as follows:

$$NPV = 0 = CF_0 + \frac{CF_1}{(1+k)} + \frac{CF_2}{(1+k)^2} + \frac{CF_3}{(1+k)^3} + \ldots + \frac{CF_N}{(1+k)^N}$$

The IRR can be found by using:
- Trial and error
- Financial calculator
- Spreadsheet software

Accept the project if IRR > minimum required return on the project. The IRR measures the return earned on funds that remain internally invested in the project – that is, it measures the profitability of investment.

Advantages of IRR are:
- Takes time value of money into account
- Uses cash flows rather than earnings
- Accounts for all cash flows
- Project IRR is a number with intuitive appeal

Disadvantages of IRR are:
- Multiple IRRs may occur
- No real solutions can be obtained

Profitability Index

The *profitability index* (PI) method computes the ratio between present values and the inflows and outflows. The PI measures the relative benefits of undertaking a project. A PI of 2 means that the project returns a present value of €2 for every €1 invested. Whenever NPV is positive, PI is greater than 1.0; whenever NPV is negative, PI is less than 1.0. NPV, IRR, and PI always agree on which projects would increase shareholder wealth. A simple rule of this method can be summarized as follows:
- Accept project if PI > 1.0
- Reject project if PI < 1.0

Payback Period

The *payback period* method determines the time in years that it will take to recover or pay back the initial investment. The payback period is equal to the number of years where the accumulated cash flow is equal to the initial investment. Management chooses a benchmark number of years to use as the hurdle. This method, however, does not take into consideration the time value of money as the other methods, and so it may be the least preferable to use. Accept the project if the payback period is less than a maximum desired time period.

The discounted payback method is derived from the payback period method where future cash flows are discounted at the cost of capital and the payback period is calculated based on these discounted values.

Advantages of payback method are:
- Computational simplicity
- Easy to understand
- Focus on cash flow only

Disadvantages of payback method are:
- Does not properly account for time value of money
- Does not properly account for risk
- Cutoff period (the maximum payback period acceptable to management) is arbitrary
- Does not lead to value-maximizing decisions

Accounting Rate of Return (ARR)

The *accounting rate of return* (ARR) can be computed from available accounting data. It needs only profits after taxes and depreciation:

$$ARR = Average\ profits\ after\ taxes/Average\ investment$$

Average profits after taxes are estimated by subtracting average annual depreciation from the average annual operating cash inflows:

$$Average\ profits\ after\ taxes = Average\ annual\ operating\ cash\ inflows$$
$$- Average\ annual\ depreciation$$

ARR uses accounting numbers, not cash flows; there is no time value of money.

Modified Internal Rate of Return

The *modified internal rate of return* (MIRR) was developed to solve some of the issues associated with IRR. MIRR will agree with NPV on the accept/reject decision. MIRR gives a single answer – there is only one MIRR. MIRR agrees with NPV rankings when the initial investments are of comparable size.

Calculation of MIRR involves the following steps:
- Find the present value of all cash outflows.
- Find the future value of all cash inflows at the end of the project's life at year n. This lump sum is called the terminal value.
- MIRR is the discount rate, which equates the present value of the outflows and the future value of the inflows:

$$\text{FV at year } n = PV(1 + MIRR)^n$$

For example, assume the cost of capital is 10%. The project has the following cash flows (in millions of euros). The duration of the project is 2 years.

Cash flows	−1.6	10	−10
End of period	0	1	2

$$0 = \frac{-1.6}{(1+IRR)^0} + \frac{10}{(1+IRR)^1} + \frac{-10}{(1+IRR)^2}$$

Let us try first 25% and then 400%. These two rates will produce a zero net present value. This occurs when the project has abnormal cash flows. The project generates a huge amount of cash outflow either in the middle or at the end of the project.

In order to correct this assumption, MIRR reinvests cash flows on the cost of capital. To this end, the following calculations are made:

$$\text{Present value of cash outflows } PVCO_0 = \sum_{t=0}^{t=n} \frac{CO_t}{(1+k)^t}$$

$$\text{Future value of cash inflows } FVCI_t = \sum_{t=0}^{t=n} CIt(1+k)^{n-t}$$

$$MIRR = \left(\frac{FVCI_n}{PVO_0}\right)^{1/n-1}$$

Where:
CI = Cash inflows
CO= Cash outflows
$FVCI_n$ = Future value of cash inflows
$PVCO_0$ = Present value of cash outflows
k = Cost of capital
$FVCI_n = 10(1+0.10)^1 = 11$
$PVCO_0 = 1.6 + 10/(1+0.10)^2 = 1.6 + 8.26 = 9.86$
$MIRR = \left(\frac{11}{9,86}\right)^{1/2} - 1 = \% 5.6$

This project should be rejected, since the MIRR is less than the cost of capital.

Calculations

For the following projects, compute the NPV, IRR, profitability index, and payback period. If these projects are mutually exclusive, which one(s) should be done? If they are independent, which one(s) should be undertaken? See Table 10.1.

Table 10.1: Data for Projects.

	A	B	C	D
Year 0	-€10,000	-€15.000	-€5,000	-€20,000
Year 1	4,000	5,000	1,000	6,000
Year 2	4.000	5,000	3,000	8,000
Year 3	4,000	7,000	2,500	2,000
Year 4	4,000	2,000	2,000	3,000
Discount rate	10%	12%	15%	8%

Project A

NPV $= €4,000 \times$ PVIFA $(10\%,4) - 10,000 = €4,000 \times 3.170 - 10,000$
$= €12,680 - 10,000 = €2,680$
PI $= €1,268/1,000 = 1.268$
IRR $= 21.86\%$ (calculator or spreadsheet solution)
Payback $= €10,000/4,000 = 2.5$ years

Project B

NPV $= €5,000(1/1.12) + €5,000(1/1.12)^2 + €7,000(1/1.12)^3 + €2,000(1/1.12)^4 - 15,000$
$= €4,464.3 + 3,986.0 + 4,982.5 + 1,271.0 - 15,000 = -€296.2$
PI $= €14,703.8/15,000 = 0.98$
IRR $= 10.99\%$ (calculator or spreadsheet solution)
Payback $= 2.71$ years

Project C

NPV $= 1,000(1/1.15) + 3,000(1/1.15)^2 + 2,500(1/1.15)^3 + 2,000(1/1.15)^4 - 5,000$
$= €869.6 + 2,268.4 + 1,643.8 + 1,143.5 - 5,000 = €925.3$

PI   = €5,925.3/5,000= 1.19
IRR   = 23.13%
Payback = 2.4 years

Project D

NPV   = €6,000(1/1.08) + 8,000(1/1.08)^2 + 2,000(1/1.08)^3 + 3,000(1/1.08)^4–20.000
          = €5,555.6 + 6,858.7 + 1,587.7 + 2,205.1–20,000 = € –3,793.0
PI   = €16,207/20,000 = 0.81
IRR   = undefined; when discount rate = 0. NPV < 0
Payback = Project never pays back the initial investment.

If *A*, *B*, *C*, and *D* are mutually exclusive, choose the project with the highest NPV: Project A. If *A*, *B*, *C*, and *D* are independent, choose the project(s) with positive NPVs: Choose Project A and Project C.

Comparison of All Investment Evaluation Techniques

Now let us compare NPV, IRR, and others.
- They will always agree on whether to accept or reject a project. So, if projects are independent, either method is acceptable.
- Sometimes they may rank projects differently. What can be done if projects are mutually exclusive and the rankings conflict? In this case, always use NPV.
- NPV > 0 always means that IRR > minimum required return and that the PI > 1.
- If one indicates we should reject the project, they will all indicate *reject*.
- NPV < 0 always means that the IRR < minimum required return and that the PI < 1.
- A project may have more than one IRR! This can occur if a project has alternative positive and negative cash flows. This is most likely to occur if a project requires substantial renovations or maintenance during its life, or if its end-of-life shut-down costs are high. İn this case, use MIRR.

But conflicts may occur between NPV, IRR, and MIRR. This is likely when:
- Projects have different cash flow patterns
- Projects with higher and earlier cash flows have higher IRR rankings than those with larger and later cash flows

10.4 Separating Project Cash Flows

The stand-alone principle features isolating a project from the rest of the company to ensure that the analysis focuses solely on the project's incremental cash flows.

Three categories of cash flows are relevant for the capital budgeting process:
- *Cannibalization.* It occurs when a project robs cash flow from a firm's existing lines of business.
- *Enhancement.* It reflects and increases in cash flows of the firm's other products due to the new project.
- *Opportunity cost.* It is the cost of passing up the next best alternative.

In estimating incremental after-tax cash flows for a project, the following procedures are important:
- Build a base case scenario outlining the firm's after-tax cash flows without the new project.
- Examine incremental after-tax cash flows representing the difference between the firm's after-tax cash flows with the new project and the firm's base case.

Two categories of cash flows that are irrelevant in capital budgeting analysis are:
- *Sunk costs.* Project-related expenses that do not depend on whether or not the project is undertaken.
- *Financing costs.* These costs are taken into consideration by the discount rate.

10.5 Approaches to Estimating Project Cash Flows

The first step in the financial analysis of a capital budgeting proposal is the construction of year-by-year projected balance sheets and income statements for the project. Cash flow statements can be constructed from the projected balance sheets and income statements.

Cash flow from operations	= Net income + Depreciation + Current asset/liability sources – Current asset/liability uses
	= Net income + Depreciation – Change in net working capital

The net income from a project can be estimated on a daily, weekly, monthly, or yearly basis, as follows:
- Project sales (usually a cash inflow)
- Project costs (usually a cash outflow)
- Depreciation (noncash expense)
- EBIT

- Interest expense (taken into consideration in cost of capital, ignored here)
- EBT
- Taxes (cash outflow)
- Net income

Note that credit sales are not cash inflows until collected; likewise, not all costs reflect cash outflows.

Cash flow from investment activities for a project typically reflects spending on fixed assets, such as property, plant, and equipment required in undertaking the project. Thus, the cash flow here is usually negative at the start of a project but may be positive at the project's conclusion if the assets are sold for salvage value.

Cash flow from financing activities is usually excluded from the cash flow of the project; capital budgeting already accounts for relevant after-tax financing costs in the discount rate (interest rate being charged on the financing) applied to the estimated projected cash flows.

The depreciation tax shield (t×Dep) represents the tax savings due to the depreciation of fixed assets. For example, at a 20% tax rate, a depreciation expense of €1,000 saves the company €200 in income tax.

Depreciation expense is deductible from income before taxes and reduces a firm's tax liability. There are two basis depreciation methods: *straight-line* and *double-declining balance* method. Assets are assigned a depreciation class based on useful life. Generally, long-lived assets require straight-line treatment. Tax laws may allow for aggressive depreciation (double-declining balance method) until it becomes advantageous to use straight-line over the asset's remaining life. If a depreciated asset is sold, proceeds may be taxable, depending on how much depreciation was taken on the asset during its use.

Let us give an example. ABC is considering an expansion. Construction will cost €90,000 and will be depreciated to zero using straight-line depreciation over five years. Earnings before depreciation are expected to be €20,000 in each of the next five years. The firm's tax rate is 20 percent. What are the project's cash flows, ignoring working capital requirements?

Depreciation = €90,000/5 = €18,000. See Table 10.2.

Table 10.2: Calculation of Net Income.

Earnings before depreciation	€ 20.000
-depreciation	18.000
Earnings before taxes	2.000
−Taxes	400
Net income (NI)	1,600

Cash flow = N1 + Depreciation = €1,600 + €18,000 = €19,600

When conducting NPV analysis, there are a number of considerations, one of which is the treatment of working capital. Working capital, or current assets minus current liabilities, is essentially financial resources available to a company for its day-to-day operations. Examples of current assets include cash, inventory, and accounts receivable. Examples of current liabilities include accounts payable and accruals. Short-term financial liabilities such as bank loans are not taken into consideration here, but in the cost of capital.

The changes in net working capital (NWC) associated with a project should be included in NPV calculations. Most projects require additional investments in working capital such as increased inventories and accounts receivable that are typically recovered at a later date. Working capital investments tie up resources that could otherwise be used to generate revenue for the business.[2] The cash flow associated with these investments, like other project cash flows, must be captured in the NPV analysis.

The choice of discount rate (cost of capital) in the calculations of NPV of a project is very important. One can either use reel cost of capital or the nominal cost of capital. It is preferable to use nominal cost of capital because all future cash flows are usually calculated in nominal terms. However, one may choose to use the real cost of capital – in which case, all future cash flows should also be expressed in real terms, which may be time consuming.[3] The important point is consistency.

Let's say that ABC Inc. is planning to expand. The additional capacity will add sales of €5,000,000 per year for the next five years. Variable costs are 80% of sales. Fixed operating costs are €300,000 per year. Additional net working capital of €450,000 will be acquired immediately. It will be liquidated at the end of the fifth year. The initial cost of expansion is €3,000,000. The fixed asset will be depreciated by the straight-line method with no salvage value. The cost of capital of ABC is 14% and it is in the 20% tax bracket. See Table 10.3.

- Prepare the modified income statement and free cash flow statement.
- Calculate the net present value.
- Calculate the internal rate of return.
- Calculate the profitability index.
- Should the expansion be undertaken?

---

2 Forecasting working capital requirement is discussed in Section 12.2.
3 See James C. van Horne, "A Note on Biases in Capital Budgeting Introduced by Inflation," *Journal of Financial and Quantitative Analysis*, vol. VI, Jan. 1971, pp. 653–658; Charles T. Horngren, *Cost Accounting: A Managerial Emphasis*, Fourth Edition, Prentice-Hall, New Jersey, 1977, pp. 388–399.

Table 10.3: A Capital Budgeting Example.

Modified Income Statement	0	1	2	3	4	5
Revenue		€5,000	€5,000	€5,000	€5,000	€5,000
Variable costs		−4,000	−4,000	−4,000	−4,000	−4,000
Fixed costs		−300	−300	−300	−300	−300
Depreciation		-600	−600	−600	−600	−600
Operating profit		100	100	100	100	100
Tax		−20	−20	−20	−20	−20
Net income		€80	€80	€80	€80	€80
FCFF Calculations	**0**	**1**	**2**	**3**	**4**	**5**
Net income		€80	€80	€80	€80	€80
Depreciation		+600	+600	+600	+600	+600
Cost of expansion	−3,000					
Change in NWC	−450					450
Salvage value						
After-tax cash flows	−3,450	680	680	680	680	1,130
Project Evaluation Tools						
Present value factors	1,0000	0,8772	0,7695	0,6750	0,5921	0,5194
Present values	−€3,450	€596	€523	€459	€403	€587
Net present value	−€882					
Internal rate of return	3.49%					
Profitability index	−0.744409					

$$NPV = (680 \times 0.8772) + (680 \times 0.7695) + (680 \times 0.6750) + (680 \times 0.5921)$$
$$+ (1,130 \times 0.5194) - 3,450$$
$$= 596 + 523 + 459 + 403 + 587 - 3,450 = -€882 \, \text{million}$$
$$IRR = 0.0349$$
$$PI = \frac{2,568}{3,450} = 0.7444$$

The expansion should not be undertaken. Since it will add more to costs than to revenues, it will not increase the shareholders' wealth.

10.6 Risk Considerations

Cash flow estimations and risk analysis go hand-in-hand with capital budgeting. Projecting cash flows is the final step in determining whether a project is worthy or not. A new project's cash flows and its capital outlay often are not known with certainty before the project starts. The process of determining the size, timing, and risk of future cash flows is often more art than science; however, success depends on getting it right.

A competitive advantage is the reason that a firm's customers are willing to purchase one company's products or services rather than another firm's products. Firms conduct extensive research on knowing their customers and understanding competitive advantage. New product development is one way to sustain competitive advantage. Cash flow estimation and risk analysis are therefore important for a company to decide what products to offer.

There are two main issues:
- Measurement of risk
- Incorporation of risk into a capital budgeting analysis

Types of Risks

There are three perspectives on risk: stand-alone risk, corporate risk, and market risk. We briefly describe each in the following section.

Stand-Alone Risk (Project Own Risk). This is a project's risk, ignoring the possibility that much of the risk will be diversified away as the project is combined with other projects and assets. Stand-alone risk is easiest to calculate. In this case, start by calculating a divisional cost of capital. Estimate the risk of the project using the techniques discussed here. Use judgment to scale up or down the cost of capital for an individual project relative to the divisional cost of capital.

It is measured by the σ^2 or CV (coefficient of variation) of NPV, IRR, or MIRR:

$$\sigma^2 = \sum_{i=1}^{n} (r_i - E(r_i))^2 \times p_i$$

Corporate Risk (Contribution-to-Firm Risk). This is the amount of risk that the project contributes to the firm as a whole. This measures the project's risk considering the diversification away of risk, but ignores the effects of diversification on the firm's shareholders. Market risk is theoretically best in most situations. However, customers, suppliers, and employees are more affected by corporate risk. Therefore, for creditors, corporate risk is also relevant. It reflects the project's effect on corporate earnings stability.

In this case, the proper measure of risk is projects' (portfolio) variance or standard deviation and is defined as follows:

$$\sigma_p^2 = \sum_{i=1}^{i=n} W_i^2 Var(R_i) + \sum_{\substack{i=1 \\ i< >j}}^{i=n} \sum_{j=1}^{i=n} W_i W_j Cov(r_i.r_j)$$

Market Risk (Systematic Risk). This is the risk of the project from the viewpoint of a well-diversified shareholder. This measure takes into account that some of the risk will be diversified away as the project is combined with the firm's other projects and in addition. Some of the remaining risk will be diversified away by the shareholders as they combine this stock with other stocks in their portfolios. Market risk is theoretically best in most situations. It reflects the project's effect on a well-diversified stock portfolio. It takes account of stockholders' other assets.

In this case, the proper measure of risk is the project's beta, which is defined as:

$$\beta = \frac{Cov(r_i.r_m)}{S_m^2}$$

Theoretically, the only risk of concern to shareholders is systematic risk. Since the project's contribution-to-firm risk affects the probability of bankruptcy for the firm, it is the relevant risk measure. Thus, we need to consider both the project's contribution-to-firm risk and the project's systematic risk.

Incorporating Risk into Capital Budgeting

We know that investors demand higher returns for riskier projects. As the risk of a project increases, the required rate of return is adjusted upward to compensate for the added risk. This *risk-adjusted discount rate* is then used for discounting free cash flows (in the NPV model) or as the benchmark required rate of return in the IRR model.

Measurement of Stand-Alone Risk

There are three widely used methods: sensitivity analysis, scenario analysis, and simulation.

Sensitivity Analysis (*What-If* Analysis). This determines how the distribution of possible net present values or internal rate of return for a particular project is affected by a change in one particular input variable. It shows how changes in a variable, such as unit sales, affect NPV or IRR. Each variable is fixed except one. Change this one variable to see the effect on NPV or IRR.

Weaknesses of sensitivity analysis are:
- It does not reflect diversification.
- It says nothing about the likelihood of change in a variable.
- It ignores the relationships among variables.

Benefits of sensitivity analysis are:
- It gives some idea of stand-alone risk.
- It identifies critical variables.
- It gives some break-even information.

Scenario Analysis. It identifies the range of possible outcomes as the worst, best, and most likely cases. It provides a range of possible outcomes. (See Table 10.4.)

Table 10.4: Inputs for Scenario Analysis.

Case	Probability	NPV
Worst	0.25	€15
Base	0.50	€82
Best	0.25	€148

This method overcomes the problems associated with sensitivity analysis. Three or four scenarios are developed (the best case, the worst case, and so on), then all variables are altered, and the outcome is measured. The problem with this method is that it results in a few point estimates.

$$E(NPV) = 0.25\ (€15) + 0.50\ (€82) + 0.25(€148) = €82$$

$$\sigma_{NPV} = [0.25(€15 - €82)^2 + 0.50(1ro82 - €82)^2 + 0.25(€148 - €82)^2]^{1/2}$$

$$= €47$$

$$CV_{NPV} = \frac{\sigma_{NPV}}{E(NPV)} = \frac{47}{82} = 0.57$$

A project's CV_{NPV} can be compared to that of a project of a different size because those CVs have been adjusted for sizes.

Simulation. *Simulation* involves the process of imitating the performance of the project under evaluation.[4] It is done by randomly selecting observations from each

---

4 For more information on simulation, see Louis Y. Pouliquen, *Risk Analysis in Project Appraisal*, World Bank Staff Occasional Papers, No. 11, The John Hopkins University Press, Baltimore, 1983; James A. Murtha, *Decisions Involving Uncertainty: An Risk Tutorial for the Petroleum Industry*, Houston TX,

of the distributions that affect the outcome of the project and continuing with this process until a representative record of the project's probable outcome is assembled. This is a computerized version of scenario analysis, which usually uses continuous probability distributions. The computer selects values for each variable based on given probability distributions, and NPV and IRR are calculated. The process is repeated many times (1,000 or more). The end result is the probability distribution of NPV and IRR based on a sample of simulated values. The end result is generally shown graphically in Figure 10.1.

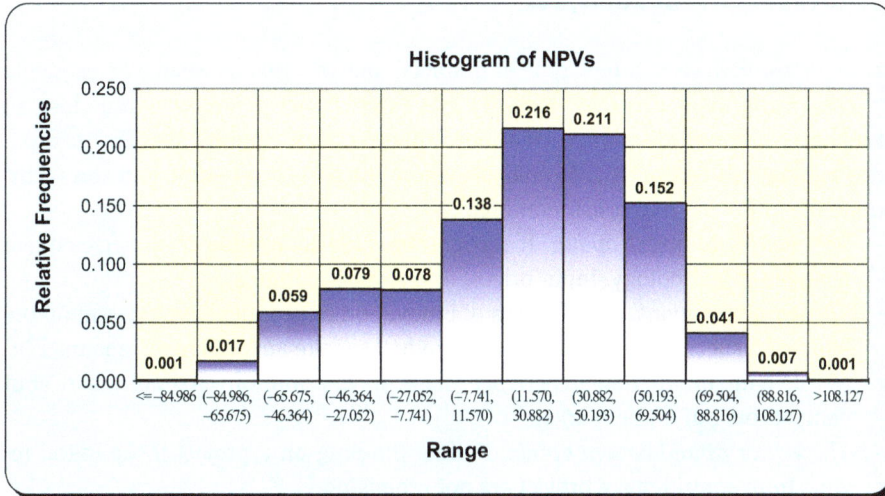

Figure 10.1: Output of a Simulation Study.

How to read this graph? For instance, the probability of NPV being higher than 108.127 is 0.001; the probability of NPV being in the range of 11.570–30.882 is 0.216.

The advantages of simulation analysis are that it:
- Reflects the probability distributions of each input
- Shows range of NPVs, the expected NPV, σ_{NPV}, and the CV_{NPV}
- Gives a sense of possible of real-life results

The disadvantages of simulation are:
- It is difficult to specify probability distributions and correlations.
- If inputs are bad, outputs will be bad, thus misleading managers.

1993; David B. Hertz, "Risk Analysis in Capital Investment," HBR Classic, *Harvard Business Review*, September–October 1979; David B. Hertz and Thomas Howard, *Practical Risk Analysis: An Approach Through Case Histories*, John Wiley and Sons, New York, 1984; and Arman T. Tevfik, *Risk Analizine Giriş*, Alfa, 1997.

Conclusions. Sensitivity scenario and simulation analyses do not provide a decision rule. They do not indicate whether a project's expected return is sufficient to compensate for its risk. Sensitivity scenario and simulation analyses all ignore diversification. Thus, they measure only stand-alone risk, which may not be the most relevant risk in capital budgeting.

CV (coefficient of variation) measures a project's stand-alone risk. High stand-alone risk usually indicates high corporate and market risks.

10.7 Real-Options Analysis

Real-options analysis is a new type of financial analysis that evaluates investments by recognizing the sources of flexibility that can enhance a project's value instead of using traditional discounted cash now analysis. Real options analysis incorporates managerial flexibility into analysis where the NPV stays static and can incorporate the following five considerations:[5]

- *The waiting-to-invest option.* It recognizes value in waiting to better evaluate changes in technology, input prices, or market conditions.
- *The learning options.* Acceleration of innovation or product development on the heels of a successful introduction of product to take advantage of consumer interest, gain production experience, lock up distribution channels, and shut competitors out of the market.
- *The exit or abandonment option.* Pulling the plug on a project if the initial results from a multi-stage project are not promising.
- *The growth-opportunities option.* Investing in future technology or opportunities as laying the groundwork for future growth market expansion and technology development.
- *The flexibility options.* Having the flexibility to, for example, shift production to different plants and switching fuel to less expensive options.

We will focus on the following options in this text:[6]

- The option to delay a decision to a future date. This is a *call option.*
- The option to abandon a project once it has been commenced. This is a *put option.*
- The option to exploit follow-up opportunities which may arise from taking on an initial project. This is also a *call option.*

---

5 Aswath Damodaran, *Applied Corporate Finance*, 1999, op. cit., pp. 196–212.
6 The models are adapted from ACCA, *Advance Financial Management Revision Notes*, ACCA, March/June 2017, pp. 113–118.

There are many methods to calculate the real option value of a project. We will explain it with the Black-Scholes model. Five variables are used in calculating the value of real options using the Black-Scholes option pricing (BSOP) model:
- The underlying asset value S, which is the present value of future cash flows arising from the project.
- The exercise price X, which is the amount paid when call options are exercised or the amount received if the put option is exercised.
- The risk-free rate r, which is normally given or taken from the return offered by the short-term Treasury bill.
- The volatility s, which is the risk attached to the project or underlying asset measured by the standard deviation.[7]
- The time t, which is time in years that is left before the opportunity to exercise ends.

Delaying the Decision to Undertake a Project

A company is considering undertaking a project which will initially cost €35m. The company forecasts the following end-of-year cash flows for the four-year project, as shown in Table 10.5.

Table 10.5: Cash Flows of the Project (€ in millions).

Year	1	2	3	4
Cash flow	20	15	10	5

The cost of capital for the project is 11% and the risk-free rate is 4.5%. The standard deviation of the project is estimated to be 50%.

The NPV without any option to delay the decision is shown in Table 10.6.

Table 10.6: NPV Calculation (€ in millions).

Year	0	1	2	3	4
Cash flow	−35	20	15	10	5
PV (11%)	−35	18.0	12.2	7.3	3.3

NPV = €5.8mm

Suppose that the company does not have to make the decision right now but can wait two years before it needs to make the decision.

The company forecasts the following end of year cash flows (see Table 10.7) for the delayed four-year project.

Table 10.7: New NPV Calculation (€ in millions).

Year	3	4	5	6
Cash flow	20	15	10	5
PV (11%)	14.6	9.9	5.9	2.7

Variables to be used in the Black-Scholes (B-S) model:
Asset value (S) = 14.6 + 9.9 + 5.9 +2.7 = €33.1m
Exercise price (X) = €35m
Exercise date (t) = 2 years
Risk free rate (r) = 4.5%
Volatility (s) = 50%

Input and the results from these values are shown in Table 10.8.

Table 10.8: Input and Output of BSOP (Values are in million euros).

Asset value	33.10
Exercise price	35.00
Exercise date (year)	2
Risk free rate	0.045
Variance	0.250
d1	0.402
N(d1)	0.656
d2	-0.305
N(d2)	0.380
Call value	9.559

As shown in Table 10.9, we add the value of the option to the project NPV to give the strategic NPV.

Table 10.9: Strategic NPV (million euros).

Project NPV	5.8
Value of the real option	9.6
Strategic NPV	15.4.

Based on the facts, the decision to invest should then be based on strategic NPV rather than the project NPV alone.

Exploiting a Follow-on Project

A company is considering a project with a small positive NPV €3m, but there is a possibility of further extension using the technologies developed for the initial project. The extension would involve undertaking a second project in four years' time. Currently, the present value of the cash flows of the second project are estimated to be €90m and its estimated cost in four years is expected to be €140m. The standard deviation of the project cash flows is likely to be 40%, and the risk-free rate of return is currently 5%.

The variables to be used in the B-S model for the second (follow-on) project are as follows:

Asset value (S) = €90m
Exercise price (X) = €140m
Exercise date (t) = 4 years
Risk free rate (r) = 5%
Volatility (s) = %40

Input and the results from these values are shown in Table 10.10.

Now we add the value of the option to the project NPV to give the strategic NPV, as shown in Table 10.11.

The overall value to the company is €23.85m when the projects are considered together. What makes the projects profitable is that a lot could happen to the cash flows, given the high volatility rate in four years' time.

Option to Abandon a Project

ABC Co. is considering a five-year project with an initial cost of €37.5m and has estimated the present values of the project's cash flows, as shown in Table 10.12.

DEF Co. has approached ABC Co. and has offered to buy the entire project for €28m at the start of year three. The risk-free rate of return is 4%. ABC's finance

Table 10.10: Input and Output of BSOP: Follow-on.

Asset value (€m)	90.00
Exercise price (€m)	140.00
Exercise date (year)	4
Risk free rate	0.05
Variance	0.160
d1	0.098
N(d1)	0.539
d2	−0.702
N(d2)	0.241
Call value (€m)	20.85

Table 10.11: Strategic NPV: Follow-on.

Project NPV (€m)	3.00
Value of the real option (€m)	20.85
Strategic NPV (€m)	23.85

Table 10.12: Present Values of the Project (€ in millions).

Year	1	2	3	4	5
PV (11%)	1.50	4.94	9.95	7.06	13.60

director is of the opinion that there are many uncertainties surrounding the project and has assessed that the cash flows vary by a standard deviation as much as 35% because of these uncertainties.

DEF Co.'s offer can be considered a real option for ABC Co. Since it is an offer to sell the project as an abandonment option, a put option value is calculated based on the finance director's assessment of the standard deviation and uses the BOSP model together with the put-call parity formula.

Although ABC Co. will not actually obtain any immediate cash flow from DEF Co.'s offer, the real option computation, as shown in Table 10.13, indicates that the project is worth pursuing because the volatility may result in increases in future values.

Table 10.13: Input and Output of BSOP: Abandonment.

Asset value (€m)	30.600
Exercise price (€m)	28.000
Exercise date (year)	2.000
Risk-free rate	0.040
Standard deviation	35%

Using these figures, the net present value of the project without option value can be estimated as follows: $-37.5 +1.50+4.94+9.95+7.06+13.60 = -€0.50m$.

The asset value of the real option is the sum of the PV of cash flows foregone in years three, four, and five if the options are exercised ($9.95 + 7.06 + 13.6 = €30.6m$).

Input and the results from these values are shown in Table 10.14.

Table 10.14: Output of BSOP: Abandonment.

Variance	0.123
d1	0.589
N(d1)	0.722
d2	0.094
N(d2)	0.537
Call value (€m)	8.204
Put value (€m)	3.451

The net present value of the project with the put option is approximately €3 (3.45 – 0.45). See Table 10.15.

Table 10.15: Strategic NPV: Abandonment.

Project NPV (€m)	−0.45
Value of the real option (€m)	3.45
Strategic NPV (€m)	3.00

If DEF Co.'s offer is not considered, then the project gives a marginal negative net present value.

10.8 Mergers and Acquisitions (M&A)

In a *merger*, one firm absorbs the assets and liabilities of the other firm. The acquiring firm retains its identity. In many cases, control is shared between the two management teams. Transactions are generally conducted on friendly terms. Mergers must comply with applicable laws. Usually, shareholders must approve the merger by a vote.

Traditionally, *acquisition* is the term described in a situation when a larger corporation purchases the assets or stock of a smaller corporation while control remains exclusively with the larger corporation.

In a *consolidation*, an entirely new firm is created. The two firms dissolve.

Often, a tender offer is made to the target firm (friendly) or directly to the shareholders (often a hostile takeover). Transactions that bypass the management are considered hostile, as the target firm's managers are generally opposed to the deal.

The important terms regarding M&A are:

- *Target* is the corporation being purchased.
- *Bidder* is the corporation that makes the purchase, also known as the acquiring firm.
- *Leveraged buyouts (LBO)* is where a buyer uses debt to finance the acquisition of a company. Usually, LBOs are a way to take a public company private or put a company in the hands of the current management.
- *Friendly takeover* is a transaction that takes place with the approval of each firm's management.
- *Hostile takeover* is a transaction that is not approved by the management of the target firm.

The following are the types of mergers:

- *Horizontal mergers* are mergers made between competing companies.
- *Vertical mergers* are mergers made between buyer-seller relationship companies.
- *Conglomerate mergers* are mergers where merged firms are in different sectors or in different geographical areas.

The Reasons of M&A

There are three main reasons for mergers and acquisitions: synergy, growth, and diversification.

Synergy. The most used word in M&A is synergy, which implies that by combining business activities, performance will increase and costs will decrease. Essentially, a business will attempt to merge with another business that has complementary strengths and weaknesses.

$$\text{Market value(A)} + \text{Market value(B)} < \text{Market value(AB)}$$

There are three sources of synergy:
- *Revenue synergy*. Market power, the larger company will attract more customers (more brand awareness), complementary products and reduce competition.
- *Cost synergy*. A large company will be able to get quantity discounts, reduce costs due to elimination of overlapping fixed assets, and departments.
- *Financial synergy*. A large company will be able to borrow at a lower cost, get higher returns for its portfolio.

Growth. Mergers can give the acquiring company an opportunity to increase its market share. Usually, these are called *horizontal mergers*. For example, a beer company may choose to buy out a smaller competing brewery, enabling the smaller company to make more beer and sell more to its brand-loyal customers.

Diversification. "Don't put all your eggs in one basket" is a famous maxim. Current finance literature seriously questions the merits of this reasoning. Why does the management know how to achieve diversification better than the shareholders? It is usually the case that shareholders can diversify much more easily than can a corporation. Individuals can easily diversify by buying shares in mutual funds.

Merger Financing

There are three ways of financing:
- *Cash transaction*. The receipt of cash for shares by shareholders in the target company.
- *Share transaction*. The offer of shares of acquiring a company or a combination of cash and shares to the target company's shareholders.
- *Going private transaction (issuer bid)*. A special form of acquisition where the purchaser already owns a majority stake in the target company.

Some Evidence on the Winners and Losers

The findings can be summarized as follows:[8]
- Shareholders of target companies almost always gain, because most mergers involve a premium being paid over the target firm's pre-merger value.

---

8 George P. Diacogiannis, *Financial Management: A Modeling Approach Using Spreadsheets*, McGraw-Hill, 1994, pp. 684–685; Glen Arnold, *The Handbook of Corporate Finance*, FT Financial Times, 2005, pp. 272–273.

- Mergers have little or no positive impact on the market values of bidding firms. The bidding firm's share price will often fall immediately after a merger is announced.
- The real winners are the lawyers, accountants, and investment dealers who make large fees from assisting the bidding or target firms.

Accounting in M&A

There are two accounting treatments for mergers:
- *Purchase method.* The assets of the target firm are revalued to their fair market values and any difference between the purchase price and the revalued assets is recorded as *goodwill*. In comparison to the pooling of interests method, the purchase method usually results in lower earnings per share because of higher levels of amortization on capital assets (because of the restated values).
- *Pooling of interests method.* The pre-merger assets and liabilities of the two firms are simply added together without any revaluation to form the post-merger balance sheet. The pooling of interests method tends to exaggerate the rates of return on assets because the assets on the merged balance sheet are valued at their historical values rather than market values. This treatment is banned in International Financial Reporting Standards.
- An example of an acquisition is presented in Tables 10.16–10.18.

ABC Inc. plans to acquire NMP Inc. The pre-merger balance-sheets are shown in Table 10.16.

Table 10.16: B-S of ABC (€ in millions) and B-S of NMP (€ in millions).

Current assets	€400	Current assets	€300
Fixed assets	900	Fixed assets	400
Total assets	1,300	Total assets	700
Current liabilities	200	Current liabilities	100
Debt	500	Debt	250
Net worth	600	Net worth	350
Total liabilities and net worth	1,300	Total liabilities and net worth	700

Now, let us construct post-merger balance sheets using both the purchase and the pooling of interest methods. Assume NMP fixed assets are undervalued by €80 million and that ABC pays €850 million for NMP. See Tables 10.17 and 10.18.

Table 10.17: Purchase Method (€ in millions).

Current assets	€700
Fixed assets*	1,380
Goodwill**	70
Total assets	2,150

Current liabilities	300
Debt	750
Net worth	1,100
Total liabilities and net worth	2,150

*NMP's fixed assets are restated from €400M to €480M.
**Purchase price (€850M – NMP's current assets and
restated fixed assets.

Table 10.18: Pooling of Interest Method (€ in millions).

Current assets	€700
Fixed assets	1,300
Goodwill	0
Total assets	2,000
Current liabilities	300
Debt	750
Net worth	950
Total liabilities and net worth	2,000

Valuing Synergy

A merger and acquisitions decision is similar to a capital budgeting decision. In order to value a target firm, one needs to know valuation, which is discussed in Chapter 5. We will only value synergy here. A procedure for valuing synergy is as follows:[9]

9 Aswath Damodaran, *Investment Valuation: Tools and Techniques for Determining the Value of Any Asset*, Third Edition, Wiley, 2012, pp. 702–739.

- The firms involved in the merger are valued independently, by discounting expected cash flows to each firm at the weighted average cost of capital for that firm.
- The value of the combined firm, with no synergy, is obtained by adding the values obtained for each firm in the first step.
- The effects of synergy are built into expected growth rates and cash flows, and the combined firm is revalued with synergy.

Value of Synergy = Value of the combined firm, with synergy – Value of the combined firm, without synergy

We will develop a model for operating and financial synergy. The general inputs of the model are as follows:

Risk-Free Rate: 2.50%

Equity Risk Premium: 4.00%

Financial inputs for bidding (GEM) and target (NEF) companies are shown in Tables 10.19 and 10.20.

Table 10.19: Financial Data.

	Bidding Co.	Target Co.
Number of Stock (in million)	250.00	100.00
Current Share Price	€ 11.75	€ 15.00
Financial Debts (€ in million)	300.00	700.00

Table 10.20: Data for Bidder and Target at t-1 period (€ in millions).

	Bidding Co.	Target Co.	Combined
Beta	1.20	0.80	1.02
Pre-Tax Cost of Debt	5.0%	5.0%	5.0%
Revenues	1.000.0	500.0	1.500.0
EBIT/Revenues	30.0%	40.0%	33.3%
Tax Rate	20.0%	20.0%	20.0%
Depreciation	50.0	25.0	75.0
Capital Expenditure	50.0	30.0	80.0
NWC Investment	40.0	30.0	70.0

Table 10.20 (continued)

	Bidding Co.	Target Co.	Combined
Length of Growth Period	5	5	5
Pre-Tax Return on Capital	15.0%	20.0%	17.6%
Reinvestment Rate	70.00%	75.00%	72.55%

Table 10.21: New Inputs (€ in millions).

New EBIT/Revenues	40.0%
New Depreciation	70.0
New Capital Expenditure	70.0
New NWC Investment	50.0

Data for bidder (GEM) and target (NEF) were given as follows:

The growth period of both firms is about 5 years. The beta of the combined firms will be 1.02. The cost of debt is 5%, while long-term Treasury bond yield is 2.5% and equity risk premium is 4%.

A merger is believed to increase New EBIT/Revenues to 40%, and the revenue growth rate will be higher than before due to the reinvestment rate. The cost of capital will decrease as the combined beta is lower. Some operating developments are summarized in Table 10.21.

Using this data, answer the following:
- Value of GEM as a stand-alone company
- Value of the two companies without synergy
- Value of the two companies with synergy
- Determine the value of synergy

According to these inputs, the combined firm's FCFF is calculated as shown in Table 10.22.

$$\text{FCFF} = \text{Revenue} \times \text{EBIT/Revenue} \times (1-t) + \text{Depreciation} - \text{New Capital Expenditure} - \text{New NWC Investment}$$
$$\text{FCFF} = 1,500 \times 0.40 \times (1-0.20) + 70 - 70 - 50 = €430\text{m}$$

As shown in Table 10.23, it is understood that they are undervalued by the market. Let us now calculate the synergy gain:

$$\text{Synergy gain} = 7,613.79 - 2,752.57 - 2,874.36 = €1,986.86 \text{ million}$$

Table 10.22: New Inputs for Valuation of Companies.

	Bidding Co.	Target Co.	Combined
FCCF (million €)	200.0	125.0	430.0
Debt/Capital Ratio	9.3%	31.8%	20.8%
Cost of Equity	7.3%	5.7%	6.6%
After-tax Cost of Debt Capital	4.0%	4.0%	4.0%
WACC	7.0%	5.2%	6.0%
After-tax Return on Capital	12.0%	16.0%	14.0%
Reinvestment Rate	70.0%	75.0%	72.6%
Expected Growth Rate	8.4%	12.0%	10.2%

Table 10.23: Valuation of Companies.

	Bidding Co.	Target Co.	Combined
PV of FCFF in high growth	249.63	151.62	530.56
Terminal Value	3,509.55	3,501.39	9,493.74
Enterprise Value	2,752.57	2,874.36	7,613.79

In mergers and acquisitions (M&A), the *share exchange ratio* measures the number of shares the acquiring company has to issue for each individual share of the target firm. For M&A deals that include shares as part of the consideration (compensation) for the deal, the share exchange ratio is an important metric. Deals can be all cash, all shares, or a mix of the two. In the event of an all-cash merger transaction, the exchange ratio is not a useful metric.

$$\text{Offer Price} = \text{Target share price} \times (1 + \text{Takeover premium})$$

$$= 15 \times (1 + 0.3531) = €\,20.30$$

The formula for calculating the exchange ratio is:

$$\text{Exchange ratio} = \text{Offer Price for the target's shares}/\text{Acquirer's share price}$$

$$= 20.30/11.75 = 1.7274$$

Number of shares to be issued for the target = Share exchange ratio × Number of shares of the target

$$= 1.7274 \times 100 = 172.74$$
$$\text{New Total Number of Shares} = 250 + 172{,}74 = 422.74 \text{ million}$$
$$\text{Equity Value} = \text{Value of Firms (Combined)} -$$
$$\text{Financial Debts (GEM)} - \text{Financial Debts (NEF)}$$
$$= 7{,}613.79 - 300 - 700 = 6{,}613.79$$
$$\text{Value Per Share} = 6{,}613.79/422.74 = \text{€}15.65$$
$$\text{Wealth of Bidder's Shareholders} = 250 \times \text{€}15.65 = \text{€}3{,}911.30$$
$$\text{Wealth of Target's Shareholders} = 172.75 \times \text{€}15.65 = \text{€}2{,}702.49$$

In a different distribution, the wealth of each company shareholders will be different. If all synergy gain is distributed to the target's shareholders, the wealth increase of target's shareholders will be huge.

10.9 Summary

Capital budgeting (investment decision) is the process of identifying, evaluating, and implementing a firm's investment opportunities.

To evaluate projects, six methods of capital budgeting are widely used: net present value (NPV), internal rate of return (IRR), profitability index, payback period, accounting rate of return, and modified internal rate of return.

The stand-alone principle features isolating a project from the rest of the company and ensures that the analysis focuses solely on the project's incremental cash flows.

The first step in the financial analysis of a capital budgeting proposal is the construction of year-by-year projected balance sheets and income statements for the project. Cash flow statements (free cash flow to firm) can be constructed from the projected balance sheets and income statements.

Cash flow estimations and risk analysis go hand-in-hand with capital budgeting. There are three perspectives on risk: stand-alone risk (project stand-alone risk), corporate risk (contribution-to-firm risk), market risk (systematic risk).

There are three widely used methods in measuring stand-alone risk: sensitivity analysis, scenario analysis, and simulation.

Real-option analysis is a new type of financial analysis that evaluates investments by recognizing the sources of flexibility that can enhance a project's value instead of using traditional discounted cash now analysis.

One firm absorbs the assets and liabilities of the other firm in a merger. The acquiring firm retains its identity. Traditionally, acquisition is the term described in a situation when a larger corporation purchases the assets or stock of a smaller corporation, while control remained exclusively with the larger corporation. In a consolidation, an entirely new firm is created. The two firms dissolve. A merger and acquisitions decision is similar to a capital budgeting decision. The valuation of M&A is also similar to firm valuation.

11 The Cost of Capital, Capital Structure, and Distributions to Stockholders

11.1 Introduction

Management must determine the financing structure that minimizes the firm's overall financial costs or its cost of capital. This chapter reviews some of the tools managers can use in the art of selecting a capital structure. Once the financing mix is selected, the firm's cost of capital – the return it should earn on its average risk projects – can be determined. The objective here again is to maximize the value of the firm. We also discuss several dividend theories such as *Modigliani and Miller (M-M) dividend irrelevance theory, bird-in-the-hand theory*, and *tax preference theory*.

11.2 Capital Structure

Before financial managers can estimate the cost of capital, two important pieces of information are required:
-   The cost of each financing source
-   The appropriate financing mix needed to fund the company

With this information, one can calculate the firm's *weighted average cost of capital* (WACC), which is the minimum required rate of return on a capital budget project. The capital structure of a firm is its mix of debt and equity. Capital structure determines the proportion of debt and equity used to estimate cost of capital. As shown in Figure 11.1, the target capital structure is important because:
-   It determines the proportion of debt and equity used to estimate a firm's cost of capital, or the minimum acceptable rate of return on a project; and,
-   The firm's optimum debt/equity mix – the proportionate use of debt or equity that minimizes the firm's cost of capital – helps the firm to maximize shareholder wealth.

A non-optimal capital structure with either too much or too little debt leads to higher financing costs; as a result, the firm may have to reject some capital budgeting projects that could have increased shareholder wealth under a more favorable financing mix. Note that a lower WACC results in higher net present values, which should lead to an increase in shareholder wealth.

In general, smaller firms use relatively more debt than larger firms. Smaller firms have a higher relative cost of equity when compared with the larger firms since the larger firms have better access to capital markets.

https://doi.org/10.1515/9783110705355-011

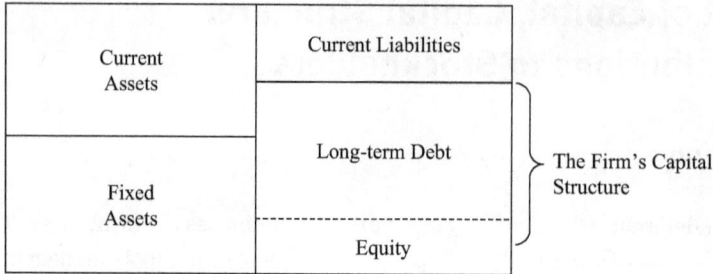

Figure 11.1: The Balance Sheet.

11.3 Required Rate of Return and the Cost of Capital

The minimum acceptable rate of return on a project is the return that it generates sufficient cash flow (expected return) to pay investors. The minimum rate of return is a weighted average of the firm's various sources of capital.

A firm's current financing costs determine its current cost of capital. We will look at costs of various sources.

Cost of Debt

The cost of debt for a firm can be determined by several methods:
- A review of the *yield to maturity* (YTM) of the appropriate-rated bonds can provide an estimate of the firm's current borrowing costs.
- If the firm has publicly traded debt, there is a public market price and yield that can be used to estimate the firm's current cost of debt.
- The firm can seek long-term debt financing from a bank or consortium of banks, which will indicate the estimated interest rate that the firm will pay on the loan.

The after-tax cost of debt, k_d, is:

$$k_d = YTM\,(1-t)$$

where t is the firm's marginal tax rate.

The cost to the firm of preferred stock financing, k_p, is:

$$k_p = D_p/(P-F_p)$$

where P is price per share, F_p is flotation cost per share, and D_p is the dividend per share.

Cost of Equity

These equations hold because cash flows are fixed. With common equity, however, this is not the case.

There are two ways to estimate the cost of common equity (k_e) or the cost of retained earnings (k_{re}):
- Using a modification of the security market line equation
- Using the constant growth dividend model

The Security Market Line (Capital Asset Pricing Model)

The security market line equation is: $E(R_i) = r_f + \beta_i\, E(r_M - r_f)$

where $E(R_i)$ is the expected return on the capital asset, r_f is the risk-free return, β_i is a measure of responsiveness of return of a stock to the market return, r_M is the market return, and $E(r_M - r_f)$ is the expected equity risk premium.

In practice,
- Government security rates are used as the risk-free rate
- Historical risk premiums are used for the risk premium
- Betas are estimated by regressing stock returns against market returns

On a risk-free asset, the actual return is equal to the expected return. Therefore, there is no variance around the expected return. For an investment to be risk-free, it has to have no default risk and no reinvestment risk.

The risk premium (r_M-r_f) is the premium that investors demand for investing in an average risk investment relative to the risk-free rate. A simple approach will be described as follows:
- Calculate geometric average returns on a stock index during the period.
- Calculate geometric average returns on a riskless security over the period.
- Calculate the difference between the two averages and use it as a premium looking forward.

The estimate for the cost of equity (k_e) is:

$$k_e = E(r_i) = r_f + \beta_i\, E(r_M - r_f)$$

Let us calculate the cost of equity for company ABC stock using the capital asset pricing model:

risk-free rate, $r_f = 0.05$, beta, $\beta_i = 1.5$, and market return, $r_M = 0.10$.

$$k_e = 0.05 + 1.5\,(0.10 - 0.05) = 0.125 = 12.5\%$$

Dividend Model. The constant growth dividend model, discussed in Chapter 5, is used to calculate the cost of equity.

The price, in this case, is:

$$\hat{P}_0 = \frac{D_0(1+g)}{k_e - g}$$

Solving this equation for the cost of equity;

$$k_e = \frac{D_0}{\hat{P}_0} + g$$

where $\hat{P}_0$ is the stock price, D_0 is the dividend in period 0 and g is the annual growth rate of the dividends.

The cost of new common stock is more expensive than that of retained earnings because of flotation costs. *Flotation costs* include accounting, legal, printing, and commission costs.

$$k_e = \frac{D_0}{(\hat{P}_0 - f)} + g$$

where f represents the flotation cost, expressed as a fraction of the issue price.

Why is the cost of internal equity from reinvested earnings cheaper than the cost of issuing new common stock?

- When a company issues new common stock, they also have to pay flotation costs to the underwriter.
- Issuing new common stock may send a negative signal to the capital markets, which may depress stock price.

Let us estimate the cost of new common equity: price of stock, P_0=€50, dividend, D_0=€4.20, growth rate, g=5%, and flotation cost, f=15%.

=4.20(1.05)/(50(1−0.15) +5% = 10.38 + 0.05 = 15.38%

11.4 Weighted Average Cost of Capital

A firm's *weighted average cost of capital* (WACC) is the minimum required rate of return on its capital budgeting projects:

$$\text{WACC} = w_d V_d + w_p k_p + w_e k_e$$

where the weights of debt, preferred equity, and common equity in the firm's capital structure are w_d, w_p, and w_e, respectively, and the firm k_d, k_p, and k_e are the firm's cost of debt, preferred, and common equity, respectively. Keep in mind that the weights must sum to 1.0.

There are two ways to measure the mix of debt and equity in the firm's capital structure:

- Using target weights of debt and equity in the firm's balance sheet.
- Using the market values of the firm's debt and equity.

Financial theory favors the second approach. Assume that you want to buy a company with no financial debt. This is in a way an investment decision. If the company is a profitable one, you will probably pay more than book value of equity. Your cost of capital will depend on what you pay (market value), not on historical value.

The composite WACC reflects the risk of an average project undertaken by the firm. Different divisions may have different risks. The division's WACC should be adjusted to reflect the division's risk and capital structure. Therefore, the composite WACC should not be used for each division.

Procedures used to determine the risk-adjusted cost of capital for a particular division are:

- Estimate the cost of capital that the division would have if it were a stand-alone firm.
- This requires estimating the division's beta, cost of debt, and capital structure.

The methods for estimating beta for a division or a project are:

- *Pure play.* Find several publicly traded companies exclusively in the project's business. Use the average of their betas as proxy for the project's beta. But it may be hard to find such companies.
- *Accounting beta.* Run the regression between the project's ROA (return on asset) and a market index ROA. Accounting betas are correlated (0.5–0.6) with market betas. But normally, one can't get data on new projects' ROAs before the capital budgeting decision has been made.

11.5 Determining the Optimal Capital Structure

The optimal capital structure is the one that maximizes the value or the company. Also, that same capital structure minimizes the WACC.

They are basically two methods of determining optimal capital structure:[1]

- *The cost of capital approach.* The optimal debt ratio is the one that minimizes the cost of capital for a firm.

---

[1] Damodaran, *Applied Corporate Finance*, 1999, op. cit., p. 163.

– *The sector approach*. The optimal debt ratio is the one that brings the firm close to its peer group in terms of a financing mix.

To estimate the optimal capital structure, we need information on how capital structure affects the costs of debt and equity.

Modigliani-Miller (MM)

The Modigliani-Miller model (MM) proves under a very restrictive set of assumptions – there is no corporate tax and no bankruptcy cost – that a firm's value is unaffected by its financing mix.[2] Therefore,

$V_L = V_U$, where;

$$V_u = \frac{EBIT}{k_{eU}}$$

V_L = value of a leveraged firm,
V_U = value of an unleveraged firm,
k_{eU} = cost of capital for an unleveraged firm.
EBIT = earnings before interest and taxes

Therefore, capital structure is irrelevant. Any increase in return on equity (ROE) resulting from financial leverage is exactly offset by the increase in risk, so WACC is constant.

Corporate tax laws favor debt financing over equity financing. With corporate taxes, the benefits of financial leverage exceed the risks – more EBIT goes to investors and less to taxes when leverage is used.[3]

MM show that: $V_L = V_U + tD$
where

$$V_u = \frac{EBIT \ (1-t)}{k_{eU}}$$

If t=20%, then every euro (€) of debt adds €0.20 of extra value to firm. Under MM with corporate taxes, the firm's value increases continuously as more debt is used.

MM theory ignores bankruptcy (financial distress) costs, which increase as more leverage is used.

At low leverage levels, tax benefits outweigh bankruptcy costs. At high levels, bankruptcy costs outweigh tax benefits. An optimal capital structure exists that balances these costs and benefits.

---

2 M. H. Miller and F. Modiglianni, "The Cost of Capital, Corporation Finance and the Theory of Investment," *American Economic Review*, No. 38, 1958, pp. 261–269.
3 M. H. Miller and F. Modiglianni, "Taxes and Cost of Capital: A Correction," *American Economic Review*, No. 53, 1963, pp. 433–443; M. H. Miller, "Debt and Taxes," *Journal of Finance*, Vol. 32, 1977, pp. 261–276; S. C. Myers, "The Capital Structure Puzzle," *Journal of Finance*, July 1984, pp. 575–592.

The New Model: Revised MM Model

Discussions with its bankers indicate that ABC can borrow different amounts, but the more it borrows, the higher the cost of its debt. See Table 11.1. Note that the percentages are based on market values.

Table 11.1: Interest Rates for ABC with Different Capital Structures.

Debt Cost Schedule

Percent financed with debt (w_d)	Percent financed with equity (w_e)	Cost of debt (r_d)
0%	100%	8.0%
10%	90%	8.0%
20%	80%	8.1%
30%	70%	8.5%
40%	60%	9.0%
50%	50%	11.0%
60%	40%	14.0%

Hamada developed his equation by combining the CAPM with the *Modigliani-Miller* model.[4] We use the model to determine beta at different amount of financial leverage, and then use the betas associated with different debt ratios to find the cost of equity associated with those debt ratios. The Hamada equation is as follows:

$$b_L = b_U \times [1 + (1 - t) \times (D/E)]$$

where b_L is the leveraged beta, b_U is the beta that the firm would have if it used no debt, t is the marginal tax rate, D is the market value of the debt, and E is the market value of the equity.

In Table 11.2, we apply the Hamada equation to ABC, given its unlevered beta and tax rate.

As the table shows, beta rises with financial leverage. With beta specified, we can determine the effects of leverage on the cost of equity and then on the WACC. Here we assume that the risk-free rate is 6% and the market risk premium is 6%. We also assume that ABC pays out all of its earnings as dividends, hence earnings

---

4 Robert Hamada, "Portfolio Analysis, Market Equilibrium, and Corporate Finance," *Journal of Finance*, March 1969.

Table 11.2: Calculation of Leveraged Beta.

bU		1
Tax rate		20%
W_d	D/E	B_1
0%	0.00	1.0000
10%	0.11	1.0889
20%	0.25	1.2000
30%	0.43	1.3429
40%	0.67	1.5333
50%	1.00	1.8000
60%	1.50	2.2000

and dividends are not expected to grow. Therefore, its stock price can be found by using the perpetuity equation:

Price = Dividends/k_e.

Risk-free rate, r_f = 6%

Market risk premium, R_M = 6%

Free Cash Flow, FCFF[5] = €40,000

In order to determine ABC's optimal capital structure, the following calculations are done Tables 11.3 and 11.4:

Table 11.3: Inputs for Cost of Capital.

Unleveraged beta	1.000
Tax rate	20.00%
Risk-free rate	6.00%
Expected market return	12.00%
FCFF/EBIT	40,000
Growth rate in FCFF	0
Leveraged beta	1.400

---

5 Or EBIT.

Table 11.4: Calculation of Optimal Capital Structure.

D/A	D/E	Leveraged Beta, β_L	kd	Kd (1-t)	Ke	Wd×kd × (1-t)	We×Ke	WACC	EBIT× (1-T)	Firm Value	Weight of Debt
0.0000	0.0000	1.0000	0.0800	0.0640	0.1200	0.0000	0.1200	0.1200	32,000	266,667	
0.1000	0.1111	1.0889	0.0800	0.0640	0.1253	0.0064	0.1128	0.1192	32,000	268,456	
0.2000	0.2500	1.2000	0.0810	0.0648	0.1320	0.0130	0.1056	0.1186	32,000	269,906	0.200
0.3000	0.4286	1.3429	0.0850	0.0680	0.1406	0.0204	0.0984	0.1188	32,000	269,360	
0.4000	0.6667	1.5333	0.0900	0.0720	0.1520	0.0288	0.0912	0.1200	32,000	266,667	
0.5000	1.0000	1.8000	0.1100	0.0880	0.1680	0.0440	0.0840	0.1280	32,000	250,000	
0.6000	1.5000	2.2000	0.1400	0.1120	0.1920	0.0672	0.0768	0.1440	32,000	222,222	

Notes:
- The D/E ratio is calculated as: $D/E = w_d / (1 - w_d)$.
- The interest rates are shown in Table 11.3. The tax rate is 20%.
- The beta is estimated using Hamada's formula.
- The cost of equity is estimated using the CAPM formula: $k_{re} = E(r_i) = r_f + \beta_i (r_M - r_f)$ where the risk-free rate is 6% and the market risk premium is 6%.
- The value of the firm is calculated using the *free cash flow to firm* (FCFF) valuation formula. It is modified to reflect the fact that ABC has zero growth:

$$V = FCFF_0 (1 + g) / (WACC - g).$$

Since ABC has zero growth, it requires no investment in capital, and its FCFF is equal to its NOPAT (Net Operating Profit After Tax). Using data in Table 11.4:

$$FCF = NOPAT + Investment\ in\ capital = EBIT(1 - t) - 0$$

$$= 40,000\,(1 - 0.2) = 32,000.$$

In this case, the formula reduces to the following:
$$V = FCFF_0 / WACC.$$

We see that the stock price is maximized and the WACC is minimized if the firm finances with 20% debt and 80% equity. This is the *optimal capital structure*.

We can graph (Figures 11.2 and 11.3) the key data in Table 11.4.

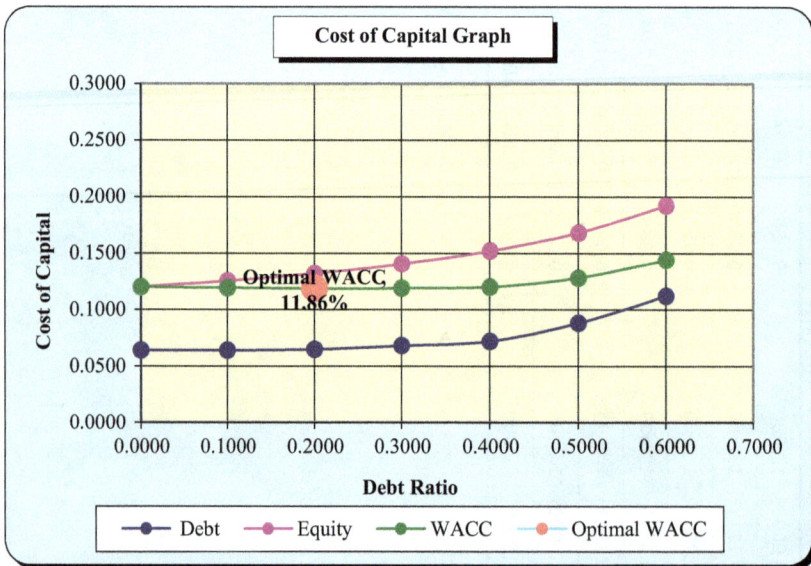

Figure 11.2: Cost of Capital Graph.

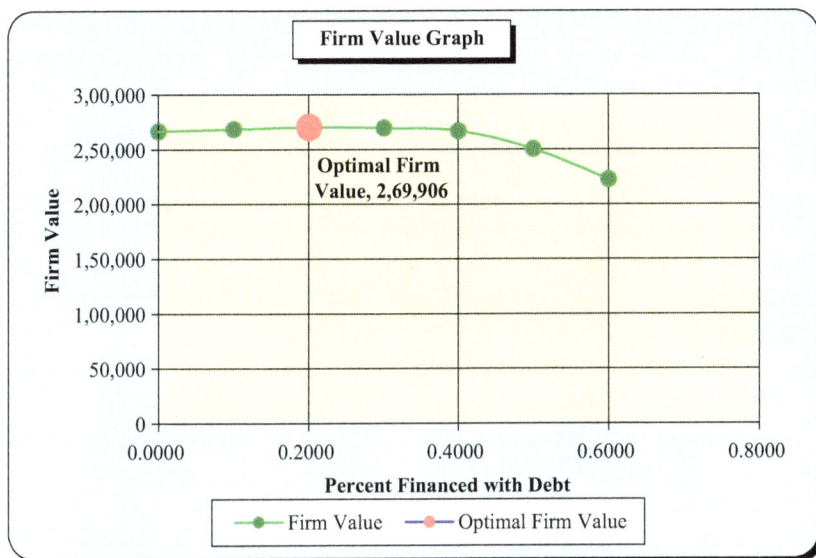

Figure 11.3: Firm Value Graph.

The next step in the financing mix decision is as follows:[6]
- *Deciding how quickly or gradually the firm should move to its optimal capital structure.* Changing debt ratio quickly can be done as follows. To decrease the debt ratio, sell operating assets and use the cash to buy back stock or pay a dividend or a special dividend. To increase the debt ratio, borrow money and buy back stock, or pay a large special dividend. The complication of changing debt ratios over time is that firm value is itself a moving target.
- *After deciding the speed of movement to optimize capital structure, design the right kind of financing to use in making this adjustment.* The objective in designing debt is to make the cash flows on debt match up as closely as possible with the cash flows that the firm makes on its assets. By doing so, we reduce our risk of default, increase debt capacity, and increase firm value.

11.6 Distributions to Shareholders: Dividends and Repurchases

If there are not enough investments that earn the hurdle rate, the firm should return the cash to stockholders. The form of returns, dividends, and stock buybacks will

---

6 For detailed information, see Aswath Damodaran, *Applied Corporate Finance*, 1999, op. cit., pp. 305–348.

depend upon the stockholders' characteristics. The objective, again, is to maximize the value of the firm.

The Basics

The most common way that companies pay dividends is in cash. Public companies usually pay regular cash dividends once a year or four times a year (advance payments). Paying a cash dividend reduces the cash balance and the retained earnings accounts on the balance sheet.

Another form of dividend payment is in the form of stock, known as a stock dividend. This merely increases the number of shares outstanding.

Timeline regarding the payment process of dividend payments is shown in Table 11.5.

Table 11.5: Dates in Dividend Payment Process.

Thursday April 15	Wednesday April 28	Friday April 30	Monday April 16
Declaration date	Ex-dividend date	Record date	Payment

- *Declaration date* marks the date of announcement by the board of directors that a dividend will be paid. The declaration date specifies the date that dividends will be paid, as well as the record date.
- *Record date* is the date when the firm prepares a list of all individuals and organizations believed to be stockholders as of the record date. All of these investors will actually receive the dividend.
- *Ex-dividend date* is the first business day at which a buyer of the stock is not entitled to receive the recently declared dividend. The ex-dividend date is typically two business days before the date of record.
- *Payment date* is the date of mailing dividend checks to the shareholders of record.

Dividend policy can be measured by three tools:
- *Dividend per share.* Amount of dividend for one share owned.
- *Dividend yield.* It is measured by *Annual dividends per share / Price per share*. This is one part of stock return. *Value investing* style often focuses on holding stocks with high dividend yield.
- *Dividend payout ratio.* It is measured by *Dividends per share / Earnings per share = 1 – Retention ratio*.

The return on a stock (r_s) consists of two elements: dividends and capital gains. In rate of return terms, the total return consists of a dividend yield plus a capital gains yield, the g (growth rate in dividends).

$$r_s = (D_1/P_0) + g$$

This equation can be transformed into the constant growth stock valuation model:

$$P_0 = D_1/(r_s - g)$$

If a company increases its dividend payout, that raises the numerator of the stock price equation, D_1, and that tends to increase the stock price. However, raising the dividend will lower the amount of earnings available for reinvestment. Thus, it will lower the growth rate which will tend to lower the stock price since, $g = (1 - \text{payout}) \times$ ROE. Then, if the payout were to increase to 100%, or 1.0, then g would drop to zero. Thus, increasing the dividend payout has two opposing effects on a firm's stock price. Management must then seek to find the payout policy that balances these two forces and thereby maximizes the stock price.

Dividend Theories

There are several dividend theories. Some of them are discussed and illustrated as follows:[7]

- *M-M Dividend Irrelevance Theory.* Proposed by *Merton Miller* and *Franco Modigliani*,[8] this theory argues that dividend policy has no effect on either the price of a firm's stock or on its cost of capital. Firm value, they claim, is determined by basic earning power and business risk. Therefore, a firm's value is based only on fundamental factors. Dividend policy is *irrelevant.*
- *Bird-in-the-Hand Theory.* Others, including *Myron Gordon*, who developed the *dividend stock valuation model*, disagreed with M-M. They argued that investors regard capital gains as being riskier than dividends, hence that a dollar of dividends contributes more to stock price than a dollar of retained earnings. According to this theory, the cost of capital would decrease, and the stock price would increase as dividend payout is increased.
- *Tax Preference Theory.* Still others argue that tax factors cause investors to prefer capital gains to dividends due to higher tax on dividends. First, long-term capital gains are taxed at a lower rate than dividends. In addition, capital gains are not taxed until the gain is realized. Due to the time value of money, taxes

---

7 For further information, see Michael C. Ehrhardt and Eugene F. Brigham, *Corporate Finance: A Focused Approach*, Fourth Edition, South-Western, 2011, pp. 564–570.
8 M. H. Miller and F. Modiglianni, "Dividend Policy, Growth and Valuation of Shares," *Journal of Business*, No. 34, 1961, pp. 411–433.

paid in the future will have a lower effective cost than those paid today. Finally, if a stock is held until death, no capital gains tax is due at all. Because of these tax advantages, investors should prefer low payout.

- *The Theories Conflict.* The three theories conflict with one another. So, managers get no clear signal from academic theories as to what their dividend payouts should be. There is some truth in each of the theories. Some investors undoubtedly prefer more dividends, some prefer fewer dividends (and more growth), and others are indifferent. This may lead managers to adopt the majority-held payout policy. Unfortunately, empirical tests have not been able to determine the preferred policy.

Illustration of the Effects of Dividend Policy

In this illustration,[9] we make several assumptions. First, the firm has a current stock price of €6, which is also the book value. Second, its ROE is 15%. So, EPS = €6(0.15) = €0.90. Third, the firm currently pays out 0% of its dividends. So DPS = €0.0. Fourth, the ROE is expected to remain constant in the future. So, its sustainable growth rate (g) is determined as the product of the ROE and the fraction of earnings retained, or (1.0–Payout %). Currently with payout = 0%, g = ROE (1.0–Payout) = 15% (1.0–0.0) = 15%. So, inputs are:

Book value = stock price = 6

ROE = 15%

EPS = 0, 90

Payout % = 0% – 100%

Alternative payout policies for €0,90 of EPS are shown in Table 11.6.

Table 11.6: Alternative Payout Policies.

% payout	% retain	DPS	g*
0%	100%	€0.00	15.0%
50%	50%	€0.45	7.5%
100%	0%	€0.90	0.0%

* g = ROE(1-Payout)

---

9 Adapted from Ehrhardt and Brigham, *Corporate Finance*, op. cit., pp. 564–570.

If MM are correct and investors are indifferent, then the firm's stock will sell for €30 regardless of its dividend policy. On the other hand, if Gordon is correct, the stock price will fall (from €30) as the payout is decreased. If the tax preference people are correct, it will rise with lower payouts.

Table 11.7 shows three possible outcomes.

Table 11.7: Possible Outcomes (only one of which can be true).

Payment	Likely Results								
	Bird in Bush			MM			Tax		
	P_0	D_1/P_0	k_s	P_0	D_1/P_0	k_s	P_0	D_1/P_0	k_s
0%	€ 6.00	0.00%	15.0%	€ 6.00	0.0%	15.0%	€ 6.00	0.0%	15.0%
50%	€ 7.00	6.43%	13.9%	€ 6.00	7.5%	15.0%	€ 5.00	9.0%	16.5%
100%	€ 8.00	11.25%	11.3%	€ 6.00	15.0%	15.0%	€ 4.00	22.5%	22.5%

The graph of these results is presented in Figure 11.4.

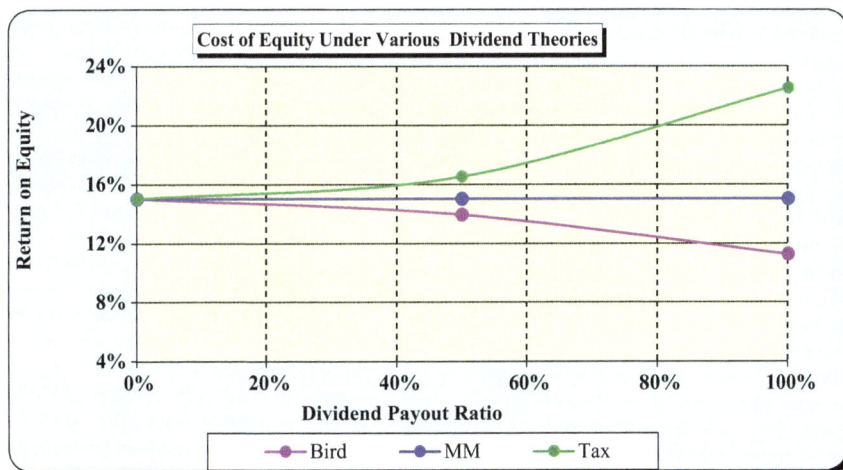

Figure 11.4: Cost of Equity Under Different Theories.

Establishing Dividend Policy in Practice

The optimal payout ratio for a firm is a function of four factors:[10]
- Investors' preferences for dividends versus capital gains

---

[10] For further information, see *Corporate Finance: A Focused Approach*, Second Edition, Thomson, 2006, pp. 520–523.

- the firm's investment opportunities
- the firm's target capital structure
- and the availability and cost of external capital

The last three elements can be combined into what has become the residual dividend model. Within the residual dividend model, firms must determine the optimal capital budget, determine the amount of equity needed to fund the capital budget (based upon the target capital structure), use retained earnings to meet equity requirements whenever possible, and pay dividends only if more earnings are available than are needed for dividends. The residual dividend model can be expressed as:

$$Dividends = Net\ income - [(Target\ equity\ ratio) \times (Total\ capital\ budget)]$$

Consider a firm whose net income for the current year is €100 million. Their target equity ratio is 60% and the expected capital budget is €50 million. What are its dividends to be paid according to the residual model?

Net income = €100

Target equity ratio = 60%

Total capital budget = €50

Dividends = Net Income − [(Target equity ratio) * (Total capital budget)]

= €100 − 60%×€50

= €70

Resulting payout = 70.0%

Assessing Dividend Policy

The steps in assessing dividend policy of a company are as follows:[11]

- Step 1: How much could the company have paid out during the period in question?
- Step 2: How much did the company actually pay out during the period in question?
- Step 3: How much do I trust the management of this company with excess cash?
  - How well did they make investments during the period in question?
  - How well has my stock performed during the period in question?

The free cash flow to equity (FCFE) is a measure of how much cash is left in the business after non-equity claimholders (debt and preferred stock) have been paid,

---

11 Aswath Damadoran, *Applied Corporate Finance*, 1999, op. cit., pp. 401–413.

and after any reinvestment needed to sustain the firm's assets and future growth. The free cash flow to equity is defined as follows:

Net income
+ Depreciation & Amortization
= Cash flows from operations to equity investors
- Preferred dividends
- Capital expenditures
- Working capital needs
- Principal repayments
+ Proceeds from new debt issues
= Free cash flow to equity

Estimating FCFE when leverage is stable can be expressed as follows:

Net Income
- $(1-d)$ (Capital expenditures – Depreciation)
- $(1-d)$ Working capital needs
= Free cash flow to equity

Where, d = Debt/Capital ratio.

Let us define proceeds from new debt issues as follows:

Proceeds from new debt issues = Principal repayments + d (Capital expenditures – Depreciation + Working capital needs)

Consider the following inputs for a company to estimate its FCFE:

- Net income = €2.176 million
- Capital expenditures (Capex) = €494 million
- Depreciation (Dep) = € 480 million
- Change in non-cash working capital (Change in NCWC) = € 35 million
- Debt ratio (DR) = 0%

FCFE = Net income – (Capex – Dep) (1-DR) – Change NCWC (1-DR)
= € 2.176 – (494–480) (1–0) – € 35 (1–0)
= € 2.127 million

By this estimation, the firm could have paid €2.127 million in dividends/stock buy-backs in that year. It paid no dividends and bought back no stock. Where will the €2.127 million show up in the firm's balance sheet? Cash and marketable securities (financial investments). The board should give a reasonable answer why such a huge amount is maintained.

Balanced View in Dividend Policy

Companies should apply the following principles in determining dividend policy:
- If a company has excess cash and few good investment opportunities (NPV>0), returning money to stockholders (dividends or stock repurchases) is *good*.
- If a company does not have excess cash and/or has several good investment opportunities (NPV>0), returning money to stockholders (dividends or stock repurchases) is *bad*.

Stock Dividends, Stock Splits, and Repurchase of Stock

Other important terms regarding dividends are as follows:
- *Stock dividends.* This is an additional distribution of stock shares. An *accounting* transfer is required at fair market from retained earnings. The par value of the stock dividend is transferred to the common stock account. Unless total cash dividends increase, the stockholder does not benefit from a stock dividend.
- *Stock split.* This is a distribution of stock that increases the total shares outstanding. Accounting transfer from retained earnings is not required. The par value of stock is reduced. Benefits to stockholders, if any, are difficult to identify. The primary purpose is to lower the stock price into a more popular trading range.
- *Repurchase of stock.* This is an alternative to the payment of dividends. It is most often used when a firm has excess cash and inadequate investment opportunities. With the exception of a lower capital gains tax, the stockholder would be as well off with a cash dividend. Management may also think that stock is selling at a very low price and that the firm buying its own stock is the best investment available.

11.7 Summary

Minimum rate of return is a weighted average of the firm's various sources of capital. Market values of each sources must be used in calculating the weighted average cost of capital.

The optimal capital structure is the one that maximizes the value or the company. Also, that same capital structure minimizes the WACC.

Although some assumptions of the Modigliani-Miller (MM) model are missing or incorrect, they paved the way to calculate optimal capital structure and company valuation.

If there are not enough investments that earn the hurdle rate, return the cash to stockholders. The form of returns, dividends, and stock buybacks will depend upon the stockholders' characteristics.

There are several dividend theories, such as MM dividend irrelevance theory, bird-in-the-hand Theory, and tax preference theory.

The optimal payout ratio for a firm is a function of four factors: investors' preferences for dividends versus capital gains, the firm's investment opportunities, the firm's target capital structure, and the availability and cost of external capital.

If a company has excess cash and few good investment opportunities (NPV>0), returning money to stockholders (dividends or stock repurchases) is good. If a company does not have excess cash and/or has several good investment opportunities (NPV>0), returning money to stockholders (dividends or stock repurchases) is bad.

12 Managing Working Capital

12.1 Introduction

Proper management of a firm's short-term assets and liabilities is essential for ongoing operations and maximizing shareholder wealth. This chapter focuses on managing current assets – specifically, cash flows that arise from a firm's day-to-day operations. The operating cycle and cash conversion cycle help show that cash is what determines the firm's ability to pay bills on time. The cash budget assists the treasurer in forecasting cash needs and planning ahead to invest funds in marketable securities or to borrow funds to cover shortfalls.

12.2 Working Capital and Working Capital Requirement

A firm can invest in both working capital and fixed capital. Working capital is a firm's current assets and includes cash, marketable securities, inventory, and accounts receivable. Fixed capital is a firm's fixed assets and includes plant, equipment, and property. Firms that cannot obtain short-term financing become candidates for bankruptcy. Management of working capital is particularly important to the entrepreneurial or venture firms because of insufficient equity.

Two important concepts in managing working capital are the operating and the cash conversion cycles:
- The *operating cycle* measures the time between receiving raw materials and collecting the cash from credit sales.
- The *cash conversion cycle* measures the time it takes to collect money from the company's customers and use it to pay its suppliers.

A graphic version of the operating cycle is presented in Figure 12.1.
Calculating three ratios will reveal the average length of these cycles:
- Inventory days = 365 / (Cost of goods sold / Average inventories)
- Accounts receivable period (average collection period) = Average accounts receivable / (Net sales / 365)
- Average payment period = Average accounts payable / (Cost of goods sold / 365)

The *operating cycle* is the inventory conversion period plus the average collection period. The *cash conversion cycle* is the operating cycle minus the average payment period Figure 12.2.

In order to determine the average investment in accounts receivable, multiply the net sales per day by the average collection period. With this number, a manager can now estimate what the investment in accounts receivable will be for the

https://doi.org/10.1515/9783110705355-012

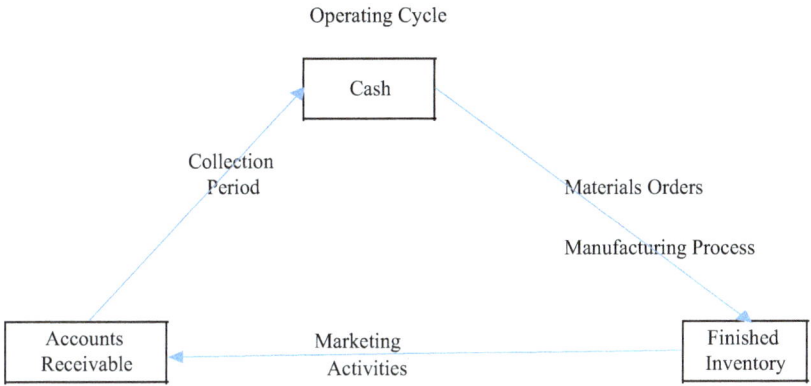

Figure 12.1: Operating Cycle.

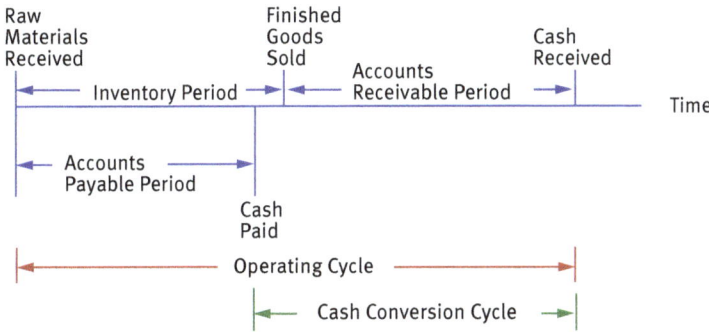

Figure 12.2: Timeline for Operating and Cash Conversion Cycles.
Source: Malicher and Norton, op. cit., p. 235.

following year, given sales increases and the average collection period. In order to determine the investment required in inventories, multiply the average cost of goods sold per day by the inventory conversion period. The required amount of accounts payable can be found by multiplying the cost of goods sold per day by the average payment period.

Tables 12.1 and 12.2 present the financial statements for the ABC Corporation for the years 20X7 and 20X8.

Calculate the firm's operating cycle and cash conversion cycle for 20X7 and 20X8. Why did they change between these years?

Inventory period = Inventory/(COGS/365)

$$= €1,000,000/(1,800,000/365) = 202.78 \text{ days } (20X8)$$
$$€900,000/(€1,560,000/365) = 210.56 \text{ days } (20X7)$$

Table 12.1: Selected Balance Sheet Information.

	20X7	20X8
Cash	€100,000	€80,000
Accounts receivable	400,000	520,000
Inventory	900,000	1,000,000
Total current assets	1,400,000	1,600,000
Bank loan. 10%	180,000	180,000
Accounts payable	260,000	340,000
Accruals	100,000	140,000
Total current liabilities	540,000	660,000
Long-term debt. 12%	600,000	800,000

Table 12.2: Selected Income Statement Information.

	20X7	20X8
Net sales	€2,600,000	€3,000,000
Cost of goods sold	1,560,000	1,800,000
Gross profit	1,040,000	1,200,000
Net income	186,000	228,000

AR period = AR/(Sales/365)

    = €520,000/(€ 3,000,000/365) = 63.27 days (20X8)

    = €400.000/(€2,600.000/365) = 56.15 days (20X7)

AP period = AP/(COGS/365)

    = €340,000/(€1,800,000/365) = 68.94 days (20X8)

    = €260,000/(€1,560,000/365) = 60.83 days (20X7)

Operating cycle = Inventory period + AR period

    = 202.78 days + 63.27 days = 266.05 (20X8)

    = 210.58 days + 56.15 days = 266.73 days (20X7)

Cash conversion cycle = Operating cycle – Average payment period

    = 266.05 days – 68.94 days = 197.11 days (20X8)

    = 266.73 days – 60.83 days = 205.90 days (20X7)

The operating cycle remained constant in 20X7 and 20X8, as a reduction in the inventory period was balanced by an increase in the average collection period. The cash conversion cycle for 20X8 was longer.

The firm expects its sales to increase by 10% in 20X9. Estimate the firm's investment in accounts receivables, inventory, and accounts payable in 20X9.

If the inventory collection and payment periods remain constant, each account should rise by 10%.

$$\text{Accounts receivable: €260,000 (1.10) = €286,000}$$
$$\text{Inventory: €500,000 (1.10) = €550,000}$$
$$\text{Accounts payable: € 170,000 (1.10) = €187,000}$$
$$\text{Net investment in working capital}_{20X9} = \text{AR + Inventory} - \text{AP}$$
$$= €286,000 + €550,000 - €187,000 = €649,000$$
$$\text{Net investment in working capital}_{20X8} = €260,000 + €500,000 - €170,000$$
$$= €590,000.$$
$$\text{Incremental net investment in working capital}_{20X9} = €649,000 - €590,000$$
$$= €50,000$$

In capital budgeting, similar calculations are done to determine *working capital requirements of the projects*. That is, the firm should have budgeted €50,000 for the year 20X9.

In capital budgeting, investment in cash also be included to the incremental net investment in working capital. The percent of *cash to net sales ratio* can also be used to estimate the investment in cash.

12.3 Cash Budgets

A *cash budget* shows the cash inflows and outflows of a firm over a specific time frame. Small firms may prepare annual or monthly cash budgets while larger firms will forecast cash flows weekly or daily. Most firms have a minimum desired cash balance that depends on the firm's ability to acquire financing on short notice, management preferences, and the predictability of cash inflows and outflows.

Estimates of cash inflows are calculated by using two main factors:
- Sales forecast, which may exhibit seasonality
- Customer payment patterns

Cash outflows will go to suppliers, payroll, taxes, operating expenses, and purchases of plant and equipment.

In order to construct the cash budget, list all expected cash inflows and then all expected cash outflows for the particular period, generating a net cash flow amount.

Seasonal or otherwise varying production and forecasting can lead to *idle plant capacity* and *laid-off workers* during the off-season. Under a level production plan, the same amount of raw material is purchased, and the same amount of finished product is manufactured every month.

Of its monthly sales, the ABC Company historically has had 25% cash sales with the remainder paid within one month. Each month's purchases are equal to

75% of the next month's sales forecast; suppliers are paid one month after the purchase. Salary expenses are €100,000 a month, except in January, when bonuses equal to 1% of the previous year's sales are paid out. Interest on a bond issue of €20,000 is due in March. Overhead and utilities are expected to be €50.000 monthly. Dividends of €90,000 are to be paid in March. ABC's 20X7 sales totaled €4 million; December sales were €400,000. ABC's estimated sales for January are €200,000; February at €400,000; March at €500,000; and April at €600,000. Relevant data and the expected cash budget are presented in Tables 12.3–12.5.

Table 12.3: Expected Cash Inflows.

What are ABC's expected monthly cash inflows during January through April?					
	Dec.	Jan.	Feb.	Mar.	Apr.
Sales	€400,000	€200,000	€400,000	€500,000	€600,000
Cash sales (25%)		50,000	100,000	125,000	150,000
1 month later (75%)		300,000	150,000	300,000	375,000
Total cash receipts		350,000	250,000	425,000	525,000

Table 12.4: Expected Cash Outflows.

What are ABC's expected monthly cash outflows during January through April?					
	Dec.	Jan.	Feb.	Mar.	Apr.
Sales	€400,000	€200,000	€400,000	€500,000	€600,000
Purchases (75% of next month's sales)	150,000	300,000	375,000	450,000	
Payments (1 month after purchase)		150,000	300,000	375,000	450,000
Salary		140,000	100,000	100,000	100,000
Interest				20,000	
Overhead and utilities		50,000	50,000	50,000	50,000
Dividends				90,000	
Total cash payments		340,000	450,000	635,000	600,000

Determine ABC's monthly cash budget for January through April. Assume a minimum desired cash balance of €80,000 and ending December cash balance of €100,000.

It is understood that the firm should obtain bank loan for months February, March, and April.

Table 12.5: Expected Cash Budget.

	Jan.	Feb.	Mar.	Apr.
Total cash receipts	€350,000	€250,000	€425,000	€525,000
Less: total cash payments	340,000	450,000	635,000	600,000
Net cash flow	10,000	−200,000	−210.000	−75,000
Beginning cash balance	100,000	110,000	80,000	80,000
Bank loan	0	170,000	210,000	75,000
Ending cash balance	110,000	80,000	80,000	80,000

12.4 Cash Management

There are three types of motives for holding cash, as described by Keynes:
- The *transactions motives* are demands for holding cash to conduct daily operations.
- *Precautionary motives* are demands that may be caused by unpredictable events such as delays in production or in the collection of receivables. Marketable securities are held in such a contingency.
- *Speculative motives* are demands for funds to take advantage of unusual cash discounts for needed materials.

Cash and marketable securities include:
- Cash itself
- Treasury bills
- Commercial paper, unsecured notes of well-known business firms
- Negotiable certificates of deposit, a receipt issued by a bank in exchange for a deposit of funds
- Bankers' acceptances, primarily used to finance exports and imports
- Eurodollar, deposits placed in foreign banks denominated in U.S. dollars

In general, managers try to speed up cash collections while slowing down the payment process. The *float* is the time between sending out payments and having them actually be charged to the bank account. The *collection float* is the time between when a payer sends payment and funds are credited to the payee's bank account. The *disbursement float* is the time between when a payer sends payment and when the funds are deducted from the payer's bank account.

Float has three components:
- *Delivery* or *transmission float* is the delay in transferring the means of payment from the payer (customer) to the payee (provider of goods/services).

- *Processing float* is time to process the transaction.
- *Clearing float* is the delay in transferring funds because of the banking system itself.

Optimal cash balances can be estimated using either the *William Baumol model* or the *Miller-Orr model*.

William Baumol Model

The model developed by William Baumol can determine the optimum amount of cash for a company to hold under conditions of certainty. The objective is to minimize the sum of the fixed costs of transactions and the opportunity cost of holding cash balances that do not yield a return. This is similar to the economic order quantity (EQQ) model used in inventory management. The total cost is expressed as:

$$\text{Total cost} = F \times (T/C) + i \times (C/2)$$

Where:
   F = Fixed costs of a transaction
   T = Total cash required for the specified time period
   i = Interest rate on marketable securities
   C = Cash balance
   The optimal level of cash is determined using the following formula (taking the derivative of the total cost with respect to cash balance C and equating it to zero):

$$\text{Optimal level of cash} = C^* = \sqrt{\frac{2T}{i} \times F}$$

For example, a company estimates a cash requirement of €1,000,000 for a one-month period. The opportunity interest rate is 12% per annum, which works out to 1% per month. The transaction cost for borrowing or withdrawing funds is €100. Then:

$$\text{Optimal level of cash} = C^* = \sqrt{\frac{2 \times 1,000,000}{0.01} \times 100} => €141,421.36$$

With this optimal transaction size, we can now find the number of transactions required:
   Number of transactions required = €1,000,000 / €141,421.36 => 7.07 or 7 transactions during the month.

Miller-Orr Model

When the cash payments are uncertain, the *Miller-Orr model* can be used. This model places upper and lower limits on cash balances. When the upper limit is reached, a transfer of cash to marketable securities (financial investments) is made. A transfer from securities to cash is made when the lower limit is reached. As long as the cash balance stays within the limits, no transaction occurs. The various factors in this model are: fixed costs of a securities transaction (F), which is assumed to be the same for buying and selling; the daily interest rate on marketable securities (i); and variance of the daily net cash flows represented by σ^2. This model assumes that the cash flows are random. The control limits in this model are d euros as an upper limit and zero dollars or some other amount at the lower limit (L). When the cash balance reaches the upper level d, z euros of securities are bought to lower the cash balance to level z. When the cash balance equals zero, z euros of securities are sold, and the new balance again reaches z. According to this model, the optimal cash balance $z*$ is computed as follows:[1]

$$z^* = \sqrt[3]{\frac{3F\sigma^2}{4i}} + L$$

$$H^* = 3Z^* - 2L$$

$$\text{Average cash balance} = \frac{4Z^* - L}{3}$$

The optimal value for d is computed as $3z$.

Average cash balance (approx.) = $(z + d)/3$

As an example, given the following, let us calculate optimal cash balance.

Fixed cost of a securities transaction = €10

Variance of daily net cash flows = €36

Daily interest rate on securities = 0.000278 (10% per annum. So, 10%/360 days = 0.000278 daily)

$$\text{Optimal cash balance} = z^* = \sqrt[3]{\frac{3 \times 10 \times 36^2}{4 \times 0.0003}} + 0 => €328.59$$

Upper limit, d = 3z = 3 × €328.59 = €985.77

Average cash balance = (4×€328.59)/3 => €438.12

---

1 For a discussion of the model, see D. Mullins and R. Homonoff, "Applications of Inventory Cash Management Models," S.C. Myers, *Modern Developments in Financial Management*, Frederick A. Praeger, Inc., New York, 1976.

So, when the upper limit of €985.77 is reached, €657.18 (€985.77 – €328.59) will be purchased. When the lower limit of zero euro is reached, €328.59 of securities will be sold to again bring it to the optimal balance of cash, calculated as approximately €328.59.

12.5 Accounts Receivable Management and Credit Analysis

In order to facilitate sales, firms often offer customers credit for purchases. This process calls in *credit analysis*. The five C's of credit analysis are:
- *Character.* The ethical quality of the applicant and the history of paying bills on time (credit checks).
- *Capacity.* The ability of the borrower to pay bills (liquidity ratios).
- *Capital.* The adequacy of the owner's equity relative to existing liabilities.
- *Collateral.* Whether assets are available to provide security.
- *Conditions.* The current economic climate and the state of the business cycle.

Trade credit is extended on purchases to a firm's customers. Sometimes, customers are given a discount if they pay early. The financial manager must be careful not to impose onerous credit terms that will alienate customers and lower sales.

With respect to global credit, the concern is foreign exchange. There are two ways to handle the issue:
- Invoice customers in the firm's home currency
- Hedge the foreign exchange risk

Let's say that ABC Corporation's year sales are €10 million, and its average collection period is 40 days. Only 10% of sales are for cash and the remainder are credit sales. Answer the following questions:
- What is ABC's investment in accounts receivable?
- If ABC extends its credit period, it estimates the average collection period will rise to 50 days and that credit sales will increase by 30% from current levels. What is the expected increase in ABC's accounts receivable balance if it extends its credit period?
- If ABC's net profit margin is 15%, the expected increase in bad debt expense is 10% of the new sale, and the cost of financing the increase in receivables is 20%. Should ABC extend the credit period?

With the relevant data given in Table 12.6, the expected increase in accounts receivables and the net profit from financing in credit sales are presented in Tables 12.7 and 12.8.

ABC should follow this policy, since the policy will increase the net profit. The increase in profit is €241,212.33.

Table 12.6: Calculation of Investment in A/R.

Year sales	€10,000,000.00	
Cash sale	€1,000,000.00	
Credit sale	€9,000,000.00	
Collection period	40 days	
A/R Turnover	365/Average Collection Period	365/40 = 9.125
Investment in A/R	Credit Sales/A/R Turnover	9,000,000/9.125 =986,301.37

Table 12.7: Expected Increase in A/R investment.

Credit sale	increase 30%	€11,700,000.00
Collection period	increased to 50 days	50
Investment in A/R	€11,700,000/ (365/50)	€1,602,739.73
Expected increase in A/R investment	€1,602,739.73– €986,301.37	€616,43836

Table 12.8: Net Profit from Financing in Credit Sale.

Increase in credit sales	€11,700,000 –€9,000,000	€2,700,000.00
Bad debt expense	€2,700,000.00	€270,000.00
Net increase in credit sales	€2,700,000.00 – €270,000.00	€2,430,000.00
Profit margin	15%	–
Increase in profit	€2,430,000.00 × 0.15	€364,500.00
Cost of financing the increase in A/R	20%	–
Cost of financing	€616,438.36× 0.20	€123,287.67
Net profit from financing in credit sale	€364,500.00 – €123,287.67	€241,212.33

12.6 Inventory Management

Inventory is the stock of goods a firm has on hand, either for production or for sale. There are three basic components of inventory:
- Raw materials
- Work in process
- Finished goods

Differing Views about Inventory

The different departments within a firm (finance, production, marketing, etc.) often have differing views about what an appropriate level of inventory is.

- *Financial managers* would like to keep inventory levels low to ensure that funds are wisely invested.
- *Marketing managers* would like to keep inventory levels high to ensure orders could be quickly filled.
- *Manufacturing managers* would like to keep raw materials levels high to avoid production delays and to make larger, more economical production runs.

Techniques for Managing Inventory

There are many techniques for managing inventory such as the *ABC system*, the *economic order quantity* (EOQ) *model, materials requirement planning* (MRP), *just-in-time system* (JIT).

The ABC System. The ABC system of inventory management divides inventory into three groups of descending order of importance, based on the euro amount invested in each group.

In a typical system, group A would consist of 20% of the number of items but 80% of the total value of the inventory, group B would consist of 30% of the number of items but 10% of the total value and so on.

Control of the group A items would be intensive because of the high euro investment involved.

The EOQ model, which we will discuss in the following section, would be most appropriate for managing items A, B, and C.

The Economic Order Quantity (EOQ) Model. This model (see Figure 12.3) assumes that relevant costs of inventory can be divided into order costs and carrying costs.

Order costs decrease as the size of the order increases, while carrying costs also increase.

The EOQ model analyzes the tradeoff between order costs and carrying costs to determine the order quantity that minimizes the total inventory cost.

$$EOQ = \sqrt{\frac{2 \times S \times O}{C}}$$

Where:

S = usage in units per period (year)
O = order cost per order
C = carrying costs per unit per period (year)

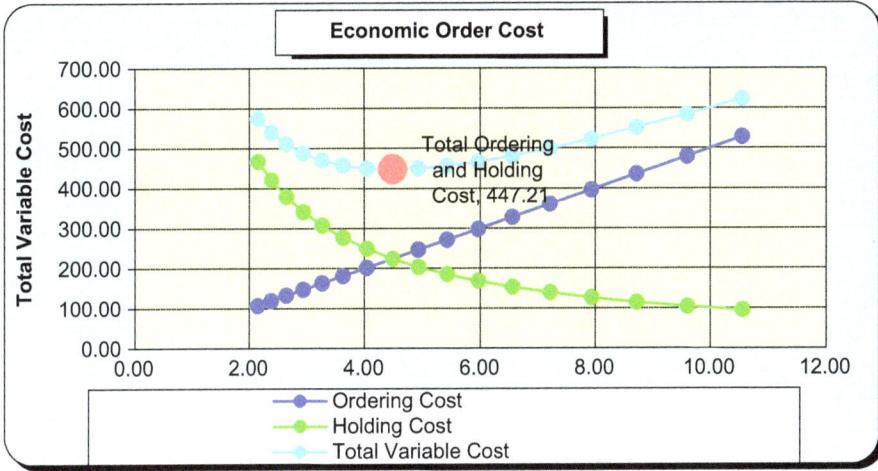

Figure 12.3: Economic Order Quantity.

Assume that ABC Inc., a manufacturer of electronic test equipment, uses 2,000 units of an item annually. Its order cost is €50 per order and the carrying cost is €1 per unit per year. Substituting into this equation, we get:

$$EOQ = \sqrt{\frac{2 \times 2,000 \times €50}{€1}} \approx 447 \ units$$

The EOQ can be used to evaluate the total cost of inventory as shown below:

$$Ordering \ costs = \frac{Cost}{Order} \times \frac{\# \ of \ Orders}{Year}$$

$$Carrying \ costs = \frac{Carrying \ costs/Year \times Order \ size}{2}$$

$$Total \ costs = Ordering \ costs + Carrying \ costs$$

Total costs are calculated for different order quantities, and the data for Table 12.9 is presented in Table 12.10.

Once a company has calculated its EOQ, it must determine *when* it should place its orders. More specifically, the reorder point must consider the lead time needed to place and receive orders.

If we assume that inventory is used at a constant rate throughout the year (no seasonality), the reorder point can be determined by using the following equation:

$$Daily \ usage = 2,000/360 = 5.55 \ units/day$$

Table 12.9: Inventory Data.

ABC Inc.

Inventory Data	
Variable	**Value**
Annual Usage	2.000
Order Cost/order	€50.00
Carrying Costs/year	€1.00

Table 12.10: Total Inventory Cost Under Different Order Quantity.

Number of Orders	Order Cost	Carrying Cost	Total Variable Cost
2.14	€106.95	€467.51	€574.46
2.38	118.83	420.76	539.59
2.64	132.04	378.68	510.72
2.93	146.71	340.81	487.52
3.26	163.01	306.73	469.74
3.62	181.12	276.06	457.18
4.02	201.25	248.45	449.70
4.47	223.61	223.61	447.21
4.92	245.97	203.28	449.25
5.41	270.56	184.80	455.36
5.95	297.62	168.00	465.62
6.55	327.38	152.73	480.11
7.20	360.12	138.84	498.96
7.92	396.13	126.22	522.35
8.71	435.75	114.75	550.49
9.59	479.32	104.31	583.64
10.55	527.25	94.83	622.08

Using the ABC example, if the company knows that it requires ten days to place and receive an order, and the annual usage is 2,000 units per year, the reorder point can be determined as follows:

$$\text{Recorder point} = 10 \times 5.55 = 55.55 \text{ or } 56 \text{ units}$$

Thus, when ABC's inventory level reaches 56 units, it should place an order for 447 units. However, if ABC wishes to maintain the safety stock to protect against stock sellouts, they would order before inventory reached 56 units.

Materials Requirement Planning (MRP). MRP systems are used to determine what to order and when to order, and what priorities to assign to ordering materials.

MRP uses EOQ concepts to determine how much to order using computer software.

It simulates each product's bill of materials structure (all of the product's parts), inventory status, and manufacturing process.

Like the simple EOQ, the objective of MRP systems is to minimize a company's overall investment in inventory without impairing production.

Just-in-Time System (JIT). The JIT inventory management system minimizes the inventory investment by having material inputs arrive exactly when they are needed for production.

For a JIT system to work, extensive coordination must exist between the firms, its suppliers, and shipping companies to ensure that material inputs arrive on time.

In addition, the inputs must be of near perfect quality and consistency, given the absence of safety stock.

Technology and Managing Working Capital. Technology is improving asset management by making available information with which managers make business decisions in a real-time setting. Technology may be the key to reducing procurement and supply chain costs. Portals are specialized and secure websites through which clients can access order and account information.

12.7 Summary

A firm can invest in both working capital and fixed capital. Working capital is a firm's current assets and includes cash, marketable securities, inventory, and accounts receivable. Fixed capital is a firm's fixed assets and includes plant, equipment, and property.

Two important concepts in managing working capital are the operating cycle and the cash conversion cycle.

A cash budget details the cash inflows and outflows of a firm over a specific time frame. In general, managers try to speed up cash collections while slowing down the payment process.

Optimal cash balances can be estimated using one of the following methods: the William Baumol model and the Miller-Orr model.

In order to facilitate sales, firms often offer customers credit for purchases. This process calls in credit analysis. The five C's of credit analysis are: character, capacity, capital, collateral, and conditions.

Inventory is the stockpile of goods a firm has on hand, either for production or for sale. There are three basic components of inventory: raw materials, work in process, and finished goods. The different departments within a firm (finance, production, marketing, etc.) often have differing views about what an appropriate level of inventory is. There are many techniques for managing inventory, such as the ABC system, the economic order quantity (EOQ) model, materials requirement planning (MRP), just-in-time system (JIT), and technology.

13 Short-Term and Intermediate-Term Business Financing

13.1 Introduction

A firm's current assets need to be financed. Many firms finance their short-term assets with short-term financing sources. The amount of short-term financing a firm uses is a strategic decision, as it has risk and return implications. Using short-term funds to finance both current and fixed assets is a high-risk, high-return strategy. The use of long-term funds to finance both current and fixed assets is a low-risk, low-return strategy. Most people may think the only short-term financing sources available to firms are trade credit (accounts payable) and bank loans. But there are many different kinds of bank-lending arrangements, and firms have other financing sources they can use besides suppliers and banks. This chapter reviews these sources and also demonstrates how to compute the effective cost of a financing source. In addition to short-term financing, we also cover intermediate-term financing such as medium-term loans and leasing.[1]

13.2 Strategies for Financing Working Capital

There are three approaches to financing working capital:
- Maturity-matching approach
- Aggressive approach
- Conservative approach

These three approaches are graphically presented in Figures 13.1–13.3:
- *Maturity-matching approach* (also called *balanced approach*) is a financing method where the financial manager tries to match the term of the loan to the life of the asset that it is financing. With maturity-matching, current assets exceed current liabilities, so the net working capital is positive.
- *An aggressive approach* is when all current assets both temporary and permanent are financed with short-term financing. Only fixed assets are financed with long-term debt and equity funds.
- A *conservative approach* utilizes long-term debt and equity funds heavily to finance current assets.

---

[1] Bond and common stock are long-term financing sources. Since we covered them before, we will not discuss them again here.

https://doi.org/10.1515/9783110705355-013

Hedging (or Maturity Matching) Approach

• Less amount financed spontaneously by payables and accruals.
•• In addition to spontaneous financing (payables and accruals).

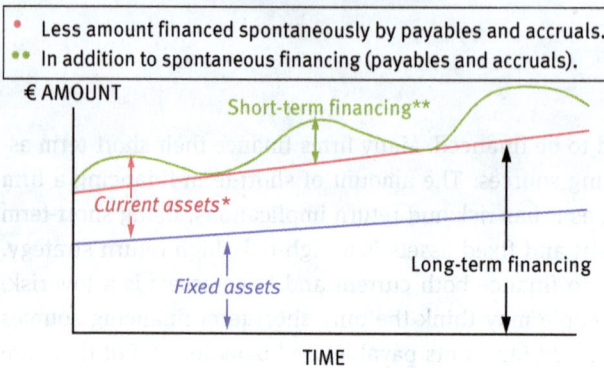

Figure 13.1: Hedging Approach.

Risks vs. Costs Trade-Off (Conservative Approach)

Firm can reduce risks associated with short-term borrowing by using a larger proportion of long-term financing.

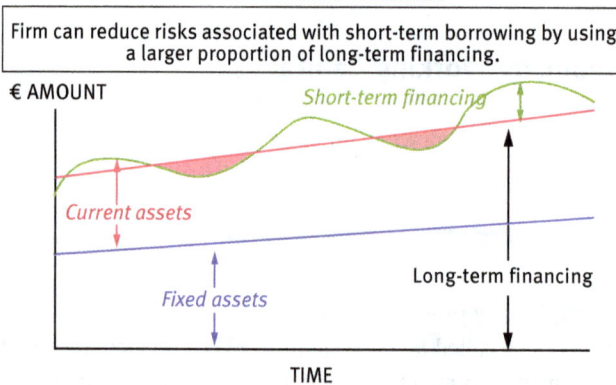

Figure 13.2: Conservative Approach.

The risk/return implications of these approaches are follows:

- An aggressive financing plan using more short-term financing generally has lower financing costs and will be more profitable as it is rolled into a new debt. However, short-term interest rates are more volatile than long-term rates.
- A conservative financing plan has a higher financing cost but a lower risk of not being able to borrow when short-term funds are needed.

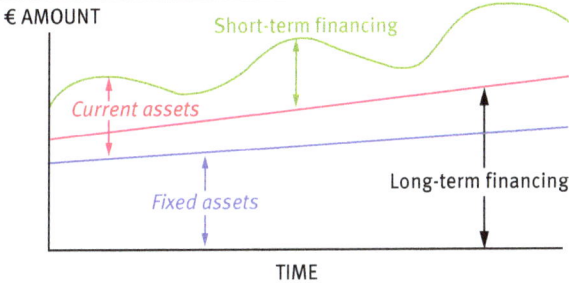

Figure 13.3: Aggressive Approach.

13.3 Factors Affecting Short-Term Financing

A firm's financing strategy depends on:
- The company's operating characteristics
- The cost of financing
- The flexibility of financing
- The ease of future financing
- Seasonal variations in sales and the growth
- Fluctuations in the business cycle
- The composition of the asset structure, or current assets versus fixed assets
- The size and age of a company and the stage of its financial life cycle
- The growth prospects of the firm

Some industries, such as utilities, iron-steel, and oil refineries, have a larger number of fixed assets than current assets and prefer to use long-term financing. Manufacturing companies generally have an equal balance between current and fixed assets. Service industries have more current assets than fixed assets.

Advantages of short-term borrowing are as follows:
- Short-term borrowing offers more flexibility than long-term loans since a business can borrow only what it needs and pay off amounts quickly if the need for financing diminishes. Long-term debt often comes with prepayment penalties.
- Short-term borrowing builds a strong relationship with a bank or other financial institution by virtue of creating a history of frequent borrowing and prompt repayment.

Disadvantages of short-term borrowing include:
- The need for frequent renewals and processing cost
- An added element of risk due to frequent maturities (non-renewal)

13.4 Short-Term Financing Sources

Three basic sources of short-term financing include:
- Bank loans
- Trade credit
- Commercial paper

Bank Loans

Bank loans may be secured or unsecured. Bank loans generally appear as notes payable on the balance sheet. Bank credit is available in three different formats: single loans, lines of credit, and revolving credit agreements.

Single loans are usually arranged for definite financing needs. The interest rate charged on a single loan is usually related to the prime rate. The effective annual percentage cost of a bank loan depends on the payment schedule and whether a compensating balance is required.

A *line of credit* is an agreement that allows the firm to borrow up to a predetermined limit at any time during the life of the agreement. A line of credit is usually negotiated for a one-year period. The interest rate on a line of credit is usually stated in terms of the prime rate and varies as the prime rate changes during the year. A line of credit may contain restrictive covenants on working capital, allowable debt, and so on.

A *revolving credit* agreement legally commits the bank to making loans up to the credit limit specified in the agreement. Revolving credit agreements are usually secured. Revolving credit agreements require the firm to pay a commitment fee on the unused portion of the funds. The effective annual interest cost on a revolving credit agreement contains both actual interest costs and the commitment fee.

Unsecured loans provided by commercial banks are the primary type of loan arrangement. Interest rates are typically stated in terms of prime rate plus a spread.

Cost of Short-Term Credit. Determining the cost of short-term financing is a five-step process:
- Determine the amount to be borrowed (consider discounting, compensating balances).
- Interest expense = interest rate × amount borrowed.
- Estimate fees and other expenses of the loan.

- Estimate the net loan proceeds.
- Financing cost = (interest expenses + fees)/net proceeds. Annualize if necessary.

The firm can borrow €100,000 for 1 year at an 10% nominal rate. Interest may be set under one of the following scenarios:
- Simple annual interest
- Discount interest
- Discount interest with 10% compensating balance

Nominal (quoted) rate = 10% in all cases. We want to compare loan cost rates and choose the lowest cost loan.

Simple annual interest. *Simple interest* means no discount or add-on. Effective annual interest rate (EAR) can be calculated as follows:

$$EAR = \frac{Interest}{Principal} = \frac{r}{1} = \frac{0.1}{1} = 0.10$$

Discount interest. The borrower receives usable funds after deducting the discount. EAR can be calculated as follows:

$$EAR = \frac{Interest\,(Discount)}{Principal - Interest} = \frac{r}{1-r} = \frac{0.1}{1-0.1} = 0.111$$

Where r is nominal discount rate.

Discount interest loan with a 10% compensating balance. EAR can be calculated as follows:

$$EAR = \frac{Interest\,(Discount)}{Principal - Interest - Compensating\ balance} = \frac{r}{1-r-c} = \frac{0.10}{1-0.1-0.1}$$

$$EAR = \frac{0.1}{0.8} = 0.125$$

As can be seen, the loan with the compensating balance feature is the most expensive option.

Trade Credit

Trade credit is accounts receivable together with longer-term notes receivable taken by manufacturers, wholesalers, jobbers, and other businesses that sell products or services to businesses. This is the least formal of all forms of financing and involves only an order for goods or services by one business and the delivery of goods or

performance of service by the business. Sales may be made on a variety of terms including:
- *Cash.* Payment due upon receipt of invoice.
- *EOM.* Payment due at the *end of the month.*
- *MOM.* Payment due at the *middle of the month.*
- *ROG.* Payment due upon *receipt of goods.*

A seller may offer attractive terms such as 2/10, net 60, meaning that if payment occurs within 10 days of shipment, a 2% discount applies; if not paid within 10 days, the net amount is due within 30 days. The cost of trade credit is high when discounts are missed. Trade credit is usually more accessible than bank credit. Effective cost (EC) of trade credit is calculated as follows:

$$EC = \% \, Discount / (100\% - \% \, Discount)$$
$$\times (365 \, days) / (Credit \ Period - Discount \ days)$$

Compute the effective cost of not taking the cash discount under the following trade credit terms: 2/10 net 40

$$2/ \, (100-2) \times 365/(40-10) = 0. \, 020408163 \times 12.16666667 = 24.83\%$$
$$\text{Interest rate period} = 2/98 = 0.0204$$
$$\text{Number of interest periods} = 365/ \, (30-10) = 18,25$$
$$\text{Effective Annual Rate} = (1.0204)^{18.25} - 1 = 0.4456 = 44.56\%$$

Commercial Paper

Commercial paper is a short-term promissory note backed solely by the credit quality of the issuer. There is no security or collateral behind the loan. Commercial paper:
- May be sold directly by the issuer to financial institutions or investors or to dealers.
- Is generally only issued by a firm that has an unquestioned reputation for sound operation that can sustain an investigation of the firm's financial position.
- Is sold on a discount basis.
- Is only issued by large, well-known, and financially stable firms.
- Cost of borrowing is generally less costly than regular bank rates.
- Is rated like bonds.
- Provides a yield slightly above short-term government security.
- Can be issued overseas in the European commercial paper (Euro CP) market.

Formulas for the calculation of discounted price and yield of a commercial paper are as follows:

$$\text{Price} = \text{Face Value}/ [1 + \text{yield} \times (\text{no. of days to maturity}/365 \text{ or } 360)]$$
$$\text{Yield} = (\text{Face value} - \text{Price})/ (\text{price} \times \text{no. of days to maturity}) \times 365 \text{ or } 360 \times 100$$

Assume that the face value of a commercial paper is €6,000,000 and the number of days to maturity is 199 days. What is the current purchase value of this instrument if yield is 7.00%?

$$\text{Price} = 6,000,000/ (1 + (0.07 \times 199/360) = €\,5,776,482.23$$
$$\text{Yield} = (€6,000,000 - €5.776.482,23)/(€\,5,776,482.23 \times 199) \times 360 = 7.00\%$$

13.5 Asset-Based Lending for Short-Term Financing

Secured lending (*asset-based lending*) means that there is collateral or security backing the loan that can be claimed or sold by the lender in the event of a default.

There are two types of accounts receivable financing: pledges, and factoring.

Pledge

A *pledge* is a means of obtaining a short-term loan by using accounts receivable as collateral. As a result, a lender will carefully examine the borrower's collection experience on its receivables and examine certain characteristics of the accounts receivable. The lender may spot-check receivables, analyze each account and study the type and quality of goods sold. The bank also charges fees for extra work needed to maintain the loan, such as periodic checks on the books of the business. As customers pay the bill on pledged accounts, the proceeds are generally turned over to the bank.

Factoring

Factoring is the selling of receivables to a financial institution, the factor, usually *without recourse*.

A factor purchases accounts receivables outright and assumes all credit risks. Factoring takes two forms:

- *Maturity factoring*. The firm selling the accounts receivable is paid on the normal collection date or net due date of the account.
- *Advance factoring*. The factor pays the firm for its receivable before the account due date.

Customers whose accounts have been sold are notified that their bills are payable to the factor. Typically, factors will exclude late receivables and only lend on 85% of the remainder.

The charge for factoring has two components:
- Interest is charged on money advanced.
- A factoring commission or service charge is figured as a percentage of the face amount of the receivables. (This charge typically ranges from 1.5% to 2% of the face amount of the accounts financed.)

Advantages of factoring for the firm include:
- The cost of doing business through credit sales is definite and can be determined in advance.
- Factoring eliminates expenses including book keeping costs to maintain a credit department and collecting on delinquent accounts.
- Factoring frees the management of a business from concern with financial matters and allows it to concentrate on production and distribution.
- Factoring supports export sales.

Disadvantages of factoring for the firm include:
- Cost is relatively high.
- There is probably an implication of financial weakness.

Let's say that ABC Inc. is evaluating proposals from two different factors that will provide receivables financing. Y Factoring will finance the receivables at an annual percentage rate (APR) of 16% discounted and charges a fee of 8%. D Factoring offers an APR of 14% (non-discounted) with fees of 2%. The average term of either loan is expected to be 40 days. With an average receivables balance of €500,000, which proposal should we accept?

ABC should accept D's offer, as its APR is lower than Y's. See Tables 13.1 and 13.2.

Other

Inventory can also be used as collateral for loans. Inventory financing is more expensive than unsecured loans partly because of warehousing operations. Assignable stocks and bonds can also be used as collateral for short-term loans.

Table 13.1: Cost of Factoring: Y Factoring.

	Data	Explanation
Amount needed	€500,000.00	
APR	16.00%	
Time of loan (in days)	40	days
Interest charge	1.7534%	=16% × (40/365)
Fee	8%	
Step 1:		
Amount to be borrowed	508,923.59	=€500,000/ (1−0.0175)
Step 2:		
Interest expense	8,923.59	=1.7534% × 508,923.59
Step 3:		
Fees and other expenses	40,713.89	=8% × €508,923.59
Step 4:		
Net proceeds	500,000.00	
Step 5:		
Interest = fees	49,637.48	=8,923.59+40,713.89
Net proceeds	500,000.00	
Financing cost	9.93%	=49,713.89/500,000.00
Annualized cost	137.19%	$= (1+0.0993)^{(365/35)}$-1

13.6 Intermediate-Term Financing

Basic sources of intermediate-term finance are the following:
- Ordinary shares (equity capital)
- Bonds (debt financing)

- Term loans (debt financing)
- Leasing (debt financing)

Table 13.2: Cost of Factoring: D Factoring.

Data	Data	Explanation
Amount needed	€500,000.00	
APR	14.00%	
Interest charge	1.53%	
Fee	4%	
Time of loan (in days)	40	days
Step 1:		
Amount to be borrowed	500,000.00	
Step 2:		
Interest expense	7,671.23	=1.53% × 500,000.00
Step 3:		
Fees and other expenses	20,000.00	=4% × 500,000.00
Step 4:		
Net proceeds	500,000.00	
Step 5:		
Interest + fees	27,671.23	=20,000.00+7,671.23
Net proceeds	500,000.00	
Financing cost	5.53%	=27,671.23/500,000.00
Annualized cost	63.48%	$= (1+0.0553)^{(365/35)}-1$

In this section, we will just explain term loans and leasing.

Term Loans

Five (5) to fifteen (15) years' term to maturity loans are often referred to as *notes* or *term loans*. They are granted by commercial and development banks, whereas insurance companies and commercial banks provide term loans in some countries. These loans are used for equipment and working capital financing.

Features of long-term loans are:

- Secured by equipment or property
- Similar to mortgage loans
- Periodic repayment of interest and principal

Repayments can be done via *straight loan reduction method* or *amortization*.

In *straight loan reduction method*, annual payment on principal can be found as follows:

Annual payment on principal = Original loan/life of loan.

The payment of the principal plus the interest cost, I, paid annually. Payments are unequal and are larger at first.

The *amortization method* creates even payments. More interest is paid in earlier years. More principal is paid in later years. The annual payment (annuity) on principal can be found as follows:

$$PMT = \frac{Amount\ Borrowed}{PVFA}$$

How do we obtain PMT? It comes from the following formula:

$$PVA = PMT \left[\frac{1 - \frac{I}{(1+i)^n}}{i} \right]$$

$$PVA = PMT \times PVFA$$

Note that PVFA represents the second term in the equation.

$$PMT = PVA/PVFA$$

where:

Amount borrowed = Present value of an annuity (Po)

PMT = annual repayment

PVFA – present value investment factor for an annuity

Possible restrictive covenants on the operations of the firm:

- The loan will come due if the present management is dissolved.
- The lender will get a receipt of some votes of stock.
- The lender imposes an upper limit on the amount of additional debt.

Benefits of term loans:
- They allow for a tailored agreement between the firm and the creditor.
- Term loans do not require annual cleanup.

Let us give an example. A bank grants a loan amounting to €6,000 to your company at an interest rate of 15% over 4 years. What will your annual payments be at the end of each year?

Payment amount can be found by solving for PMT using PV of annuity formula, as discussed in Chapter 3:

$$PVA = PMT\left[\frac{1 - \frac{I}{(1+i)^n}}{i}\right]$$

$$6.000 = PMT\,(2.855)$$
$$PMT = 6.000/2.855$$
$$= €2,101.58$$

An example is provided in Table 13.3.

Table 13.3: Amortization Schedule: End of Period.

End of period	Interest to be paid	Principal to be paid	Balance
0			6.000
1	900	1,202	4,798
2	720	1,382	3,417
3	512	1,589	1,827
4	274	1,827	0

Leasing

Leasing is an alternative to buying. The *lessor* is the owner of the property or equipment. The *lessee* is the user of the property or equipment. The *lease* is the contractual agreement.

Operating lease is a contract for the use of equipment and generally includes a service clause. *Capital or financial lease* is a contract for expected life of the asset. No maintenance clause is attached. The lease payment is designed to earn a set return for the lessor.

In a *sale and lease back contract*, assets are sold to a second party, then leased back to the original owner. The main reason is a tax advantage.

Characteristics of leasing:
- The lessor owns the asset legally, but gives up the economic value.
- The contract life equals the economic life in financial leasing.
- The lessor receives the cost of the assets plus a profit.
- The contract contains the lease terms:
    - Duration of lease
    - Payments
    - Any renewal or purchase option
    - Special arrangements (for example, maintenance insurance)

Advantages of leasing:
- Flexibility
- Elimination of protective covenants associated with debt
- Higher leverage and get up to 100% financing without a down payment
- The lessor's priorities are below the creditor's in bankruptcy
- Tax advantages
- Lease information is frequently disguised

Disadvantages of leasing:
- The residual value goes to the lessor
- Interest cost is higher than debt financing
- Financial risk of the firm is increased

The decision to lease depends on present value of the cash outflows associated with leasing compared to the present value of the cash outflows associated with borrowing and owning.

A capital budgeting framework is employed to decide whether to lease or buy an asset:
- *Step 1.* Find the after-tax cash outflows under the lease alternative.
- *Step 2.* Find the after-tax cash outflows under the purchase alternative.
- *Step 3.* Calculate the PV of expected future cash flows, using the firm's after-tax cost of debt, under each alternative, and select the alternative with the lower present value of expected cash outflows.

Although the analysis approach is similar to capital budgeting decision, the decision is not a capital budgeting (investment) decision, but a *financing decision*.

Leasing was considered an example of *off-balance sheet* financing. But this is not possible according to *International Financial Reporting Standards*. If the lease essentially provides the benefits of ownership, the lease must be *capitalized*. The present value of the lease payments is put on the lessee's balance sheet as a fixed asset. The same amount is credited to a medium- to long-term liability account, which is called *lease liability*.

Let us give an example. ABC Inc. has decided to acquire a new data system for its home office. The equipment costs €2,000,000, and if it were purchased, ABC could obtain a term loan for the full purchase price at an 8% interest rate. The system will be depreciated in 5 years. If the system were purchased, a 5-year maintenance contract could be obtained at a cost of €50,000 per year, payable at the beginning of each year. The equipment would be sold after 5 years, and the best estimate of its residual value at that time is €200,000.

As an alternative to the borrow-and-buy plan, the equipment manufacturer informed ABC that XYZ Leasing would be willing to write a 5-year guideline lease on the equipment, including maintenance, for payments of €450,000 at the beginning of each year. ABC's marginal corporate tax rate is 20 percent. ABC will depreciate the new equipment by *double declining balance* method. You have been asked to analyze the lease-versus-purchase decision, and, in the process, you should answer the following questions:

- What is the present value cost of owning the equipment? (Set up a timeline which shows the net cash flows over the period $t = 0$ to $t = 5$, and then find the PV of these net cash flows, or the PV cost of owning.)
- Leasing is similar to debt financing in that the cash flows have relatively low risk because most are fixed by contract. Therefore, the firm's 10% cost of debt is a good start. The tax shield of interest payments must be considered. 8% $(1-t) = 10\%\ (1-0.2) = 6.4\%$.
- What is the net advantage to leasing (NAL)? Does your analysis indicate that ABC should buy or lease the equipment? Explain.

First, we want to show depreciation calculations. See Table 13.4.

Table 13.4: Depreciation Calculations.

Year	Depreciation Expense, Straight Line (SL)	Depreciation Expense, DoubleDeclining Balance (DDB)	SL Shield	DDB Shield
1	€360	800	72	160
2	360	480	72	96
3	360	288	72	58
4	360	173	72	35
5	360	259	72	52
NPV @8%			287.48	337.61

Depreciation shields are calculated as:

Depreciation shield = Depreciation Expense × Tax Rate

Since the PV of DDB Shield is larger than SL Shield, ABC adopts DDB method.

In Tables 13.5 and 13.6, we show the amortization tables of two alternatives. In a leasing case, the present value of rental payment gives us the debt. The PV of debt was obtained using the annuity due formula.

Table 13.5: Loan Amortization Schedule, End of the Period.

End of the Period	Interest to be Paid	Principal to be Paid	Balance of Principal
0			2.000
1	€160	341	1.659
2	133	368	1.291
3	103	398	893
4	71	429	464
5	37	464	0

Table 13.6: Leasing Amortization Schedule, Beginning of the Period.

Beginning of the Period	Interest to be Paid	Principal to be Paid	Balance of Principal
1		€450	€1.490
2	119	331	1.160
3	93	357	802
4	64	386	417
5	33	417	0

Since the NPV of leasing is less than NPV of borrowing, ABC should adopt the leasing alternative. See Tables 13.7 and 13.8. However, in building the models, we have made such assumptions:
- We have ignored VAT and the like.
- Annual interests are paid at the end the year.
- Annual rentals are paid at the beginning of the year.
- DDB shield is input into the model.

Table 13.7: NPV of Cost of Owning.

Year			End of the Period			
	0	1	2	3	4	5
Equipment cost	−€2,000.00					
Loan amount	€2,000.00					
Annuity Payment		−€500.91	−€500.91	−€500.91	−€500.91	−€00.91
Tax savings from interest		€32.00	€26.55	€20.65	€ 14.29	€.42
Depreciation shield		€160.00	€96.00	€57.60	€ 4.56	€ 1.84
Maintenance		−€50.00	−€50.00	−€50.00	−€ 0.00	−€50.00
Tax savings on maintenance		€10.00	€ 0.00	€10.00	€10.00	€10.00
Residual value						€200.00
Tax on residual value						−€40.00
Net cash flow		−€348.91	−€418.37	−€462.66	−€ 92.06	−€321.65
PV ownership cost	−€1,701.37					

Table 13.8: NPV of Leasing.

Year			Beginning of the Period		
	0	1	2	3	4
Lease payment	−€450.00	−€ 450.00	−€ 450.00	−€ 450.00	−€ 450.00
Tax savings from lease İnterest Expense		€ 23.85	€ 18.56	€ 12.84	−€ 6.67
Depreciation shield		€ 160.00	€ 96.00	€ 57.60	€ 34.56
Net cash flow	−€ 450.00	−€ 266.15	−€ 335.44	−€ 379.56	−€ 422.11
PV of leasing	−€ 1,640.90				

13.7 Summary

There are three approaches to financing working capital: the maturity-matching approach, aggressive approach, and conservative approach. A firm's financing strategy depends on many factors.

Three basic sources of short-term financing include: bank loans, trade credit, and commercial paper. Unsecured loans provided by commercial banks are the primary type of loan arrangement. Interest rates are typically stated in terms of prime rate plus a fixed number like Libor+1. A line of credit is the loan limit that the bank establishes with each of its business customers.

Trade credit is accounts receivable together with longer-term notes receivable taken by manufacturers, wholesalers, jobbers, and other businesses that sell products or services to businesses.

Commercial paper is a short-term promissory note backed solely by the credit quality of the issuer; there is no security or collateral behind the loan.

Secured lending (asset-based lending) means there is collateral or security backing the loan that can be claimed or sold by the lender in the event of default.

There are two types of accounts receivable financing: pledges and factoring. A pledge is a means of obtaining a short-term loan by using accounts receivable as collateral.

Factoring is the selling of receivables to a financial institution, the factor, usually without recourse.

Basic sources of (long-term) finance are the following: ordinary shares (equity capital), bonds (debt financing), term loans (debt financing), and leasing (debt financing).

Term to maturity loans are often referred to as notes or term loans. It is granted by commercial and development.

Leasing is an alternative to borrowing and owning. A lessor is the owner of the property or equipment. A lessee is the user of the property or equipment. A lease is the contractual agreement. The decision to lease depends on the present value of the cash outflows associated with leasing compared to the present value of the cash outflows associated with borrowing and owning.

14 International Financial Management

14.1 Introduction

Today, it is not possible for a country to live in isolation from other countries. Financial capital flows freely from country to country depending on interest rates, inflation, and political stability. Individuals want to be able to buy goods and services at the lowest prices for a given quality wherever the goods and services are available. This chapter begins with a discussion of the international monetary system. Our other focus is on the characteristics of and the difficulty in achieving a balance in international payments. A summary of *European Unification* is provided. A description of currency exchange rate relationships between countries and international parity relations is presented. Arbitrage is also described. Multinational companies, overseas investments, and capital budgeting are explained briefly. We then turn our attention to the management of foreign exchange exposure by businesses. This is followed by a discussion of how international trade is financed both for exporters and importers. We finally present some information on international financial institutions.

14.2 International Monetary System

The *international monetary system* is a system of institutions and mechanisms that exist in order to foster trade, manage the flow of financial capital, and determine exchange rates. This system is especially important in today's business environment because business is truly global. Developments in the international monetary system are summarized as follows:[1]

- A *gold standard* was the monetary system where currency was convertible into gold at fixed exchange rates prior to the start of World War II.
- *The International Monetary Fund* (IMF) was created to promote world trade by fostering monetary cooperation, securing financial stability, and making loans to countries facing balance of trade and payments problems.
- *The International Bank for Reconstruction and Development*, or *World Bank*, was created to help economic growth in developing countries.
- *The Bretton Woods System*, or exchange rate agreement, is an international monetary system in which individual currencies are tied to gold through the U.S. dollar via fixed or pegged exchange rates.
- However, by the 1960s, the value of U.S. gold stock was less than the number of foreign holdings of dollars, calling into question the viability of the Bretton Woods

---

[1] For further information, see Michael H. Muffet, Arthur I. Stonehill, and David K. Eitman, *Fundamentals of Multinational Finance*, Addison Wesley, 2003, pp. 22–43.

https://doi.org/10.1515/9783110705355-014

system. In 1970, as a response, the IMF created *Special Drawing Rights* (SDRS), a reserve asset consisting of a basket of portfolio of currencies that could be used to make international payments. Beginning in March 1973, major currencies were allowed to *float* against one another. By mid-1970, the gold standard was abandoned in favor of a system of flexible exchange rates, where currency exchange rates are determined by supply and demand forces. This is the system in use today.[2]

14.3 Balance of Payments

The *balance of payments* of a country is a document that shows all payments and receipts of the country vis-a-vis the rest of the world for a year. The balance of payments accounts is compiled using a *double entry accounting system* by central banks. Receipts are recorded as credits and payments are recorded as debits.

The balance of payments records all types of international transactions of a country over a certain period of time. It contains a wide variety of accounts. However, a country's international transactions can be grouped into the following five main categories:
- Current account
- Capital account
- Finance account
- Statistical discrepancy (net errors and omission)
- Official reserve account

The Current Account

This includes the export and imports of goods and primary net income as in Table 14.1, resulting in a deficit of 480 million U.S. dollars. For example, *Smalland* (a fictional country) thus had a balance of payments deficit on the current account in 20X8. The current account deficit implies that Smalland imported more than it exported. This deficit was realized by borrowing from foreigners or its reserves.

The current account is divided into four subcategories as in Table 14.1.
- *Balance of trade in goods*. It shows the most traditional international economic activity. The current account is typically dominated by this component, which is known as the *balance of trade* (BOT).

---

2 For the current exchange regime, see Nicholas Sunday, *Principles of International Finance*, Grin, 2013, pp. 12–13.

Table 14.1: Summary of the Balance of Payments of Smalland for 20X8 ($ in millions).

	20X8
CURRENT ACCOUNT BALANCE	−480
Export f.o.b.	1,209
Import f.o.b.	−1,774
Balance of trade in goods	−565
Exports of services	340
Imports of services	−195
Balance of trade in goods and services	−420
Primary income inflow	44
Primary income outflow	−118
Balance of trade in goods, Services and Income	−494
Current transfers (net)	14
CAPITAL ACCOUNT	−1
FINANCE ACCOUNT	578
Direct Investment Inflow	−15
Direct Investment Outflow	92
Portfolio Investment Assets	−36
Portfolio Investment Assets	196
Other Investments-Assets	70
Other Investment-Liabilities	271
Current, Capital, and Financial Accounts	97
NET ERRORS AND OMISSIONS	46
	0
GENERAL BALANCE	143
RESERVE ASSETS	−143
Official Reserves	−119
IMF Loans	−24
Financing of Balance of Payment	

- *Services.* These are the *export* and *import* of services, including financial services provided by banks to foreign importers and exporters, travel services of airlines, and construction services of domestic firms in other countries.
- *Primary income.* The dividend incomes from subsidiaries are the income receipts. The wages and salaries paid to nonresident workers are income payments.
- *Current transfers.* Any transfer between countries that is one-way – such as a gift or grant – is termed a current transfer. For example, funds provided by a developed country as an aid to a less-developed nation, or money sent home by migrants and permanent workers abroad is a unilateral transfer.

The current account balance, especially trade balance, tends to be sensitive to exchange rate charges when a country's currency depreciates against the currencies of major trading partners. The country's exports rise while the imports fall, improving the trade balance.

The effect of currency depreciation on a country's trade balance can be more complicated than the case described here. Indeed, following a depreciation, the trade balance may at first deteriorate for a while. Eventually, however, the trade balance will tend to improve over time. See Figure 14.1. This particular reaction pattern of the trade balance to a depreciation is referred to as the *J-Curve effect.*

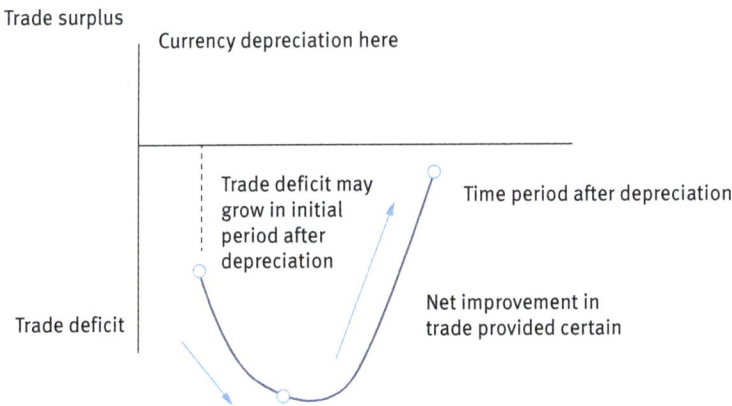

Figure 14.1: J-Curve Effect.

A depreciation will begin to improve the trade balance immediately, if imports and exports are responsive to the exchange rate changes. On the other hand, if imports and exports are inelastic, the trade balance will worsen following a depreciation. Following a depreciation of the domestic currency and the resultant rise in import prices, domestic residents may still continue to purchase imports because it is difficult to change their consumption habits in a short period of time. Even if domestic residents are willing to switch to less expensive domestic substitutes for foreign imports, it may take time for domestic producers to supply import substitutes. Likewise, foreigners' demand for domestic products, which become less expensive with a depreciation of the domestic currency, can be inelastic essentially for the same reasons. In the long run, however, both imports and exports tend to be responsive to exchange rate changes, exerting positive influences in the trade balance.

The Capital Account

The *capital account* balance shows the country's sales of assets to foreigners and the country's purchase of foreign assets.

Sales or exports of assets are recorded as credit, as they result in capital inflow. On the other hand, the country's purchases (imports) of foreign assets are recorded as debit, as they lead to capital outflow. There is payment, as shown in Table 14.1.

Finance Account

Unlike trades in goods and services, trade in financial assets affect future payments and receipt of factor income.

As the previous exhibit shows, Smalland had a finance account surplus of $580 million in 20X8, implying that there was a capital inflow of this amount into Smallland.

Clearly, the current account deficit was almost entirely offset by the finance account surplus. A country's current account deficit must be paid for either by borrowing from foreigners or selling off post foreign investments.

In the absence of the government's reserve transactions, the current account balance must equal the capital and finance accounts balance but with the opposite sign. When nothing is excluded, a country's balance of payments must balance.

The finance account can be divided into three subcategories:
- Direct investments
- Portfolio investments
- Other investments

Direct investment occurs when the investor acquires controlling interest of a foreign business.

Portfolio investments mostly represent the sale and purchases of foreign financial assets such as stock and bonds that do not involve a transfer of control. Portfolio investments comprise equity securities and debt securities that include corporate shares, bonds, notes, money market instruments, and financial derivatives such as options.

Other investments include transactions such as currency bank deposits and trade credits. These investments are quite sensitive to both changes in relative interest rates between countries and the anticipated change in exchange rates.

Statistical Discrepancy (Net Errors and Omissions)

Statistical discrepancy refers to the estimate of foreign exchange flow on account of either variations in the collection of related figures or unrecorded illegal transaction of foreign exchange. An FX inflow of $46 million is reported in Table 14.1.

Official Reserve Account

The *official reserve account* is the reserve held by central banks. When a country must make payments to foreigners because of a balance of payments deficit, the central bank of the country should either run down its official reserve assets, such as gold, foreign exchanges, and special drawing rights (SDRs), or borrow from foreign central banks.

On the other hand, if a country has a surplus balance of payments, its central bank will either retire some of its foreign debts or increase its reserves.

The official reserve account includes transactions undertaken by authorities to finance the overall balance and intervene in foreign exchange markets.

International reserve assets comprise:
- Gold
- Foreign exchange
- Special drawing rights (SDRs)
- Reserve positions in the IMF

As seen in Table 14.1, Smalland officials used reserves to pay off its debts decreasing the reserves by $143 million.

Contrary to the accounting mechanism previously discussed, foreign currency inflows are recorded as debit and foreign currency outflows are recorded as credit.

Special Drawing Rights (SDRs). In the late 1960s, neither gold nor major foreign currencies were available in sufficient quantities to support the growing volume of international transactions. Therefore, an agreement was reached among the industrial and developing countries to create an *artificial currency* named *special drawing rights* (SDRs) in 1967. SDRs are credits extended to importing countries and are monitored by an international organization called the *International Monetary Fund* (IMF), located in Washington, DC. Each country has a credit quota depending on the volume of its exports and imports. SDRs are exchanged only among central banks and are convertible into other currencies.

The value of an SDR was initially determined by sixteen major currencies, each of which had a different weight depending on its volume in international trade. The method of valuation was changed in 1981, and the value of an SDR now is basically the weighted average of four currencies: the U.S. dollar, euro, Japanese yen, and UK pound sterling.

14.4 European Unification

The *European Union*, often referred to as the EU, is an economic and political partnership[3] involving 28 European countries. It began after World War II to foster economic cooperation with the idea that countries that trade together were more likely to avoid going to war with each other. It traces its origins to the establishment of the *European Economic Community* (EEC) by six European nations in the post–World War II years.

The aim of the European Union was also to pursue closer economic cooperation on the European continent with the intent of preventing wars. In this respect, the EU has proven its worth: Western Europe has never before enjoyed such a long period of peace. Although the EU began as a purely economic community, cooperation has expanded in the intervening years to include areas such as asylum, migration, justice, safety, energy, environment, and foreign policy, developing into a unique political organization.

The list of members of EU and some information on the members are presented in Table 14.2.

Table 14.2: Members of EU.

Country	Accession	Population (in millions)	Area (km2)	Seats in European Parliament	Votes in EU Council
Austria	1995	8.8	83,879	18	10
Belgium	1957	11.3	30,528	21	12
Bulgaria	2007	7.1	110,370	17	10

---

3 For an economic analysis of the European Union, see Susan Grant and Colin G. Bamford, *The European Union*, Fifth Edition, Heinemann, 2006.

Table 14.2 (continued)

Country	Accession	Population (in millions)	Area (km2)	Seats in European Parliament	Votes in EU Council
Croatia	2013	4.2	56,594	11	7
Cyprus	2004	0.8	9,251	6	4
Czechia	2004	10.6	78,868	21	12
Denmark	1973	5.7	42,924	13	7
Estonia	2004	1.3	45,227	6	4
Finland	1995	5.5	338,446	13	7
France	1957	67	633,187	74	29
Germany	1957	82.5	357,376	96	29
Greece	1981	10.8	131,957	21	12
Hungary	2004	9.8	93,011	21	12
Ireland	1973	4.8	69,797	11	7
Italy	1957	60.6	302,073	70	29
Latvia	2004	1.9	64,573	8	4
Lithuania	2004	2.8	65,286	11	7
Luxembourg	1957	0.6	2,586	6	4
Malta	2004	0.5	315	6	3
Netherlands	1957	17.1	41,542	26	13
Poland	2004	38	312,679	51	27
Portugal	1986	10.4	92,226	21	12
Romania	2007	19.6	238,391	32	14
Sweden	1995	10	438,574	19	10
Slovakia	2004	5.5	49,035	13	7
Slovenia	2004	2	20,273	8	4
Spain	1986	46.5	505,944	54	27
United Kingdom*	1973	65.8	248,528	73	29
Total		511.5	4,463,440	747	352

*will leave the Union in 2020.
Source: DEA, https://www.eda.admin.ch/dea/en/home/eu/europaeische-union/mitgliedstaaten-eu.html, 08.10.2018.

It has since grown to become a *single market*, allowing goods and people to move around as if the member states were one country. It has its own currency, the *euro*, which is used by 19 of the member countries, its own parliament. It now sets rules in a wide range of areas, including on the environment, transport, consumer rights, and even things such as mobile phone charges.

Euro

The *euro*, introduced as legal tender, is used by almost 340 million EU citizens today. It has been in the pockets of EU citizens since January 2002. The creation of the single European currency took decades of preparation.

Rationale for euro:
- It is easier for goods, people, and services traveling across national borders.
- It eliminates exchange costs when trading between countries.
- It eliminates the uncertainty associated with exchange rate fluctuations.
- It eliminates cost differences for goods in different countries.
- It is easier to compare prices and reduce the discrepancies.

14.5 Currency Exchange Markets and Rates

Currency exchange markets, also called *foreign exchange markets*, are *electronic markets* where banks and institutional traders buy and sell various currencies on behalf of businesses, other clients, and themselves. A currency exchange rate indicates the value of one currency relative to another currency. Exchange rates are stated in two basic ways:
- The *direct quotation method* indicates the value of one unit of a foreign currency in terms of a home country's currency; or
- The *indirect quotation method* indicates the number of units of a foreign currency needed to purchase one unit of the home country's currency.

An *American currency quotation* is how much U.S. currency it takes to buy one unit of foreign currency. In a currency pair, the first currency listed is one unit, and the listed rate is how much of the second currency it takes to buy the single unit of the first. For example, an American currency quote would be $0.84 USD per $1 CAD. This shows that it will take 0.84 U.S. dollars to purchase a single unit of Canadian currency. To purchase $1,000 CAD, it would cost $840 USD. The currency pair involved is the CAD/USD.

The opposite of an American currency quotation is a European currency quotation where the foreign currency is the stated per-unit measure of the U.S. dollar. Using the Canadian dollar again as an example, assume a rate of $1.35 CAD per $1 USD. This explains that it will take 1.35 Canadian dollars to purchase a single U.S. dollar. In this case, the pair involved flips to the USD/CAD.

The first currency of the pair is always called *base currency*. The second currency is called *counter currency* (or quote currency). Currency pair quotes are always expressed in units of the counter currency to get one unit of the base currency.

Traders more often refer to quotes as direct or indirect, rather than American or European, although all the terms are used.

Depreciation of Danish krone against a foreign currency means that more Danish kroners will be paid to buy the same amount of foreign currency. For instance, if 1 USD is worth of dk.6,000, while it was dk.5,950 yesterday, it means that Danish krone has depreciated today. For instance, if 1 USD is worth of dk.6,000, while it was Dk.6,100 yesterday, it means that Danish krone has appreciated today.

Change (appreciation or depreciation) in the value of local and foreign currency can be calculated as follows:[4]

$$\% \text{ change} = (\text{Beginning rate} - \text{Ending rate})/\text{Ending rate}$$

For instance, if USD was worth of dk.4,000 in the beginning of the year, worth dk.5,000 at the end of the year? Or initially dk.1=\$0.25, later dk.1=\$0.20. What is the change in dk. and dollars? Assume that dk. is the local currency.

First, let us calculate these figures will be 4,000 and 5,000 terms of direct quotation (dk.):

Change = (4,000 – 5,000)/5,000 = – 0.20. In this case, dk.has depreciated by 20%.

Now let us calculate in terms of indirect quotation:

Change = (0.2500 – 0.20)/0.20 = 0.25. In this case USD has appreciated by 25%.

The difference between the bid and ask price is called a *spread*. A *pip* is the smallest amount a price can move in any currency quote. For example, for the quote, EUR/USD 1.2700/05, the spread would be 0.0005 or 5 pips, which are also called *points*. Exchange rates between TL and some selected currencies are presented in Table 14.3.

Table 14.3: Danish Krone Exchange Rates Table.

Danish Krone	1.00 dk.	inv. 1.00 dk.
US Dollar	0.149422	6.692444
Euro	0.133810	7.473274
British Pound	0.118470	8.440935

---

4 In the flexible exchange rate system, appreciation and depreciation terms are used instead of revaluation and devaluation in the fixed exchange rate system.

Table 14.3 (continued)

Danish Krone	1.00 dk.	inv. 1.00 dk.
Indian Rupee	11.029201	0.090668
Australian Dollar	0.237030	4.218876
Canadian Dollar	0.206294	4.847439
Singapore Dollar	0.210395	4.752963
Swiss Franc	0.141216	7.081352
Malaysian Ringgit	0.639342	1.564108
Japanese Yen	15.906767	0.062866

Source: https://www.x-rates.com/table/?from=
Dk.&amount=1, 13.03.2020.

A *spot exchange rate* is the rate being quoted for the immediate delivery of the currency. The supply and demand balance involving two currencies is in balance, or at equilibrium, at the current of spot exchange. A *forward exchange rate* is the rate for the purchase or sale of a currency where delivery will take place at a future date. Currency exchange rates depend on relative inflation rates, interest rates, and political and economic risks. Note that currency rates tend to change often. See Table 14.4.

Table 14.4: Currency Table.

Currency	Last	Day High	Day Low	% Change	Bid	Ask
EUR/USD	▲ 1.1707	1.1725	1.1676	▲ +0.19%	1.1707	1.1710
GBP/USD	▼ 1.3254	1.3292	1.3225	▲ +0.17%	1.3254	1.3258
USD/JPY	▼ 112.34	112.55	112.14	▼ −0.02%	112.34	112.37
USD/CHF	▼0.99750	1.0024	0.99720	▼ −0.41%	0.99750	0.99790
USD/CAD	▼ 1.3154	1.3162	1.3137	▼ −0.04%	1.3154	1.3160
AUD/USD	▼0.74230	0.74420	0.74080	▼ +0.00%	0.74230	0.74280

Source: https://www.reuters.com/finance/currencies/quote?srcCurr=TRY&destCurr=USD.
16.7.2018.

The forward exchange rate is the fixed price that applies for contracts with delivery in the future. The forward premium or discount is useful for comparing against the interest rate differentials between two countries. The forward premium or discount can be expressed in American or European terms.

On a certain date in 20X8, the agreement to trade dollars for pounds one month later was a specified forward price of $1.5924/£. Spot rate was $1.5955/£.

$$\frac{F-S}{S} = \frac{\$1.5924/£ - \$1.5955/£}{\$1.5955/£} = -0.194\%$$

$$\text{Annualized forward discount} = -0.194\% \times (360/30)$$

$$\text{Annualized forward discount} = -2.33\%$$

The *Foreign Exchange Market* is organized as an over-the-counter market. It is a network of telephone and computer connections among banks, foreign exchange dealers, and brokers.

The FX market operates at three levels:[5]
- *Level 1.* Customers buy and sell foreign exchange through their banks.
- *Level 2.* Banks buy and sell foreign exchange from other banks in the same commercial center.
- *Level 3.* Banks buy and sell foreign exchange from banks in commercial centers in other countries (cities such as New York, London, Zurich, Frankfurt, Hong Kong, Singapore, and Tokyo).

An example of multi-level trading is:
- Importer buys Japanese yen from a bank in California for payment to a Japanese supplier.
- California bank purchases the Japanese yen from a bank in New York.
- The New York bank buys the yen from another bank in New York.

14.6 International Parity Relations

In economics, *parity* is the equality in price, rate of exchange, purchasing power, or wages. In international exchange, parity refers to the exchange rate between the currencies of two countries, making the purchasing power of both currencies substantially equal. Theoretically, exchange rates of currencies can be set at a parity or par level and adjusted to maintain parity as economic conditions change. An understanding of parity relationships provides insights into:

---

5 Cheol S. Eun, Bruce G. Resnick, *International Financial Management*, Third Edition, McGraw, 2004, p. 76.

- How foreign exchange rates are determined.
- How to forecast foreign exchange rates.

Arbitrage can be defined as the act of simultaneously buying and selling the same or equivalent assets or commodities for the purpose of making certain guaranteed profits. As long as there are profitable arbitrage opportunities, the market cannot be in equilibrium. Such well known parity relationships as *interest rate parity* and *purchasing power parity*, in fact, present arbitrage equilibrium conditions.

Interest Rate Parity Theory: Short-Term Determination of FX Rates

Interest rate parity theory states that the forward premium or discount (except for the effects of small transaction costs) should be equal and opposite in size to the difference in the national interest rates for securities of the same maturity.

Expected spot rate (domestic currency per unit of foreign currency)	= Current spot rate (domestic currency per unit of foreign currency)	× (1 + expected domestic interest rate)/ (1 + expected foreign interest rate)

In other words, because of arbitrage, the interest rate differential between two countries must be equal to the difference between the forward and spot exchange rates.

Let e_o be the current spot rate (the dollar value of euro, say), and f_1 the end-of-period forward rate. Let r_h and r_f be the prevailing interest rates in New York and Brussels, respectively.

Assume that the interest rate in the United States is 10% and 8% in the European Union. Let the spot rate for the euro be $1.20. If the interest rate parity holds, what is the 90-day forward rate? The forward rate is given by the following:

$$f_1 = (1 + r_h) \times e_0/(1 + r_f) = (1 + 0.025) \times 1.20/(1 + 0.02) = \$1.2059$$

Thus, the annualized forward premium is $(1.2059 - 1.20) \times 4/1.20 = 1.95\%$.

Purchasing Power Parity Theory (PPP): Long-Term Determination of FX Rates

In the long run, exchange rates adjust so that the purchasing power of each currency tends to be the same. The exchange rate changes tend to reflect international differences in inflation rates.

Countries with high rates of inflation tend to experience declines in the value of their currency. Thus, according to PPP:

Expected spot rate = Current spot rate × Expected difference in inflation rate.

Expected spot rate (domestic currency per unit of foreign currency)	=	Current spot rate (domestic currency per unit of foreign currency)	×	(1 + expected domestic inflation rate)/ (1 + expected foreign inflation rate)

PPP is based on the *law of one price*, a proposition in competitive markets in which there are no transportation costs or barriers to trade. The same goods sold in different countries sell for the same price if all the different prices are expressed in terms of the same currency.

Let i_h and i_f be the periodic price level increases (rates of inflation) for the home country and the foreign country, respectively. Let e_0 be the current spot rate (the dollar value of euro, say) and e_t the spot exchange rate in period t. Then:

$$e_t/e_0 = (1+i_h)^t/(1+i_f)^t$$

The one-period version of the relation is as follows:

$$e_1 = (1+i_h) \times e_0/(1+i_f)$$

Suppose the inflation rate is 4% in the United States and 3% in the European Union. If the initial value of the euro is $1.15, the dollar value at the end of one year will be as follows:

$$e_1 = (1+i_h) \times e_0/(1+i_f) = \$(1.04) \times 1.15/1.03 = \$1.1612$$

That is, the euro will appreciate by (1.1612–1.15)/1.15 = 0.97%.

International Fisher Effect

The *International Fisher Effect* states that the real interest rate should be the same all over the world, with the differences in nominal rate resulting from differences in expected inflation rates.

Thus, investing in a foreign bond with the highest interest rate may simply mean investing in a country with the highest rate of inflation.

According to the Fisher effect, the nominal interest rate R is made up of two components:
- Real required returns are assumed to be the same in both countries.
- Inflation premium equals the expected rate of inflation.

If the real required return is the same across countries, then the following equation is true:

$$\frac{1+R_{for}}{1+R_{dom}} = \frac{[1+E(i_{for})]}{[1+E(i_{dom})]}$$

Where:

R_{for} = Nominal interest rate in foreign country,
R_{dom} = Domestic nominal interest rate,
I_{for} = Nominal inflation rate in foreign country,
I_{dom} = Domestic nominal inflation rate.

Assume that expected inflation in the United States equals 3% and expected inflation in Italy is 8%. A one-year risk-free rate in the U.S. is 3.2%. What should the one-year interest rate be to maintain the real interest rate parity?

$$\frac{1+R_{Italy}}{1+0.032} = \frac{(1+0.08)}{(1+0.03)} \quad R_{Italy} = 8.20\%$$

Deviations from real interest rate parity occur because of limits to arbitrage.

Forecasting Exchange Rates

In forecasting exchange rates, there are three approaches:
-   Efficient markets approach
-   Fundamental approach
-   Technical approach

Efficient Markets Hypothesis (EMH) Approach. Financial markets are *efficient* if prices reflect all available and relevant information. If this is so, exchange rates will only change when new information arrives. Predicting exchange rates using the efficient markets approach is not possible.

Fundamental Approach. This approach involves econometrics to develop models that use a variety of explanatory variables. This involves three steps:[6]
-   *Step 1:* Estimate the structural model.
-   *Step 2:* Estimate the future parameter values.
-   *Step 3:* Use the model to develop forecasts.

---

6 For a developed model, see Jae Shim, *Financial Management of Multinational Corporations*, Global Professional Publishing, 2009, pp. 100–102.

The downside is that fundamental models do not work any better than the forward rate model or the random walk model.

Technical Approach. *Technical* analysis looks for patterns in the past behavior of exchange rates. It is based upon the premise that history repeats itself. Thus, it is at odds with the EMH.

14.7 Arbitrage

Arbitrage is the simultaneous purchasing of commodities, securities, or bills of exchange in one market and selling them in another where the price is higher. The effect of arbitrage on exchange rates is to eliminate the price discrepancy between the markets.

Foreign exchange quotes in two different countries must be in line with each other. Otherwise, a trader could make a profit by buying in the market where the currency was cheaper and selling it in the other.

The process of buying and selling in more than one market to make a riskless profit is called *arbitrage*. Such opportunities do not exist for a long time due to the arbitrage process.

Types of arbitrage:
- *Simple.* Eliminates exchange rate differentials across the markets for a single currency.
- *Triangular.* Eliminates exchange rate differentials across the markets for all currencies.
- *Covered-interest.* Eliminates differentials across the currency and interest-rate markets.

Simple. As a speculator in the financial markets, you notice that for the last few minutes, Swiss francs are being quoted in New York at a price of $0.5849 and in Frankfurt at $0.5851. Assuming that you have access to international trading facilities, what action might you take? Purchase Swiss francs in New York at $0.5849 and simultaneously sell francs in Frankfurt at $0.05851 in order to *lock* a profit of $0.0002 per franc. Such an arbitrage activity involving one million francs would produce a profit of $200,000.

Triangular arbitrage. We will now discuss *triangular arbitrage*. The cross-exchange rate is the exchange rate between two currencies other than USD. Divide the dollar exchange rate for one currency by the dollar exchange rate for another currency.

Assume you are quoted the following exchange rates: SF1.50/$; €1.00/$; F1.25/€.

$$\text{Cross} - \text{exchange rate}(SF/€) = SF1.50/\$: €1.00/\$ = 1.50 \ SF/\$ \times \$/€1.00$$

$$= 1.50 \ SF/1.00€$$

Since the cross-exchange rate (1.50 SF/1.00€) is different from quoted rate (SF1.25/€) there might be arbitrage opportunity.
-   Exchange $1.000.000 into SF1.500.000 (at SF1.50/$)
-   Trade SF1.500.000 for €1.200.000 (at €0.80/SF)
-   Convert €1.200.000 into $1.200.000 (at $1.00/€)

You could make a riskless, instant profit of $200.000.

Covered Interest. When *Interest Rate Parity Theory* (IRP) holds, you will be indifferent between investing your money in the U.S. and investing in the UK with forward hedging. When IRP does not hold, the situation also gives rise to covered interest arbitrage opportunities, which is illustrated as follows:

$$\text{Current spot rate} = C\$\,2.00/£$$

$$\text{Forward rate} = C\$\,2.05/£$$

Annualized interest rate on a six-month Canadian government bond is 6%.
    Rate on similar UK instrument is 2%.

$$\frac{C\$2.05/£}{C\$2/£} > \frac{1.03}{1.01}$$

This means the Canadian interest rate is too low or the UK interest rate is too high, which implies the existence of an arbitrage opportunity.
    The process is as follows:
-   Borrow $1,000,000 CAD at 6% per year and convert it into 500,000 pounds.
-   This will increase to 505,000 pounds in six months, at which time you convert back at the forward rate to $1,035,250 CAD.
-   Next, repay the Canadian loan, which takes $1,030,000 CAD.
-   Arbitrage profit is $5,250 CAD.

14.8 Multinational Corporations (MNCs)

A *multinational corporation* is a firm that operates in two or more countries.[7] Five reasons that companies go international are to:[8]

---

7 A. A. Groppelli, Eksan Nikbakht, *Finance*, Barron's Educational Series, 2000, p. 509.
8 Vyuptakesh Sharan, *International Financial Management*, Sixth Edition, PHI Learning, 2012, pp. 1–2.

- Seek new markets
- Seek raw materials
- Seek new technology
- Seek production efficiency
- Avoid political and regulatory hurdles

There are six factors that distinguish managerial (corporate) finance as practiced by firms operating entirely within a single country (domestic managerial finance) from management of firms operating in several different countries (international financial management). They are as follows:[9]
- Different currency denominations
- Economic and legal ramifications
- Language differences
- Cultural differences
- Role of governments
- Political risk

14.9 Investing Overseas

Individuals and companies in a country are affected by international finance in at least two ways:
- Growth or recession overseas affects jobs in domestic markets.
- Foreign investment in a country affects financial markets and interests.

The following risks affect the value of a currency:
- *Political risk.* Risk that governments might confiscate or expropriate assets held by foreigners.
- *Economic risk.* Risk of slow negative or variable economic growth, unstable exchange rates, and high inflation.

The risk can be defined, as tomorrow's exchange rate will differ from today's rate. Exchange rate risk affects:
- *International trade contracts.* You are expecting to receive 1 million euros next year from exports. The future value of euros in dollars is uncertain and depends on future exchange rate. If euro = $1.25, you will receive $1.25M, but if the Euro depreciates to $0.90, your contract is worth only $90M.

---

9 Cheol Eun, Bruce G. Resnick, *International Finance*, Seventh Global Edition, McGraw-Hill, 2014, pp. 5–8.

- *Foreign portfolio investments.* The future return on a portfolio is unknown as investments in securities are risky. Thus, investing in euro market could yield positive and negative results. In addition, the investor is exposed to USD and €/Euro exchange rate fluctuation. Thus, if the euro investment yields 10% but the euro depreciates during the period, the net return will be less than 10%, depending on the extent of euro depreciation.
- *Direct foreign investment.* In a *direct foreign investment* (DFI), a parent company invests in assets denominated in foreign currency. The U.S.-based parent company receives the repatriated profit stream from the subsidiary in dollars. Thus, the exchange rate risk arises due to fluctuations in the dollar value of the assets located abroad and fluctuations in the home currency-denominated profit stream.

14.10 International Capital Budgeting

A hypothetical Denmark-based multinational company ABC is trying to determine whether the project is profitable or not. The Danish firm will set up a new plant to produce soap and detergents in Kyrgyzstan.

The project initially requires 100m coms of capital expenditure and will generate the cash flows, net of tax, during the life of the investment shown in Table 14.5.

Table 14.5: Cash Flows
(in million coms).

Year	Cash flows
1	30
2	40
3	50
4	60
5	100

The current spot rate is 25 coms per dk. (1 com = dk.0.04). The risk-free rates in Denmark and Kyrgyzstan are estimated to be 2% and 8%, respectively. The company's hurdle rate is 15%. Tax rate in Kyrgyzstan and Denmark are 10% and 30%, respectively. Should the firm undertake this project? Our answer will depend on the NPV of the project.

How do we calculate the NPV of such a project? They are two basic methods: local currency method and foreign currency method.[10] We will just examine the local currency method here. See Table 14.6.

Table 14.6: NPV of Project for the Subsidiary income.

Years	0	1	2	3	4	5
Subsidiary Point of View (million com)						
Capital Expenditures	−100	–	–	–	–	–
Net Operating Cash Flow	–	30	40	50	60	100
Management Commissions	–	1	1	1	1	1
Cash Flow	–	29	39	49	59	99
Tax to be withheld	–	2.9	3.9	4.9	5.9	9.9
Net Cash Flow	–	26.1	35.1	44.,1	53.1	89.1
Net Present Value	52.89	–	–	–	–	–

We will have to use the estimated foreign currency (FX) rates in the local currency method. According to *interest rate parity*, the forward FX rate for period t can be estimated as follows:

$$S_t = S_0 \times ((1 + r_d)/(1 + r_f))^t$$

where.

S_0= Spot rate in time 0
r_d= Nominal risk-free rate in local currency
r_f= Nominal risk-free rate in foreign currency
In our case, S_0= dk. 0.04, r_d = 2%, r_f = 8%.
By using these inputs, we can calculate the estimate of forward FX rates, as shown in Table 14.7.
By using estimated spot rates, the company's cash flows are converted into euros, as shown in Table 14.8.

---

10 There is one more approach, called the *adjusted present value* method, which we do not discuss here. For further information, see Donald R. Lessard, "Evaluating International Projects: An Adjusted Present Value Approach." Donald R. Lessard (ed.), in *International Financial Management: Theory and Application*, Second Edition, New York: Wiley, 1985, pp. 570–84.

Table 14.7: Estimated Spot Rates.

Year	Estimated spot rate
1	$0.04 \times (1.02/1.08)^1 = 0.0378$
2	$0.04 \times (1.02/1.08)^2 = 0.0357$
3	$0.04 \times (1.02/1.08)^3 = 0.0337$
4	$0.04 \times (1.02/1.08)^4 = 0.0318$
5	$0.04 \times (1.02/1.08)^4 = 0.0301$

Table 14.8: NPV of Project for the Parent in com and dk.

Parent's Point of View (million com)	0	1	2	3	4	5
Operating Cash Flow of the Subsidiary	–	29	39	49	59	99
Tax to Be Withheld	–	2.9	3.9	4.9	5.9	9.9
Remitted, net	–	26.1	35.1	44.1	53.1	89.1
dk./com FX Rate	0.0400	0.0378	0.0357	0.0337	0.0318	0.0301

Parent's Point of View (million dk.)						
Capital Expenditures	−4.00	–	–	–	–	–
Remitted, net	–	0.99	1.25	1.49	1.69	2.68
Tax to Be Paid in Denmark	–	0.30	0.38	0.45	0.51	0.80
After-Tax Cash	–	0.69	0.88	1.04	1.18	1.87
Management Commission Received	–	0.04	0.04	0.03	0.03	0.03
Net Cash Flow	–	0.73	0.91	1.07	1.21	1.90
Net Present Value	**−0.33**					

$$NPV = -4 + 0.73/(1.15)^1 + 0.91/(1.15)^2 + 1.07/(1.15)^3 + 1.21/(1.15)4$$
$$+ 1.9/(1.15)^5 = -dk.0.33M$$

The project with a dk.-033M NPV seems unprofitable. In this hypothetical example, all cash flows are assumed to be remitted to the parent company. In real life, this is not the case. Governments may put restriction on remittances. Those funds that are not remitted are called *blocked funds*. In this case, the NPV is calculated using *remitted funds*. In addition, we ignored the tax effect of incoming cash flows.

14.11 Exposure to Exchange Rate Risk

There are three measures of foreign exchange exposure: translation exposure, transaction exposure, and economic exposure.

Translation Exposure

Translation exposure risk arises because the foreign operations of MNCs have financial statements denominated in the local currencies of the countries in which the operations are located. These denominations must be converted into the MNC's home currency at the prevailing exchange rate.

Translation methods are summarized as follows:
- *Current/noncurrent method.* All monetary balance sheet accounts (cash, marketable securities, accounts receivable, etc.) of a foreign subsidiary are translated at the current exchange rate. All other (non-monetary) balance sheet accounts (owners' equity, land) are translated at the historical exchange rate in effect when the account was first recorded.
- *Temporal method.* Balance sheet accounts are translated at the current spot exchange rate if they are carried on the books at their current value. Items that are carried on the books at historical costs are translated at the historical exchange rates in effect at the time the firm placed the item on the books.
- *Current rate method.* All balance sheet items (except for stockholder's equity) are translated at the current exchange rate. A "plug" equity account called the *cumulative translation adjustment* is used to make the balance sheet balance.

Some hedging techniques for translation exposure are:
- Hard currencies are those currencies whose value is likely to appreciate; soft currencies are those currencies whose value is likely to depreciate. Increase hard-currency assets – for example, increase dollar-denominated receivables.
- Decrease hard-currency debts – for example, pay off dollar-denominated debts.
- Decrease soft-currency assets. Increase soft-currency debts.

Transaction Exposure

Transaction exposure refers to the net contracted foreign currency transactions (such as receivables, payables, fixed price sales, or purchase contract) for which the settlement amounts are subject to changing exchange rates.

Transaction exposure can be hedged by using money market hedge, forward contracts, futures contracts, or options:

– Use futures or forwards when the quantity of a foreign currency cash flows is known. Use options when the quantity of a foreign currency cash flows is unknown.
– Money market hedge: To hedge payables, borrow home currency and invest in currency in which the payables will be settled. To hedge receivables, borrow foreign currency and invest in home currency asset.
– A variety of swap agreements can be used for transaction exposure management.

Economic Exposure

Economic exposure refers to the overall impact of exchange rate changes on the value of the firm. This change in value may be caused by a rate-change-induced decline in the level of expected cash flows or by an increase in the riskiness of these cash flows. Economic exposure to exchange rate changes depends on the competitive structure of the markets for a firm's inputs (purchases/expenses) and outputs (sales) and how these markets are influenced by changes in exchange rates. For example, the profits of a Canadian company that used coal in its production process was influenced indirectly by the Yen/USD exchange rate, as the price of coal depended on Japanese demand for coal, which in turn depended on the Yen/USD exchange rate.

International firms can use five techniques to reduce their economic exposure:
– A company can reduce its manufacturing costs by taking its production facilities to low-cost countries.
– A company can outsource its production or apply low-cost labor.
– A company can diversify its products and services and sell them to clients from around the world.
– A company can continually invest in research and development. Subsequently, it can offer innovative products at a higher price.
– A company can use derivatives and hedge against exchange rate changes.

14.12 Conducting International Business

Firms that do business overseas must accept the uncertainties of working in an unfamiliar environment. In order to reduce exposure to foreign exchange fluctuations, companies may utilize the tools in the following areas:
– Hedging
– Adjusting accounts receivable and payable procedures
– Cash management
– Borrowing and lending activities

International Financing and Investment Decisions

MNC has access to both domestic and foreign markets for financing. Foreign host countries may often provide low-cost subsidized financing to attract investments. Because of its international presence, MNC can also access external currency markets such as *Eurodollar*, *Eurocurrency*, or *Asian* dollar markets.

The decision process for *direct foreign investment* (DFI) is similar to capital budgeting decisions in the domestic context. Risks in domestic capital budgeting arise from two sources: business risk and financial risk. In international capital budgeting problems, we also have to incorporate political risk and exchange risks.

Political risk arises because the foreign subsidiary conducts business in a political system different from that of the home country.

Some examples of such risk include:
- Expropriation of assets without compensation.
- Non-convertibility of the subsidiary's foreign earnings into the currency of the parent company.
- Changes in the laws governing taxation.
- Restrictions on sale price, wage rates, local borrowing, extent of local ownership, hiring of personnel, and transfer payments made to the parent.

In summary, exchange rate risks can have significant effect on cash flows and earnings.

Multinational Working-Capital Management

Basic principles of working-capital management for a multinational corporation are similar to those of a domestic firm. Tax rates and exchange rates are additional considerations.

There are two techniques used for managing working capital:
- Leading and lagging strategies
- Cash management and positioning of funds

Leading and Lagging Strategies. *Holding* a net asset (long) position in a weak or potentially depreciating currency is not desirable. *Leading* means selling these assets and converting the funds into a stronger currency. *Lagging* means delaying the collection against a net asset position in a strong currency. In case of a net liability (short) position, two things can be done:
- In case of a weakening currency, the payment should be delayed.
- In case of a strengthening currency, the payment should be expedited.

Cash Management and Positioning of Funds. Funds may be transferred from a subsidiary of the multinational company in country A to another subsidiary in country B such that the foreign exchange exposure and the tax liability is mini-mized. The transfer of funds among subsidiaries and the parent company is done via royalties, fees, and transfer pricing. Transfer pricing is the price charged by a subsidiary or a parent company to other companies that are part of the multina-tional company for its goods and services.

14.13 International Financial Markets

The term *international financial markets* refers to various financial institutions around the world in which multinational firms and governments participate to borrow money or invest surplus funds. The two major international financial markets are the Eurodollar market (Euromarket) and the international bond (Eurobond) market.

The Euromarket

The Eurodollar market offers short-term and intermediate loans denominated in the U.S. dollar. The maturity date of Eurodollar loans is usually less than 5 years. *Eurodollars* by definition are U.S. dollars traded outside U.S. borders. The Eurodollar market is an alternative to domestic banks for financing the business operations of international firms. Instead of using commercial banks in the United States, an American firm may find it cheaper and easier to borrow dollars outside this country to finance its foreign or domestic subsidiaries. Borrowing through the Euromarket has become very popular because the banking procedure is not controlled by the host government. Credit terms are also more flexible and sometimes cheaper than those for domestic loans. These flexible and relatively cheaper terms are sometimes attributed to greater availability of funds and more efficiency in the Euromarket as compared to domestic banking.

The International Bond Market

Whereas the Euromarket deals with short-term and intermediate loans, the interna-tional bond market lends long-term funds outside the country of the borrower. For instance, a firm in Brazil may issue long-term bonds denominated in the U.S. dollar in European countries. Such bonds, denominated often in most major currencies and issued outside the borrowing country, are called *international bonds* or *Eurobonds*.

How Eurodollars Are Created

Eurodollars are created when deposit accounts in the United States transfer to deposit accounts outside the country and maintain the denomination in the U.S. dollar. Suppose the XYZ Corporation in New York decides to transfer $500,000 of deposits from Citibank in New York to the Westminster Bank in London. If this deposit is maintained in terms of the U.S. dollar, the XYZ Corporation becomes the owner of $500,000 Eurodollars as a result. Westminster Bank in London becomes liable to the XYZ Corporation and Citibank to Westminster Bank. Note that Eurodollars, despite being traded outside the United States, keep their origin with a bank in the United States.

Another characteristic of Eurodollars is that they may continuously create more credit. To illustrate, in the previous example, the Westminster Bank in London may lend the 500,000 Eurodollars to a firm either within or outside England. Suppose the borrowing firm is located in France and it decides to keep the loan in the form of a deposit with Credit Lyonnais in Paris. What happens in the United States is simply a change in liability of the Citibank from Westminster to Credit Lyonnais. As long as deposits are maintained in the U.S. dollar, Eurodollars may grow without limit in the form of new loans. The reason is that Eurodollar banks need not maintain reserve requirements. The absence of reserve requirements could be a major reason for the substantial growth of Eurodollar loans in the last decade.

Eurodollars are U.S. dollars traded outside the geographical boundaries of the United States. Eurodollars are created when a deposit is transferred outside the United States and is maintained in U.S. dollars. The origin of Eurodollars always remains with a bank in this country. Eurodollars may grow continuously as long as Eurodollar loans are not converted into other currencies.

14.14 Export Financing

Every company that is involved in exporting goods or services abroad needs to secure some kind of financing during international transactions. The same is also valid for the companies that are involved in import transactions. The trade cycle of an export/import transaction is longer than a similar domestic transaction and it also carries additional risks. Some of the factors that make these kinds of transactions longer and riskier than their domestic counterparts are longer transit time, different custom regulations for each country, different business or banking rules and regulations, creditworthiness of the buyer/seller, and exchange rate risk as well as the political risk of a specific country.

Methods of Payment

One of the complicated aspects of international finance is the system of payments or settlements. An exporter cannot claim that he or she has actually sold merchandise until the sales proceeds are received and deposited in a bank account. In export financing, there are a number of payment methods with varying flexibility in terms and conditions for the buyer and the seller. These methods differ in a number of ways, including the timing of the legal transfer of ownership, the date of the payment, the risk exposure of the buyer, and the risk exposure of the seller. Methods of payment are summarized as follows:

Cash in Advance or Payment in Advance. Payment in advance or cash in advance carries the least degree of risk for an exporter. In this scenario, the exporter receives the payment before shipping the goods. With this method, the exporter is protected from any default of the buyer as well as all other risks. Although this method seems to be reasonable in some specific cases (such as highly customized product orders), for high-credit-risk customers or politically unstable countries, it is not perceived as the best arrangement by importers, especially in established economics or markets since it shifts all the risks to the importer.

Letter of Credit (LC). As opposed to a cash in advance payment, which shifts most risks to the importer, the letter of credit provides a means of safety for both parties. A letter of credit is a contract between the banks representing the exporter and the importer and including all the terms and conditions of the sale. In a basic letter of credit transaction, the buyer (importer) sends a request to a bank to open an account (letter of credit) and to notify the bank of the seller (exporter) that the total amount of sales will be paid upon the submission of certain documents. Among the documents required are the *bill of lading*, a *detailed invoice*, and a *third-party inspection report* (it stated in the contract). Thus, the exporter is assured that once the documents are submitted, the export proceeds will be paid by the importer's bank and the importer is assured of the delivery of the ordered goods. While the documents related to the transaction are examined by the banks, the goods are not inspected by any party in this process. An example of an LC is presented in Figure 14.2. There are different types of letter of credit that vary the risk exposure of the exporter and the importer:

- *Irrevocable letter of credit.* The purpose of an irrevocable letter of credit is to ensure that the arrangement is not canceled or changed by either the buyer or the seller; therefore, irrevocable letters of credits cannot be canceled or amended without the consent of all parties involved, whereas revocable letters of credit can be changed any time by the issuer bank without any notification to the seller.
- *Confirmed letter of credit.* In this case, both the issuing bank and a third party are obligated to make the export payments upon submission of certain documents. Since the seller usually works with a domestic bank, it is always safer

> **New York First Bank, Inc.**
> (Name of the issuing bank)
>
> Date: September 4, 2019
> L/C Number 123457
>
> New York First Bank, Inc. hereby issues this irrevocable documentary letter
> of credit to *Nut Exporters, Inc.* (name of the exporter) for US$600,000
> payable 90 days after sight by a draft drawn against New York First Bank,
> Inc. in accordance with Letter of Credit number 123457.
> The draft is to be accompanied by the following documents:
> 1. Commercial invoice in triplicate
> 2. Packing list
> 3. Clean on-board order bill of lading
> 4. Insurance documents, paid for by the buyer
>
> At maturity, New York First Bank, Inc. will pay the face amount of the draft
> to the bearer of that draft.
>
> Authorized Signature

Figure 14.2: Letter of Credit.

for the exporter to have the domestic bank assume the responsibility of the payment. This is a double-insured export financing arrangement. A confirmed, irrevocable letter of credit provides even a greater protection to the exporting
party. In an advised letter of credit, the second bank does not guarantee the
funds, but acts as an advisor to the exporter in its relations with the foreign
bank that has issued the letter of credit and guaranteed the payment. Advising
activities consist of reviewing and submitting the documents to the issuer
bank. In case the issuer bank defaults on its obligations, the exporter's bank
does not take any action. Therefore, the degree of protection to the exporter is
relatively lower.
- *Revolving letter of credit.* To avoid repetitious requests to open letters of credit,
  the importer may request, under certain terms and conditions, that a revolving
  letter of credit be opened for a number of orders for the same supplier and at
  the same time.

Drafts. After establishing a credit line with the bank, an importer can send a notification to the exporter requesting that payments be made upon submission of a
draft. A *draft* is basically a formal collection request through a bank. Note that the
bank is only an intermediary and it simply serves as a collection agent; therefore,
unlike the case of a letter of credit, the bank has no obligation for final payments.
Sight drafts are common among firms with years of business relations and established trust. From the buyer's point of view, the draft eliminates the risk of accepting goods before confirming that the goods are received in the proper condition and

agreed quantity. On the other hand, a sight draft creates an extra risk for the seller in the event that the buyer does not honor the payments. An example of a draft is presented in Figure 14.3.

Nut Exporters, Inc.
(Name of Exporter)

Date: September19, 2019
Draft number 7990

Ninety (90) days after sight of this First of Exchange, pay to the order of Commercial Bank of Rome (name of exporter's bank) thesum of Six-hundred thousand U.S. dollars for value received under New York First Bank, Inc. letter of credit number 123457.

Nut Exporters, Inc.

(Signature of Exporter)

Figure 14.3: Draft.

In this case, the seller has to pay for the shipment of the goods back to the warehouse or dispose of the goods in certain situations.

A *time draft* is a specific draft in which the buyer is given an extra period of time before the buyer submits the payment for this transaction. This gives the buyer an opportunity to check and try the goods before any payment is made. At the same time, this opportunity for the importer (buyer) increases the cost and risk for the exporter (seller).

Open Account. An open account is the opposite side of a cash in advance option in terms of sharing risk between the buyer and the seller. In an open account, an exporter ships the goods to an importer and bills the importers account with the transaction amount to be paid within a certain period of time. This transaction places all the risk on the seller's side.

Consignment. An exporter can also send the goods on consignment where the exporter holds the title of the goods until it is fully paid. A consignment arrangement expedites the sale of goods and increases the turnover ratio of the inventory. However, the exporter takes full risk if the buyer decides not to buy the shipment. A well-established business relationship and mutual trust are needed for successful arrangements in the case of consignments in international trade. If the importer does not sell the goods, the exporter can either ship the goods back to the warehouse or dispose of them at their entire cost.

Financial Tools

There are many financial tools used in international trade. Some of them are discussed briefly in the following section.

Banker's Acceptance. A very popular method of raising funds in export financing is issuing debts through banks by submitting export or import bills. Depending on the future cash flows involved, commercial banks may accept the documents and lend a portion of the future proceeds to the exporter/importer. The instrument generated through this process is called a *banker's acceptance*, which can be traded in a secondary market.

Financing through Receivables. An exporter can borrow money against the export receivables and pay it back with the interest at the end of the term. If the exporter insures the receivables, it may be negotiated with the tender for a lower interest rate on the loan. Borrowing against receivables is generally used for increasing the working capital and it does not decrease any of the risks imposed on the exporter.

As long as the exporter can find a bank to buy its receivables, it can totally liquidate them. However, in this case, the bank that buys the receivables will contact the customer directly on the due date. The exporter should evaluate the consequences of this process in terms of its customer relationship and future transactions.

Factoring or Outsourcing Receivables. Factoring firms offer services to the exporters who want to outsource their receivables departments by paying a factored fee per receivable. Factoring firms buy the receivables and carry out the tasks of credit investigation, collection, book keeping, and statements. The exporter contracts a local factoring firm and transfers the receivables; in turn, the local factoring firm begins to work with an associate factoring firm in the foreign country. This arrangement provides access to the credit records of the importer, leading to a more efficient collection process for all parties involved.

Forfaiting (Customized Factoring). *Forfaiting* is a form of factoring customized to finance medium-term accounts receivables based on a fixed interest rate. It has been a major instrument used in Europe and is becoming popular among American financial institutions. Forfaiting offers a simpler documentation process compared to contracts. The importer issues a series of semi-annual notes in the form of drafts against the balance. The forfaiting firm finds a bank or a guarantor who endorses the note itself, thereby avoiding the costs of preparing and signing a contract.

14.15 An Example of Trade Financing: Letter of Credit

A U.S.-based firm, *Atlanta Nuts Importers*, buys hazelnuts from an Italian firm *Nut Exporters, Inc*. The steps of the process are as follows:
- After the importer and exporter agree on the sales terms, a sales contract is signed by the importer and exporter. The sales contract specifies the amount and type of hazelnut, price, shipping date, and payment method.
- *Atlanta Nuts Importers* requests LOC from *NY First Bank*.
- NY First Bank issues LOC.
- The exporter's bank, *Commercial Bank of Rome*, advises the exporter that LOC is in good order.
- Hazelnuts are shipped.
- The exporter gives shipping documents and bank draft drawn on NY First Bank.
- Commercial Bank of Rome sends LOC shipping documents and bank draft to NY First Bank.
- When NY First Bank accepts the draft, a bankers' acceptance is created, and NY First Bank pays a discounted amount to Commercial Bank of Rome.
- Commercial Bank of Rome pays the exporter the discounted amount.
- NY First Bank presents shipping documents to importer and *Atlanta Nuts Importers* takes possession of nuts.
- NY First Bank sells the BA to an investor.
- At maturity, the importer pays *Atlanta Nuts Importers* the full amount due, and the bank pays the investor.

14.16 International Institutions

The three global organizations playing a major role in international economic relations are: the International Monetary Fund (IMF), the World Bank, and the World Trade Organization (WTO). Let's take a closer look at the functions of these organizations.[11]

---

[11] For an introductory analysis of international institutions, see Michael Taillard, *101 Things Everyone Needs to Know about the Global Economy*, Adams Media, 2013, pp. 38–56.

The International Monetary Fund (IMF)

The *International Monetary Fund* (IMF)[12] was founded at the *Bretton Woods* meetings amongst the *Allies* in July 1944. Each member is allotted a quota of SDRs (Special Drawing Rights), depending on its size and its position in the world economy.

The IMF was established to:
- Promote international monetary cooperation
- Promote exchange stability and orderly exchange arrangements
- Foster growth and high levels of employment
- Provide temporary financial assistance to countries to help ease the balance of payments adjustment

If a crisis occurs when a country runs out of foreign exchange reserves, IMF lends that country. *IMF conditionality* means the requirement for the borrowing member to carry out economic reforms in exchange for a loan. This is the main criticism of the IMF.[13]

The World Bank

The *World Bank* was also founded at the Bretton Woods Conference as the International Bank for Reconstruction and Development (IBRD). The World Bank has 184 members.[14]

The main function of the bank is development lending. Today, IBRD is one of the four subgroups making up the World Bank Group:
- International Development Association (IDA)
- International Finance Corporation (IFC)
- Multilateral Investment Guarantee Agency (MIGA)
- International Center for Settlement of Investment Disputes (ICSID)

The main criticism is that the World Bank charges high interest rates on loans even granted by governments.[15]

---

12 www.imf.org.

13 For more information on the criticisms of IMF, see M. Maria John Kennedy, *International Economics*, PHİ Learning, 2014, p. 249.

14 For more information, see Kenneth A. Reinert, *An Introduction to International Economics*, Cambridge University Press, 2012, pp. 413–434.

15 For more information on the criticisms of the World Bank, see Kennedy, *International Economics*, op. cit., pp. 257–258.

From GATT to WTO

The GATT functioned through trade rounds – interstate negotiations to reduce tariffs and other barriers to trade. After the *Tokyo Round* of the 1970s, tariffs were brought to record lows. However, the *Uruguay Round* was launched in 1986 to address previously neglected trade issues such as agriculture and textiles, as well as new trade issues such as intellectual property rights and trade in services.

The Uruguay Round Agreement was signed in 1994. It established the WTO:
–   164 members as of 1 January 2019
–   Reaches beyond GATT to new trade issues
–   Has a more effective dispute settlement mechanism
–   Monitors national trade practices more consistently

The main tasks of the WTO are:
–   Administering WTO trade agreements
–   Serving as a forum for trade negotiations
–   Handling trade disputes
–   Monitoring national trade policies
–   Providing technical assistance and training for LDCs
–   Fostering cooperation with other international agencies

Interdependence norms of WTO are:
–   *Liberalization.* Negotiations are conducted to reduce protection.
–   *Nondiscrimination.* Adopted the concept of most favored national status (MFN): every WTO member must treat each of its trading partners as it treats its most favored partner.
–   *National treatment.* Imports must be given a similar treatment on the domestic market as domestically produced goods.

Sovereignty norms of WTO are:
–   *Reciprocity.* Negotiations proceed in terms of exchange of *concessions* of substantially equivalent value.
–   *Safeguards.* The right of the government to preserve economic stability through (nondiscriminatory) protection is recognized.

Some of the criticisms of the WTO are:[16]
- Free trade benefits for developed countries are more than those for developing countries.
- Free trade gives an unfair advantage to multinational companies.
- Free trade fails to reduce tariffs on agriculture.
- Free trade does not help developing countries to diversify into other sectors' diversification.
- Free trade ignores cultural and social factors.
- The WTO is criticized for being undemocratic.
- Trade rounds have been notoriously slow and difficult to reach an agreement.

President Donald Trump has threatened to withdraw the U.S. from the World Trade Organization, claiming it treats the U.S. unfairly. His warning about a possible U.S. pull-out from the WTO highlights the conflict between his *protectionist trade policies* and the *open trade system* that the WTO oversees.[17] In this context, the U.S. has introduced tariffs on a number of goods imported into the U.S.

Regional Trade Agreements

Besides economic organizations, regional trade agreements form a key part of the institutional structure of the world economy. Regional trade agreements have proliferated around the world since the beginning of the 1990s.

Five types of regional trade agreements are:
- *Partial trade agreement.* Two or more countries liberalize trade in a selected group of product categories.
- *Free trade area* (FTA). Trade-in goods and services are fully liberalized between two or more countries, as in the North American Free Trade Agreement (NAFTA).
- *Customs Union* (CU). A free trade area (FTA) with common external tariff (CET) like the European Union in the 1980s and MERCOSUR in South America.
- *Common Market* (CM). A customs union with free mobility of factors of production like the European Union after the 1990s.
- *Economic Union* (EU). Common market with coordination of macroeconomic policies like the European Union in the 2000s.

---

16 Tejvan Pettinger, *Criticisms of WTO*, https://www.economicshelp.org/blog/4/trade/criticisms-of -wto/, Oct. 29, 2017.
17 BBC, *Trump threatens to pull US out of World Trade Organization*, https://www.bbc.com/news/ world-us-canada-45364150, Jan. 22, 2019.

Opposition to International Institutions

International institutions receive two types of criticism:
- Globalization may be problematic and may not cure all problems. However, how would curtailing economic and social interactions between people from different countries be beneficial?
- International institutions are undemocratic. Decision-making is closed to participation by civic and social groups, and thus doesn't focus on the most vulnerable groups. However, global institutions were created to resolve technical economic problems. They have thus been slow to respond to social problems. International institutions today are heavily focused on social issues such as fostering education and health standards, and civil and human rights.

14.17 Summary

The international monetary system is a system of institutions and mechanisms that exist in order to foster trade, manage the flow of financial capital, and determine exchange rates.

The balance of payments of a country is a document that shows all payments and receipts of the country vis-a-vis the rest of the world for a year. The balance of payments accounts are compiled using the double entry accounting system by central banks. Receipts are recorded as credits and payments are recorded as debits. International transactions can be grouped into the following five main types: current account, capital account, finance account, statistical discrepancy (net errors and omission), and the official reserve account.

The European Union (EU) is a political and economic association of 28 European sovereign states. The euro, introduced as legal tender, is used by almost 340 million EU citizens today. It has been in the pockets of EU citizens since January 2002. Britain is leaving the European Union. This process is called Brexit.

Currency exchange markets, also called foreign exchange markets, are electronic markets where banks and institutional traders buy and sell various currencies on behalf of businesses, other clients, and themselves.

A currency exchange rate indicates the value of one currency relative to another. Currency exchange rates are stated in two basic ways: the direct quotation method indicates the value of one unit of a foreign currency in terms of a home country's currency; the indirect quotation method indicates the amount of units of a foreign currency needed to purchase one unit of the home country's currency.

In international exchange, parity refers to the exchange rate between the currencies of two countries, making the purchasing power of both currencies substantially equal. Such well-known parity relationships as interest rate parity and purchasing power parity, in fact, present arbitrage equilibrium conditions. Interest rate parity theory states that the forward premium or discount (except for the effects of small transaction costs) should be equal and opposite in size to the difference in the national interest rates for securities of the same maturity. In the long run, exchange rates adjust so that the purchasing power of each currency tends to be the same. The exchange rate changes tend to reflect international differences in inflation rates. The *International Fisher Effect* states that the real interest rate should be the same all over the world, with the differences in nominal rate resulting from differences in expected inflation rates. In forecasting exchange rates, there are three approaches: the efficient markets approach, fundamental approach, and technical approach.

The process of buying and selling in more than one market to make a riskless profit is called arbitrage. Such opportunities do not exist for a long time due to the arbitrage process. Types of arbitrage are simple, triangular, and covered-interest.

A multinational corporation is a firm that operates in two or more countries.

The FX risk can be defined, as tomorrow's exchange rate will differ from today's rate. The exchange rate risk affects the exchange rate risk in international trade contracts, in foreign portfolio investments, and in direct foreign investment.

How do we calculate the NPV of such a project? There are two basic methods in international capital budgeting decisions: the local currency method and the foreign currency method. In the local currency method, the exchange rate is estimated by interest rate parity.

There are three measures of foreign exchange exposure: translation exposure, transaction exposure, and economic exposure. Firms that do business overseas must accept the uncertainties of working in an unfamiliar environment. In order to reduce exposure to foreign exchange fluctuations, companies may utilize the tools in the following areas: hedging, adjusting accounts receivable and payable procedures, cash management, and borrowing and lending activities.

MNC has access to both domestic and foreign markets for financing. Foreign host countries may often provide low-cost, subsidized financing to attract investments.

Basic principles of working-capital management for a multinational corporation are similar to those of a domestic firm. Tax rate and exchange rates are additional considerations. There are two techniques used for managing working capital: leading and lagging strategies, and cash management and positioning of funds.

The term *international financial markets* refers to various financial institutions around the world in which multinational firms and governments can participate to borrow money of invest then surplus funds. The two major international financial markets are the Eurodollar market (Euromarket) and the international bond (Eurobond) market.

International trade is more difficult and is riskier. The exporter may not know whether the importer is a good credit risk. Additionally, political instability makes it risky to ship merchandise abroad. From the importer's perspective, it is risky to make an advance payment for goods that may never be shipped by the exporter. Some of the factors that make these kinds of transactions longer and riskier than their domestic counterparts are longer transit time, different custom regulations for each country, different business or banking rules and regulations, creditworthiness of the buyer/seller, and the exchange rate risk as well as the political risk of a specific country.

The three global organizations playing a major role in international economic relations are the International Monetary Fund (IMF), the World Bank, and the World Trade Organization (WTO).

Part IV: **Management of Financial Institutions**

15 Management of Financial Institutions: The Basics

15.1 Introduction

In this chapter, the terms *bank management* and *financial institution management* are used interchangeably.[1] Topics covered include the bank balance sheet, basics of banking, general principles of bank management, off-balance sheet activities, and measuring bank performance.

The main roles of banks are to transfer funds from savers to firms and individuals. However, to promote a better understanding of this issue, bank financial statement analysis is introduced first. The main operations of banks are then explained using simple accounting entries.

15.2 The Bank Balance Sheet and Income Statement

The balance sheet is a list of a bank's assets and liabilities. *Total assets = Total liabilities + capital.* A bank's balance sheet lists sources of bank funds (liabilities) and uses to which they are put (assets). Banks invest these liabilities (sources) into assets (uses) in order to create value for their capital providers.

The balance sheet (statement of financial position) consists of the following:
- Assets: cash assets, loans, securities, and fixed assets
- Liabilities: deposit funds and non-deposit funds
- Capital: equity capital, subordinated notes, debentures, and loan loss reserves

The income statement (statement of income statement) consists of the following:
- Interest income
- Non-interest income
- Interest expenses
- Non-interest expenses (including provision for loan losses)
- Net profit

Examples of a bank income statement and a balance sheet are provided in Tables 15.1 and 15.2.

---

[1] Since banks are the most dominant financial institution, we approach financial institutions management from a commercial bank perspective. The discussions in this chapter and the next chapter can be applied well to almost all financial institutions. Therefore, the term *bank* is used instead of *financial institution* in many instances.

https://doi.org/10.1515/9783110705355-015

Table 15.1: Income Statement of ABC Commercial Bank, End of 20X8 (amounts in millions of euros).

Interest and fees on loans	€130
Interest on securities	24
Total interest income	**€154**
Interest paid on deposits	98
Interest on non-deposit borrowings	12
Total interest expense	**€110**
Net interest income	44
Provision for loan losses	4
Noninterest income and fees	14
Noninterest expenses:	
Salaries and employee benefits	24
Overhead expenses	10
Other noninterest expenses	6
Total noninterest expenses	**40**
Net noninterest income	**−26**
Pre-tax operating income	**14**
Securities gains (or losses)	2
Pre-tax net operating income	**€16**
Taxes	2
Net operating income	**€14**
Net extraordinary income	−2
Net income	**€12**

Table 15.2: Balance Sheet of ABC Commercial Bank, End of 20X8 (amounts in millions of euros).

Assets		Liabilities and Stockholder's Equity	
Cash and due from banks	€200	Demand deposits	€380
Investment securities	300	Savings deposits	360
Interbank funds sold	20	Time deposits	940
Net loans	1,340	Interbank funds purchased	120
Plant and equipment	100	Total liabilities	€1,800
		Common stock	40
		Share premium	50
		Retained earnings	70
		Common equity	€160
Total assets	€1,960	Total liabilities and stockholders' equity	€1,960
Memo:			
Total earnings assets	€1,660	Interest bearing deposits	€1,300

Assets

Basic asset items are described in the following sections.[2]

Reserves and cash items. They include the following:

- *Cash.* Cash consists of vault cash, deposits at other financial institutions, and cash in the process of collection. Large banks hold a larger percentage of cash to meet their comparatively high reserve requirements.
- *Reserves.* They represent deposits at the Central Bank.
- *Interbank funds.* This is the excess reserve kept at the Central Bank to fund other banks. The interbank rate is an indicator of liquidity in bank markets. Interbank funds sold are assets while the Central Bank funds purchased are liabilities.

---

2 For a detailed explanation about financial statement items, see T. Ravi Kumar, *Asset Liability Management*, Second Edition, Vision Books, 2005, pp. 12–22. The financial statements we present here are in concise form. Actual financial statements prepared in accordance with International Financial Reporting Standards by banks have many items. For a more complete treatment of financial statement items, see The Hong Kong Institute of Bankers, *Bank Asset and Liability Management*, Wiley-Singapore, 2018, pp. 9–13; Mario Massari, Gianfranco Gianfrate, and Laura Zanetti, *The Valuation of Financial Companies: Tools and Techniques to Value Banks and Other Financial Institutions*, Wiley, 2014, pp. 15–60.

- *Repurchase agreements (repos).* They are short-term sale of Treasury bills or other liquid securities repurchased at a higher price at a later date.
- *Assets held in trading accounts.* These are securities that are traded by large banks. Securities must appear on the balance sheet at market value, with any market value losses or gains reflected in income.
- *Investment securities.* These are securities which provide additional income and long-term liquidity.

Loans. Gross loans and leases report the book value of loans and leases. *Allowance for loan losses* records an offsetting account to cover expected loan losses. Actual net charge-offs are subtracted from allowance for loan losses. Additions to allowance for loan losses are made yearly through provisions for loan loss expense. Net loans and leases report gross loans minus the allowance for loan losses.

Other assets. These are bank premises and equipment, and other intangible assets.

Liabilities

Basic liability items are described as follows.
- *Demand deposits.* These deposits include all accounts that allow the owner (depositor) to write checks to third parties. Examples include non-interest-earning checking accounts (known as demand deposit accounts), interest earning negotiable orders of withdrawal accounts, and money-market deposit accounts, which typically pay the most interest among checkable deposit accounts. Checkable deposits are a bank's lowest cost funds because depositors want safety and liquidity and will accept a lesser interest from the bank in return.
- *Time deposits.* These are the overall primary source of bank liabilities and are accounts from which the depositor cannot write checks. Examples include savings accounts and time deposits. Time deposits are generally a bank's highest cost funds because banks want deposits which are more stable and predictable and will pay more to the depositors.
- *Borrowings.* Banks can obtain funds from the central bank, other banks, and corporations. These borrowings are called: discount loans/advances (from the central bank), interbank loans (from other banks), interbank offshore deposits (from other banks), repurchase agreements (repos from other banks and companies), commercial paper, and notes (from companies and institutional investors). Certain borrowings can be more volatile than other liabilities depending on market conditions.

– *Equity.* This is the source of funds supplied by the shareholders, either directly through the purchase of ownership shares or indirectly through the retention of earnings. Since assets minus liabilities equals equity, equity is seen as protecting the liability suppliers from asset devaluations or write-offs. Equity is also called the balance sheet's *shock absorber* – thus, capital level is important.

Income Statement Items

They include the following:
– *Interest income* (II). *Interest income* is interest earned on interest-earning assets. An income statement normally itemizes the source of interest by type of asset. It separates interest income into interest on loans, interbank funds sold, repos, and deposits at other institutions. Note that interest on loans contributes the most to interest income because loans are the bank's dominant asset and pay the highest gross yields. In general, interest income increases when the level of interest rates increases and/or when a bank can book more earning assets. It decreases when loan balances decline and/or when rates fall.
– *Interest expense* (IE). *Interest expense* is interest paid on time and savings deposits, other purchased liabilities, and subordinated debt.
– *Net interest income.* *Net interest income* is interest income minus interest expense. It plays a crucial role in determining how profitable a bank is in any period. Variations in net interest income are also used to measure how successful a bank has been in managing its interest rate risk.
– *Provision for loan losses* (PL). *Provision for loan losses* represents a deduction from income for transfers to a bank's loan loss reserve. It is a non-cash expense that indicates management's estimate of potential revenue losses from *non-performing loans* (NPL). Increases in provisions thus reported lower net income. Banks that understate potential losses effectively overstate net income and eventually have to raise provisions in recognition that their past income has been overstated. The income statement reports net interest income after provision to account for estimated loan losses.
– *Non-interest income* (NOI). *Non-interest income* consists primarily of service charges, fees and commissions, merchant service fees, and gains (or losses) from securities sales. Large banks that operate securities and foreign exchange desks also report trading account profits. Fees arise from loan commitments, standby letters of credit, and trust department services. Most banks have concentrated on increasing non-interest income as an alternative source of earnings, service charges, and fees, which have generally increased. These alternative sources primarily include revenues derived from mortgage banking, credit card, insurance, and electronic or treasury banking operations.

- *Non-interest (overhead) expense* (NOI). *Non-interest or overhead expense* is composed primarily of personnel, occupancy, equipment, and other expenses. These expenses consist of salaries and fringe benefits paid to employees, rent, depreciation, maintenance on equipment and premises, and other operating expenses including utilities and insurance premiums. At most banks, non-interest income falls far below non-interest expenses. A bank's burden is the difference, measured as non-interest expense minus non-interest income. Improving a bank's burden by raising fees and controlling unit-operating costs has been a major source of bank profits.
- *Income before taxes* (IBT). A bank's *income before taxes* thus equals net interest income minus provision for loan losses less burden. Net income is then obtained by subtracting taxes.
- *Taxes* (T). This is a corporate *tax* paid on income before taxes (pre-tax net operating income).

15.3 Measuring Bank Performance

Bank performance can be measured by two tools:
- Internal performance
- External performance (financial ratios)

Internal performance evaluations based on economic profit are:
- Risk-Adjusted Return on Capital (RAROC)
- Economic Value Added (EVA)

Internal Performance Evaluations

There are basically two methods: risk-adjusted return on capital (RAROC) and economic value added (EVA).[3] We will explain each briefly.

Risk-Adjusted Return on Capital (RAROC). An example is presented in Table 15.3. In this example, if the loan rate is 12%, the bank will earn the target return on equity of 16%. Of course, if the bank can price the loan at a rate higher than 12%, it will earn a profit over the target level of equity returns. In this case, an economic profit is earned in that the value of equity is increased.

---

3 For a simple comparison of both approaches, see J. Dermine and Y. F. Bissade, *Asset & Liability Management: A Guide to Value Creation and Risk Control*, FT Prentice-Hall, 2002. pp. 20–23.

Table 15.3: Risk-Adjusted Capital.

Cost of funds	8.00%
Provision for loan losses	1.00%
Direct expense	0.50%
Indirect expense	0.25%
Overhead	0.25%
Total charges before capital charge	10.00%
Capital charge*	2.00%
Total required loan rate	12.00%

Note: The capital charge is determined by multiplying the equity capital allocated to the loan times the opportunity cost of equity and then converting to a pre-tax level. Assume that the allocated equity to loan ratio is 10% and the opportunity cost of equity is 16%, such that the after-tax capital charge is 1.6% if the tax rate for the bank is 0.2, the pre-tax capital charge is 1.6/(1.0−0.2) or 2.00.

Economic Value Added (EVA). EVA can be defined as follows:

EVA = Adjusted earnings (Net Operating Income, 20X8) – Opportunity cost of capital (in)

where adjusted earnings are net income after taxes, and the opportunity cost of capital equals the cost of equity times equity capital.

Let us give you the inputs required to calculate economic value added. See Table 15.4.

Table 15.4: Inputs for EVA.

Cost of equity capital	0.16
Market value of equity capital, 20X8 (Price per share × Number of shares=5×40)	200
Pre-tax operating income*	14

*From the income statement above.

$$EVA = 14 - 200 \times 0.16 = 14 - 32 = -€18m$$

The bank incurred a loss of €18m.

Comparison of RAROC and EVA:

- Both methods are beneficial in assessing managerial performance and developing incentives and compensation schemes compatible with shareholder wealth goals.

– RAROC has a short-run perspective (i.e., business unit profit is compared to the unit's capital at risk).
– EVA has a long-run perspective (i.e., business unit profit is compared to the cost of capital of the bank).

External Performance Evaluations

In finance, we generally assume that markets are efficient or that the stock price incorporates all available information about a company. Therefore, when it is available, the stock price is the best indicator of a financial institution's performance. Unfortunately, few banks have widely traded stock.

External performance evaluation is conducted with ratios. Following are definitions of bank ratios:[4]

Profitability Ratios. When stock prices are not available for other reasons, a financial institution's performance can be analyzed using financial ratios.

Return on assets (ROA) measures efficiency, or how well the institution is using its assets to generate income.

$$\text{ROA} = \frac{\text{Net Income After Taxes}}{\text{Total Assets}} = \text{ROE} \times \frac{\text{Total Equity Capital}}{\text{Total Assets}}$$

Return on equity (ROE) measures returns to shareholders.

$$\text{ROE} = \frac{\text{Net Income After Taxes}}{\text{Total Equity Capital}}$$

$$= \text{Profit Margin} \times \text{Asset Utilization} \times \text{Equity Multiplier}$$

This is the famous DuPont equation we discussed in Chapter 9 to show how a company could increase its return on equity.

$$= \text{ROA} \times \frac{\text{Total Assets}}{\text{Total Equity Capital}}$$

$$\text{Profit Margin} = \frac{\text{Net Income After Taxes}}{\text{Operating Income}}$$

4 For a detailed treatment of ratios, see Arman T. Tevfik and Gürman Tevfik, *Bankalarda Finansal Yönetime Giriş*, Bankalar Birliği, 1997, pp. 213–219; Marcia Millon Cornett and Anthony Sounders, *Fundamentals of Financial Institutions Management*, McGraw-Hill, 1999, pp. 145–177; and Timothy W. Koch, *Bank Management*, The Dryden Press, 1995, pp. 92–149.

Asset Utilization Ratios. Asset utilization is affected by:
- Mix of loans
- Investments
- Liquidity

Asset utilization is measured by the following ratio:

$$\text{Asset Utilization} = \frac{\text{Operating Income}}{\text{Total Assets}}$$

It indicates the income-generating power of assets.

Equity multiplier is a measure of capital structure. It is measured by the following ratio:

$$\text{Equity Multiplier} = \frac{\text{Total Assets}}{\text{Equity Capital}}$$

It shows the degree to which assets are financed by equity.

Net operating margin (NOM) represents operating efficiency. It shows the portion of the institution's revenues flowing to net income.

$$\text{Net Operating Margin(NOM)} = \frac{[\text{Total Operating Income} - \text{Total Operating Expense}]}{\text{Total Assets}}$$

Yield spread and *net interest margin* (NIM) provide information on how profitably the institution is providing financial intermediation. These measures compare the rate earned on credits and the cost of funds.

Yield Spread = Percent yield on interest earning assets − Percent cost on interest bearing funds.

$$\text{Net Interest Margin(NIM)} = \frac{[\text{Total Interest Income} - \text{Total Interest Expense}]}{\text{Total Assets}}$$

Interest before securities gains or losses (IBSG) is similar to ROA except that gains and losses on securities are added back into the net income. This removes the effects of portfolio manipulation by financial institution managers.

$$\text{IBSG} = \frac{\text{Income before Securities Gains or Losses}}{\text{Total Assets}}$$

Efficiency and Expense Control Ratios. These ratios describe how well the financial institutions control expenses relative to producing revenues and how productive employees are in terms of generating income, managing assets, and handling accounts.

$$\text{Operating Efficiency Ratio} = \frac{\text{Total Operating Expenses}}{\text{Total Assets}}$$

$$\text{Cost of Funds} = \frac{\text{Total Interest Expense}}{\text{Total Deposit and Nondeposit Borrowing}}$$

$$\text{Income Productivity(per employee)} = \frac{\text{Total Income After Taxes}}{\text{Number of Full Time Equivalent Employees}}$$

Tax Management Ratios. These ratios describe how well the financial institution is managing its tax burden.

$$\text{Tax Exempt Assets Ratio} = \frac{\text{Investment in Tax Exempt Assets}}{\text{Total Assets}}$$

$$\text{Tax Ratio} = \frac{\text{Total Income Tax Payments}}{\text{Income before Taxes}}$$

$$\text{Provision Ratio} = \frac{\text{Loan Loss Provision}}{\text{Total Assets}}$$

Liquidity Ratios. Financial institutions (banks) must meet investors' demands for liquidity. However, there is a tradeoff, given that more liquid assets generally yield lower returns.

The following ratios describe the institution's liquidity position.

$$\text{Demand} - \text{to} - \text{Time Deposits} = \frac{\text{Total Demand Deposits}}{\text{Total Time and Saving Deposits}}$$

$$\text{Demand/Deposits Ratio} = \frac{\text{Total Demand Deposits}}{\text{Total Assets}}$$

$$\text{Nondeposit Borrowing Ratio} = \frac{\text{Nondeposit Borrowings}}{\text{Total Assets}}$$

Risk Ratios. Financial institutions face many risks, including losses on loans and losses on investments. The financial institution's managers must limit these risks in order to avoid the failure of the institution (bankruptcy).

The following ratios provide some information concerning the risk of the institution:

$$\text{Equity Ratio} = \frac{\text{Total Equity Capital}}{\text{Total Assets}}$$

A high value of this ratio indicates this bank is better prepared to confront risks. It also shows the debt burden of the bank.

$$\text{Loan Loss Allowance Ratio} = \frac{\text{Allowance for Possible Loan Losses}}{\text{Total Assets}}$$

Using these statements, calculate the following performance measures: ROE, ROA, NIM, NIMPLL, net non-interest margin, NPM, AU, EM, tax management efficiency, efficiency ratio, and fee income ratio.

$$\text{ROE} = \frac{\text{Net Income}}{\text{Total Equity Capital}} = \frac{12}{160} = 0.075 = 7.5\%$$

$$\text{ROA} = \frac{\text{Net Income}}{\text{Total Assets}} = \frac{12}{1,960} = 0.00612 = 0.612\%$$

$$\text{Net Interest Margin} = \frac{\text{Net Interest Income}}{\text{Total Assets}} = \frac{22}{1,960} = 0.0224 = 2.24\%$$

NIMPLL = (Net Interest Income – Provision for Loan Losses)/Total Assets = $(44-4)/1,960 = 0.0204 = 2.04\%$

$$\text{Net NoninterestMargin} = \frac{\text{Net Noninteret Income}}{\text{Total Assets}} = \frac{-26}{1,960} = -0.0133 = -1.33\%$$

$$\text{Net Profit Margin} = \frac{\text{Net Income}}{\text{Total Operating Revenues}} = \frac{12}{168} = -0.0714 = 7.14\%$$

$$\text{Asset Utilization} = \frac{\text{Total Operating Revenue}}{\text{Total Assets}} = \frac{154+14}{1,960} = -0.0857 = 8.57\%$$

$$\text{Equity Multiplies} = \frac{\text{Total Asset}}{\text{Total Equity Capital}} = \frac{1,960}{160} = 12.25x$$

$$\text{Tax Management Efficiency} = \frac{\text{Net Income}}{\text{Pre Tax Income}} = \frac{12}{14} = 0.857 \text{or} 85.7\%$$

Fee Income Ratio = Non-interest Income/ (Net Interest Income + Non-interest Income) = $(14/ (44 + 14) = 0.2414 = 24.14\%$

Efficiency Ratio = Non-interest Expense/ (Net Interest Income + Non-interest Income) = $(40/ (44 + 14) = 0.6897 = 68.97\%$

Ratios Financial Institution Management Can Control. Many external factors affect the performance of financial institutions, including:
- Technology changes
- Competition
- Regulation
- Government policies (fiscal and monetary policies)

Financial institution managers cannot control these factors. The best they can do is try to anticipate future changes and position the institution to best take advantage of these changes.

Many internal factors, however, can be controlled by financial institutions managers. The ratios described here focus on some of these internal factors, such as:
- Operating efficiency
- Expense control
- Tax management
- Liquidity
- Risk

15.4 Basics of Banking: T-Account Analysis

For a better explanation the main role of banks, which is fund transformation, it is helpful to understand some of the simple accounting associated with the process of banking.[5]

The following is an example of T-account Analysis: Let's say that Mr. Brown opens a checking account with DEF Bank by depositing €1,000 cash. See Table 15.5.

Table 15.5: T-account Analysis.

DEF Bank

Assets		Liabilities	
Reserves	+€1.000	Deposits	+€1.000

When the bank receives the deposit, its reserves increase by an equal amount; when the bank loses deposits, its reserves decrease by an equal amount.

This simple analysis gets more complicated when we add bank regulations to the picture. With excess reserves (coming from regulation), the balance-sheet will be as follows:

Table 15.6: T-account Analysis: Deposit of €1,000 Cash into DEF Bank.

DEF Bank

Assets		Liabilities	
Required reserves	+€100	Checkable deposits	+€1.000
Excess reserves	+€900		

---

5 For a detailed explanation, see Frederic S. Mishkin and Stanley G. Eakins, *Financial Markets and Institutions*, Seventh Edition, Prentice-Hall, 2012, pp. 403–405.

As we can see in Table 15.6, €1,000 of the deposit must remain with the bank to meet regulations. Now, the bank is free to work with the €900 to its customers.

15.5 General Principles of Bank Management

The principle function of a bank is to transfer the funds it collects from depositors, shareholders, and other sources to investors with a view of maximizing the profits within the rules and regulations issued by relevant authorities, especially in relation to capital adequacy. Thus, a bank has to manage four principle areas:[6]

- *Liquidity management.* It focuses on maintaining enough liquid assets to meet obligations to depositors (for cash withdrawals).
- *Asset management.* It deals with managing assets (loan portfolio) to achieve diversification and minimize default risk/credit risk and interest rate risk.
- *Liability management.* The objective is to acquire/attract funds (deposits) at the lowest possible cost.
- *Capital adequacy management.* It tries to maintain the appropriate net worth to meet regulations and prevent bank failure.

Liquidity Management

The management of bank reserves is very important, since it involves the management of excess reserves and insufficient reserves.

The bank is holding non-interest-bearing assets, and reserves pay zero interest. Loans generate interest income. The opportunity cost of excess reserves is the lost or foregone interest income. Banks, therefore, want to minimize excess reserves. However, if a bank has insufficient reserves, there could be a costly readjustment process. Banks want to hold the optimal amount of excess reserves, which is not zero. An example is provided here, with required accounting entries in Tables 15.7–15.10.

Assume that banks are required to hold minimum reserves equal to 10% of checking and savings deposits.

- *Scenario #1: Bank initially has excess reserves.* Required reserves are €100 million, actual reserves are €200 million, excess reserves are in the amount of €100 million. Assume a deposit outflow of €100 million. People could move to Italy for the summer and withdraw €100m from ABC Bank. Or, in the case of a stock market

---

6 Discussions regarding these four areas are adapted from Mishkin and Eakins, *Financial Markets and Institutions*, op. cit., pp. 405–414.

boom, people transfer money from checking to mutual funds. Or there is a natural disaster (flood, earthquake, hurricane, etc.) and there is a large deposit outflow. The bank can handle the €100 million deposit outflow and still meet the 10% reserve requirement without having to make any other changes in its balance sheet.

- *Scenario #2: Bank has no excess reserves.* The deposit outflow is €100 million. The bank now has *no* reserves and the required reserves are €90 million.

There are four options for the bank to meet the reserve requirement:

- Borrow €90 million from other banks in the Interbank market on interbank funds rate.
- Sell €90 million of securities (T-bills). Disadvantages of these transactions are costs and converting interest-bearing assets to non-interest-bearing assets.
- Borrow €90 million from the Central Bank at a discount rate. The discount rate is usually lower than the Interbank rate.
- Reduce loans by €90 million by calling them in, but not actually renewing them. For example, many commercial loans are short-term and are renewable at short intervals. Customers will be upset and will go to other banks or sell €90 million of loans to other banks.

Table 15.7: Liquidity Management.

Assets		Liabilities	
Liquidity Management *Initial Position*			
Reserves	€200 million	Deposits	€1,000 million
Loans	800 million	Bank capital	100 million
Securities	100 million		
Liquidity Management *Deposits outflow of €100 million*			
Reserves	€100 million	Deposits	€900 million
Loans	800 million	Bank capital	100 million
Securities	100 million		

Assuming the bank has no excess reserves:

Table 15.8: No Excess Reserves.

Assets		Liabilities	
Reserves	€100 million	Deposits	€1,000 million
Loans	900 million	Bank capital	100 million
Securities	100 million		
Deposit outflow of €100 million			
Reserves	€0 million	Deposits	€900 million
Loans	900 million	Bank capital	100 million
Securities	100 million		

Table 15.9: Liquidity Management: Borrowing Case.

Borrow from other banks or corporations			
Assets		Liabilities	
Reserves	€90 million	Deposits	€1,000 million
Loans	900 million	Borrowings	90 million
Securities	10 million	Bank capital	100 million
Sell securities (€90 million)			
Assets		Liabilities	
Reserves	€90 million	Deposits	€900 million
Loans	900 million	Bank Capital	100 million
Securities	100 million		
Borrow from Central Bank (€90 million)			
Assets		Liabilities	
Reserves	€90 million	Deposits	€900 million
Loans	900 million	Discount loans	90 million
Securities	100 million	Bank capital	100 million
Call in or sell off loans			
Assets		Liabilities	
Reserves	€90 million	Deposits	€900 million

Table 15.9 (continued)

Loans	810 million	Bank capital	100 million
Securities	100 million		

Conclusion: As shown in Tables 15.8 and 15.9, excess reserves are insurance against 4 costs from deposit outflow.

Asset Management

Banks want to manage their assets to maximize profits by carefully managing the following:

- *Creditworthiness of customers.* Banks should assess creditworthiness of loan customers to avoid costly defaults. If more defaults occur, capital can be eroded, and the bank may go bankrupt.
- *Purchase right securities.* Banks should purchase securities, subject to banking regulations. They are usually restricted to treasury securities.
- *Diversify assets.* Banks should diversify short- and long-term securities. Diversification should cover loan portfolios, such as commercial, auto, mortgage, and credit card.
- *Manage assets to ensure liquidity.* Banks should hold sufficient liquid assets like T-bills in case of large deposit outflows or loss of reserves. T-bills are so safe and liquid that they are considered *secondary reserves*. The bank has to balance liquidity (holding reserves and T-bills) against increased earnings from less liquid assets (holding loans).

Liability Management

Liability management is the process by banks to maintain a balance between the maturities of their assets and liabilities to meet liquidity requirements, and to lend to investors with a view of profitability and maintain a healthy balance sheet. Liabilities include deposits and funds borrowed from other institutions. In this context, liabilities include depositors' money as well as funds borrowed from other financial institutions (such as other banks or Central Bank) with careful hedging against interest rate changes.

In recent years, the interbank market developed. So, banks had access to a new source of funds: other banks. Banks also began to issue negotiable CDs, commercial bills, and bonds which allowed banks access to another source of funds besides deposits. Banks now placed higher emphasis on liability management due to increased flexibility for attracting sources of funds. They no longer needed to rely exclusively on checking and demand deposits. They now set goals for asset (growth) and then acquired funds (issuing liabilities) as they needed for new loans. Suppose ABC Bank has an attractive €10m loan opportunity. It would take a long time to get €10m in new deposits. However, it could issue a €10m CD or commercial paper to attract funds.

Or suppose there is an unexpected deposit outflow. Banks can now use the interbank market to easily and efficiently acquire sufficient reserves.

Important changes over the last 40 years in bank balance sheets are:
- Negotiable CDs, bonds, and bank borrowing (interbank market) now account for a large percent of bank liabilities.
- Checking deposits have declined in importance as a source of bank liabilities.
- Increased alternatives and higher flexibility in liability management, have given banks higher flexibility to manage assets profitably. Banks have increased the percentage of assets held as loans.

Capital Adequacy Management

Bank capital is a cushion that prevents bank failure. The higher the bank capital, the lower the return on equity. Let's look at the following ratios:
- Return on Assets (ROA)=Net Profits/Assets
- Return on Equity (ROE)=Net Profits/Equity Capital
- Equity Multiplier (EM)=Assets/Equity Capital
- ROE=ROA × EM.

As equity capital increases, equity multiplies and return on equity will decrease. A tradeoff between safety (high capital) and ROE should be sought. Banks also hold capital to meet capital requirements.

Strategies for managing capital are:
- Sell or retire stock
- Change dividends to change retained earnings
- Change asset growth

The role of capital is:
- To cushion an unexpected loss
- Maintain public confidence in the banking system
- Protection for non-insured deposits and other liabilities

The safety of deposits is of paramount importance from the point of view of bank regulators and depositors. Bank capital adequacy refers to the amount of equity capital and other securities a bank holds as reserves against risky assets to reduce the probability of a bank failure.

Basel Agreement is an effort to apply uniform standards and minimum levels of capital for banks. It requires capital to be held for each class of asset.

The basic calculations and related requirements are as follows:
- Common equity Tier I ratio ≥ 4.5%
- Tier I Capital Ratio ≥ 6%
- Capital Adequacy Ratio ≥ 8%

Where:

Common equity Tier I is comprised of an ordinary share issued by the bank, a share issue premium arising from issuance of instruments classified as common equity Tier I, and retained profits and other relevant reserves.

Additional Tier II Capital is defined as instruments such as convertible or hybrid securities, which can be converted into equity when relevant events occur.

However, the Basel Committee introduced two additional requirements: *capital conservation buffer* and *counter cyclical buffer*. With the addition of these requirements:

Minimum Tier I Ratio + Minimum Tier II Ratio + Capital Conservation Ratio was set to 10.5%. With the addition of of the counter cyclical buffer, the ratio was increased to 13%.[7]

In determining risk-weighted assets, four categories of risky assets are weighted differently. More risky assets receive a higher weight. Government obligations are weighted at zero percent. Short-term interbank assets are weighted at 20 percent. Residential mortgages are weighted at 50 percent, and other assets at 100 percent.

$$\text{Capital adequacy ratio} = \frac{\text{Core capital} + \text{Supplemental capital}}{\text{Risk weighted assets}}$$

Banks should maintain the following ratios from Jan. 1,2013, on:

Core capital / Risk weighted assets	3.5%
Supplemental / Risk weighted assets	4.5%
Total capital / Risk weighted assets	8.0%

7 An excellent and detailed summary of Basel III is provided in Hofbauer G., Klimontowicz M., and Nocon A., "Basel III Equity Requirements and a Contemporary Rating Approach," *Copernican Journal of Finance and Accounting*, 5(1), 91–105. http://dx.doi.org/10.12775/CJFA.2016.005

Let us develop a simple example. The assets of bank and respective risk weight are shown in Table 15.10.[8]

Table 15.10: Assets (in millions of euros) and Risk Weights.

Assets	Amounts	Risk weights	Risk weighted assets
Treasury bills	1,500	0%	0
Corporate loans	15,000	10%	1,500
Loans to small firms	8,000	20%	1,600
Guaranties and off balance-sheet obligations	6,000	10%	600
Total assets	30,500		3,700

Core (Tier I) and supplemental capital (Tier II) of the bank are €200 and €300 million, respectively. Using these inputs, let us now calculate the ratio.

$$\text{Total capital of the bank} = €200 + €300 = €500 \text{ million}$$

$$\text{Risk} - \text{weighted exposures} = €1,500 \times 0\% + €15,000 \times 10\% + €8,000 \times 20\%$$

$$+ €6,000 \times 10\% = €3,700 \text{ million.}$$

$$\text{Capital adequacy ratio} = €500/€3,700 = 13.5\%.$$

If the national regulator requires a capital adequacy ratio of 10%, the bank is safe. However, if the required ratio is 15%, the bank might have to face regulatory actions.

Due to some shortcomings of the *1998 accord*, an amendment was made in 1996 which requires commercial banks engaging in significant trading activity to set aside additional capital to cover the *market risks* inherent in their trading accounts. It allows sophisticated banks to use internally developed portfolio models to assess adequate capital requirements. Instead of using a *rules-based* approach to determine adequate bank capital, a *risk-focused* approach that relies on a modern portfolio may be used. The bank's portfolio is the monetary value of its own and off-balance sheet trading account positions.

The *value at risk* (VaR) technique is used and is a loss that will be exceeded with a specified probability over a specified time horizon.

8 Capital Adequacy Ratio, http://accountingexplained.com/financial/specialized-ratios/capital-adequacy-ratio, access date: 10.3.2015. For further information, see Richard Apostolik, Chistopher Donohue, and Peter Went, *Foundations of Banking Risk*, Wiley, 2009, pp. 203–228.

The amendment requires VaR to be calculated according to the criterion that there will only be a 1% chance that the maximum loss over a 10-day time period will exceed the bank's capital:

$$VaR = Portfolio\ Value \times Daily\ Standard\ Deviation\ of\ Return \\ \times Confidence\ Interval\ Factor \times Horizon$$

The confidence interval factor is the appropriate z-value from the standard normal density functions associated with the maximum level of loss that is tolerable.

For example, the 1% VaR for a portfolio of €800 million with a daily portfolio standard deviation of 0.75% for a 10-day planning horizon is €44.14 million = €800 million × 0.0075 × 2.326 × √10, where 2.326 is the z-value associated with a one-tail 99% confidence level. That is, there is only a 1% chance that the loss during a 10-day period will exceed €44.14 million. In addition to capital required, the bank should provide €44.14 million extra capital to cover market risk.

There are many methods to measure operating risk. We will show the simplest approach here.[9] The Basel Committee proposes to retain 15% of the average gross income (GI) over the last three years. The required capital (or capital requirement) is then equal to:

$$Required\ capital = \alpha \times GI$$

The coefficient α is set at 15%

Assume that gross income of the bank amounts to €2,440M, then the required capital will be (0, 15 × €2,440 =) €366M.

New capital adequacy ratio = €500/ (€3.700 +€44+ €366) = 500/4,110 =12.17%.

If required ratio is below 12.17%, there is no need for new capital, because the capital the bank possesses is above the required capital.

15.6 Off-Balance-Sheet Activities

Some of the off-balance-sheet activities and income generated by them are:[10]
- Fee income from:
    - Foreign exchange trades for customers
    - Servicing mortgage-backed securities
    - Guarantee of debt
    - Backup lines of credit

---

9 Fatima Zahra El Arif and Said Hinti, "Methods of Quantifying Operational Risk in Banks: Theoretical Approaches," *American Journal of Engineering Research (AJER)*, 3(3), 2014, pp. 238–244.
10 Mishkin and Eakins, *Financial Markets and Institutions*, op. cit., pp. 414–416.

- Financial futures and options
- Foreign exchange trading
- Interest rate swaps

All these activities involve risks which should be managed. FI's net worth or economic value is linked not only to the value of its traditional on-balance-sheet activities but also to the contingent asset and liability values of its off-balance-sheet activities. The risks and returns of several off-balance-sheet items are such as loan commitments, commercial and standby letters of credit, derivative contracts (futures, options, and swaps), and forward purchases are obvious. In all cases, it is clear that these instruments have a major impact on the future profitability and risk of an FI. Two other risks associated with off-balance-sheet activities, settlement risk and affiliate risk, are also important. Although off-balance-sheet activities can be risk-increasing, they can also be used to hedge on-balance-sheet exposures, resulting in lower risks as well as generating fee income to the FI.

15.7 Summary

A bank balance sheet (statement of financial position) consists of the following: assets (cash assets, loans, and securities, fixed assets), liabilities (deposit funds and non-deposit funds), and capital (equity capital, subordinated notes, debentures, and loan loss reserves).

An income statement (statement of income statement) consists of the following: interest income, non-interest income, interest expenses, non-interest expenses (including provision for loan losses), and net profit.

Bank performance can be measured by two tools: internal performance and external performance (financial ratios). Internal performance evaluations based on economic profit are as follows: risk-adjusted return on capital (RAROC) and economic value added (EVA).

External performance evaluation is conducted with ratios such as profitability ratios, asset utilization ratios, efficiency and expense control ratios, tax management ratios, liquidity ratios, and risk ratios.

When the bank receives deposits, reserves increase by an equal amount; when the bank loses deposits, reserves decrease by an equal amount.

The management areas in banking are as follows: liquidity management, asset management, liability management, and capital adequacy management.

Liquidity management focuses on maintaining enough liquid assets to meet obligations to depositors (for cash withdrawals).

Asset management deals with managing assets (loan portfolios) to achieve diversification and minimize default risk/credit risk and interest rate risk.

Liability management aims at acquiring and attracting funds (deposits) at the lowest possible cost.

Capital adequacy management tries to maintain the appropriate net worth to meet regulations and prevent bank failure.

Off-balance-sheet activities of banks, while making money for the bank, involve risk which should be managed.

16 Risk Management in Financial Institutions

16.1 Introduction

Risk is the probability that the outcome of an event will result in the reduction of wealth. It implies a loss of wealth or income. Any firm is subjected to different types of risks, which will diminish the value of the firm. Any environment in which a firm is in constant change may have negative influences on entities in that environment. In this chapter, we will review basic risks such as credit risk, liquidity risk, interest rate risk, market risk, off-balance-sheet risks, foreign exchange, country risk, technological risk, operational risks, insolvency risks, and derivatives such as options, futures, and swaps to manage most of the risks that financial institutions face.

16.2 The Risks

Most financial firms are intermediaries. They channel the funds of the savers to the borrowers and investors and hence they provide an essential service for the proper functioning of the economy. They need to continue to make a reasonable income for their stockholders and they also need to be able to pay their depositors or lenders when required. They borrow from millions of savers, they lend to millions of customers (including other financial institutions), and they perform other financial services to both individuals and corporations. They face many changes. There may be internal changes, such as management changes, infrastructural changes, and changes in the ownership structure. There may be changes in the sector such as many new entrants. There may be changes in basic economic variables such as the exchange rates, interest rates, unemployment rate, and inflation rate. There may be changes in the legal structure concerning the sector. Lastly, there may be changes in the world economy. The financial institutions (FIs) will be affected by degrees by all of these changes which may negatively affect the entities.

The risks associated with all of these changes are classified as:[1]

- *Credit risk.* The risk that the money lent may not be fully paid back.
- *Liquidity risk.* FI may not have enough liquid funds on hand to pay the obligations.
- *Interest rate risk.* Interest rates may change, causing a decline in the value of the entity.
- *Market risk.* Risk involving the trading of assets and liabilities because of changes in interest rates and exchange rates.

1 Anthony Saunders and Marcia Millon Cornett, *Financial Institutions Management: A Risk Management Approach*, Sixth Edition, McGraw-Hill/Irwin, 2008, pp. 168–188.

https://doi.org/10.1515/9783110705355-016

- *Off-balance-sheet risks*. Risks associated with balance sheet obligations, such as the payment of a letter of guarantee because the customer failed to accomplish a task.
- *Foreign exchange risk*. Risks associated with the changes of the exchange rates. Such changes will change the values of assets and liabilities, causing a change in the value of the bank.
- *Country risk*. Risk that the company in which the entity is formed or operates may undergo political changes that will negatively affect the entity.
- *Technological risk*. Risk that new technologies introduced into the entity may have negative results.
- *Operational risks*. Risks that the current infrastructure of the entity will not support the healthy functioning of the entity.
- *Insolvency risks*. Risk that the capital of the entity is not enough to support a sudden decline in the value of its assets.

Due to the introductory nature of this book, we will briefly summarize the credit risk, interest rate risk, market risk, foreign exchange risk, technology and operational risk, country (sovereign) risk, liquidity risk, and hedging instruments.

The management of risk in financial institutions is known as *asset and liabilities management* (ALM). ALM includes a set of tools that ensure that value is created for shareholders and that risks are under control.[2] The ultimate goal of ALM is to manage risks associated with mismatches between assets and liabilities.[3]

16.3 Managing Credit Risk

A major part of the business of financial institutions is making loans. The major risk with loans is that the borrower will not repay the loan and or the interest.

Credit risk is the risk that a borrower will not repay a loan according to the terms of the loan, either defaulting entirely or making late payments of interest or principal.

Once again, the concepts of *adverse selection* and *moral hazard* will provide our framework to understand the principles that financial managers must follow to minimize credit risk.

Adverse selection is a problem in the market for loans because those with the highest credit risk have the biggest incentives to borrow from others.

2 J. Dermine and Y. F. Bissade, *Asset & Liability Management: A Guide to Value Creation and Risk Control*, FT Prentice-Hall, 2002, p. ix.
3 The Hong Kong Institute of Bankers, *Bank Asset and Liability Management*, Wiley-Singapore, 2018, p. 4.

Moral hazard plays an important role as well. Once a borrower has a loan, the borrower has an incentive to engage in risky projects to produce the highest pay-offs, especially if the project is financed with debt.

Both of these risks exist because of the problem of *asymmetric information*, which means that the lender does not possess complete information on the borrower to make the right decision.

Financial managers have a number of tools available to assist in reducing or eliminating the risk posed by the asymmetric information problem:[4]

- *Screening.* FI will try to collect reliable information about prospective borrowers. This has also led some institutions to specialize in regions or industries such as gaining expertise in evaluating particular firms or individuals. The balance sheet, income statement, and other relevant information from the borrower are obtained and analyzed. The problem is that the information provided may not be correct for companies which are not audited by independent auditors. Other information from the tax authorities, social security office, and suppliers to the borrower are obtained, if available.
- *Monitoring.* FI periodically verifies that the borrower is complying with the terms of the loan contact, like paying the interest due at the due date.
- *Long-term customer relationships.* Past information contained in checking accounts, savings accounts, and previous loans provides valuable information to more easily determine credit worthiness.
- *Collateral.* FI wants a pledge of property or other assets that must be surrendered if the terms of the loan are not met. This procedure is also routine for most loans. However, this may not be necessary for loans like car or mortgage loans, since they are already secured.
- *Compensating balances.* These are reserves that a borrower must maintain in an account that acts as collateral, should the borrower default. This is also a routine procedure. The compensating balance acts not only as collateral but as an item which reduces the cost funds lent since the bank does not pay interest on compensating balances.
- *Credit rationing.* Lenders will refuse to lend to some borrowers regardless of how much interest they are willing to pay. Some lenders will only finance part of a project, requiring that the remaining part comes from equity financing.

---

4 For further information, see Mishkin and Eakins, *Financial Markets and Institutions*, op. cit., pp. 565–573.

Banks usually use four ways to minimize credit risk:

- *Accurate pricing of loans*. More risky loans may be priced higher than the less risky loans.
- *Credit limits*. Credit limits may be imposed on the borrower according to their wealth or potential income in the near future.
- *Collateral or security*. Loans should be properly secured against the wealth or assets of the borrower (for example, houses or shares).
- *Diversification*. Risky loans can be backed up through new capital injection or diversification through finding new loan markets.

The *quantitative method* of credit risk analysis requires the use of financial data to predict the probability of default by the borrower. The methods, which are commonly used, are *discriminant analysis* and *logit and probit models*. These methods are statistical techniques and involve methods similar to regression. The probability of defaults is calculated on the basis of some important predetermined variables such as age, marital status, residence, and qualification.

Firm-specific credit risk refers to the likelihood that specific individual assets may deteriorate in quality, while systematic credit risk involves macroeconomic factors that may increase the default risk of all firms in the economy. Thus, if a rating company lowers its rating on a certain stock and an investor is holding only this particular stock, the company may face significant losses as a result of this downgrading. However, *portfolio theory* in finance has shown that firm-specific credit risk can be diversified away if a portfolio of well-diversified stocks is held. Similarly, if an FI holds well-diversified assets, the FI will face only systematic credit risk that will be affected by the general condition of the economy.[5] The risks specific to any one customer will not be a significant portion of the FI's overall credit risk.

16.4 Managing Interest-Rate Risk

Financial institutions – banks, in particular – specialize in earning a higher rate of return on their assets relative to the interest paid on their liabilities. A simple example will suffice to explain that risk.

Suppose a financial institution buys a long-term bond after valuing it by discounting the related cash inflows from the bond at a certain interest rate (discount rate). However, if the discount rate changes due to an external reason, the value of the bond will decline, causing a loss.

---

5 For further information, see David J. Moore, *Dr Moores' Perspectives in Finance: Financial Institutions*, CreateSpace, 2010, pp. 155–161.

As interest rate volatility has increased in the last 30 years, interest-rate risk exposure has become a concern for financial institutions.

To see how financial institutions can measure and manage interest-rate exposure, we will examine the balance sheet for DEF Bank. We will develop two tools: *income gap analysis* and *duration gap analysis*[6] to assist the financial manager in this effort.

Income Gap Analysis

Income gap analysis measures the sensitivity of a bank's current year net income to changes in interest rate.

It requires determining which assets and liabilities will have their interest rates change as market interest rates change. Let's see how that works for DEF Bank (see Tables 16.1 and 16.2).[7]

Table 16.1: Balance Sheet of DEF Bank.

DEF Bank			
Assets		**Liabilities**	
Reserves and cash items	+€50 million	Checkable deposits	+€150 million
Securities		Money market deposit	
Less than1 year	+€50 million	accounts	+€50 million
1 to 2 years	+€50 million	Savings deposits	+€150 million
Greater than 2 years	+€100 million	CDs	
Residential mortgages		Variable-rate	+€100 million
Variable rate	+€100 million	Less than 1 year	+€150 million
Fixed-rate (30 year)	+€100 million	1 to 2 years	+€50 million
Commercial loans		More than 2 years	+€50 million
Less than 1 year	+€150 million	Central Bank funds	+€50 million
1 to 2 years	+€100 million	Borrowings	

---

6 These models are adapted from Mishkin and Eakins, *Financial Markets and Institutions*, op. cit., pp. 573–585.

7 Adapted from Mishkin and Eakins, *Financial Markets and Institutions*, op. cit., pp. 574–576.

Table 16.1 (continued)

DEF Bank

Assets		Liabilities	
Greater than 20 years	+€250 million	Less than 1 year	+€100 million
Physical capital	+€50 million	1 to 2 years	+€50 million
		More than 2 years	+€50 million
		Bank capital	+€50 million
Total	+€1,000 million	Total	+€1,000 million

Table 16.2: Determining Rate Sensitive Items for DEF Bank.

Assets	Liabilities
Assets with maturity less than one year	Money market deposits
Variable-rate mortgages	Variable-rate CDs
Short-term commercial loan	Short-term CDs
Portion of fixed-rate mortgages (say 20%)	Interbank (Central Bank) funds
	Short-term borrowings
	Portion of checkable deposits (10%)
	Portion of savings (20%)

Rate-Sensitive Assets (RSA) = €50m + €100m + €150m + (20% × €100m)

RSA= €320M

Rate-sensitive liabilities (RSL) = €50m + €250m + €50m + €100m + (10% × €150m + 20% × €150m

RSL= €495M

If interest rates go up by 5%, then

Asset Income = +5% × €320m =+€ 16m

Liability Costs = +5% × €495m =+€ 24.75m

Income = €16m – € 24.75 = – €8.75m

Then, If RSL > RSA, then if *i* increases income come falls and vice versa.
Or, more generally:

$$GAP = RSA - RSL$$

$$= €320\,m - €495m = -\ €175m$$

$$\text{Change in Income} = GAP \times i$$

$$= -\ \text{€}175m \times 5\% = -\ \text{€}8.75m$$

This is essentially a short-term focus on interest rate risk exposure. A longer-term focus uses duration gap analysis.

Duration Gap Analysis

Shareholders and managers care about the impact of interest rate exposure on current net income. They are also interested in the impact on net worth.

The concept of duration which first appeared in bond valuation plays an important role here.

Duration gap analysis measures the sensitivity of a bank's current year net income to changes in interest rates, which requires determining the duration for assets and liabilities, whose market value will change as interest rates change.

Let's see how this looks for DEF Bank (see Table 16.3).

Table 16.3: Duration of the DEF Bank's Assets and Liabilities.

	Amount (€ millions)	Duration (years)	Weighted Duration (years)
Assets			
Reserves and cash items	50	0.0	0.00
Securities			
Less than1 year	50	0.4	0.02
1 to 2 years	50	1.6	0.08
More than 2 years	100	7.0	0.70
Residential mortgages			
Variable rate	100	0.5	0.05
Fixed-rate (30 year)	100	6.0	0.60
Commercial loans			
Less than 1 year	150	0.7	0.11
1 to 2 years	100	1.4	0.14
More than 20 years	250	4.0	1.00
Physical capital	50	0.0	0.00

Table 16.3 (continued)

	Amount (€ millions)	Duration (years)	Weighted Duration (years)
Average duration			2.70
Liabilities			
Checkable deposits	150	2.0	0.32
Money market deposit accounts	50	0.1	0.01
Savings deposits	150	1.0	0.16
CDs			
Variable-rate	100	0.5	0.05
Less than 1 year	150	0.2	0.03
1 to 2years	50	1.2	0.06
More than 2 years	50	2.7	0.14
Fed funds	50	0.0	0.00
Borrowings			
Less than 1 year	100	0.3	0.03
1 to 2 years	50	1.3	0.07
More than 2 years	50	3.1	0.16
Average duration			1.03

The basic equation for determining the change in market value for assets or liabilities is:

$$\% \text{ Change in Value} = -DUR \times [\Delta i/(1+i)] \text{ or}$$

$$\text{Change in Value} = -DUR \times [\Delta i/(1+i)] \times \text{Original Value}$$

Consider a change in rates from 10% to 15%. Using the value from Table 16.3, we see that (notice that the total value of assets is 1,000):

Assets:

$$\Delta \text{Asset Value} = -2.7 \times .05/(1+.10) \times €1,000m$$

$$= -€123m$$

Liabilities:

$$\Delta Liability\ Value = -1.03 \times .05/(1+.10) \times €950m$$

$$= -€45m$$

Net Worth:

$$\Delta NW = \Delta Assets - \Delta Liabilities$$

$$\Delta NW = -€123 - (-€45m) = -€78m$$

For a rate change from 10% to 15%, the net worth of DEF Bank will fall by €78m.

Recall from the balance sheet that DEF Bank has *capital* totaling €50m. Following such a dramatic change in rate, the capital would fall to – €28m. More generally:

For DEF Bank, with a rate change of Δi (say, from 10% to 15%), these equations are:

$$DURgap = DUR_{Assets} - [L/A \times DURL]$$

$$\%\Delta NW = -DUR_{gap} \times \Delta i/(1+i)$$

Where DUR_{Assets} and $DUR_{Liabilities}$ represents duration of asset and the duration of liabilities. Numerically:

$$DURgap = DUR_{Assets} - [L/A \times DURL]$$

$$= 2.7 - [(950/1{,}000) \times 1.03]$$

$$= 1.72$$

$$\%\Delta NW = -DUR_{Gap} \times \Delta i/(1+i)$$

$$= -1.72 \times .05/(1+.10)$$

$$= -.078.\ or\ -7.8\%$$

So far, we have focused on how to apply income gap analysis and duration gap analysis in a banking environment. The same analysis can be applied to other financial or nonfinancial institutions.

Other Topics

Problems with GAP analysis:
- It is assumed that slope of yield curve does not change and is flat.
- Managers estimate the percentage of fixed-rate assets and liabilities that are rate-sensitive. This not an easy task.

Strategies for managing interest-rate risk are as follows:
- In the previous example, shorten the duration of bank assets or lengthen the duration of bank liabilities.
- To completely immunize the net worth from the interest-rate risk, set $DUR_{Gap} = 0$.
- Reduce $DUR_{Assets} = 0.98 \Rightarrow DUR_{Gap} = 0.98 - [(950/1,000) \times 1.03] = 0$
  Raise $DUR_{Liabilities} = 2.80 \Rightarrow DUR_{Gap} = 2.7 - [(950/1,000) \times 2.80] = 0$.

16.5 Market Risk Management

There are two types of risk: systematic and unsystematic risks.
- *Systematic risks* are the risks due to the changes from political, social, and macroeconomic factors. They are all uncontrollable.
- *Unsystematic risks* refer to risks associated with controllable and known variables.

For example, a bank can be exposed to market risk (general and specific) in relation to debt and service, fixed and floating rate debt instruments such as bonds, debt derivatives, futures and options on debt instruments, interest rate and cross-country swaps, forward foreign exchange positions, equities, equity derivatives (equity swaps), futures, options on equity indices, options, and futures warrants.

Banks participate in the buying and selling of financial instruments in various and diverse markets around the globe. Adverse changes in the price of these instruments can expose the banks significantly and effect the values of their portfolio. This is called *market risk*.

Two common methods to calculate the exposure of market risk are:
- *Value at Risk* (VaR), which calculates the market risk faced by a bank in an everyday, normal market condition.
- *Stress testing* calculates the market risk in an abnormal market condition.

We will discuss each approach in some detail.

Value at Risk (VaR) Approach

A bank might calculate that the daily *VaR* of its trading portfolio is €35 million at a 99%. A relatively new approach for measuring the market risk, VaR calculates the worst possible loss that a bank could expect to suffer over a time interval, under normal market conditions, on the basis of some specific confidence level (e.g. % confidence interval). This means that there is only 1 chance in 100 that a loss > €35 million would occur on any given day.

VaR can be calculated for any portfolio of assets or liabilities for which market values are available on a periodic basis and price volatilities (σ) can also be estimated.

In its most general form, the VaR measures the potential loss in value of a risky asset or portfolio over a defined period for a given confidence interval. Thus, if the VaR on a portfolio is €100 million at a one-day, 95% confidence level, there is only a 5% chance that the value of the portfolio will drop more than €100 million over any given day. Another way of putting this is to say that on 95 days out of every 100, the value of the portfolio will drop by no more than €100 million. Note that the VaR is not a measure of the worst-case scenario. As with a 95% confidence interval, 5 days out of every 100, the losses over one day on the portfolio will exceed €100 million.

To calculate the VaR for an asset or portfolio, the distribution of returns on the asset or portfolio needs to be specified. This distribution can be determined from *historic data*, from assuming that returns follow a *normal distribution*, or by a technique called the *Monte Carlo simulation*.[8]

Historical Method. The *historical method* is based on an evaluation of the past performance of the asset or portfolio on the assumption that the past performance is a fairly accurate predictor of future performance. The return performances of the asset or portfolio are then ordered, and the desired percentile is read off. For example, consider a dealer working for a bank with a €20 million portfolio. Assume the dealer has compiled from historical information the following information about the change in the value of a portfolio over a one-day period (see Table 16.4).

Table 16.4: Data for Historical Simulation.

Change in Value	Probability
< -€10,000,000	.01
-€5,000,000 to -€9,999,999	.04
-€250,000 to -€4,999,999	.20
€0 to -€2,499,999	.25
€1 to €2,499,999	.25
€2,500,000 to €4,999,999	.20
€5000,000 to €9,999,999	.04
> £ €10,000,000	.01

8 See M. Buckle and E. Beccalli, *Principles of Banking and Finance*, London School of Economics and Political Science, 2011, pp. 132–134.

From this table, we can easily define the daily VaR at a 95% confidence interval, which is -€5,000,000. There is a 4% chance of a loss of between €5,000,000 and €9,999,999 plus a 1% chance of a loss of at least €10 million. Thus, the bank can expect to lose at least €5,000,000 at 5% of the time. Or 95% of the time, the loss to the bank will be no more than €5,000,000. The bank can then set aside an appropriate amount of capital to cover this potential loss.

One problem with the historical method is that the historical data used to produce the distribution should be representative of all possible states of the portfolio. To achieve this would require many years of data on returns, which may not be available or may not exist at all.

Normal Distribution. The second approach is to assume the returns on the asset or portfolio follow some statistical distribution (e.g. normal, lognormal, etc.). A typical distribution used for estimating a VaR is the *normal distribution* as in Figure 16.1. The advantage of this approach is that relatively little information is needed to construct the distribution and compute the VaR – just the mean and standard deviation of the distribution.

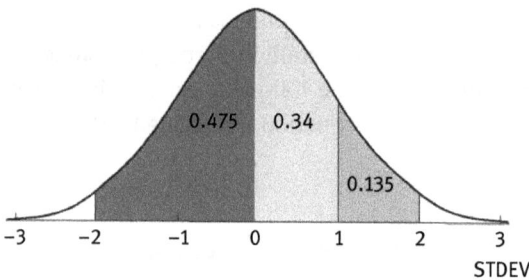

Figure 16.1: Standard Normal Distribution.

If a 95% confidence level is required, meaning we wish to have 5% of the observations in the left-hand tail of the normal distribution, this means that the observations in that area are 1.645 standard deviations away from the mean.

To take an example, if a portfolio of assets of value €100 million has a standard deviation of returns of 12.48% (note this standard deviation will have been calculated using a portfolio approach and knowledge of the covariances or correlations between returns on assets in the portfolio. The 95% VaR is equal to $1.645 \times 0.1248 = 0.205296$. In € terms, the VaR = €100 million $\times 0.205295 = $ €20,529,500.

A stricter VaR would be one with a 99% confidence interval, which implies that 1% of observations would lie in the left-hand tail of the distribution. This would mean that the losses incurred would exceed the VaR on only 1 day out of every 100. In this case, assuming a normal distribution, the observations in the left-hand tail of the distribution would be 2.33 standard deviations away from the mean.

The main drawbacks of this approach are:
- The *variance-covariance approach* assumes stable correlations over time. We saw in the recent financial crisis that during times of financial stress, the correlations between asset returns tend to move toward +1.
- It assumes a normal distribution, which is not always appropriate. Returns in markets are widely believed to have "fatter tails" than those of a normal distribution. A fatter tail implies that extreme events have a higher probability (that is, a greater chance of occurring) than that predicted by a normal distribution.

Monte Carlo Simulation. The last technique of the *Monte Carlo simulation* basically involves the development of a model for the returns on an asset or portfolio and then randomly generating outcomes for returns to determine the distribution of outcomes.

Portfolio Stress Testing

This is a relatively new technique that relies on computer modeling of different worst-case scenarios and computation of effects of those scenarios on a bank's portfolio position. The advantage of this technique is that it can allow risk managers to evaluate possible scenarios that may be completely absent from historical data. All assets in portfolio are revalued using a changed environment, and a modified estimate for the return on the portfolio is created.

Such scenarios can lead to many exercises and a range of values for return on the portfolio is derived. By specifying the probability for each scenario, managers can then generate a distribution of portfolio returns from which VaR can be measured.

16.6 Foreign Exchange or Currency Risk

Under flexible exchange rates, a bank with global operation faces such a type of risk. It usually arises due to an adverse exchange rate fluctuation, which effects the bank foreign exchange position taken on its own account or on the behalf of its customers.

Foreign exchange risk involves the adverse effect on the value of an FI's assets and liabilities, which are denominated in foreign currencies when the exchange rate changes. An FI is *net long* in foreign assets when the foreign currency-denominated assets exceed the foreign currency denominated liabilities. An FI will suffer potential losses if the domestic currency strengthens relative to the foreign currency when repayment of the assets will occur in the foreign currency. If an FI is *net short* in foreign assets when the foreign currency-denominated liabilities exceed the foreign currency denominated assets, the FI will suffer potential losses. An FI will suffer potential

losses if the domestic currency weakens relative to the foreign currency when repayment of the liabilities will occur in the domestic currency.

If the Danish krone (dk.) is expected to depreciate in the near future, would a
FI in Copenhagen prefer to be net long or net short in its asset positions? The FI
would prefer to be net long (liabilities less than assets) in its asset position. The depreciation of the dk. relative to the euro means that the FI would increase its net
asset position. This will bring about *exchange rate profit*.

If an FI has the same amount of foreign assets and foreign liabilities (neutral position) in the same currency, the FI has no foreign currency risk. However, matching the
size of the foreign currency book will not eliminate the risk of the international transactions if the maturities of the assets and liabilities are mismatched. To the extent that
the asset and liabilities are mismatched in terms of maturities or, more importantly,
durations, the FI will be exposed to a foreign interest rate risk.

Exchange rate changes can systematically affect the value of the bank by influencing its operating cash flows as well as the domestic currency values of its assets
and liabilities.

Types of exposures[9] are:
- *Economic Exposure.* This can be defined as the extent to which the value of the
  bank would be affected by unanticipated changes in exchange rates. Any anticipated changes in exchange rates would have been already discounted and reflected in the bank's value. Changes in exchange rates can have a profound
  effect on the bank's competitive position in the market and thus on its cash
  flows and market value. When the bank's assets or operating cash flows exhibit
  sensitivity to exchange rate movements, the bank is exposed to currency risk.
  Exposure to currency risk thus can be properly measured by the *sensitivities* of
  the future home currency values of the assets and operating cash flows.
- *Transaction Exposure.* This can be defined as the sensitivity of realized domestic
  currency values of the bank's contractual cash flows denominated in foreign currencies to unexpected exchange rate changes. Since settlements of these contractual cash flows affect the bank's domestic currency cash flows, transaction
  exposure is sometimes regarded as a short-term economic exposure. This exposure
  arises from fixed-price contracting in a world where exchange rates are changing
  randomly. There are many ways of heading transaction exposures. One way is to
  use financial contracts which include forward market hedge, money market
  hedge, option market hedge, and swap market hedge. Most of these contracts are
  discussed before and at the end of this chapter.

---

9 For detailed information, see Cheol Eun and Bruce G. Resnick, *International Financial
Management*, McGraw-Hill, 2001, pp. 293–297. We discussed types of exposures in the context of an
international financial management in Chapter 14. Here, we focus on types of exposures from a
banking perspective.

–   *Translation Exposure*. This refers to the potential that the bank's consolidated fi-
    nancial statements can be affected by changes in exchange rates. Consolidation
    involves translation of the subsidiaries' financial statements from local currencies
    to the home currency. For instance, assume that a Danish MNC has subsidiaries in
    Bulgaria and Albania. Each subsidiary will produce financial statements in its
    local currency. To consolidate financial statements worldwide, the firm must
    translate the subsidiaries' financial statements in local currencies into the dk., the
    home currency. However, not all items in the financial statements are translated
    at the current exchange rate. Which items are to be translated at the current ex-
    change rate? This is a key question related to translation exposure. The answer
    depends on the translation method followed by the parent bank.

16.7 Technology and Operational Risk

Technology risk occurs when investments in new technologies do not generate a net
cost savings expected in the expansion in financial services. Economies of scale
occur when the average cost of production decreases with an expansion in the
amount of financial services provided. Economies of scope occur when an FI is able
to lower overall costs by producing new products with inputs similar to those used
for other products. In financial service industries, the use of data from existing customer databases to assist in providing new service products is an example of economies of scope.

   Operational risk refers to the failure of the back-room support operations necessary to maintain the smooth functioning of the operation of FIs, including settlement, clearing, and other transaction-related activities. For example, computerized
payment systems such as *SWIFT* allow modern financial intermediaries to transfer
funds, securities and messages across the world in real-time. This creates the opportunity to engage in global financial transactions rapidly and in an extremely cost-
efficient manner. However, the interdependence of such transactions also creates
settlement risk. Typically, any given transaction leads to other transactions involving funds and securities across the globe. A transmittal failure or high-tech fraud
affecting any one of the intermediate transactions could cause an unraveling of all
subsequent transactions.

16.8 Country (Sovereign) Risk

A *country risk* involves the interference of a foreign government in the transmission
of fund transfers to repay a debt by a foreign borrower. A lender FI has very little
recourse in this situation unless the FI is able to restructure the debt or demonstrate

influence over the future supply of funds to the country in question. This influence likely would involve significant working relationships with the IMF and the World Bank.

There are basically three ways to assess country risk:

- Debt ratios of the country in question are used to make the assessment. The following ratios are extensively used:[10]

  Import ratio = Total imports/Total foreign reserves
  Debt service ratio = Interest and principal payments/Exports
  Import ratio = Total imports/Total foreign reserves
  Investment ratio = Real investments/Gross national product
  Variance of exports = σ^2 Exports
  Increase in money supply = $\Delta M/M$

- Some publications, such as *Euromoney*, determine the overall creditworthiness of most countries around the world. The overall creditworthiness depends on economic factors, political factors, and foreign relations.
- Some rating agencies like *Moody's Investor Service, Fitch,* and *Standard & Poor's* assign letter ratings to indicate the quality of bonds issued by most sovereign governments.

16.9 Liquidity Risk

Liquidity risk is the uncertainty that an FI may need to obtain large amounts of cash to meet the withdrawals of depositors or other liability claimants. In times of normal economic activity, depository FIs meet cash withdrawals by accepting new deposits and borrowing funds in the short-term money markets. However, in times of harsh liquidity crises, the FI may need to sell assets at significant losses in order to generate cash quickly.

A bank, at all times, must be able to meet cash flow obligations arising from deposit withdrawals.

The best way to deal with this type of risk in modern banking is to use the gap analysis. To control this risk, banks usually plan cash flows (in and out) over a short interval of time.

---

10 Marcia Millon Cornett and Anthony Saunders, *Fundamentals of Financial Institutions Management*, 1999, pp. 707–715.

16.10 Hedging with Financial Derivatives

We now examine how the markets for derivatives work and how they are used by financial managers to reduce risk. Topics include:[11]
- Hedging
- Forward markets
- Financial futures markets
- Hedging FX risk
- Stock index futures
- Options
- Interest-rate swaps

Hedging

Hedging involves engaging in a financial transaction that reduces or eliminates risk. Some definitions are:
- *Long position.* An asset which is purchased or owned shows a long position. A purchase increases the long position and sale of an asset reduces that position. However, the return on these assets are usually risky. Thus, a long position exposes the company to risk if the return on the assets is reduced.
- *Short position.* An asset which must be delivered to a third party as a future date, or an asset which is borrowed and sold, but must be replaced in the future. For example, foreign exchange denominated loans from other banks expose the bank to foreign exchange risk. The devaluation of the local money increases the debt of the bank in local currency, thus resulting in the decrease of the income of the bank.

Hedging risk involves engaging in a financial transaction that offsets a long position by taking an additional short position or offsets a short position by taking an additional long position. For example, if a bank has received loans in a foreign currency, it may lend an equal amount in the same currency. Thus, it has a *neutral* position, implying that whatever happens to the exchange rate, the bank remains unaffected.

A hedge is called *micro-hedge* if it is used only for one asset. In most cases, a micro-hedge involves taking an offsetting position in that single asset. Offsetting positions can include taking short positions in futures contracts of that same asset.

It is called a *macro-hedge* if it is used to protect an entire portfolio. A macro-hedge is an investment technique used to mitigate or eliminate downside systemic

---

[11] We discuss these instruments from the bank's perspective. More information on these instruments can be found in Chapter 7.

risk from a portfolio of assets. Macro-hedging strategies typically involve using derivatives.

In the following section, we will examine how both approaches are used in different financial markets.

Forward Markets

Forward contracts are agreements by two parties to engage in a financial transaction at a future point in time. Although the contract can be written, the contract usually includes:
- The assets to be delivered and the location of delivery
- The price paid for assets
- The date when the assets and cash will be exchanged

An example of an interest-rate contract can be shown as follows:
- A company needs $100,000 in the future. The manager knows the exchange rate will be different in the future and wants to make sure how much they will pay in Danish krone for the $100,000 now. This protects the company from any fluctuations in rate.
- The company purchases a forward contract with a bank stating that the bank will sell the dollars at a certain rate in the future (say $/dk.4) regardless of the market rate.
- The company and the bank settle the contract at the specified future date at specified exchange rate. The total amount of dk. to be paid to the bank will be Dk.400.000 and this is known by both parties now.
- The bank loses money if the market rate on the settlement date is dk.4.5. The company loses if the market rate is dk.3.5.

It is apparent that a forward contract protects the company from exchange rate being higher than the market rate, but not the other way around.

Financial Futures Markets

Financial futures contracts are similar to forward contracts in that they are an agreement by two parties to engage in a financial transaction at a future point in time. However, they differ from forward contracts in several significant ways.

Features of a financial futures contract are:
- Specifies delivery of type of security at a future date
- Specifies the quantity
- Specifies the price

– Traded on exchanges
– Involves a margin account

Advantages of futures over forwards are:
– Futures are more liquid, standardized contracts that can be traded.
– Delivery of range of securities reduces the chance that a trader can corner the market.
– Mark-to-market daily avoids default risk.
– Parties don't have to deliver. A holder of a future contract can sell an equal amount of the same type to net out their position.

Hedging FX Risk. An example of an FX futures contract can be shown as follows: A manufacturer expects to be paid 10 million euros in two months for the sale of equipment in Europe. Currently, $1 = €1 and the manufacturer would like to lock-in that exchange rate. So, the manufacturer wants to have 10 million dollars at the end of two months.

The manufacturer can use the FX futures market to accomplish this.
– The manufacturer sells 10 million euros of futures contracts. Assuming that one (1) contract is for €250,000 in euros, the manufacturer takes as short position in 40 contracts.
– The exchange will require the manufacturer to deposit cash into a margin account. For example, the exchange may require €2,000 per contract, or €80,000.
– As the exchange rate fluctuates during the two months, the value of the margin account will fluctuate. If the value in the margin account falls too low (below €80,000, in this case), additional funds may be required. This is how the contract is marked-to-market. If additional funds are not deposited when required, the position will be closed by the exchange.
– Assume that actual exchange rate is $0.96 = €1 at the end of the two months. The manufacturer receives the 10 million euros and exchanges them in the spot market for $9,600,000.
– The manufacturer also closes the margin account, which has €480,000 in it: $400,000 for the changes in exchange rates, plus the original $80,000 required by the exchange (assuming no margin calls).
– In the end, the manufacturer has the $10,000,000 desired from the sale.

Stock Index Futures. Financial institution managers – particularly those who manage mutual funds, pension funds, and insurance companies – also need to assess their stock market risk, which occurs due to fluctuations in equity market prices. One instrument to hedge this risk is stock index futures.

Stock index futures are a contract to buy or sell a particular stock index starting at a given level. Contacts exist for most major indexes, including the S&P 500, Dow Jones Industrials, FTSE-100, and Russell 2000.

The best stock futures contract to use is generally determined by the highest correlation between returns to a portfolio and returns to a particular index. An example of hedging transaction is as follows:

RAS Bank has a stock portfolio worth €100 million which tracks closely with the *FTSE 100*. The portfolio manager fears that market will decline, and they want to hedge their portfolio over the next year if the *FTSE 100* currently is 1,000. How can they hedge their portfolio?

Value of the Index Futures Contract = 250 × index.

$$\text{Currently } 250 \times 1{,}000 = €250{,}000$$

To hedge €100 million of the stocks that move 1 for 1 (perfect correlation) with *FTSE 100* currently selling at 1000, they would sell €100 million of index futures = 400 contracts.

Suppose after the year, the *FTSE 100* is at 900 and the portfolio is worth €90 million. The futures position is up €10 million. If instead, the *FTSE 100* is at 1100 and portfolio is worth €110 million, the futures position is down €10 million. Either way, the net position is €100 million.

Note that the portfolio is protected from downside risk – the risk that the value in the portfolio will fall. In doing so, however, the manager has also eliminated any upside potential.

Options

An *options contract* gives the owner right to buy (call option) or sell (put option) an instrument at the exercise (strike) price up until the expiration date (American) or on the expiration date (European).

Options are available on a number of financial instruments, including individual stocks and stock indexes.

To hedge with options, buy the same number of put option contracts as you would sell of futures, but at a price which is called the *option premium*.

Factors affecting the premium (Black and Scholes) are:
- *Higher strike price.* Lower premium on call options and higher premium on put options.
- *Higher term to expiration.* Higher premiums for both call and put options.
- *Higher price volatility of underlying instrument.* Higher premiums for both call and put options.

Continuing with the same example:

Value of the Index Option Contract = 100 × index.

$$\text{Currently } 100 \times 1{,}000 = €100{,}000$$

To hedge €100 million of stocks that move 1 for 1 (perfect correlation) with *FTSE 100* currently selling at 1,000, you would buy €100 million of Index, and put options = 1,000 contracts.

The premium would depend on the strike price. For example, a strike price of 950 might have a premium of €200 per contract, while a strike price of 900 might have a strike price of only €100.

Let's assume RAS Bank chooses a strike price of 950. Then RS must pay €200,000 for the position. This is non-refundable and comes out of the portfolio value (now only €99.8 million).

Suppose after the year, the Index is at 900 and the portfolio is worth €89.8 million. The options position is up €5 million (since 950 strike price). In net, the portfolio is worth €94.8 million.

·If instead, the *FTSE 100* is at 1100 and the portfolio is worth €109.8 million, the options position expires worthless and the portfolio is worth €109.8 million.

Note that the portfolio is protected from any downside risk (the risk that the value in the portfolio will fall) in excess of €5 million. However, to accomplish this, the manager has to pay an upfront premium of €200,000.

Interest-Rate Swaps

Interest-rate swaps involve the exchange of one set of interest payments (like fixed rate) for another set of interest payments (like variable rate) all denominated in the same currency.

The simplest type, called a plain *vanilla* swap, specifies:
- The rates being exchanged
- Type of payments
- Nominal amount

Let's say RAS Bank wishes to hedge rate changes by entering into variable-rate contracts. ABC Bank wishes to hedge some of its variable-rate debt with some fixed-rate debt. There is a notional principle of €1 million and a term of 10 years. RAS swaps 7% payment for T-bill + 1% from ABC.

Reduce the interest-rate risk for both parties. RAS Bank converts €1m of fixed rate assets to rate-sensitive assets, thus lowering GAP. ABC Bank does the opposite.

Advantages of swaps are:
- Reduce risk, while not changing balance sheet
- Longer term than futures or options

Disadvantages of swaps are:
- Lack of liquidity
- Subject to default risk

Financial intermediaries help reduce disadvantages of swaps (but at a cost).

16.11 Summary

Management of risk in financial institutions (FI) is known as *asset and liabilities management* (ALM). The ultimate goal of ALM is to manage risks.

Credit risk is the risk that the money lent may be paid back fully.

Liquidity risk involves that FI may not have enough liquid funds on hand to pay the obligations.

Interest rate risk arises when interest rates may change, causing a decline in the value of the entity.

Market risk involves the trading of assets and liabilities because of changes in interest rates and the exchange rates.

Off-balance-sheet risks are associated with balance sheet obligations such as the payment of a letter of guarantee because the customer failed to accomplish a task.

A foreign exchange risk is associated with the changes of the exchange rates. Such changes will change the values of assets and liabilities, causing a change in the value of the bank.

A country risk is a risk that the company in which the entity is formed or operates may undergo political changes that will negatively affect the entity.

Technological risk is a risk that new technologies introduced into the entity may have negative results.

Operational risks are risks that the current infrastructure of the entity will not support the health functioning of the entity.

Insolvency risks are risks that the capital of the entity may not be enough to support a sudden decline in the value of its assets.

Derivatives such as options, futures, and swaps can also be used to manage most of the risks we have described.

Appendix A: Basic Calculus

Frequently used principles of calculus are reviewed below.[1]

Functions

The concept of function is a very important in mathematics. The word *function* implies that the value of a variable depends on the value of another variable. It could well be that the value of a variable depends not on one variable but on many variables. The value of the variable that can freely take on any value is called an *independent variable* – for example, the number of study hours by a student. The student can freely choose the hours they can study. The *dependent variable* is the variable whose value depends on the value of the independent variable(s) chosen. The mark the student gets depend on the number of hours they chose to study. We can write this dependence as:

Mark = a function of hours studied. More mathematically:

$y = 20x$, where x represents the numbers of hours studied while y represents the mark received. More generally:

$y = f(x)$, meaning that the value of the independent variable y is a function of (f) the independent variable (x). The function $f(x)$ can be of any form: linear, non-linear exponential, and so on.

For example, if the student studied 4 hours $(x=4)$, they will get a mark of 80 $(=20 \times 4)$.

The set of values where the independent variables come from is defined as the *domain*. The domain could be any range of values. One can plot $f(x)$ by finding different values of y by assigning different values of x and identifying each pair on the x, y space. This is called a *graph*.

Some functions most commonly used are:

- $y = a$, a constant
- $y = ax$, linear
- $y = ax^2 + bx + c$, quadratic-nonlinear
- $y = a_0 + a_1x + a_2x^2 + a_3x^3 + \cdots + a_nx^n$, polynomial
- $y = ae^x$, *or* $Y = ax^n$, exponential
- $y = a\ln x$, logarithmic (natural logarithm)

---

1 For a more complete treatment of calculus for business, see Ian Jacques, *Mathematics for Economics and Business*, Fifth Edition, Pearson Education, 2006; Mike Rosser, *Basic Mathematics for Economists*, Second Edition, Routledge, 2003. For a quick survey of mathematics for business, see Ian Jacques, *Quantitative Methods: Economics Express*, Pearson, 2013.

https://doi.org/10.1515/9783110705355-017

Power. *Power* is a term that simply explains how many times a number or a variable is multiplied by itself. For example, if the variable x is multiplied by n times by itself, the result can be written as:

Y=xxxxxxx . . . . . . =n^n which implies that x multiplied by itself n times.

Y=x^6 if the x is multiplied by itself 6 times. Some examples of power functions are: $x^4 x^3 x^2 = (xxxx)(xxx)(xx) = x^9$ which means that to multiply the power functions, all we need to do is to sum the powers. Similarly, we can write $x^7/x^2 = xxxxxxx/xx = x^5$ which means that we can divide power functions by simply subtracting the power of the variable x in the denominator from that of the numerator. The resulting power can be negative, zero, or positive.

Root. The *nth root* of a number is the number that if we take its nth power, we get that number. For example, if the 4th root of a number is A, we can find the number by A^4. Or,

A=Y$^{1/4}$ or, similarly, A=$\sqrt[4]{Y}$, we can find Y by taking the 4th power of A, that is, $A^4 = (\sqrt[4]{Y})^4$ =Y.

The number n can be negative or positive. Negative numbers have imaginary (complex variable) roots.

Logarithms. *Logarithms* are functions are used to simplify operations involving large numbers. For example, working with a number such as 1,000,000 may be difficult or cumbersome. Taking the logarithm (base 10) of 1,000,000 =10^6 means finding a number which, when the number 10 is raised to this number, gives us the original number. In our example here, the number will be 6. We get 1,000,000 when we take the 6th power of 10.

The base can be different than 10 which is commonly used. For example, if the base was 4, the logarithm of 64 will be calculated as:

Log$_4$64=log$_4$4^3=3

The natural logarithm is a special case of logarithm when the base is e = 2.71828 and it is denoted as *ln* or *log$_e$*. Some properties of it are:

$$\ln xy = \ln x + \ln y, \ln x^n y^m = n \ln x + m \ln y$$

$$\ln x/y = \ln x - \ln y, \ln x^{1/n} = (1/n) \ln x$$

$$\ln x^n = n \ln x$$

$$e^{\ln m} = m, \ln e^a = a$$

Derivative of a Function

The derivative of a function $y(x)$ at a point x_0 is the slope of the straight-line tangent to the function $y(x)$ at point $(x_0, y(x_0))$. (See Figure A.1.) Then it is approximately defined as:

$$\frac{\Delta y}{\Delta x} = \frac{f(x_0 + \Delta x) - f(x_0)}{\Delta x}$$

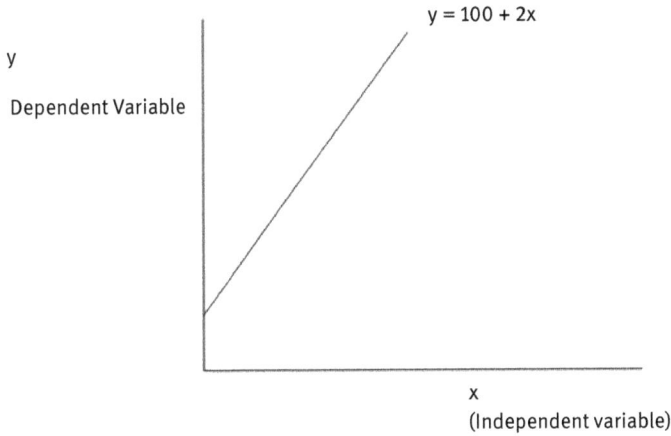

Figure A.1: Graph of Linear Function.

More precisely is defined as:

$$\frac{dy}{dx} \equiv f'(x) \equiv \lim_{\Delta x \to 0} \frac{f(x_0 + \Delta x) - f(x_0)}{\Delta x}.$$

It is evident that the function $f(x)$ has to be continuous for the derivative to exist. For example, the derivative for the following function would be calculated as:

$$y = 100 + 2x$$

$$f(x_0 + \Delta x) = 100 + 2(x_0 + \Delta x)$$

$$f(x_0) = 100 + 2x_0$$

$$f(x_0 + \Delta x) - f(x_0) = 2\Delta x$$

Then, using this definition;

$$dy/dx = 2$$

In case the function is not linear but nonlinear (see Figure A.2), the derivative at point A is the slope of the line tangent to the curve at point A. Suppose the function is $f=x^2$. Then its derivative at point A, which can be denoted as x_0 and y_0, can be calculated using the definition.

y

Dependent variable

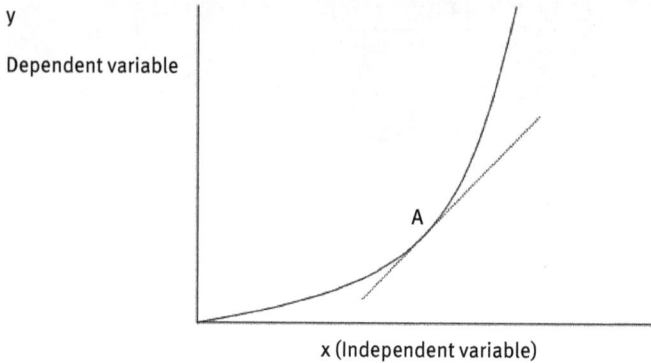

x (Independent variable)

Figure A.2: Graph of Non-Linear Function.

So, $\lim_{\Delta x \to 0} f(x_0+\Delta x)-f(x_0)/ \Delta x =((x_0+\Delta x)^2 -x_0^2)/ \Delta x=2x_0$ or more precisely, 2x evaluated at x_0.

Rules of Differentiation

1. Constant functions, $y = f(x) = ax^0 = a$. Then;

$$\frac{dy}{dx} = f'(x) = 0$$

2. Power functions: $y = f(x) = ax^b$. Then;

$$\frac{d}{dx} = f'(x) = abx^{b-1}$$

A more generalized power function as $f(x)=(g(x))^n$ will have a derivative

$$f'(x)=n(g(x))^{n-1}g'(x)$$

3. Sum of two functions: $y = f(x) = g(x) + h(x)$. Then:

$$\frac{dy}{dx} = f'(x) = g'(x) + h'(x)$$

4. Multiplication of two functions: $y = f(x) = g(x) \cdot h(x)$. Then:

$$\frac{dy}{dx} = f'(x) = g'(x) \cdot h(x) + g(x) + h'(x)$$

5. Division of two functions: $y = f(x) = \frac{g(x)}{h(x)}$. Then:

$$\frac{dy}{dx} = f'(x) = \frac{g'(x) \cdot h(x) - g(x) \cdot h'(x)}{[h(x)]^2}$$

6. Chain rule: if $y = g(z)$ and $z = h(x)$, Then, $y = f(z) = g(h(x))$. Then:

$$\frac{dy}{dx} = f'(x) = \frac{dy}{dz}\frac{dz}{dx} = g'(h(x)) \cdot h'(x)$$

7. Polynomials: $y = f(x) = a_0 + a_1 x + a_A x^A + a_3 x^3 + \ldots + a_n x^n$. Then:

$$\frac{dy}{dx} = f'(x) = a_1 + 2a_2 x + 3a_3 x^2 + \cdots + n a_n x^{n-1}$$

8. Logarithmic functions:

$y = f(x) = log_a g(x)$. Then:

$$\frac{dy}{dx} = f'(x) = \frac{g'(x)}{g(x) \ln a}$$

Natural logarithm: $y = f(x) = \ln g(x)$. Then:

$$\frac{dy}{dx} = f'(x) = \frac{g'(x)}{g(x)}$$

Higher Order Derivatives

Taking the derivative of a derivative of a function $f(x)$ n times is called the nth order derivative. For example, if $f'(x)$ is the derivative of the function f, the second derivative of function will be:

$f''(x) = \frac{df'(x)}{d(x)} = \frac{d^2 y}{dx^2}$. The nth derivative will be $f^{n(x)} = \frac{d^n y}{dx^n}$

As a simple example, the derivative of a function $f(x)=x^3$ will be $f'(x)=3x^2$. Then the second derivative of the function f will be:

$$f''(x)=d(f'(x))/dx=6x$$

Optimization

First-degree and second-degree derivatives are commonly used in optimization. Optimization usually refers to finding the minimum or the maximum of a function with constraints. Maximization or minimization refers to finding the value of the independent variable which makes a function minimum or maximum without any constraints. In this section, we will discuss the basics of maximization or minimization without constraints.

Two concepts need to be explained:

- *Necessary condition.* These are the conditions that have to be met for a maximum or a minimum. This condition is for the first derivative to be zero. At this point, we know that the slope of the line tangent to the function of which we are trying to find the maximum or minimum is zero. This implies that the function has reached its maximum or minimum. However, we do not know whether that point is the minimum or the maximum. Therefore, we need another condition to make sure it is either the maximum or the minimum. That condition is called the sufficient condition.
- *Sufficient condition.* For a point which satisfies the necessary condition to be the maximum, any departure from it should decrease the value of the function. For that, we need:

$$\frac{d^2y}{dx^2} = f''(x) < 0$$

evaluated at the point where the first derivative is zero (for the maximum), which is the definition of strict concavity.

For the minimum, any departure from the point where the first derivative is zero, the function must increase:

$\frac{d^2y}{dx^2} = f''(x) > 0$, which is the definition of strict convexity.

Derivatives of Functions with Many Variables

Up to now, only functions with one variable were considered. Now functions with many variables will be considered.

Suppose the function is $z = f(x, y)$

That is, the value of z depends on the values of x and y. In this case, there is no such thing as derivative. We can only talk about the partial derivative with respect to one or the other variable (x or y). The rules of partial derivative are the same as the rules of derivative except when taking the partial derivative – with respect to one independent variable, the other variables are assumed to remain constants.

The partial derivative with respect to x and y of a function, z, is as follows:

$$z = ax^3y + bx^2y^4$$

$$\frac{\delta z}{\delta x} = 3ax^2y + 2bxy^4$$

$$\frac{\delta z}{\delta y} = ax^3 + 4bx^2y^3$$

Integrals

We will briefly review indefinite and definite integrals in this section.

Indefinite Integrals. The easiest definition of an *indefinite integral* is that it is the area under a curve of a function. It is also explained as the reverse of derivative. For example, we know that the acceleration is the derivative of speed. So, the question may be: What is the speed if the acceleration is given?

So, if the speed of a vehicle is:

$v = F (x) = ax^2$ where x represents time, the acceleration is:

$$dv/dx = F'(x) = f(x) = 2ax$$

Then, if the acceleration is given, we can calculate the speed as:

$$F(x) = \int f(x)dx$$

These integrals are called indefinite integrals because the end point values of x are not specified.

In our case:

$F(x) = \int 2ax\, dx = ax^2 + c$ where the parameter c is called the constant of integration because the derivative of $F(x)$ for any value of c will result in v=2ax. We need another condition on $F(x)$ to specify c.

Some examples of integration are:

$$F(x) = \int x^n dx = \frac{1}{n+1}x^{n+1} + c$$

$$F(x) = \int x^2 dx = \frac{1}{3}x^3 + c$$

$$F(x) = \int af(x)dx = a\int f(x)dx$$

$$F(x) = \int [f(x) + g(x)]dx = \int f(x)dx + \int g(x)dx$$

Definite Integrals. An integral is called a *definite integral* if the end point values of x are speeding, in which case:

$$[F(x)]_a^b = \int_a^b f(x)dx = F(b) - F(a)$$

As an example:

$$\int_1^2 x^2 dx = (x^3/3)^2_1 = 8/3 - 1/3 = 7/3$$

Appendix B: Introduction to Matrix Algebra

A matrix is a mathematical expression, shown as the following. Matrices are employed as such in a wide variety of analytical studies.[1]

$$A = \begin{bmatrix} a_{11} & a_{12} & \ldots a_{1n} \\ a_{21} & a_{22} & \ldots a_{2n} \\ \ldots & \ldots & \ldots \\ a_{m1} & a_{m2} & \ldots a_{mn} \end{bmatrix}$$

The matrix has m rows and n columns and hence it is called an m by n matrix. M by n is the dimension of the matrix. It is called a *square matrix* if m and n are the same. In the case m=1, the matrix is a *row matrix*, and if n=1, the matrix is a *column matrix*.

The letters a are called the *cells* of a matrix. They are also called the *members* of a matrix. Generally, a cell is denoted as aij, where i=1, m and j=1, n and the matrix as:

$$A = \begin{bmatrix} a_{ij} \end{bmatrix}, \quad i = 1, \ \ldots, \ m$$

$$j = 1, \ \ldots, \ n$$

Equal Matrices

$A = \begin{bmatrix} a_{ij} \end{bmatrix}$ ve $B = \begin{bmatrix} b_{ij} \end{bmatrix}$ are equal only if $a_{ij} = b_{ij}$ for all I and j.

Addition and Subtraction. This operation can be carried out only if the matrices are of equal size.
For example,

$$\begin{bmatrix} 4 & 8 \\ 2 & 1 \end{bmatrix} + \begin{bmatrix} 2 & 0 \\ 0 & 7 \end{bmatrix} = \begin{bmatrix} 6 & 8 \\ 2 & 8 \end{bmatrix}$$

More generally:

$$\begin{bmatrix} a_{ij} \end{bmatrix} + \begin{bmatrix} b_{ij} \end{bmatrix} = \begin{bmatrix} c_{ij} \end{bmatrix} \text{ implies } c_{ij} = a_{ij} + b_{ij}$$

In addition: A + B = B + A (commutativity), (A + B) + C = A + (B + C) – associativity,

$$A(B + C) = AB + AC - \text{distributivity}$$

Similar rules apply to subtraction of matrices.

---

[1] For a more complete treatment of the matrix algebra, see Jacques, *Mathematics for Economics and Business*, op. cit., and Rosser, *Basic Mathematics for Economists*, op. cit. For a quick survey of the matrix algebra for business, see Jacques, *Quantitative Methods*, op. cit.

https://doi.org/10.1515/9783110705355-018

Matrix Operations

Scalar Multiplication. This is a simple operation where each of the cells of the matrix is multiplied by the scalar. For example:

$$7 \begin{bmatrix} 3 & 1 \\ 0 & 5 \end{bmatrix} = \begin{bmatrix} 21 & -7 \\ 0 & 35 \end{bmatrix}$$

$$-2 \begin{bmatrix} 0 & -3 \\ 4 & 1 \end{bmatrix} = \begin{bmatrix} 0 & +6 \\ -8 & -2 \end{bmatrix}$$

$$-3 \begin{bmatrix} a_{11} & a_{12} \\ a_{21} & a_{22} \end{bmatrix} = \begin{bmatrix} -3a_{11} & -3a_{12} \\ -3a_{21} & -3a_{22} \end{bmatrix}$$

More generally: $k[a_{ij}] = [ka_{ij}] = [a_{ij}]k$.

Matrix Multiplication. The dimension of the matrices to be multiplied is important. We need to have the number of columns in the first matrix equal to the number of rows in the second matrix. The resulting matrix will have the same number of rows as the first matrix and the same number of columns as the second matrix. For example, let us take the following pair of matrices:

$$\underset{2\times 2}{A} \quad \underset{2\times 3}{B} \qquad \underset{7\times 5}{A} \quad \underset{5\times 4}{A}$$

$$\underset{1\times 2}{A} \quad \underset{2\times 3}{A} \qquad A = [a_{11}a_{12}] \quad B = \begin{bmatrix} b_{11} & b_{12} & b_{13} \\ b_{21} & b_{22} & b_{23} \end{bmatrix}$$

These pairs can be multiplied because the requirement is met.
Suppose we have the following matrices to multiply.

$$A = [a_{11}\ a_{12}] \text{ ve } B = \begin{bmatrix} b_{11} & b_{12} & b_{13} \\ b_{21} & b_{22} & b_{23} \end{bmatrix}$$

These matrices can be multiplied since the number of columns in the first matrix (2) is the same as the rows (2) in the second matrix. The resulting matrix will have a size of 1x3.

$$AB = C = [c_{11}\ c_{12}\ c_{13}]$$

Where:

$$c_{11} = a_{11}b_{11} + a_{12}b_{21}$$

$$c_{12} = a_{11}b_{12} + a_{12}b_{22}$$

$$c_{13} = a_{11}b_{13} + a_{12}b_{23}$$

$$[a_{11}\ a_{12}] \begin{bmatrix} b_{11} & b_{12} & b_{13} \\ b_{21} & b_{22} & b_{23} \end{bmatrix}$$

Take the following example:

$$\underset{2\times 2}{A} = \begin{bmatrix} 3 & 5 \\ 4 & 6 \end{bmatrix} \quad \underset{2\times 2}{B} = \begin{bmatrix} -1 & 0 \\ 4 & 7 \end{bmatrix}$$

$$AB = \begin{bmatrix} 3 & 5 \\ 4 & 6 \end{bmatrix} \begin{bmatrix} -1 & 0 \\ 4 & 7 \end{bmatrix} = \begin{bmatrix} 3\times -1+5\times 4 & 3\times 0+5\times 7 \\ 4\times -1+6\times 4 & 4\times 0+6\times 7 \end{bmatrix} = \begin{bmatrix} 17 & 35 \\ 20 & 42 \end{bmatrix}$$

$$BA = \begin{bmatrix} -1 & 0 \\ 4 & 7 \end{bmatrix} \begin{bmatrix} 3 & 5 \\ 4 & 6 \end{bmatrix} = \begin{bmatrix} -1\times 3+0\times 4 & -1\times 5+6\times 0 \\ 4\times 3+7\times 4 & 4\times 5+7\times 6 \end{bmatrix} = \begin{bmatrix} -3 & -5 \\ 40 & 62 \end{bmatrix} \neq AB$$

Notice that AB is not equal to BA.

Unit and Null Matrices

Unit matrix is a square matrix where all cells on principal diagonal are 1. All other cells are zero. The following are examples of unit matrix.

$$I_2 = \begin{bmatrix} 1 & 0 \\ 0 & 1 \end{bmatrix} \quad I_3 = \begin{bmatrix} 1 & 0 & 0 \\ 0 & 1 & 0 \\ 0 & 0 & 1 \end{bmatrix}$$

An important property of unit matrix is that multiplication of it by another matrix (given that this possible) leaves the non-unit matrix unchanged. This is something like if a number or variable is multiplied by one, the number or the variable remains unchanged.

The following are some examples of this property.

Given, $A = \begin{bmatrix} 1 & 2 & 3 \\ 0 & 2 & 2 \end{bmatrix}$, then,

$$I_2\ A = \begin{bmatrix} 1 & 0 \\ 0 & 1 \end{bmatrix} \begin{bmatrix} 1 & 2 & 3 \\ 0 & 2 & 2 \end{bmatrix} = \begin{bmatrix} 1 & 2 & 3 \\ 0 & 2 & 2 \end{bmatrix} = A$$

$$AI_3 = \begin{bmatrix} 1 & 2 & 3 \\ 0 & 2 & 2 \end{bmatrix} \begin{bmatrix} 1 & 0 & 0 \\ 0 & 1 & 0 \\ 0 & 0 & 1 \end{bmatrix} = A$$

Null matrix is one where all cells have the value zero. It has a role similar to zero algebra.

Transpose of a Matrices

The transpose of a matrix A is denoted $A' = A^T = A$. It is obtained by taking the rows of the original matrix and creating a new matrix by placing them as columns in the new matrix. Then if the original matrix is n by m, the transpose will be m by n.

$$A = \begin{bmatrix} 3 & 8 & -9 \\ 1 & 0 & 4 \end{bmatrix} \Rightarrow A' = \begin{bmatrix} 3 & 1 \\ 8 & 0 \\ -9 & 4 \end{bmatrix}$$

Some properties of matrices related to transposing are given as follows:
- $(A')' = A$: Transpose of a transpose results in the original matrix.
- $(A + B)' = A' + B'$: Transpose of sum of matrices is equal to the sum of the transpose of each matrix.
- $(AB)' = B' + A'$: Transpose of the multiplication of two matrices is equal to the multiplication of transposed matrices in reverse order.

Inverse of a Matrix

The inverse of a matrix, denoted by A^{-1}, is a matrix which when a *square matrix* is multiplied it (or vice versa), the resulting matrix is a unit matrix. Mathematically:

$$AA^{-1} = A^{-1}A = I$$

The following points are important for inverse of matrices.
- Not every square matrix has an inverse. The inverse of a matrix is only possible for square matrices. However, the inverse does not have to exist.
- If A is $n \times n$ then, A^{-1} is also $n \times n$.
- A matrix has only one matrix

Some properties of an inverse function are:
- $(A^{-1})^{-1} = A$: Inverse of an inverse results in the original matrix.
- $(AB)^{-1} = B^{-1}A^{-1}$: Inverse of multiplication of matrices are equal to the multiplication of the inverse.
- $(A')^{-1} = (A^{-1})'$: Inverse of a transpose is equal to the transpose of the inverse.

Some numerical examples are:

$$A = \begin{bmatrix} 3 & 1 \\ 0 & 2 \end{bmatrix} \text{ and } B = \frac{1}{6} \begin{bmatrix} 2 & -1 \\ 0 & 3 \end{bmatrix} \text{ are the original matrices, then;}$$

$$AB = \begin{bmatrix} 3 & 1 \\ 0 & 2 \end{bmatrix} \frac{1}{6} \begin{bmatrix} 2 & -1 \\ 0 & 3 \end{bmatrix}$$

$$= \frac{1}{6} \begin{bmatrix} 3 & 1 \\ 0 & 2 \end{bmatrix} \begin{bmatrix} 2 & -1 \\ 0 & 3 \end{bmatrix}$$

$$= \frac{1}{6} \begin{bmatrix} 6 & 0 \\ 0 & 6 \end{bmatrix} = \begin{bmatrix} 1 & 0 \\ 0 & 1 \end{bmatrix}$$

$$\text{ve } BA = \frac{1}{6} \begin{bmatrix} 2 & -1 \\ 0 & 3 \end{bmatrix} \begin{bmatrix} 3 & 1 \\ 0 & 2 \end{bmatrix} = \begin{bmatrix} 1 & 0 \\ 0 & 1 \end{bmatrix}$$

$$\Rightarrow B = A^{-1}$$

Determinants

The determinant of a square matrix is a single number that characterizes the matrix. It can be thought of as the *value* of the matrix. So, if the matrix A, the value is as follows:

$$A = \begin{bmatrix} a_{11} & a_{12} \\ a_{21} & a_{22} \end{bmatrix}$$

The determinant of this matrix is calculated as:

$$|A| = \begin{bmatrix} a_{11} & a_{12} \\ a_{21} & a_{22} \end{bmatrix} = a_{11}a_{22} - a_{12}a_{21}.$$

Appendix C: Review of Statistics

This appendix is intended to be a summary of basic descriptive statistics and regression analysis.[1] Descriptive statistics provides basic information about variables in a data set and highlights potential relationships between variables. A simple regression is an extension of the correlation/covariance concept. It attempts to explain one variable, which is called the *dependent variable*, as a function of another variable, called the *independent variable*. A multiple regression attempts to explain one variable, which is called the dependent variable, using the other variables, called the independent variables.

Descriptive Statistics

In this section, measures of central tendency, random variables, expected values, variance, and covariance will be considered.

The following are numbers generated by a random distribution to be used in the following examples. They can be grades obtained by students in an examination, temperatures taken in a certain environment, or prices of a certain commodity at different markets.

20	18	25	26	15	24	25	23	19	20

The most used statistic is the average. However, there are different definitions of the average.

Arithmetic Average. It is simply the sum of the observed numbers divided by the total number of observations:

$$\bar{X} = \frac{\sum_1^n}{n} = \frac{X_1 + X_2 + \cdots + X_n}{n}$$

Where $\bar{X}$ is the arithmetic average, X_i's are the observations. The letter n denotes the number of observations. The average for the population is denoted as μ. Using the data:

$$\bar{X} = \frac{20 + 18 + 25 + 26 + 15 + 24 + 25 + 23 + 19 + 20}{10}$$

$$= 21.50$$

---

[1] For a more complete treatment of statistics in finance, see R. A. DeFusco, D. W. McLeavey, J. E. Pinto, and D. E. Runkle, *Quantitative Investment Analysis* (CFA Institute Investment Series), Wiley, Second Edition, 2007; R. A. DeFusco, D. W. McLeavey, J. E. Pinto, and D. E. Runkle, *Quantitative Investment Analysis: Workbook* (CFA Institute Investment Series), Wiley, Second Edition, 2007.

https://doi.org/10.1515/9783110705355-019

Thus, the average of the measurements taken above was 21,50, if the data represents the room temperature. The student will notice that some of the measurements will be above this number while the others will be below.

Geometric Average. This central tendency measure is used to calculate the average when the observations are percentages and the measurements are taken over a long period of time. For example, the growth rate of an economy is such a measure. The formula for this statistic is:

$$G = (x_1 x_2 ....x_n)^{1/n}$$

where $X_i > 0$ and $i = 1, 2, n$. Again, the letter n denotes the number of observations. For example, if an economy grew by the numbers given, the average geometric growth per year would be calculated as:

$$G = \sqrt[10]{20 \times 18 \times 25 \times 26 \times 15 \times 24 \times 25 \times 23 \times 19 \times 20}$$

$$= 21.21$$

$R_g = \sqrt[n]{(1 + R_1) \times (1 + R_2) \times \cdots \times (1 + R_n)} - 1$ However, it is quite possible that some of the observations can be negative – in which case, the formula will be:

Notice that, in this case, the numbers should be expressed as percentages since adding 1 to a large negative number will be still negative.

The geometric average can also be calculated as:

$$R_g = (V_n / V_0)^{1/n} - 1$$

Instead of observations every year, we have two observations for, say, wealth, one at the beginning of a period (V_0), and one at the end (V_n).

This statistic is often used in yield calculations of investments. Assume that an investor invests €100 in a stock for two years. Assume also that they earn 100% in the first year but lose 50% in the second year. They earn €100 in the first year increasing the value of their investment to €200. They lose €100 in the second year. At the end of the second year, they just have €100, the original investment on hand. Therefore:

Their first-year return = (200/100) – 1 = 100%
Their second-year return = (100/200) – 1 = –50%
Therefore, their geometric return is:

$$R_g = [(1 + 1)(1 - 0.5)]^{1/2} - 1 = 0$$

Or;
$$R_g = (100/100)^{1/2} - 1 = 0$$

Whereas the arithmetic average would be:

$$\bar{R} = (1 - 0.5)/2 = 0.25$$

As is obvious, the geometric return is a better measure of return than the arithmetic mean return.

Weighted average, harmonic average, median, and mode are other central tendency measures.

Weighted Average. This measure is frequently used in finance and operations research, and it is calculated as:

$$\bar{X}_W = \sum_{i=1}^{n} w_i X_i$$

where X_is are the observed values, and ws are the weights of the sample where Xs come from. For example, if a company has three types of debt – the weight of which are w_1, w_2, w_3 in the total debt (50%, 20%, 30%) and the cost of each type of debt is c_1, c_2, c_3 (10%, 12%, 15%) – the weighted average cost (cow) of the total debt of the company will be:

$$C = \sum_{1}^{3} cow = 0.5 \times 0.1 + 0.20 \times 0.12 + 0.3 \times 0.15 / (0.5 + 0.2 + 0.30) = 11.9\%$$

Harmonic Average (HA). Harmonic average is calculated as:

$$HO = \frac{n}{\frac{1}{x_1} + \frac{1}{x_2} + \dots \dots \dots \dots + \frac{1}{x_n}}$$

Harmonic average is used when speeds are involved. For example, if a driver drove his car at 20, 18, 25 . . . .19, and 20 km per hour stopping at different restaurants along the way, the harmonic speed would be calculated as follows:

$$HO = \frac{10}{(1/20) + (1/18) + (1/25) + (1/26) + (1/15) + (1/24) + (1/25) + (1/23) + (1/19) + (1/20)} = 20$$

Median. Median is the number where half of the observations are below that number or conversely where half of the numbers are above this number. A simple method to find the medium is to order the numbers from low to high, and then find the average of 1 and the number of observations. The result will give the rank of the approximate rank of the median, then find the average of the numbers whose ranks are just and above the calculated rank of the median. Obviously, if the number of observations is large, the median will be equal to average. For example, if we use the data points given at the beginning of this chapter, we have:

20	18	25	26	15	24	25	23	19	20

Then, if we order these numbers from lowest to highest, we get:

15	18	19	20	20	23	24	25	25	26
1	2	3	4	5	6	7	8	9	10

Then the order of the median will be $\frac{10+1}{2}$ = 5.5. Therefore, the median is between the numbers ordered number 5 and number 6. Then the median is between 20 and 23, or it is approximately (20+23)/2 = 21.5.

Mode. Mode is the value of observation with the highest frequency. There may be one or more modes in a sample, or there may also be no mode.

For example, in the original data given, the number with the highest frequency is 20.

Variance. Variance shows how widely the observations in a sample are distributed around the mean. The variance of a sample is denoted as s^2. It is calculated as:

$$s^2 = \frac{1}{n-1}\sum_{i=1}^{n}(X_i - \overline{X})^2$$

Variance would be zero if all the numbers in a sample were equal. The variance of a population is denoted as δ^2.

Standard deviation is the square root of the variance. However, n-1 is used instead of n when calculating the standard deviation of a sample because of the degrees of freedom – the number of sample values that can change freely. For example, if the mean of a sample of size n is calculated and therefore fixed, one can change only n-1 number of observations to calculate other statistics concerning the sample data. It is reduced by one when calculating the average. Standard definition can be roughly interpreted as the range where 95% of the sample falls between that range.

Standard Error of the Mean. Standard error of the mean is calculated as:

se $(\overline{x}) = s_X/\sqrt{n}$, where s_x is the standard deviation of the sample.

Range. Range is the difference between the lowest and the highest values in the sample. Mathematically:

$$R_X = X_H - X_L$$

X_H is the highest value and X_L is the lowest value in the sample. The range for the sample data is R_X=26−15=11.

Confidence Level. Given the sample data, the confidence interval for the population mean would be:

$\overline{X} \pm t_{1-\alpha/2,n-1}(s_X/\sqrt{n})$, where $t_1.\alpha/2$ would be t value that corresponds to 1-α percent confidence level where α represents the probability that the population mean is outside this interval when in fact it is in this interval.

Kurtosis. Kurtosis shows how the tails behave. High values of kurtosis imply that tails are fat. Kurtosis is calculated as:

$$k = \frac{1}{n-1}\sum_{t=1}^{n}\frac{(X_t - \overline{X})^4}{s^4}$$

Skewness. Skewness indicates whether the data leans right or left. More precisely, it shows the symmetry of the distribution. It is calculated as:

$$sk = \sum_{1}^{n} (X_i - \bar{X})^3 / s^3$$

Coefficient of Variation. This statistic measures the variation as a multiple of the mean. It is possible to compare the variations of different distributions by using it.

Other statistics. Some other descriptive statistics are:
-   *Maximum.* Represents the observation with the highest value.
-   *Total.* Represents the sum of all of the values of observations.
-   *Sample size.* Represents the number of observations or the sample size.

Random Variables, Expected Values, Variance and Covariance

Random variable X is a variable which has a probability of having a certain value within a defined range of values (discrete), or has a probability of having a value between two values (continuous).

For example, a dice has six faces and the numerals 1 to 6 are inscribed on each face. The probability of a face with 1 inscribed on it coming at a throw is one in six, because there are only six faces that can possibly come up and only one of them has a 1 inscribed on it. However, the height of a person chosen from a population can be any number between a reasonable range of 1500 mm–2000 mm, for example. Then the probability of their height being exactly 1800 mm is not possible to be calculated. However, assuming we know the distribution of the heights of persons in a population, we can make a statement of the probability of their height being between two different values, such as 1800 mm and 1880 mm is P (1800 mm < X < 1880 mm) = 0.22.

The expected value of a random variable is the mean of the distribution of the random variable and is defined as:

$\mu = E(X) = \sum_{i=1}^{n} X_i P(X_i)$ for the whole population. It will be denoted as $\bar{X}$ if it is calculated for a sample of n variables. This is also named the first moment of the distribution. The summation sign will be replaced by an integral sign if the distribution is continuous.

The variance or the second moment of the distribution would be calculated as:

$\sigma^2 = Var(X) = \sum_{i=1}^{n} (X_i - \mu)^2 P(X_i)$ for the population or s^2 when a sample is concerned (use $\bar{X}$ in this case).

The square root of the variance is the standard deviation.

The measure of correlation between two random variables is called *covariance* and is calculated as:
-   If X and Y are $|cov\ (X,Y) = \sum_{i=1}^{n} \Pr(i)(X - \bar{X})(X - \bar{Y})$
-   If X and Y are positively correlated, then Cov (X, Y) > 0, implying that they move together in the same direction.

- If X and Y are negatively correlated, then Cov (X, Y) < 0, implying that they move in opposite directions.

However, the existence of a relationship does not imply a dependence of one variable on the other.

The *correlation coefficient* measures the covariance between two variables as a percentage of product of standard deviation of the variables. It is calculated as:

$$r = \frac{\operatorname{cov}(X,Y)}{S_X S_Y}$$

where,

$$S_X = \sqrt{\frac{\sum_{i=1}^{n}(X_i - \bar{X})^2}{n-1}}$$

The properties of the correlation coefficient between two variables are:
- It is independent of the units of measurement of both variables.
- It is between −1 and 1.
- $r = -1$ indicates a perfectly negative relationship between the variables.
- $r = 1$ indicates a perfectly positive relationship between the variables.
- $r = 0$ implies that there is no relationship between the variables.

Univariate Regression-Least Squares Method

Regression is the method of expressing the relationship between two variables taking into account the causality.[2] For example, there may be a very strong relationship between the heights of the cows in Holland and the height of the female population. In fact, the correlation coefficient, a statistic that defines this relationship, may indicate that this relationship is one implying a perfect relationship. In reality, there is no reason that should be so. There is no causality between the two variables. However, there may be a relationship between the number of study hours and the grades of the students. In this case, it is clear that the grades depend on the study hours of the students. Grades is the dependent variable and the study hours is the independent variable. Regression, in this case, is to find this relationship mathematically using sampled data. The relationship can be linear or nonlinear. For ease of explanation, we will assume that it is linear.

[2] For detailed treatment of regression analysis in finance, see Chris Brooks, *Introductory Econometrics for Finance*, Cambridge, 2014.

$$Y_i = \alpha + \beta X_i + e_i$$

Where:

Y = the values of the dependent variable.

X = the values of independent variable,

α = the value of Y when X is zero. Intercept of Y, a population parameter.

β = the tangent of the linear line, a population parameter.

e_i = the value of other random variables that effect the value of Y. It is assumed that the expected value is zero.

The objective here is to estimate α and β using sample data using the *least squares method* (LSM). Suppose that α and β are estimated as a and b. Then the estimated relationship between Y and X will be;

$$\hat{Y}_i = a + bX_i$$

Then the error between the observed values of Y and the estimated Ys is:

$$u_i = Y_i - \hat{Y}_l$$

The objective should be to choose a and b such that the sum of squares of the errors made should be minimum. However, since some errors are positive and some are negative, the minimization of the sum of errors may not be reasonable since negative errors and positive errors may negate each other, resulting in a very small sum of errors when in fact there are many positive and negative errors. Positive errors are errors as well as the negative errors. Therefore, one has to find a better definition of error to be able to count both positive and negative errors as separate errors. Squaring the errors is a way to do it. In doing so, we will be able count both types of errors as errors. Then the sum of the squares of errors is:

$\sum u^2 = \sum (Y_i - a - bX_i)^2$, which has to be minimized by choosing a and b accordingly. Noticing that this is a function of a and b, we take its partial derivative with respect to a and b and equate them to zero. This gives a system of two equations and two unknowns. Solving these equations, we get:

$$a = \bar{Y} - b\bar{X}$$

$$b = \sum_0^n (Y_i - \bar{Y})(X_i - \bar{X}) / \sum_0^n (X_i - \bar{X})^2$$

Regression Statistics. Regression analysis is a statistical method and it does not give precise estimates. Other statistics are used to define the precision of estimate and its degree of confidence related to the estimate. They are:

- The *standard deviation of regression statistics* measures the dispersion of real data around the estimated regression line and it is calculated as:

$$S_{yx} = \left(\left(\sum_0^n Y_i^2 - a \sum_0^n Y_i - b \sum_0^n X_i Y_i \right) / (n-2) \right)^{1/2}$$

- The *coefficient of determination* measures the ratio of explained variation to the total variation, and it is calculated as:

$r^2 = \Sigma(\hat{Y} - \overline{Y})^2 / \left(\Sigma(Y_i - \overline{Y})^2 \right)$, it is a measure of goodness of the fit.

- Another relevant measure is the *correlation coefficient*, which is defined as the square root of the coefficient of determination.
- The *standard error of the estimate* is calculated as:

$$S_e^2 = \frac{\sum_{i=1}^n e_i 2}{n-k}$$

$$S_e^2 = \frac{\sum_{i=1}^n (Y_i - \hat{Y}_i)^2}{n-2}$$

- The *interval estimate* at a given level of confidence is defined as:

$$\hat{Y} \pm t S_p \text{ where } S_p = S_{YX}(1 + 1/n + \left(X - \overline{X} \right)^2 / \sum^{(X_i - \overline{X})^2})^{1/2}$$

t is the value of t from its distribution at a given level of confidence.

Test of the Hypotheses that b Is Zero. To test this, we first calculate the value of the relevant t as follows:

$$t(b) = \frac{b - \beta}{s(b)}$$

This t shows how many standard errors away b is from zero. Generally, if this number is greater than 2, it shows that the probability of having β greater than zero is about 5%. Therefore, if t is greater than 2, the hypotheses that β is zero is rejected and therefore there is a relationship between Y and X. This procedure is true if the number of observations in the sample is greater than 30.

Multivariate Regression and Related Statistics

Multivariate regression is utilized if a variable is thought to be dependent on two variables, such as:

$Y = a + b X_1 + c X_2 + u$ meaning that the value of an observation depends on a constant, two independent variables, and the error term, the expected value of which is assumed to be zero.

The following statistics have to be analyzed for the multivariate regression.

- t-statistics
- Adjusted R^2 and F-statistics

- Linearity measures
- Autocorrelation

t-Statistics. This statistics was explained in the univariate regression section earlier.

Adjusted R² and F Statistics. R² increases as the number of constants to be calculated increases (and the number of freedoms decreases). To adjust for the degrees of freedom, *Adjusted* R² is used, which measures the impact of the added variable. It is calculated as:

$$Adjusted\ R^2 = R^2 - (1-R^2)\frac{k-1}{n-k}$$

F-Statistics. F-statistics is used to measure the explanatory power of the estimated equation. It tests the hypothesis that the constants are all zero. It is calculated as:

$$F = \frac{Total\ explained\ variation/m}{Total\ unexplained\ variation/(n-m-1)} \quad or,\ mathematically;$$

$$F = \frac{R^2/m}{(1-R^2)/(n-m-1)}$$

Where m is the number of independent variables and n is the sample size.

Then, if the calculated F value is greater than the value found from the F distribution tables at a given confidence level (where k-1 is used in the numerator while n-k is used in the denominator), then the estimated line is good and valid.

Autocorrelation. The statistics used to test the randomness of the error terms is called the *Durbin–Watson* (DW) test and is calculated as:

$$DW = \frac{\sum_{t=2}^{t=n}(\hat{u}_t - \hat{u}_{t-1})^2}{\sum_{t=2}^{t=n}\hat{u}_t^2}$$

DW takes on a value of 2 if the error terms are random. Generally, the error terms are presumed to be random if the DW is between 1.5 and 2.5. This implies that there is no autocorrelation.

The existence of autocorrelation implies that the changes in the dependent variable cannot be explained by the changes in the independent variables. In this case, other models should be used.

Multicollinearity and Other Aspects of Regression Analysis. Multicollinearity occurs if there are linear relationships between the explanatory variables themselves, which is detrimental to the robustness of the estimation. This is tested by variance inflation factor (VIF).[3] Another important aspect of linear regression is *specification bias*, meaning the model is not correctly specified. This can be addressed by careful analysis of data by transforming the observed data (logarithm, square, exponential). Yet another aspect of regression is that the relationship may not be stable for different periods.

An Application

Beta is a well-known term in financial literature, which defines the sensitivity of a given stock's return on the return of the market's return. In Table C.1, X denotes the return of the market and Y denotes the return of a given stock. The objective is to find the beta for the stock X. In other words, find a and b for the estimated line $Y=b_1+b_2X$. Here, Y denotes stock returns and X denotes BIST-100 Index returns.

In Table C.1, some data and related calculations are presented. In Table C.2, the constant b_1 and b_2 (beta), standard errors, related to t-statistics related to them are given. F and R^2, Durbin-Watson, d, values are presented at the bottom of the table. The beta value of 1,448 shows that this stock is riskier than the market and the estimated regression is robust.

---

3 VIF defined as follows: $VIF=1/(1-R^2)$. Each independent variable is regressed with each other. VIF values are obtained from calculated R^2 values. IF VIF values are less than 5, multicollinearity is said to be non-existent.

Table C.1: Data for X and Y.

Period	Y_i	X_i	$(Y_i-\bar{Y})$	$(X_i-\bar{X})$	$(Y_i-\bar{Y})^2$	$(X_i-\bar{X})^2$	$(Y_i-\bar{Y})(X_i-\bar{X})$	$\hat{Y}_i$	e_i	e_i^2	(e_t-e_{t-1})	$(e_t-e_{t-1})^2$
1994	1.380	0.420	1.174	0.364	1.377	0.132	0.427	0.733	0.647	0.419		
1995	0.140	0.150	-0.066	0.094	0.004	0.009	-0.006	0.342	-0.202	0.041	-0.849	0.721
1996	0.000	-0.150	-0.206	-0.206	0.043	0.043	0.043	-0.092	0.092	0.009	0.294	0.087
1997	-0.180	-0.120	-0.386	-0.176	0.149	0.031	0.068	-0.049	-0.131	0.017	-0.223	0.050
1998	0.360	-0.050	0.154	-0.106	0.024	0.011	-0.016	0.052	0.308	0.095	0.439	0.192
1999	0.080	0.010	-0.126	-0.046	0.016	0.002	0.006	0.139	-0.059	0.004	-0.367	0.135
2000	-0.290	-0.100	-0.496	-0.156	0.246	0.024	0.078	-0.020	-0.270	0.073	-0.211	0.044
2001	0.150	-0.040	-0.056	-0.096	0.003	0.009	0.005	0.067	0.083	0.007	0.353	0.125
2002	-0.090	-0.080	-0.296	-0.136	0.088	0.019	0.040	0.009	-0.099	0.010	-0.182	0.033
2003	0.050	-0.070	-0.156	-0.126	0.024	0.016	0.020	0.023	0.027	0.001	0.126	0.016
2004	0.670	0.650	0.464	0.594	0.215	0.352	0.275	1.066	-0.396	0.157	-0.422	0.178
Totals	2.270	0.620	0.000	0.000	2.190	0.649	0.939	2.270	0.000	0.830	-1.043	1.581
Averages	0.206	0.056										
# of observation	11											

Table C.2: Output.

	Constant	Market
b	0.125	1.448
s(b)	0.094	0.377
t	1.327	3.839
p-value	0.217	0.004

Variance Analysis Table

Source	Squares	df	Mean Square	F	F_{critic}	p-value	
Regression	1.360	1	1.360	14.735	5.117	0.004	s 0.304
Residual	0.830	9	0.092				
Total	2.190	10	0.219				
				R^2 0.621		Adjusted R^2 0.579	

Durbin-Watson, d 1.904

Appendix D: Time Value of Money Tables

https://doi.org/10.1515/9783110705355-020

Table D.1: Present Value Table.

Present Value of €1 Due at the End of N Periods

Peridod	Interest Rate											
	1%	2%	3%	4%	5%	6%	7%	8%	9%	10%	11%	12%
1	0.99010	0.98039	0.97087	0.96154	0.95238	0.94340	0.93458	0.92593	0.91743	0.90909	0.90090	0.89286
2	0.98030	0.96117	0.94260	0.92456	0.90703	0.89000	0.87344	0.85734	0.84168	0.82645	0.81162	0.79719
3	0.97059	0.94232	0.91514	0.88900	0.86384	0.83962	0.81630	0.79383	0.77218	0.75131	0.73119	0.71178
4	0.96098	0.92385	0.88849	0.85480	0.82270	0.79209	0.76290	0.73503	0.70843	0.68301	0.65873	0.63552
5	0.95147	0.90573	0.86261	0.82193	0.78353	0.74726	0.71299	0.68058	0.64993	0.62092	0.59345	0.56743
6	0.94205	0.88797	0.83748	0.79031	0.74622	0.70496	0.66634	0.63017	0.59627	0.56447	0.53464	0.50663
7	0.93272	0.87056	0.81309	0.75992	0.71068	0.66506	0.62275	0.58349	0.54703	0.51316	0.48166	0.45235
8	0.92348	0.85349	0.78941	0.73069	0.67684	0.62741	0.58201	0.54027	0.50187	0.46651	0.43393	0.40388
9	0.91434	0.83676	0.76642	0.70259	0.64461	0.59190	0.54393	0.50025	0.46043	0.42410	0.39092	0.36061
10	0.90529	0.82035	0.74409	0.67556	0.61391	0.55839	0.50835	0.46319	0.42241	0.38554	0.35218	0.32197
11	0.89632	0.80426	0.72242	0.64958	0.58468	0.52679	0.47509	0.42888	0.38753	0.35049	0.31728	0.28748
12	0.88745	0.78849	0.70138	0.62460	0.55684	0.49697	0.44401	0.39711	0.35553	0.31863	0.28584	0.25668
13	0.87866	0.77303	0.68095	0.60057	0.53032	0.46884	0.41496	0.36770	0.32618	0.28966	0.25751	0.22917
14	0.86996	0.75788	0.66112	0.57748	0.50507	0.44230	0.38782	0.34046	0.29925	0.26333	0.23199	0.20462
15	0.86135	0.74301	0.64186	0.55526	0.48102	0.41727	0.36245	0.31524	0.27454	0.23939	0.20900	0.18270
16	0.85282	0.72845	0.62317	0.53391	0.45811	0.39365	0.33873	0.29189	0.25187	0.21763	0.18829	0.16312
17	0.84438	0.71416	0.60502	0.51337	0.43630	0.37136	0.31657	0.27027	0.23107	0.19784	0.16963	0.14564
18	0.83602	0.70016	0.58739	0.49363	0.41552	0.35034	0.29586	0.25025	0.21199	0.17986	0.15282	0.13004
19	0.82774	0.68643	0.57029	0.47464	0.39573	0.33051	0.27651	0.23171	0.19449	0.16351	0.13768	0.11611
20	0.81954	0.67297	0.55368	0.45639	0.37689	0.31180	0.25842	0.21455	0.17843	0.14864	0.12403	0.10367
25	0.77977	0.60953	0.47761	0.37512	0.29530	0.23300	0.18425	0.14602	0.11597	0.09230	0.07361	0.05882
30	0.74192	0.55207	0.41199	0.30832	0.23138	0.17411	0.13137	0.09938	0.07537	0.05731	0.04368	0.03338
35	0.70591	0.50003	0.35538	0.25342	0.18129	0.13011	0.09366	0.06763	0.04899	0.03558	0.02592	0.01894
40	0.67165	0.45289	0.30656	0.20829	0.14205	0.09722	0.06678	0.04603	0.03184	0.02209	0.01538	0.01075
50	0.60804	0.37153	0.22811	0.14071	0.08720	0.05429	0.03395	0.02132	0.01345	0.00852	0.00542	0.00346

Periodod

	Interest Rate											
	13%	14%	15%	16%	17%	18%	19%	20%	21%	22%	23%	24%
1	0.88496	0.87719	0.86957	0.86207	0.85470	0.84746	0.84034	0.83333	0.82645	0.81967	0.81301	0.80645
2	0.78315	0.76947	0.75614	0.74316	0.73051	0.71818	0.70616	0.69444	0.68301	0.67186	0.66098	0.65036
3	0.69305	0.67497	0.65752	0.64066	0.62437	0.60863	0.59342	0.57870	0.56447	0.55071	0.53738	0.52449
4	0.61332	0.59208	0.57175	0.55229	0.53365	0.51579	0.49867	0.48225	0.46651	0.45140	0.43690	0.42297
5	0.54276	0.51937	0.49718	0.47611	0.45611	0.43711	0.41905	0.40188	0.38554	0.37000	0.35520	0.34111
6	0.48032	0.45559	0.43233	0.41044	0.38984	0.37043	0.35214	0.33490	0.31863	0.30328	0.28878	0.27509
7	0.42506	0.39964	0.37594	0.35383	0.33320	0.31393	0.29592	0.27908	0.26333	0.24859	0.23478	0.22184
8	0.37616	0.35056	0.32690	0.30503	0.28478	0.26604	0.24867	0.23257	0.21763	0.20376	0.19088	0.17891
9	0.33288	0.30751	0.28426	0.26295	0.24340	0.22546	0.20897	0.19381	0.17986	0.16702	0.15519	0.14428
10	0.29459	0.26974	0.24718	0.22668	0.20804	0.19106	0.17560	0.16151	0.14864	0.13690	0.12617	0.11635
11	0.26070	0.23662	0.21494	0.19542	0.17781	0.16192	0.14757	0.13459	0.12285	0.11221	0.10258	0.09383
12	0.23071	0.20756	0.18691	0.16846	0.15197	0.13722	0.12400	0.11216	0.10153	0.09198	0.08339	0.07567
13	0.20416	0.18207	0.16253	0.14523	0.12989	0.11629	0.10421	0.09346	0.08391	0.07539	0.06780	0.06103
14	0.18068	0.15971	0.14133	0.12520	0.11102	0.09855	0.08757	0.07789	0.06934	0.06180	0.05512	0.04921
15	0.15989	0.14010	0.12289	0.10793	0.09489	0.08352	0.07359	0.06491	0.05731	0.05065	0.04481	0.03969
16	0.14150	0.12289	0.10686	0.09304	0.08110	0.07078	0.06184	0.05409	0.04736	0.04152	0.03643	0.03201
17	0.12522	0.10780	0.09293	0.08021	0.06932	0.05998	0.05196	0.04507	0.03914	0.03403	0.02962	0.02581
18	0.11081	0.09456	0.08081	0.06914	0.05925	0.05083	0.04367	0.03756	0.03235	0.02789	0.02408	0.02082
19	0.09806	0.08295	0.07027	0.05961	0.05064	0.04308	0.03670	0.03130	0.02673	0.02286	0.01958	0.01679
20	0.08678	0.07276	0.06110	0.05139	0.04328	0.03651	0.03084	0.02608	0.02209	0.01874	0.01592	0.01354
25	0.04710	0.03779	0.03038	0.02447	0.01974	0.01596	0.01292	0.01048	0.00852	0.00693	0.00565	0.00462
30	0.02557	0.01963	0.01510	0.01165	0.00900	0.00697	0.00541	0.00421	0.00328	0.00257	0.00201	0.00158
35	0.01388	0.01019	0.00751	0.00555	0.00411	0.00305	0.00227	0.00169	0.00127	0.00095	0.00071	0.00054
40	0.00753	0.00529	0.00373	0.00264	0.00187	0.00133	0.00095	0.00068	0.00049	0.00035	0.00025	0.00018
50	0.00222	0.00143	0.00092	0.00060	0.00039	0.00025	0.00017	0.00011	0.00007	0.00005	0.00003	0.00002

To find the present value of a future amount, locate the year on the first column and the interest rate on the first row. The number in the matrix corresponding to that year and that interest rate is the present value of €1. For example, to find the present value of €100 at 5% compound interest, look up 5 years on the first column and 5% interest on the first row which is 0.78353. Then the present value of €100 is 100× 0.78353 = €78.353

Table D.2: Present Value an Annuity Table.

Present Value of €1 per Period for N Periods

Period						Interest Rate						
	1%	2%	3%	4%	5%	6%	7%	8%	9%	10%	11%	12%
1	0.99010	0.98039	0.97087	0.96154	0.95238	0.94340	0.93458	0.92593	0.91743	0.90909	0.90090	0.89286
2	1.97040	1.94156	1.91347	1.88609	1.85941	1.83339	1.80802	1.78326	1.75911	1.73554	1.71252	1.69005
3	2.94099	2.88388	2.82861	2.77509	2.72325	2.67301	2.62432	2.57710	2.53129	2.48685	2.44371	2.40183
4	3.90197	3.80773	3.71710	3.62990	3.54595	3.46511	3.38721	3.31213	3.23972	3.16987	3.10245	3.03735
5	4.85343	4.71346	4.57971	4.45182	4.32948	4.21236	4.10020	3.99271	3.88965	3.79079	3.69590	3.60478
6	5.79548	5.60143	5.41719	5.24214	5.07569	4.91732	4.76654	4.62288	4.48592	4.35526	4.23054	4.11141
7	6.72819	6.47199	6.23028	6.00205	5.78637	5.58238	5.38929	5.20637	5.03295	4.86842	4.71220	4.56376
8	7.65168	7.32548	7.01969	6.73274	6.46321	6.20979	5.97130	5.74664	5.53482	5.33493	5.14612	4.96764
9	8.56602	8.16224	7.78611	7.43533	7.10782	6.80169	6.51523	6.24689	5.99525	5.75902	5.53705	5.32825
10	9.47130	8.98259	8.53020	8.11090	7.72173	7.36009	7.02358	6.71008	6.41766	6.14457	5.88923	5.65022
11	10.36763	9.78685	9.25262	8.76048	8.30641	7.88687	7.49867	7.13896	6.80519	6.49506	6.20652	5.93770
12	11.25508	10.57534	9.95400	9.38507	8.86325	8.38384	7.94269	7.53608	7.16073	6.81369	6.49236	6.19437
13	12.13374	11.34837	10.63496	9.98565	9.39357	8.85268	8.35765	7.90378	7.48690	7.10336	6.74987	6.42355
14	13.00370	12.10625	11.29607	10.56312	9.89864	9.29498	8.74547	8.24424	7.78615	7.36669	6.98187	6.62817
15	13.86505	12.84926	11.93794	11.11839	10.37966	9.71225	9.10791	8.55948	8.06069	7.60608	7.19087	6.81086
16	14.71787	13.57771	12.56110	11.65230	10.83777	10.10590	9.44665	8.85137	8.31256	7.82371	7.37916	6.97399
17	15.56225	14.29187	13.16612	12.16567	11.27407	10.47726	9.76322	9.12164	8.54363	8.02155	7.54879	7.11963
18	16.39827	14.99203	13.75351	12.65930	11.68959	10.82760	10.05909	9.37189	8.75563	8.20141	7.70162	7.24967
19	17.22601	15.67846	14.32380	13.13394	12.08532	11.15812	10.33560	9.60360	8.95011	8.36492	7.83929	7.36578
20	18.04555	16.35143	14.87747	13.59033	12.46221	11.46992	10.59401	9.81815	9.12855	8.51356	7.96333	7.46944
25	22.02316	19.52346	17.41315	15.62208	14.09394	12.78336	11.65358	10.67478	9.82258	9.07704	8.42174	7.84314
30	25.80771	22.39646	19.60044	17.29203	15.37245	13.76483	12.40904	11.25778	10.27365	9.42691	8.69379	8.05518
35	29.40858	24.99862	21.48722	18.66461	16.37419	14.49825	12.94767	11.65457	10.56682	9.64416	8.85524	8.17550
40	32.83469	27.35548	23.11477	19.79277	17.15909	15.04630	13.33171	11.92461	10.75736	9.77905	8.95105	8.24378
50	39.19612	31.42361	25.72976	21.48218	18.25593	15.76186	13.80075	12.23348	10.96168	9.91481	9.04165	8.30450

Period						Interest Rate						
	13%	14%	15%	16%	17%	18%	19%	20%	21%	22%	23%	24%
1	0.88496	0.87719	0.86957	0.86207	0.85470	0.84746	0.84034	0.83333	0.82645	0.81967	0.81301	0.80645
2	1.66810	1.64666	1.62571	1.60523	1.58521	1.56564	1.54650	1.52778	1.50946	1.49153	1.47399	1.45682
3	2.36115	2.32163	2.28323	2.24589	2.20958	2.17427	2.13992	2.10648	2.07393	2.04224	2.01137	1.98130
4	2.97447	2.91371	2.85498	2.79818	2.74324	2.69006	2.63859	2.58873	2.54044	2.49364	2.44827	2.40428
5	3.51723	3.43308	3.35216	3.27429	3.19935	3.12717	3.05763	2.99061	2.92598	2.86364	2.80347	2.74538
6	3.99755	3.88867	3.78448	3.68474	3.58918	3.49760	3.40978	3.32551	3.24462	3.16692	3.09225	3.02047
7	4.42261	4.28830	4.16042	4.03857	3.92238	3.81153	3.70570	3.60459	3.50795	3.41551	3.32704	3.24232
8	4.79877	4.63886	4.48732	4.34359	4.20716	4.07757	3.95437	3.83716	3.72558	3.61927	3.51792	3.42122
9	5.13166	4.94637	4.77158	4.60654	4.45057	4.30302	4.16333	4.03097	3.90543	3.78628	3.67310	3.56550
10	5.42624	5.21612	5.01877	4.83323	4.65860	4.49409	4.33893	4.19247	4.05408	3.92318	3.79927	3.68186
11	5.68694	5.45273	5.23371	5.02864	4.83641	4.65601	4.48650	4.32706	4.17692	4.03540	3.90185	3.77569
12	5.91765	5.66029	5.42062	5.19711	4.98839	4.79322	4.61050	4.43922	4.27845	4.12737	3.98524	3.85136
13	6.12181	5.84236	5.58315	5.34233	5.11828	4.90951	4.71471	4.53268	4.36235	4.20277	4.05304	3.91239
14	6.30249	6.00207	5.72448	5.46753	5.22930	5.00806	4.80228	4.61057	4.43170	4.26456	4.10816	3.96160
15	6.46238	6.14217	5.84737	5.57546	5.32419	5.09158	4.87586	4.67547	4.48901	4.31522	4.15298	4.00129
16	6.60388	6.26506	5.95423	5.66850	5.40529	5.16235	4.93770	4.72956	4.53637	4.35673	4.18941	4.03330
17	6.72909	6.37286	6.04716	5.74870	5.47461	5.22233	4.98966	4.77463	4.57551	4.39077	4.21904	4.05911
18	6.83991	6.46742	6.12797	5.81785	5.53385	5.27316	5.03333	4.81219	4.60786	4.41866	4.24312	4.07993
19	6.93797	6.55037	6.19823	5.87746	5.58449	5.31624	5.07003	4.84350	4.63460	4.44152	4.26270	4.09672
20	7.02475	6.62313	6.25933	5.92884	5.62777	5.35275	5.10086	4.86958	4.65669	4.46027	4.27862	4.11026
25	7.32998	6.87293	6.46415	6.09709	5.76623	5.46691	5.19515	4.94759	4.72134	4.51393	4.32324	4.14742
30	7.49565	7.00266	6.56598	6.17720	5.82939	5.51681	5.23466	4.97894	4.74627	4.53379	4.33909	4.16010
35	7.58557	7.07005	6.61661	6.21534	5.85820	5.53862	5.25122	4.99154	4.75588	4.54114	4.34472	4.16443
40	7.63438	7.10504	6.64178	6.23350	5.87133	5.54815	5.25815	4.99660	4.75958	4.54386	4.34672	4.16590
50	7.67524	7.13266	6.66051	6.24626	5.88006	5.55414	5.26228	4.99945	4.76156	4.54524	4.34769	4.16658

To find the present value of annuity of €1, locate the year on the first column and the interest rate on the first row. The number in the matrix corresponding to that year and that interest rate is the present value of annuity of €1. For example, to find the present value of an annuity of €100 at 5% compound interest for five years, look up 5 years on the first column and 5% interest rate on the first row which is 4.32948. Then the present value of €100 is 100 ×
4.32948 = 432.948

Table D.3: Future Value Table.

Future Value of €1 at the End of N Periods

Period	Interest Rate											
	1%	2%	3%	4%	5%	6%	7%	8%	9%	10%	11%	12%
1	1.01000	1.02000	1.03000	1.04000	1.05000	1.06000	1.07000	1.08000	1.09000	1.10000	1.11000	1.12000
2	1.02010	1.04040	1.06090	1.08160	1.10250	1.12360	1.14490	1.16640	1.18810	1.21000	1.23210	1.25440
3	1.03030	1.06121	1.09273	1.12486	1.15763	1.19102	1.22504	1.25971	1.29503	1.33100	1.36763	1.40493
4	1.04060	1.08243	1.12551	1.16986	1.21551	1.26248	1.31080	1.36049	1.41158	1.46410	1.51807	1.57352
5	1.05101	1.10408	1.15927	1.21665	1.27628	1.33823	1.40255	1.46933	1.53862	1.61051	1.68506	1.76234
6	1.06152	1.12616	1.19405	1.26532	1.34010	1.41852	1.50073	1.58687	1.67710	1.77156	1.87041	1.97382
7	1.07214	1.14869	1.22987	1.31593	1.40710	1.50363	1.60578	1.71382	1.82804	1.94872	2.07616	2.21068
8	1.08286	1.17166	1.26677	1.36857	1.47746	1.59385	1.71819	1.85093	1.99256	2.14359	2.30454	2.47596
9	1.09369	1.19509	1.30477	1.42331	1.55133	1.68948	1.83846	1.99900	2.17189	2.35795	2.55804	2.77308
10	1.10462	1.21899	1.34392	1.48024	1.62889	1.79085	1.96715	2.15892	2.36736	2.59374	2.83942	3.10585
11	1.11567	1.24337	1.38423	1.53945	1.71034	1.89830	2.10485	2.33164	2.58043	2.85312	3.15176	3.47855
12	1.12683	1.26824	1.42576	1.60103	1.79586	2.01220	2.25219	2.51817	2.81266	3.13843	3.49845	3.89598
13	1.13809	1.29361	1.46853	1.66507	1.88565	2.13293	2.40985	2.71962	3.06580	3.45227	3.88328	4.36349
14	1.14947	1.31948	1.51259	1.73168	1.97993	2.26090	2.57853	2.93719	3.34173	3.79750	4.31044	4.88711
15	1.16097	1.34587	1.55797	1.80094	2.07893	2.39656	2.75903	3.17217	3.64248	4.17725	4.78459	5.47357
16	1.17258	1.37279	1.60471	1.87298	2.18287	2.54035	2.95216	3.42594	3.97031	4.59497	5.31089	6.13039
17	1.18430	1.40024	1.65285	1.94790	2.29202	2.69277	3.15882	3.70002	4.32763	5.05447	5.89509	6.86604
18	1.19615	1.42825	1.70243	2.02582	2.40662	2.85434	3.37993	3.99602	4.71712	5.55992	6.54355	7.68997
19	1.20811	1.45681	1.75351	2.10685	2.52695	3.02560	3.61653	4.31570	5.14166	6.11591	7.26334	8.61276
20	1.22019	1.48595	1.80611	2.19112	2.65330	3.20714	3.86968	4.66096	5.60441	6.72750	8.06231	9.64629
25	1.28243	1.64061	2.09378	2.66584	3.38635	4.29187	5.42743	6.84848	8.62308	10.83471	13.58546	17.00006
30	1.34785	1.81136	2.42726	3.24340	4.32194	5.74349	7.61226	10.06266	13.26768	17.44940	22.89230	29.95992
35	1.41660	1.99989	2.81386	3.94609	5.51602	7.68609	10.67658	14.78534	20.41397	28.10244	38.57485	52.79962
40	1.48886	2.20804	3.26204	4.80102	7.03999	10.28572	14.97446	21.72452	31.40942	45.25926	65.00087	93.05097
50	1.64463	2.69159	4.38391	7.10668	11.46740	18.42015	29.45703	46.90161	74.35752	117.39085	184.56483	289.00219

Period						Interest Rate						
	13%	14%	15%	16%	17%	18%	19%	20%	21%	22%	23%	24%
1	1.13000	1.14000	1.15000	1.16000	1.17000	1.18000	1.19000	1.20000	1.21000	1.22000	1.23000	1.24000
2	1.27690	1.29960	1.32250	1.34560	1.36890	1.39240	1.41610	1.44000	1.46410	1.48840	1.51290	1.53760
3	1.44290	1.48154	1.52088	1.56090	1.60161	1.64303	1.68516	1.72800	1.77156	1.81585	1.86087	1.90662
4	1.63047	1.68896	1.74901	1.81064	1.87389	1.93878	2.00534	2.07360	2.14359	2.21533	2.28887	2.36421
5	1.84244	1.92541	2.01136	2.10034	2.19245	2.28776	2.38635	2.48832	2.59374	2.70271	2.81531	2.93163
6	2.08195	2.19497	2.31306	2.43640	2.56516	2.69955	2.83976	2.98598	3.13843	3.29730	3.46283	3.63522
7	2.35261	2.50227	2.66002	2.82622	3.00124	3.18547	3.37932	3.58318	3.79750	4.02271	4.25928	4.50767
8	2.65844	2.85259	3.05902	3.27841	3.51145	3.75886	4.02139	4.29982	4.59497	4.90771	5.23891	5.58951
9	3.00404	3.25195	3.51788	3.80296	4.10840	4.43545	4.78545	5.15978	5.55992	5.98740	6.44386	6.93099
10	3.39457	3.70722	4.04556	4.41144	4.80683	5.23384	5.69468	6.19174	6.72750	7.30463	7.92595	8.59443
11	3.83586	4.22623	4.65239	5.11726	5.62399	6.17593	6.77667	7.43008	8.14027	8.91165	9.74891	10.65709
12	4.33452	4.81790	5.35025	5.93603	6.58007	7.28759	8.06424	8.91610	9.84973	10.87221	11.99116	13.21479
13	4.89801	5.49241	6.15279	6.88579	7.69868	8.59936	9.59645	10.69932	11.91818	13.26410	14.74913	16.38634
14	5.53475	6.26135	7.07571	7.98752	9.00745	10.14724	11.41977	12.83918	14.42099	16.18220	18.14143	20.31906
15	6.25427	7.13794	8.13706	9.26552	10.53872	11.97375	13.58953	15.40702	17.44940	19.74229	22.31396	25.19563
16	7.06733	8.13725	9.35762	10.74800	12.33030	14.12902	16.17154	18.48843	21.11378	24.08559	27.44617	31.24259
17	7.98608	9.27646	10.76126	12.46768	14.42646	16.67225	19.24413	22.18611	25.54767	29.38442	33.75879	38.74081
18	9.02427	10.57517	12.37545	14.46251	16.87895	19.67325	22.90052	26.62333	30.91268	35.84899	41.52331	48.03860
19	10.19742	12.05569	14.23177	16.77652	19.74838	23.21444	27.25162	31.94800	37.40434	43.73577	51.07368	59.56786
20	11.52309	13.74349	16.36654	19.46076	23.10560	27.39303	32.42942	38.33760	45.25926	53.35764	62.82062	73.86415
25	21.23054	26.46192	32.91895	40.87424	50.65783	62.66863	77.38807	95.39622	117.39085	144.21013	176.85925	216.54199
30	39.11590	50.95016	66.21177	85.84988	111.06465	143.37064	184.67531	237.37631	304.48164	389.75789	497.91286	634.81993
35	72.06851	98.10018	133.17552	180.31407	243.50347	327.99729	440.70061	590.66823	789.74696	1053.40184	1401.77690	1861.05403
40	132.78155	188.88351	267.86355	378.72116	533.86871	750.37834	1051.66751	1469.77157	2048.40021	2847.03776	3946.43049	5455.91262
50	450.73593	700.23299	1083.65744	1670.70380	2566.21528	3927.35686	5988.91390	9100.43815	13780.61234	20796.56145	31279.19532	46890.43461

To find the future value of €1, locate the year on the first column and the interest rate on the first row. The number in the matrix corresponding to that year and that interest rate is the future value of €1. For example, to find the future value of €100 at 5% compound interest at the end of five years, look up 5 years on the first column and 5% interest to on the first row which is 1.276268. Then the future value of €100 is 100 × 1.27628 = 127.628

Table D.4: Future Value an Annuity Table.

Future Value of €1 per Period at the End of N Periods

Period	1%	2%	3%	4%	5%	6%	7%	8%	9%	10%	11%	12%
						Interest Rate						
1	1.00000	1.00000	1.00000	1.00000	1.00000	1.00000	1.00000	1.00000	1.00000	1.00000	1.00000	1.00000
2	2.01000	2.02000	2.03000	2.04000	2.05000	2.06000	2.07000	2.08000	2.09000	2.10000	2.11000	2.12000
3	3.03010	3.06040	3.09090	3.12160	3.15250	3.18360	3.21490	3.24640	3.27810	3.31000	3.34210	3.37440
4	4.06040	4.12161	4.18363	4.24646	4.31013	4.37462	4.43994	4.50611	4.57313	4.64100	4.70973	4.77933
5	5.10101	5.20404	5.30914	5.41632	5.52563	5.63709	5.75074	5.86660	5.98471	6.10510	6.22780	6.35285
6	6.15202	6.30812	6.46841	6.63298	6.80191	6.97532	7.15329	7.33593	7.52333	7.71561	7.91286	8.11519
7	7.21354	7.43428	7.66246	7.89829	8.14201	8.39384	8.65402	8.92280	9.20043	9.48717	9.78327	10.08901
8	8.28567	8.58297	8.89234	9.21423	9.54911	9.89747	10.25980	10.63663	11.02847	11.43589	11.85943	12.29969
9	9.36853	9.75463	10.15911	10.58280	11.02656	11.49132	11.97799	12.48756	13.02104	13.57948	14.16397	14.77566
10	10.46221	10.94972	11.46388	12.00611	12.57789	13.18079	13.81645	14.48656	15.19293	15.93742	16.72201	17.54874
11	11.56683	12.16872	12.80780	13.48635	14.20679	14.97164	15.78360	16.64549	17.56029	18.53117	19.56143	20.65458
12	12.68250	13.41209	14.19203	15.02581	15.91713	16.86994	17.88845	18.97713	20.14072	21.38428	22.71319	24.13313
13	13.80933	14.68033	15.61779	16.62684	17.71298	18.88214	20.14064	21.49530	22.95338	24.52271	26.21164	28.02911
14	14.94742	15.97394	17.08632	18.29191	19.59863	21.01507	22.55049	24.21492	26.01919	27.97498	30.09492	32.39260
15	16.09690	17.29342	18.59891	20.02359	21.57856	23.27597	25.12902	27.15211	29.36092	31.77248	34.40536	37.27971
16	17.25786	18.63929	20.15688	21.82453	23.65749	25.67253	27.88805	30.32428	33.00340	35.94973	39.18995	42.75328
17	18.43044	20.01207	21.76159	23.69751	25.84037	28.21288	30.84022	33.75023	36.97370	40.54470	44.50084	48.88367
18	19.61475	21.41231	23.41444	25.64541	28.13238	30.90565	33.99903	37.45024	41.30134	45.59917	50.39594	55.74971
19	20.81090	22.84056	25.11687	27.67123	30.53900	33.75999	37.37896	41.44626	46.01846	51.15909	56.93949	63.43968
20	22.01900	24.29737	26.87037	29.77808	33.06595	36.78559	40.99549	45.76196	51.16012	57.27500	64.20283	72.05244
25	28.24320	32.03030	36.45926	41.64591	47.72710	54.86451	63.24904	73.10594	84.70090	98.34706	114.41331	133.33387
30	34.78489	40.56808	47.57542	56.08494	66.43885	79.05819	94.46079	113.28321	136.30754	164.49402	199.02088	241.33268
35	41.66028	49.99448	60.46208	73.65222	90.32031	111.43478	138.23688	172.31680	215.71075	271.02437	341.58955	431.66350
40	48.88637	60.40198	75.40126	95.02552	120.79977	154.76197	199.63511	259.05652	337.88245	442.59256	581.82607	767.09142
50	64.46318	84.57940	112.79687	152.66708	209.34800	290.33590	406.52893	573.77016	815.08356	########	########	########

Period	13%	14%	15%	16%	17%	18%	19%	20%	21%	22%	23%	24%
						Interest Rate						
1	1.00000	1.00000	1.00000	1.00000	1.00000	1.00000	1.00000	1.00000	1.00000	1.00000	1.00000	1.00000
2	2.13000	2.14000	2.15000	2.16000	2.17000	2.18000	2.19000	2.20000	2.21000	2.22000	2.23000	2.24000
3	3.40690	3.43960	3.47250	3.50560	3.53890	3.57240	3.60610	3.64000	3.67410	3.70840	3.74290	3.77760
4	4.84980	4.92114	4.99338	5.06650	5.14051	5.21543	5.29126	5.36800	5.44566	5.52425	5.60377	5.68422
5	6.48027	6.61010	6.74238	6.87714	7.01440	7.15421	7.29660	7.44160	7.58925	7.73958	7.89263	8.04844
6	8.32271	8.53552	8.75374	8.97748	9.20685	9.44197	9.68295	9.92992	10.18299	10.44229	10.70794	10.98006
7	10.40466	10.73049	11.06680	11.41387	11.77201	12.14152	12.52271	12.91590	13.32142	13.73959	14.17077	14.61528
8	12.75726	13.23276	13.72682	14.24009	14.77325	15.32700	15.90203	16.49908	17.11892	17.76231	18.43004	19.12294
9	15.41571	16.08535	16.78584	17.51851	18.28471	19.08585	19.92341	20.79890	21.71389	22.67001	23.66895	24.71245
10	18.41975	19.33730	20.30372	21.32147	22.39311	23.52131	24.70886	25.95868	27.27381	28.65742	30.11281	31.64344
11	21.81432	23.04452	24.34928	25.73290	27.19994	28.75514	30.40355	32.15042	34.00131	35.96205	38.03876	40.23787
12	25.65018	27.27075	29.00167	30.85017	32.82393	34.93107	37.18022	39.58050	42.14158	44.87370	47.78767	50.89495
13	29.98470	32.08865	34.35192	36.78620	39.40399	42.21866	45.24446	48.49660	51.99132	55.74591	59.77883	64.10974
14	34.88271	37.58107	40.50471	43.67199	47.10267	50.81802	54.84091	59.19592	63.90949	69.01001	74.52796	80.49608
15	40.41746	43.84241	47.58041	51.65951	56.11013	60.96527	66.26068	72.03511	78.33049	85.19221	92.66940	100.81514
16	46.67173	50.98035	55.71747	60.92503	66.64885	72.93901	79.85021	87.44213	95.77989	104.93450	114.98336	126.01077
17	53.73906	59.11760	65.07509	71.67303	78.97915	87.06804	96.02175	105.93056	116.89367	129.02009	142.42953	157.25336
18	61.72514	68.39407	75.83636	84.14072	93.40561	103.74028	115.26588	128.11667	142.44134	158.40451	176.18832	195.99416
19	70.74941	78.96923	88.21181	98.60323	110.28456	123.41353	138.16640	154.74000	173.35402	194.25350	217.71163	244.03276
20	80.94683	91.02493	102.44358	115.37975	130.03294	146.62797	165.41802	186.68800	210.75836	237.98927	268.78531	303.60062
25	155.61956	181.87083	212.79302	249.21402	292.10486	342.60349	402.04249	471.98108	554.24216	650.95513	764.60545	898.09164
30	293.19922	356.78685	434.74515	530.31173	647.43912	790.94799	966.71217	1181.88157	1445.15066	1767.08134	2160.49070	2640.91639
35	546.68082	693.57270	881.17016	1120.71295	1426.49102	1816.65161	2314.21372	2948.34115	3755.93789	4783.64474	6090.33437	7750.22511
40	1013.70424	1342.02510	1779.09031	2360.75724	3134.52184	4163.21303	5529.82898	7343.85784	9749.52483	12936.53527	17154.04560	22728.80260
50	3459.50712	4994.52135	7217.71628	10435.64877	15089.50167	21813.09367	31515.33633	45497.19075	65617.20162	94525.27933	135992.15356	195372.64423

To find the future value of annuity of 1€, locate the year on the first column and the interest rate on the first row. The number in the matrix corresponding to that year and that interest rate is the future value of 1€. For example, to find the future value of €100 at 5% compound interest for 5 years look up 5 years on the first column and 5% interest rate on the first row which is 5.52563. Then the future value of annuity €100 is 100 × 5.52563 = 552.563

Appendix E: Cumulative Standard Normal Distribution Table

d	–	0.01	0.02	0.03	0.04	0.05	0.06	0.07	0.08	0.09
–	0.5000	0.5040	0.5080	0.5120	0.5160	0.5199	0.5239	0.5279	0.5319	0.5359
0.10	0.5398	0.5438	0.5478	0.5517	0.5557	0.5596	0.5636	0.5675	0.5714	0.5753
0.20	0.5793	0.5832	0.5871	0.5910	0.5948	0.5987	0.6026	0.6064	0.6103	0.6141
0.30	0.6179	0.6217	0.6255	0.6293	0.6331	0.6368	0.6406	0.6443	0.6480	0.6517
0.40	0.6554	0.6591	0.6628	0.6664	0.6700	0.6736	0.6772	0.6808	0.6844	0.6879
0.50	0.6915	0.6950	0.6985	0.7019	0.7054	0.7088	0.7123	0.7157	0.7190	0.7224
0.60	0.7257	0.7291	0.7324	0.7357	0.7389	0.7422	0.7454	0.7486	0.7517	0.7549
0.70	0.7580	0.7611	0.7642	0.7673	0.7704	0.7734	0.7764	0.7794	0.7823	0.7852
0.80	0.7881	0.7910	0.7939	0.7967	0.7995	0.8023	0.8051	0.8078	0.8106	0.8133
0.90	0.8159	0.8186	0.8212	0.8238	0.8264	0.8289	0.8315	0.8340	0.8365	0.8389
1.00	0.8413	0.8438	0.8461	0.8485	0.8508	0.8531	0.8554	0.8577	0.8599	0.8621
1.10	0.8643	0.8665	0.8686	0.8708	0.8729	0.8749	0.8770	0.8790	0.8810	0.8830
1.20	0.8849	0.8869	0.8888	0.8907	0.8925	0.8944	0.8962	0.8980	0.8997	0.9015
1.30	0.9032	0.9049	0.9066	0.9082	0.9099	0.9115	0.9131	0.9147	0.9162	0.9177
1.40	0.9192	0.9207	0.9222	0.9236	0.9251	0.9265	0.9279	0.9292	0.9306	0.9319
1.50	0.9332	0.9345	0.9357	0.9370	0.9382	0.9394	0.9406	0.9418	0.9429	0.9441
1.60	0.9452	0.9463	0.9474	0.9484	0.9495	0.9505	0.9515	0.9525	0.9535	0.9545
1.70	0.9554	0.9564	0.9573	0.9582	0.9591	0.9599	0.9608	0.9616	0.9625	0.9633
1.80	0.9641	0.9649	0.9656	0.9664	0.9671	0.9678	0.9686	0.9693	0.9699	0.9706
1.90	0.9713	0.9719	0.9726	0.9732	0.9738	0.9744	0.9750	0.9756	0.9761	0.9767
2.00	0.9772	0.9778	0.9783	0.9788	0.9793	0.9798	0.9803	0.9808	0.9812	0.9817
2.10	0.9821	0.9826	0.9830	0.9834	0.9838	0.9842	0.9846	0.9850	0.9854	0.9857
2.20	0.9861	0.9864	0.9868	0.9871	0.9875	0.9878	0.9881	0.9884	0.9887	0.9890
2.30	0.9893	0.9896	0.9898	0.9901	0.9904	0.9906	0.9909	0.9911	0.9913	0.9916
2.40	0.9918	0.9920	0.9922	0.9925	0.9927	0.9929	0.9931	0.9932	0.9934	0.9936
2.50	0.9938	0.9940	0.9941	0.9943	0.9945	0.9946	0.9948	0.9949	0.9951	0.9952

https://doi.org/10.1515/9783110705355-021

(continued)

2.60	0.9953	0.9955	0.9956	0.9957	0.9959	0.9960	0.9961	0.9962	0.9963	0.9964
2.70	0.9965	0.9966	0.9967	0.9968	0.9969	0.9970	0.9971	0.9972	0.9973	0.9974
2.80	0.9974	0.9975	0.9976	0.9977	0.9977	0.9978	0.9979	0.9979	0.9980	0.9981
2.90	0.9981	0.9982	0.9982	0.9983	0.9984	0.9984	0.9985	0.9985	0.9986	0.9986
3.00	0.9987	0.9987	0.9987	0.9988	0.9988	0.9989	0.9989	0.9989	0.9990	0.9990

The values in the table correspond to the area under the curve of a standard normal random variable for a value at or below. If $d_1 = 0.4$, the corresponding z value will be 0.6554. If d_1 is a negative number, 1 minus the corresponding z value of the positive value of this number will give us the z value.

References

ACCA. *Advance Financial Management Revising Notes*, ACCA, March/June 2017.

Akgüç, Öztin. *Banka Finansal Tabloların Analizi*, Genişletilmiş 2. Baskı, Arayış Basım ve Yayıncılık, 2012.

Apostolik, Richard, Chistopher Donohue, and Peter Went. *Foundations of Banking Risk*, Wiley, 2009.

Arnold, Glen. *The Handbook of Corporate Finance*, FT Financial Times, 2005.

BBC, "Trump threatens to pull US out of World Trade Organization," https://www.bbc.com/news/world-us-canada-45364150, Jan. 22, 2019.

Benninga, Simon. *Financial Modelling*, The MIT Press, Fourth Edition, 2014.

Bill Neale, Trofer McElroy. *Business Finance: A Value Based Approach*, Prentice-Hall, 2004.

Black, F. M.Scholes. "The Pricing of Options and Corporate Liabilities," *Journal of Political Economy*, May–June, 1973.

Blackwell, David W., Mark D. Griffiths, Drew B. Winters. *Modern Financial Markets: Prices, Yields, and Risk Analysis*, Wiley, 2007.

Bodie, Zvi and Robert C. Merton. *Finance*, Preliminary Edition, Prentice-Hill, 1998.

Bodie, Zvi, Alex Kane, Alan J. Marcus. *Investments*, Third Edition, Irwin, 1996.

Bretani, Chiristine. *Portfolio Management in Practice*, Elsevier, 2004.

Brooks, Chris. *Introductory Econometrics for Finance*, Cambridge, 2014.

Buckle, M., E. Beccalli. *Principles of Banking and Finance*, London School of Economics and Political Science, 2011.

Capital Adequacy Ratio, http://accountingexplained.com/financial/specialized-ratios/capital-adequacy-ratio, access date: 10.3.2015.

Ceylan, Ali, Turhan Korkmaz. *Uygulamalı Portföy Yönetimi*, Ekin, 1993.

Chandra, Prassanna. *Projects: Planning, Analysis, Financing, Implementation, and Review, Implementation*, Fifth Edition, Tata McGraw-Hill, New Delhi, 2002.

Cornett, Marcia Millon, Anthony Saunders. *Fundamentals of Financial Institutions*, Management, McGraw-Hill, 1999.

Cox, John C., Stephen Ross and Mark Rubinstein. "Option Pricing: A Simplified Approach", *Journal of Financial Economics*, 7, Sep 1979.

Damadoran, Aswath. *Applied Corporate Finance*, Wiley, 1999.

Damadoran, Aswath. *Dark Side of Valuation*, Financial Times Prentice Hall, 2002, Aswath Damodaran, *Investment Valuation*, Wiley, 1996.

Damadoran, Aswath. http://pages.stern.nyu.edu/~adamodar/New_Home_Page/datacurrent.html, April 2018.

Damadoran, Aswath. *Investment Valuation: Tools and Techniques for Determining the Value of Any Asset*, 3rd Edition, Wiley, 2012.

Davies, Phillip R., Michael C. Ehrhardt, and Ronald E. Shieves. *Corporate Valuation: A Guide for Managers and Investors*, Cengage Learning 2004.

DEA, https://www.eda.admin.ch/dea/en/home/eu/europaeische-union/mitgliedstaaten-eu.html, 08.10.2018.

DeFusco, R. A., D. W. McLeavey, J. E. Pinto, D. E. Runkle. *Quantitative Investment Analysis*, Second Edition (CFA Institute Investment Series), Wiley, 2007.

DeFusco, R. A., D. W. McLeavey, J. E. Pinto, D. E. Runkle. *Quantitative Investment Analysis: Workbook*, Second Edition *(CFA Institute Investment Series)*, Wiley, 2007.

Dermine, J., Y. F. Bissade. *Asset & Liability Management: A Guide to Value Creation and Risk Control*, FT Prentice-Hall, 2002.

https://doi.org/10.1515/9783110705355-022

Diacogiannis, George P. *Financial Management: A Modeling Approach Using Spreadsheets*, McGraw-Hill, 1994.

Dow, S. "Why the banking system should be Regulated," *Economic Journal*, 106(436), 1996.

Ehrhardt, Michael C., Eugene F. Brigham. *Corporate Finance: A Focused Approach*, South Western, 2002.

Ehrhardt, Michael C., Eugene F. Brigham. *Corporate Finance: A Focused Approach*, Fourth Edition, South-Western, 2011.

El Arif, Fatima Zahra, Said Hinti. "Methods of Quantifying Operational Risk in Banks: Theoretical Approaches," *American Journal of Engineering Research* (AJER), 3(3), 2014.

Eun, Cheol S., Bruce G. Resnick. *International Financial Management*, Third Edition, McGraw, 2004.

Eun, Cheol S., Bruce G. Resnick. *International Finance*, Seventh Global Edition, McGraw Hill, 2014.

Fama, Eugene. "Random Walks in Stock Market Prices," *Financial Analysts Journal*, Sep.–Oct. 1965.

Fama, Eugene. "The Behavior of Stock Market Prices," *Journal of Finance*, 38(1), Jan. 1965.

Farber, André. *Corporate Finance Lecture Notes*, Vietnam, 2004. http://www.ulb.ac.be/cours/solvay/farber/vietnam.htm, 01.05.2005.

Fernandes, Nuno. *Finance for Executives: A Practical Guide for Managers*, 2014.

Fischer, Donald E., Ronald J. Jordan. *Security Analysis and Portfolio Management*, Sixth Edition, Prentice-Hall, 1995.

Garman, M., S. Kohlhagen. "Foreign Currency Option Values," *Journal of International Money and Finance*, 2, 1983.

Grant, James L. *Foundations of Economic Value Added*, Frank Fabozzi and Associates, 2002.

Grant, Susan, Colin G. Bamford. *The European Union*, Fifth Edition, Heinemann, 2006.

Gray, Garry, Patrick J. Cusatis, and J. Randall Woolridge. *Valuing a Stock*, McGraw-Hill, 1999.

Gray, Garry, Patrick J. Cusatis, and J. Randall Woolridge. *Valuing A Stock*, Second Edition, McGraw-Hill, 2004.

Groppelli, A., Eksan Nikbakht. *Finance*, Barron's Educational Series, 2000.

Hamada, Robert. "Portfolio Analysis, Market Equilibrium, and Corporate Finance," *Journal of Finance*, March 1969.

Haugen, Robert A. *The Inefficient Stock Market: What Pays Off and Why*, Prentice-Hall, 1999.

Haugen, Robert A. *The New Finance: The Case Against Efficient Markets*, Second Edition, Prentice-Hall, 1999.

Hertz, David B. "Risk Analysis in Capital Investment," HBR Classic, *Harvard Business Review*, September–October 1979.

Hertz, David B., Thomas Howard. *Practical Risk Analysis: An Approach Through Case Histories*, John Wiley and Sons, New York, 1984.

Hofbauer G., Klimontowicz M., and Nocon A. "Basel III Equity Requirements and a Contemporary Rating Approach," *Copernican Journal of Finance and Accounting*, 5(1),91–105. http://dx.doi.org/10.12775/CJFA.2016.005.

Horngren, Charles T. *Cost Accounting: A Managerial Emphasis*, Fourth Edition, Prentice-Hall, New Jersey, 1977.

Howells, Peter, Keith Bain, *Financial Markets and Institutions*, Fifth Edition, Pearson Education, 2007.

http://ralphwakerly.com/investing/the-risk-return-tradeoff/fi360 Asset Allocation Optimizer: Risk-Return Estimates.

https://zanders.eu/en/latest-insights/how-do-you-value-a-credit-default-swap/, 21.10.2020.

Hull, John C. *Fundamentals of Futures and Options Market*, Fifth Edition, Pearson Prentice-Hall, 2005.

Jacques, Ian. *Mathematics for Economics and Business*, Fifth Edition, Pearson Education, 2006.

Jacques, Ian. *Quantitative Methods: Economics Express*, Pearson, 2013.

Kahneman, D., A. Tvorski. "Prospect Theory: An Analysis of Decisions under Risk," *Econometrica*, XLVII.

Kennedy, M., Maria John. *International Economics*, PHİ Learning, 2014.

Keown, Arthur J., John D. Martin. J. William Petty, and David F. Scott, Jr. *Financial Management: Principles and Applications*, Tenth Edition, Pearson, 2011.

Koch, Timothy W. *Bank Management*, The Dryden Press, 1995.

Kondak, Nuray. The Efficient Market Hypothesis: Some Evidence from the Istanbul Stock Exchange, Capital Market Board of Turkey, No. 83, 1997.

Kumar, T. Ravi. *Asset Liability Management*, Second Edition, Vision Books, 2005.

Lessard, Donald R. "Evaluating International Projects: An Adjusted Present Value Approach." Donald R. Lessard (ed.), in International *Financial Management: Theory and Application*, Second Edition, New York: Wiley, 1985.

Lintner, John. "The Aggregation of Investor's Diverse Judgements and Preferences in Purely Competitive Security Markets," *Journal of Financial and Quantitative Analysis*, IV, no. 4, Dec. 1969.

Lukasz, Snopek. *The Complete Guide to Portfolio Management*, Wiley, 2012.

Malicher, Ronald W., Edgar A. Norton. *Finance: Foundations of Financial Institutions and Management*, Wiley, 2007.

Malkiel, Burton G. "Expectation, Bond Prices, and the Term Structure of Interest Rates," *Quarterly Journal of Economics*, 76, May 1962.

Markowitz, Harry M. "Portfolio Selection," *Journal of Finance*, March 1952.

Markowitz, Harry. *Portfolio Selection: Efficient Diversification of Investments*, Wiley, 1959.

Martinsen, John E. *International Macroeconomics for Business and Political Leader*, Routledge, 2017.

Massari, Mario, Gianfranco Gianfrate, and Laura Zanetti. *The Valuation of Financial Companies: Tools and Techniques to Value Banks, and Other Financial Institutions*, Wiley, 2014.

Miller, M. H. and F. Modiglianni. "Dividend Policy, Growth and Valuation of Shares," *Journal of Business*, No. 34, 1961.

Mishkin, Frederic S., Stanley G. Eakins. *Financial Markets and Institutions*, Seventh Edition, Prentice-Hall, 2012.

Moore, David J. *Dr Moores' Perspectives in Finance: Financial Institutions*, CreateSpace, 2010.

Mossin, Jan. "Equilibrium in Capital Asset Market, *Econometrica*, 34, Oct. 1996.

Muffet, Michael H., Arthur I. Stonehill, David K. Eitman. *Fundamentals of Multinational Finance*, Addison Wesley, 2003.

Mullins, D. and R. Homonoff. "Applications of Inventory Cash Management Models," S.C. Myers, *Modern Developments in Financial Management*, Frederick A. Praeger, Inc., New York, 1976.

Murtha, James A. *Decisions Involving Uncertainty: A Risk Tutorial for the Petroleum Industry*, Houston, TX, 1993.

Muzere, Mark Legge. *Multinational Financial Management Lecture Notes*, Sawyer School of Management, 2004, http://www.suffolkfin.org/mmuzere, 10.10.2005.

Peterson, Pamela P., David R. Peterson. *Company Performance and Measures of Value Added*, The Research Foundation of the Institute of Chartered Financial Analysts, 1996.

Pettinger, Tejvan. *Criticisms of WTO* , https://www.economicshelp.org/blog/4/trade/criticisms-of-wto/, Oct. 29, 2017.

PinoyMoneyTalk, *Credit Ratings by S&P, Moody's, and Fitch Ratings*, https://www.pinoymoneytalk.com/meaning-of-credit-ratings/

Pouliquen, Louis Y. *Risk Analysis in Project Appraisal*, World Bank Staff Occasional Papers, No. 11, The John Hopkins University Press, Baltimore, 1983.

Ragsdale, Cliff T. *Spreadsheet Modelling and Decision Analysis: A Practical Introduction to Management Science*, Course Technology, 1995.

Readhead, Keith. *Introducing Investments: A Personal Finance Approach*, Prentice Hall Financial Times, 2003.

Reinert, Kenneth A. *An Introduction to International Economics*, Cambridge University Press, 2012.

Rosser, Mike. *Basic Mathematics for Economists*, Second Edition, Routledge, 2003.

Saunders, Anthony, Marcia Millon Cornett. *Financial Institutions Management: A Risk Management Approach*, Sixth Edition, McGraw-Hill/Irwin, 2008.

Sharan, Vyuptakesh. *International Financial Management*, Sixth Edition, PHI Learning, 2012.

Sharpe, W.F. "Capital Asset Prices: A Theory of Market Equilibrium Under Conditions of Risk," *Journal of Finance*, Sept. 1964.

Sharpe, William F., Gordon J. Alexander. *Investments*, Fourth Edition, Prentice Hall, 1990.

Sharpe, William. "A Simplified Model for Portfolio Analysis," *Management Science*, Vol. 9, Jan. 1963.

Sharpe, William. "Capital Asset Prices: A Theory of Market Equilibrium under Conditions of Risk," *Journal of Finance*, Vol. 19, Sept. 1964.

Shim, Jae. *Financial Management of Multinational Corporations*, Global Professional Publishing, 2009.

Stewart III, G. Bennett. *The Quest for Value*, HarperCollins, 1991.

Sunday, Nicholas. *Principles of International Finance*, Grin, 2013.

Tahsin Özmen. *Dünya Borsalarında Gözlemlenen Anomoliler ve İstanbul Menkul Kıymetler Borsası Üzerine Bir Deneme*, Sermaye Piyasası Kurulu, No. 61, 1997.

Taillard, Michael. *101 Things Everyone Needs to Know about the Global Economy*, Adams Media, 2013, pp. 38–56.

Tevfik, Arman T, Gürman Tevfik. *Bankalarda Finansal Yönetime Giriş*, Bankalar Birliği, 1997.

Tevfik, Arman T, Gürman Tevfik. *Lotus 1-2-3 ile Menkul Değer Yatırımlarına Giriş*, Ekonomik Araştırmalar Merkezi, 1996.

Tevfik, Arman T. *Excel ile Hisse Senedi Değerlemesi*, Literatür, 2012.

Tevfik, Arman T. *Risk Analizine Giriş*, Alfa, 1997.

Tevfik, Arman T. *Yatırım Projeleri*, Literatür, 2012.

The Hong Kong Institute of Bankers, *Bank Asset and Liability Management*, Wiley-Singapore, 2018.

U.S. Inflation Rate, $1 in 2008 to 2017, http://www.in2013dollars.com/2008-dollars-in-2017?amount=1

Van Horne, James C. "A Note on Biases in Capital Budgeting Introduced by Inflation," *Journal of Financial and Quantitative Analysis*, vol. VI, Jan. 1971.

Wakeman, MacDonald. "The Real Function of Bond Rating Agencies," in *The Revolution in Corporate Finance*, Editor: Joel M. Stern and Donald H. Chew, Jr, Blackwell, 1998.

Index

https://doi.org/10.1515/9783110705355-023